Pinay on the Prairies

Glenda Tibe Bonifacio

Pinay on the Prairies
Filipino Women and Transnational Identities

UBCPress · Vancouver · Toronto

21 20 19 18 17 16 15 14 13   5 4 3 2 1

Printed in Canada on FSC-certified ancient-forest-free paper
(100% post-consumer recycled) that is processed chlorine- and acid-free.

Library and Archives Canada Cataloguing in Publication

Bonifacio, Glenda Tibe, author
    Pinay on the prairies : Filipino women and transnational identities /
Glenda Tibe Bonifacio.

Includes bibliographical references and index.
Issued in print and electronic formats.
ISBN 978-0-7748-2579-5 (bound); ISBN 978-0-7748-2580-1 (pbk.)
ISBN 978-0-7748-2581-8 (pdf); ISBN 978-0-7748-2582-5 (epub)

    1. Filipino Canadian women – Prairie Provinces – Ethnic identity. 2. Filipino
Canadian women – Prairie Provinces – Social conditions. 3. Prairie Provinces –
Emigration and immigration. 4. Prairie Provinces – Social conditions. I. Title.

FC3250.F4B65 2013   305.48'8992109712   C2013-905691-2
                                                       C2013-905692-0

Canadä

UBC Press gratefully acknowledges the financial support for our publishing program of the Government of Canada (through the Canada Book Fund), the Canada Council for the Arts, and the British Columbia Arts Council.

This book has been published with the help of a grant from the Canadian Federation for the Humanities and Social Sciences, through the Awards to Scholarly Publications Program, using funds provided by the Social Sciences and Humanities Research Council of Canada, and with the help of a University of Lethbridge Research Dissemination Grant.

UBC Press
The University of British Columbia
2029 West Mall
Vancouver, BC V6T 1Z2
www.ubcpress.ca

This book is dedicated to the memory
of Tatay Walding,
who supported our journey beyond the Pacific seas.

Salamat

Contents

Figures and Tables

Tables

Abbreviations

CARNA	College and Association of Registered Nurses of Alberta
CCR	Canadian Council for Refugees
CenPEG	Center for People Empowerment in Governance
CIC	Citizenship and Immigration Canada
CFO	Commission on Filipinos Overseas
CMA	census metropolitan area
CRNE	Canadian Registered Nurse Examination
DFA	Department of Foreign Affairs
ECCC	Ethno-Cultural Council of Calgary
FIDWAM	Filipino Domestic Workers Association of Manitoba
FILCAS	Filipino-Canadian Association of Saskatoon
FNAA	Filipino Nurses Association in Alberta
HRSDC	Human Resources and Skills Development Canada
ICMW	International Convention on the Protection of the Rights of All Migrant Workers and Members of Their Families
IMF-WB	International Monetary Fund and World Bank
IWAM	Immigrant Women's Association of Manitoba
LCP	Live-in Caregiver Program
LSIC	Longitudinal Survey of Immigrants to Canada
NAPWC	National Alliance of Philippine Women in Canada
NAICS	North American Industry Classification System
NOC-S	National Occupation Classification for Statistics
NSO	National Statistics Office
OFW	Overseas Filipino Worker
OPA	Overseas Performing Artist
PAM	Philippine Association of Manitoba

PAS	Philippine Association of Saskatchewan
PCCM	Philippine Canadian Centre of Manitoba
PCW	Philippine Commission on Women
PNP	Provincial Nominee Program
POEA	Philippine Overseas Employment Administration
TESDA	Technical Education and Skills Development Authority
TFW	temporary foreign worker

Acknowledgments

One never makes a journey alone. The road ahead is where one meets new people, which in turn affects the turns that we make. In completing this book, I met a number of people, strangers at first, whose inspiring stories shaped my thoughts about the Filipino diaspora. To these unnamed individuals, my sincere appreciation and gratitude for the accounts they shared about living away from the Philippines.

I am most thankful to the following for their immeasurable support during my work on this research project and manuscript: Jean Guiang and Tess Newton in Manitoba; Eusebio Koh in Saskatchewan; Flora Diloy, Zandra Ricarte, and Fromensio Bensing in Alberta; Abdie Kazemipur for lending his expertise, and James Falconer for compiling the statistical profile of Filipino migration to Canada; Connie Swenson for her superb editorial assistance; Bev Garnett and Leanne Wehlage-Ellis for administrative support; Emily Andrew of UBC Press for her patience and guidance; and the peer reviewers for their positive insights and comments. The financial assistance provided by the following institutions is greatly appreciated: Faculty of Arts and Science, University of Lethbridge; Prairie Metropolis Centre, University of Alberta; University of Lethbridge Research Dissemination Grant; Canadian Federation for Humanities and Social Sciences; and the Social Sciences and Humanities Research Council of Canada.

My fondest appreciation to my husband, Ike, for making the journey with me and sharing the joys and pains of caring for our five daughters – Charmaine, Czarina, Charelle, Czyna, and Charithe – now all adults who have been shaped by our trans-Pacific crossings and who never fail to assist me in many ways to see the day through, including caring for our canine friends Charly and Niro. To my parents, family, and friends scattered around the world for their continued expressions of goodwill. Above all, to the Supreme Reality for always showing me the way in the roads I take.

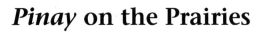

Pinay on the Prairies

Introduction

Kumusta (How are you?) is a familiar word among Filipinos. It is a sure way to connect with Filipinos scattered across more than 150 countries and territories, traversing busy airports, crowded shopping malls, isolated bus stops, and fast food outlets, and even hunkering down in the most unlikely of cold winter havens. *Kumusta* evokes not only joy and comfort at meeting a *kababayan* (compatriot) in a strange land but also sadness in recognition of sacrifices made. Tears flow in brief conversations, with shared stories of children left behind, of struggles to survive in hostile communities, and of people building new lives on their own. *Kumusta* fosters relationships among strangers drawn together by migration; it defines the experiences of Filipino women, also known as Filipinas and colloquially referred to as *Pinay*, who have become quite visible in the global labour diaspora of the twenty-first century.

I left the Philippines in March 2000 to take up a PhD scholarship at the University of Wollongong in New South Wales, Australia. As a university student, I had travelled intermittently in many parts of Asia, Australia, and Canada for various youth leadership activities sponsored by the Asia Alliance of YMCAs, YMCA International, and the Philippine government, but came to truly sense a community of Filipinos only when we – my husband, five young daughters, and I – settled in the beautiful south coast city of Wollongong. When I first met my longtime friend Zenaida in one of the nearly deserted small thrift stores on the Princess Highway, our conversation began with a single word – *kumusta*. It turned out we both came from Tacloban City, and Zenaida had a younger brother who happened to be a former student of mine at the University of the Philippines Tacloban College. Meeting Zenaida and many other Filipino women while doing research in New South Wales transformed our temporary physical sojourn into a permanent space of *Filipino-ness* where food, companionship, and rituals bound all of us together in a society where whiteness was the norm.

We moved to Canada in September 2003. Flying through Seoul on our way from Sydney to Toronto, I must have heard *kumusta* a thousand times that single day. It reverberated in the air among throngs of people lining up with passports and luggage in tow. Today, after a year in Mississauga, Ontario, and nearly six years in Lethbridge, Alberta, the same connectivity is still forged by *kumusta*. Being Filipino is "identity becoming" beyond national borders – that distinct sense of who we are away from home.

This book is inspired by these encounters. Filipino women are, undeniably, the most visible mobile group of temporary foreign workers in Canada and elsewhere today. They are also the most highly socially integrated group of women from Asia due to intermarriage (Hunt and Coller 1957; Cahill 1990; Constable 2003) and a Western colonial legacy. Over 300 years of Spanish rule and 50 years of American tutelage have made the Filipinos "little brown Americans" (Wolff 1992), whose use of the English language, practice of liberal-democratic politics, and adherence to Catholicism shape their trajectories as "citizens of the world" (Ang 2005, cited in Docot 2009, 129) and as preferred non-white workers and immigrants in Western societies, "at home in the world" (Aguilar 2002).

Over 8 million Filipinos live outside the Philippines. The two major groupings of overseas Filipino Workers (OFWs) by Philippine government agencies – land-based workers (such as nurses, domestic workers, and caregivers) and sea-based workers (such as ships' crews) – demonstrate a gendered topographical occupation distribution. Filipino women comprise the majority of land-based OFWs, whereas Filipino men predominate among sea-based OFWs. A gendered approach necessitates the inclusion of Filipino men in exploring the particular subjectivities of Filipinos in migration. I acknowledge the significance of Filipino masculinity in the comparative relational construct of Filipino women in the global labour diaspora, an important subject area in Philippine migration studies. This book, however, focuses on the lives of Filipino women for several reasons. First, Filipino girls and women comprise almost half of the Philippine population as of 2010 (45,368,660 females and 46,459,318 males) (NSO 2013), and more women than men leave the country as OFWs and registered emigrants combined: 206,299 Filipino women compared with 202,767 Filipino men in 2008 (Philippine Overseas Employment Administration [POEA] 2008; Commission on Filipinos Overseas [CFO] 2011). Permanency of migration has been greater for Filipino females than Filipino males since 1981; for example, the gender ratio of Filipino emigrants in 2010 was 73 males for every 100 females (CFO 2011). This gender disparity needs closer examination relative to migration as the labour productivity of the female Philippine population tends to be directed outside the country, with significant social consequences. Second, Filipino migrant women in host societies such as Canada tend to initiate the process of reunification. More importantly, it is the construct of "Filipino women" that shapes the ideas about this group of racialized immigrants in Canada. This does not mean, however, that Filipino men are not included in the discussion in appropriate contexts in the chapters that follow.

This book explores the migration, identity, and community of *Pinays* in Western Canada, particularly the Prairie provinces of Alberta, Manitoba, and Saskatchewan. Although Filipino women have become the mainstay group for case studies on the Live-in Caregiver Program (LCP) in Canada and its consequent phenotypical constructs of the "nanny," "caregiver," and "domestic worker" (Pratt 1999), I extend the prevailing dominant discourse of their positioning as "servants of globalization" (Parreñas 2001a) to the grounded experiences of community participation, activism, volunteerism, and negotiation of multiple identities in discerning the meanings of their quotidian transnational lives. I embark on a new path by presenting Filipino women of different migration statuses together in this book, thus shifting away from the usual research projects where temporary foreign workers, permanent residents, or citizens are studied separately in Canada or elsewhere. In the ordinariness of life, Filipino women become a collective, with shared experiences of migration. Their migration status (temporary or permanent) is an important indicator of their different paths of integration, however, and will be highlighted whenever necessary in subsequent chapters. For example, migrant workers with temporary status have different access to services, rights, and class position than permanent residents in Canada.

The economics of migration provide the impetus for many Filipino women to start anew in Canada. Their migration and community participation outside the three metropolitan census areas of Montreal, Toronto, and Vancouver are underexplored, however, and have not been treated as significant areas of interest by mainstream migration scholars. Of course, these cities, with their high concentrations of diverse ethnic groups, are the favoured destinations of immigrants, including Filipinos, but their predominance in scholarly work obscures the experiences of migration in other parts of Canada, which can be quite variable. A cross-provincial study of Filipino women leads to a deeper understanding of their ways of belonging, and to the finding of similarities and differences in their civic engagements as immigrant women, mothers, workers, and citizens. Particularly in the era of globalization, their lives deserve further scrutiny beyond their market value as contributors to the annual billion-dollar remittances to the Philippines, or their hapless struggles as commodified subjects of corporations and middle-class employers around the world. A nuanced approach to how racialized Filipino women negotiate the limiting social structures of inclusion will lead to broader appreciation of the meaning of migration in their lives, and better treatment of historical patterns of Filipino migration to the Canadian Prairies.

This book explores the ways in which migration shapes identity and community participation among Filipino women in Canada. It is divided into six chapters. Chapter 1 places gender in migration studies in context and pushes for the recognition of *Pinayism* or *Pinay peminism* in Filipino women's transnational studies using feminist perspectives. It presents the approaches, methods, and challenges of doing feminist research with immigrant and migrant *Pinays* in the Prairies. A profile of the participants in my research is included to show the diversity of Filipino women's education, occupation, regional origin, language abilities, age, and migration status in Canada.

Chapter 2 outlines the migration trajectories of Filipinos to Canada and the rest of the world. It highlights the destination, occupation, and migration status of Filipino women from a global perspective, and the demographic profile of Filipinos in Canada and in the Prairie provinces. Their exodus from the Philippines in the second half of the twentieth century was influenced by increasingly intertwined global economic networks and domestic politics. Personal motivations to leave their country and families behind in search of better opportunities in foreign lands are based not just on practical reasons but also on a complex combination of compelling cultural, economic, and political factors, including gender roles.

Chapter 3 examines the relationship between space and meaning, and how place of migration creates new meanings in the lives of Filipino women. Envisioned as a multicultural society, Canada presumably offers a "welcoming space" to newcomers that encourages many Filipinos to carve a niche for themselves in the community. This chapter explores three areas in which "welcoming Prairies" manifest during the initial stages of settlement: seeking employment, housing and accommodation, and social interactions in the community.

Chapter 4 examines the formation of Filipino identities in the cultural matrix of Canada. While Filipino is a national ethnic identity, it does not encompass all identities among Filipinos. In this chapter, the negotiation of multiple identities of Filipino women – as *Pinay*, wife, citizen, immigrant, migrant – combined with known social categories based on class, religion, ethnolingusitic origin, and sexuality are explored. Identities shape the meanings attached to migration, settlement, and belonging of Filipino women in Canada, particularly their perceptions of Filipino Canadian identity and Canadian citizenship under the rubric of multiculturalism. In constructing new meanings of "Filipino womanhood," this chapter presents the perspectives of changing gender role expectations brought about by migration.

In Chapter 5, I analyze *Pinay* activism in the Prairies through personal politics and grounded volunteerism rooted in their experiences of migration, settlement, and integration. The categories of grounded volunteerism include those motivated by faith, work, professions, schools, community building, social justice, and even pure circumstance. Noted *Pinay* community leaders are included in the discussion to provide concrete examples of grounded volunteerism and *peminism* in diaspora, demonstrating how these leaders' contribution and involvement in community organizations ultimately enable them to build links with the larger society. The role of women in Filipino community associations and changing ideas about gender and leadership in the context of migration and cultural values are also explored in this chapter.

Finally, Chapter 6 offers the notion of "vested transnationalism" in the lives of Filipino women. This means that transnational practices are vested in personalism and a sense of community, essentially translating into a symbolic attachment to an "imagined" nation (Anderson 1991), both in Canada and in the Philippines. Whether members of the immediate family or members of the extended kinship system, including associational relations through the patronage system, many are the beneficiaries of the personal and collective activities of the hometown associations and local churches through which Filipino women traverse transnational spaces. This chapter also explores the forms of Filipino transnationalism – as seen in families, remittances, *balikbayan* (returnee) goods, media and popular culture, dual citizenship, and absentee voting – and *Pinay* transnational practices in Canada, emphasizing their multiple levels of belonging, such as philanthropy, mission work, and advocacy.

A concluding chapter reviews the major points raised in each of the earlier chapters and provides a synthesis of how gender, migration, identity, and community impact the lives of Filipino women outside the immigration hubs in Canada. It interweaves an exploration of the gendered nature of quotidian expressions of identities and practices of Filipino women's migration to Canada, particularly in the Prairie context, in the era of heightened globalization and increasing transnationalism. Included are insights into resistance, common bases of civic engagement, and empowerment in the lives of Filipino women trying to make Canada their home, which provide a general synthesis of *Pinay peminism* in local and national spaces. This is our springboard towards a holistic understanding of *Pinay* migration and the Filipino community in Canada.

1

Gender, Migration, and Feminism

Women are "birds of passage" (Morokvasic 1984). In many parts of the world, for example, they are often the first to move from their homes or migrate to other communities for marriage (Chagnon 2000). Today, women in Western and non-Western societies alike leave home to seek paid employment or for other reasons. Despite the apparent mobility of women, they were "largely invisible" (Knörr and Meier 2000, 9) in scholarly discourses until the mid-1970s. The limitations were defined by the terms of movement itself. According to Ravenstein (1885, 199), in·the late nineteenth century, "females are more migratory than males within the Kingdom of their birth, but males more frequently venture beyond" (cited in Boyle and Halfacree 1999, 2). Earlier studies saw men as the main actors in migration, or the movement beyond their locales of origin. Women and children were assumed to simply follow the path taken by the male migrant as his dependents. The inclusion of women in migration studies in the 1970s was the earliest recognition of their "neglected role" (Pedraza 1991, 303) and has stirred debate about the use of gender as a variable in analysis since the 1980s (Hondagneu-Sotelo and Cranford 1999; Donato et al. 2006; Mahler and Pessar 2006).

Gender appeared as an analytical category in the latter half of the twentieth century, primarily to distinguish between biological sex and socially constructed roles (Pilcher and Whelehan 2004). For example, a woman is expected to care for her children while a man is expected to protect the home and secure its economic survival. Inevitably, our lives are shaped by gender from the moment life begins. Each step from infancy to adulthood is coded in gendered terms. Biology remains the major determinant of sexual differences based on which culture assigns female- and male-oriented spheres in daily lives. Smith (2007, 5) points out that the "gender of an individual is not independent of her sex" since behaviour often "result[s] from the interaction of biological and social forces." Kessler and McKenna (1978, 6) argue that "gender is an anchor" from which other people interpret one's actions as determined by "cultural genitals" (Kessler 1998, 86). The sex/gender divide continues in feminist scholarship (Harrison 2006), with much more interest of late in transgender, transsexual, and intersexed people – all new topics unexplored in migration discourse (Cantú 2009).

Gendered norms and social expectations are not static assignments but vary from one culture to another. As cultures and loci of residence change, so do the roles of men and women within families and in other institutions that manifest new social realities. However, gender is not simply about behavioural competencies in given cultural contexts; it is also "a process, as one of several ways humans create and perpetuate social differences" (Pessar and Mahler 2003, 813). Gender intersects with other categories such as race, ethnicity, age, and class, or what DiPalma and Ferguson (2006, 134) call the "vectors of power."

Intersectionality, or the interactions between and among social variables of identities such as gender, race, and class, is a "central tenet in feminist thinking" (Shields 2008, 301). Since Kimberle Crenshaw coined the word in 1989 (Phoenix and Pattynama 2006, 187), intersectionality has become the "buzzword" in feminist scholarship (Davis 2008). In particular, the embodied lives of people of colour and other marginalized groups, and their inclusion or exclusion in structures, institutions, and practices relative to the normative white middle class in Western societies, are best illuminated by intersectionality (Brah and Phoenix 2004; Davis 2008). More importantly, the identities and subjectivities of racialized women such as Filipinos in countries like Canada are mutually constituted by their multiple categories of belonging, for example, their being non-white women from a developing country and their migration status. Hence, intersectionality represents a paradigm that is followed through in the succeeding chapters to capture the multiple levels of oppression, resistance, and negotiation of *Pinays* in the Prairies.

In migration studies, gender is a "decisive variable" (Lipszyc 2004, 3) that shapes migration flows, impacts the decision to migrate, and defines settlement experiences in host communities. Indeed, migration is a "gendered phenomenon" (Donato et al. 2006, 4), but one that requires an understanding of its processes beyond the sex-based binaries. Contemporary scholars have raised the levels of analysis on the gendered nature of relations in origin and destination countries as they intersect with other identities, structures, and practices in changing economic and political conditions (Anthias and Lazaridis 2000; Arya and Roy 2006). According to Piper (2008, 1), "migrants *leave* and *enter* gendered and stratified societies." Or, better yet, the emphatic statements of Macklin (2009, 276): "Borders are gendered" and "Gender is bordered." These point to the prevailing practice of admitting immigrant women based on their "relationships to a man" and the "enforcement of gender identity" among faith-based communities or minority cultures (ibid.).

With regard to labour migration, the demand for particular skills and modes of entry remain gender-specific and regulated in many countries. For example, Filipino domestic workers are highly sought after in Greece, Hong Kong, Italy, and Singapore; live-in caregivers in Canada; nurses in the United States; and engineers in Saudi Arabia.[1] Of the 191 million immigrants in the world, half are women (Yinger 2007). From 1960 to 2000, female migrants were as numerous as male migrants with almost the same gap: 85 million females and 90 million males in 2000 (Zlotnik 2003).

Economic globalization, or in its present economic restructuring phase (Marchand 2003), international division of labour, and the rise of service-related industries have facilitated the increasing "feminization of migration" in modern times (Castles and Miller 1998, 9). The growth in women's participation in "global circuits," especially those coming from the developing South into certain sectors of the "shadow economy," has become what Sassen (2004, 90-91) calls the "counter-geographies of globalization," which is very much indicative of the "feminization of survival" brought about by uneven global development. Labour migration, sometimes ending in human trafficking for sex purposes and in slavelike labour conditions (Zheng 2010), coupled with the push towards foreign exchange earnings by governments highly indebted to the International Monetary Fund and World Bank (IMF-WB), promote what I call, following Appadurai (2003), the "female-scapes" of international migration.[2]

The "state of the field" of gender in migration studies is "fundamentally healthy" (Donato et al. 2006, 6). There is steady momentum in research related to gender and migration with new insights and approaches since the 1980s (Sweetman 1998; Kofman 2004). The question of how gender impacts processes of migration and globalization has now entered the discourse in various disciplines (Song 2006). Women from different countries of origin in Africa, Asia, Europe, Latin America, and North America – including Filipino women – have all become regular features in many recent case studies (Meng and Meurs 2009).

Pinays in Migration Studies

Scholarly interest in Filipino women in migration has increased exponentially in the last three decades. A number of dissertation projects have also been undertaken in many universities in the West since the 1990s on topics related to labour migration, domestic workers, nurses, and recruitment into the international sex industry and even as partners in intermarriage.[3] Indeed, the plight of Filipino women, one of the most visible groups of migrant workers and immigrants in the world, has attracted much attention from scholars, practitioners, and policy makers. Published research in English can be classified into four categories: labour migration, international marriage, settlement and integration, and health and well-being. The first two categories have predominated in the literature since the 1980s, including multimedia reports about the abuse and exploitation of Filipino women. The latter two categories have to do with post-migration challenges in host societies.

Labour migration has defined the global exodus of Filipino women (Gonzales 1998; Lan 2003; Lindio-McGovern 2003; Piper and Roces 2003; Tyner 2004; Parreñas 2008a). In particular, studies have tended to be organized according to the women's occupation in destination countries, such as domestic workers in Hong Kong, caregivers in Canada, nurses in the United States, and entertainers in Japan. Entry into these types of work is regulated by immigration policies to fill domestic demand for cheap but trained and highly qualified professionals.[4] In Canada, "caregivers" appears to be a popular euphemism for domestic workers, although the Live-in Caregiver Program (LCP) specifies care work for children, the sick, and the elderly. Studies of Filipino live-in caregivers in Canada have shown the precarious labour situation of live-in work and the lack or absence of support from host governments (federal, provincial, and local) and the Philippine government in protecting the caregivers' rights and welfare.[5] Care work provided by Filipino live-in caregivers in Vancouver (Pratt 1997, 1999) occurs in the private confines of the home of employers, which makes any monitoring of public regulation of labour standards difficult. Their contribution to Canadian society as workers is devalued and consequently accorded low wages.

Nursing constitutes another occupational trajectory of Filipino women, mainly in the United States and other Western countries, and relevant studies demonstrate the movement of health care professionals from developing countries to fill in the labour shortage in this sector in developed countries.[6] These well-trained nurses face tremendous challenges as racialized and commodified workers in the global economy. Filipino women migrating as entertainers or Overseas Performing Artists (OPA), mainly to Japan, have been explored in numerous studies that speak of their sexual exploitation as victims of human trafficking or as foreign brides of Japanese farmers, the status of Japanese-Filipino children born out of wedlock, and the capacity of the Philippine government to negotiate the workers' rights and welfare in Japan.[7] They appear as modern "Cinderella girls" (Mackie 1998) whose lives are curtailed by state policies and controlled by the organized Japanese sex industry, but whose purpose in becoming an OPA is rooted in the collective well-being of their families.

The rise of the mail-order bride industry and the international marriage market phenomenon involving women from developing countries and men from developed states has generated much scholarly discussion. Filipino women appear to figure prominently in studies of international marriages based on social constructs of docility and being good homemakers compared with Western women.[8] The use of the Internet has increased the vulnerability of Filipino women in marriage-for-migration schemes.

Pinay migration to the Western hemisphere is considered primarily a post–Second World War phenomenon. The settlement and integration of Filipino women in host countries, particularly Australia, Canada, and the United States, constitute a burgeoning area of study.[9] Research underscores the various challenges in the labour market, acculturation and cross-cultural issues, intergenerational conflict, and community formation. Depending on their occupational categories and modes of entry, Filipino women face particular difficulties in seeking employment. For example, under a strict program like the LCP, live-in caregivers in Canada have limited opportunities for retraining since most would enter the open labour market at a later age (Kelly et al. 2011). Levels of expectations for internationally recruited professionals like Filipino nurses in Australia often become an adjustment issue (Brunero, Smith, and Bates 2008). As with other immigrant groups whose cultural values differ from those of the host society, teaching daughters "not to sleep around like white girls do" (Espiritu 2003b) is a nightmare for many first-generation immigrant Filipino mothers. Despite the many challenges of living in adopted communities, however, immigrant Filipino women have been seen as "agents of change" (Zaman 2006, 135), and in Canada their engagement in policy reforms and activism vis-à-vis the LCP has been noted (Kelly 2007a; Pratt et al. 2010).

Scholarly attention has also increasingly focused on the health and well-being of Filipino women (Farrales and Chapman 1999; Kelaher, Williams, and Manderson 2001). The fusion of Western health practices with traditional cultural beliefs in the psychological, emotional, and physical care of Filipino women reflects a significant dimension of health care delivery. For example, many immigrant Filipino women have "extreme modesty" (Holroyd 2007, 192), which impacts their access to reproductive health services. On the other hand, the care practices of Filipino women contribute significantly to lower infant mortality rates in the United States (DeSantis 1998, 454).

The scope of *Pinay*-related themes in the migration literature demonstrates their relevance to various disciplines and the appropriateness of taking Filipino women as a subject of research and analysis in today's increasingly feminized state of human mobility. The field of *Pinay* migration studies appears to attract interest in certain discourses and provides opportunities for new insights and interpretations from emerging scholars. The complexity of migration at different stages of women's lives in changing social landscapes is indeed a vibrant area of study.

Pinayism

In the title of this book, I use the informal word *Pinay* in referring to Filipino women, a choice that speaks to the manner in which this study came about. Threaded through the narratives of lived experiences that form what Haraway

(2004) calls "situated knowledges" about migration, *Pinay* gives voice to an empowered, embodied postcolonial subject long perceived as a victim of contemporary globalization. Whereas the formal name "Filipino" has the Spanish colonial undertone of a subjected people (Bautista 2002), *Pinay* evokes a grounded voice of women's experiences as a base on which to construct alternative modalities of engagement. It embraces the seed of scholarly discourse planted by *Pinay Power: Theorizing the Filipina/American Experience* (2005). The subtitle of this edited collection by Melinda de Jesus, *Peminist Critical Theory*, uses the letter "p" instead of "f" in the word "feminist." In her introduction, de Jesus states: "*Peminism* describes Filipina American consciousness, theory, and culture ... It demarcates the space for Filipina American struggles against the cultural nationalist, patriarchal narratives that seek to squash our collective voice in the name of 'ethnic solidarity'" (2005, 5). *Peminism*, de Jesus further argues, subverts "white feminist hegemony" in dealing with constraining issues of "racism, sexism, imperialism, and homophobia and struggles for decolonization, consciousness and liberation" (ibid.). *Peminism* is Filipino women's own form of feminist consciousness, knowledge, and action, referred to as *Pinay peminism*, or *Pinayism*. *Peminism* recognizes the same activist underpinnings of feminism in the West but draws on Filipino women's particular histories of oppression. Like the feminist articulations of women of colour, *Pinay peminism* asserts its own "oppositional politics" (ibid.) of Filipino women's subordinated identities as former colonized subjects of the United States who are now negotiating their own space as racialized women and as members of particular communities within a national polity.[10] De Jesus further claims that *peminism* is grounded in its analysis of the "legacy of American imperialism," which parallels "negotiation of the 'borderlands,' the emergence of mestiza consciousness, the simultaneous struggle to fight racism in the women's movement and sexism in our ethnic communities, as well as the pressure to 'pledge allegiance' to *either* culture *or* gender, but not both" (ibid., 6). *Peminism* addresses the "imperial trauma" or the "Philippines' dual colonizations by Spain and the United States" and Filipino women's "resistance to imperialism's lingering effects: colonial mentality, deracination, and self-alienation" (ibid.). These effects remain central to the discussion of nation building and questions of national identity in the Philippines.

Whiteness historically means power, domination, authority, and control in many colonized countries and indigenous communities. Although Canada, unlike the United States, has never been a colonial power in the Philippines, it shares the North American orbit of whiteness with its French and British heritage. Hence, an undeniable social link of racially defined struggles of Filipinos exists between the two neighbouring countries. Both, as white-settler societies, have continuing immigration programs that have contributed immensely to their current multicultural polities, and both have been favoured destinations of skilled Filipino immigrants since the 1960s (Espiritu 1995; Choy 2003a).

This book embraces *Pinayism,* which, according to Tintiangco-Cubales (2005, 139), does not follow a singular epistemology but "draws from a potpourri of theories and philosophies, including those that have been silenced and/or suppressed." Although not clear about any specific theory, obscured or not, she adds that "Pinayism is a revolutionary action. Pinayism is a self-affirming condition or conduct. Pinayism is a self-determining system or belief" (140). In other words, *Pinayism* is praxis. Although the context of her discussion lies in the "contradiction and opposition" (139) of Filipino-American lives, she claims that "Pinayism is not just a Pinay form of feminism and/or womanism. Pinayism is beyond looking at gender politics as a major focus. Pinayism aims to look at the complexity of the intersections where race/ethnicity, class, gender, sexuality, spirituality/religion, educational status, age, place of birth, Diasporic migration, citizenship, and love cross" (141).

The introduction of the term *Pinayism* is a powerful effort to reposition a group of women of colour/Third World women from the hegemonic label used in feminist discourses (Narayan 1998; Mohanty 2003). Particular world views have become the norm for all other women to follow and, according to Mohanty (1988, 242), women are assumed to form a "coherent group with identical interests and desires, regardless of class, ethnic or racial location," and the experiences of white, middle-class women in the West are "applied universally and cross-culturally." In this new wave of deconstruction of the hegemonic ideas of "other" women, *Pinayism* signals a move to claim a space in feminist theorizing, this time by Filipino women themselves. Women's lives are complex and unique, and *Pinayism* focuses on the particular experiences of Filipino women along a continuum of multiple systems of inequality and subordination within and across their communities. *Pinayism* is in its infancy or "only at the beginning stages of creation" (Tintiangco-Cubales 2005, 147), but the "endless possibilities" of "the multiplicity of what it means to be Pinay and a Pinayist" (40) generate a continuing dialogue.

Following Tintiangco-Cubales, I extend the term *Pinayism* beyond Pinay studies, or "Filipina American feminist theorizing" (de Jesus 2005, 5), and beyond the American cultural and political spheres. I argue that while the context of Filipino women's struggles may differ from one state to another, the underlying challenge remains the same: the struggle against limiting social structures based on difference. Tintiangco-Cubales writes that "although Pinayism is localized as a US concept, this does not mean that the issues of Pinays in diaspora are not part of the Pinayism conversation. There is a failure to recognize the interconnectedness between the problem of Pinays in and outside the United States" (2005, 142). *Pinayism* is not only a discursive tool of feminist theorizing but also a lived practice based on culture-specific consciousness and action central to the lives of Filipino women. *Pinay peminism* in diaspora, I argue, is rooted in Filipino women's own negotiation of their cultural heritage and of their resources for inclusion in host communities amid exclusionary practices such as racism or discrimination. In this context, *Pinay peminism* stakes a claim to *culture and gender*, contrary to the *either culture or gender* positioning of white feminism, as sites for negotiation of these limiting social practices. As immigrants in the West, Filipino women seem unfamiliar with the cultural values of native-born white women and therefore use their own particular cultural ethos to find meanings in their migration experiences and to empower themselves. *Pinayism* as praxis recognizes culture as part of the gendered and racialized identity, activism, and struggle for change – individually or with a group – in host societies.

Pinayism is also a trajectory in defining the "woman question" in the Philippines (Lindio-McGovern 1997). Mananzan (1997) provides the cornerstone of feminist historical theorizing in the Philippines, which points to the "religious roots of women's oppression" and the Spanish colonial female prototype of the saint-martyr (cited in Roces 2010, 40). Philippine feminist scholars revisit the precolonial indigenous woman who, compared with other cultures in Asia, enjoyed more freedom and rights and the esteemed high status as *babaylan* (priestess, religious leader) (Mangahas and Llaguno 2006). The pre-Hispanic story of *Malakas at Maganda* (literally, the strong and the beautiful), about the creation of the first man, *Malakas*, and the first woman, *Maganda*, who emerged together from a split bamboo points to a semblance of equality between the genders, contrary to the biblical positioning of Eve as a product of Adam's rib. The *babaye* (woman) is, according to Santiago (1995, 110), "a whole person, separate from, yet born together with *lalaki* (man)." A growing body of historical scholarship situates the "golden age" of women in the Philippines prior to Spanish colonization, a time of possible egalitarian practices that was characterized by the absence of religious-based prototypes of "good" or "bad" women, divorce, bilateral character of kinship relations, and fluidity of work (Chant and McIlwaine 1995; Feliciano 1996; Santiago 1996).

The quest for a "Filipino approach" to understanding women in the Philippines has begun to "dismantle gender stereotypes" of wife and mother, or even the beauty queens and moral guardians, and envisions the "future Filipina" as someone with "political and economic power, and reproductive rights" (Roces 2010, 46). Roces (2012, 2) examined the representations of the Filipino woman from the mid-1980s to 2008, and how women's groups "refashioned the Filipina in their campaign to improve women's status in the legal and cultural contexts." Although the "woman question" in the

Philippines has been influenced by the Western feminist movement, it does not fit entirely any of the conventional labels such as socialist, liberal, and radical feminists (Roces 2010). The popular democratic struggles have shown the dynamic participation of grassroots women's organizations in the civil rights movement and the "broader public realm" of women in Philippine politics during and after the Marcos dictatorship (Tapales 1992a, 18). The democratization process that ensued after 1986 has led to policy changes and gender mainstreaming in government development initiatives akin to "state feminism" (Angeles 2003, 283).[11]

Although women's organizations in the Philippines differ in their orientations (for example, moderate, conservative, progressive), they seek to address the issues related to the "woman question" and the national struggle. Santiago (1995, 122) observes that the issues confronting Filipino women "could not be subordinate or secondary relative to national and social liberation." For example, the issue of prostitution was integrated into the campaign against the US military bases in Subic Bay and Olongapo City in the 1980s, and presently under the global sex tourism industry (Enloe 1990; Chant 1997; Ralston and Keeble 2009). Filipino women's issues are situated in the broader context of national and global systems (Simms 1989; Hilsdon 1995; Aguilar 1998). Francisco (2000) argues that women's work and social reproduction in developing states like the Philippines are impacted by the global trade markets controlled by Western countries. Structural inequalities fostered by globalization further entrench gender inequalities in terms of "access to and benefits from resources, capacities and potentials" (Francisco 2007, 103). Feminist responses to women's "capitalist recolonization" in the international political economy have shaped their particular histories of struggle and organizing (Alexander and Mohanty 2010, 23).

Exploration of the Filipino "woman question" reveals that the intersecting realities of gender, class, and nation appear embedded in these women's struggle against oppression. Roces (2012, 3) argues that Filipino feminists employ the "double narrative" or the "deployment of two contrasting discourses – a narrative of victimization and a narrative of activism." The double narrative of "victim/survivor," Roces adds, "reflect two sides of the same coin; although they are contradictory, women's movements have tapped on both opposing discourses for feminist ends" (ibid.).

According to Arnado (2008, 310), "Filipino feminism" is distinguished from Western feminism "not so much [in] the basic ideas of gender equality, but how they contextualize feminist ideals within the Filipino cultural, political, and economic milieu." Patriarchy and its resultant systems of privilege such as heterosexism are articulated concepts among Filipino feminist scholars (Rodriguez 1990; Tadiar 2004). Filipino feminism, however, also points to "three tiers of oppression" – national oppression, class oppression, and gender oppression – which are not all shared by white feminists in the West (Arnado 2008, 305-6). Western feminism tends to homogenize women's problems and consider them to be the same for all women, discounting particular histories of colonialism and the global capitalist enterprise (Mohanty 1988). National oppression based on histories of colonialism, political regimes, and economic marginalization, as well as the Philippines' current role as a global pool of human labour, shape Filipino women's practice of feminism based on class and levels of engagement. A different national historiography and experience make such practice quite different from that in the West (Lanzona 2009). However, the "ambiguous relationships" (Stasiulis 1999, 182) between nationalism and feminism cause the Filipino "woman question" to be sidetracked with a *bayan muna* (nation first) perspective.

In the twenty-first century, *Pinayism* presents new ways of theorizing about the embedded subjectivities of the increasingly visible Filipino women as migrant bodies in globalization. Such women have become transnational subjects with multiple belongings in terms of migration status, race or ethnicity, regional origin, and occupational sector, to name a few. According to Yuval-Davis (1997, 91), these "social attributes" affect the "specific positioning of people within and across communities." *Pinayism* is a useful perspective in examining the status of Filipino women within these sets of social collectivities in particular contexts. For instance, *Pinayism* in Filipino-American lives as postcolonial subjects is different from that in Filipino-Canadian lives as skilled immigrants or migrant workers. But *Pinayism* in Canada and the United States offers similarities in Filipino women's engagement as racialized immigrants in Western societies, facing a panoply of institutional hurdles in seeking professional recognition and, as transnational Filipinos, continued border crossings and "ambivalent returns" (Constable 1998). *Pinayism* thus underscores the interrelatedness of historical precedents in the social and national constructions of the "Filipina," the contemporary labour dispersal of Filipinas under globalization, and the manifest importance of culture in exercising personal agency and collective action in host communities.

Pinayism in the Prairies situates the complex intersectionality of gender, race, and other identities of Filipino women with space and place making. Filipino women living in the Prairies are outside the two most favoured destinations of Filipinos (Toronto and Vancouver) and face challenges that may or may not be the same as those faced by their counterparts in these metropolitan centres. The following chapters demonstrate the geospecificity of *Pinay* lives in the Prairies and my sense of their *Pinayism* from the personal to the public realms: their identities and sense of community in local, national, and transnational contexts.

Doing *Peminist* Research

Claiming a space for *Pinay peminism* within the dominant discourse on gender and migration introduces another aspect of feminist analysis and research practice. Dill (1987, 97) asserts that "critical accounts of women's situation in every race, class and culture" must be foregrounded in analyses that "define problematic [sic], generate concepts and theories." The situation of Filipinos in international migration continues to attract many scholars across disciplines (Tyner 2000; James 2007), but a feminist approach to the gendered migration patterns from the Philippines is fairly recent (Parreñas 2000; Pratt 2004; Angeles and Sunanta 2007) and still marginal compared with the paramount importance accorded to the politics and economics of managing labour flows in both sending and receiving states. Filipino women are often sidelined in mainstream discourses, which tend to classify their experiences into foreign domestic labour and transnational care practices, among others; rarely is a holistic consideration of their lives as immigrants or residents in host communities given space in scholarly literature. It is as though the migration of Filipino and other immigrant women were deemed relevant only in connection with challenges to unfair policies and practices in host countries (Lutz 1997; Freedman 2003). I contend that Canada, with its long history of racializing certain groups of people and "othering" labels such as "visible minority" (Huo 2004; Jain 2008) or "coloured people" (Bannerji 2000a; Thobani 2003), will be slow to nurture genuine bonds of cooperation and integration with its diverse racialized groups if it continues to view the "popular bits and pieces" of their lives in relation to the larger society. A narrow focus on or a selective study of an aspect of immigrants' lives tends to limit appreciation of the normalcy of their existence. Through the case of Filipino women in the Prairies, I hope to show a forward-looking attitude that enables lives altered by migration to follow certain pathways in overcoming structures of exclusion and becoming whole again.

I frame this book using a personal/collective paradigm of engagement with host societies. The basic premise is grounded in how the personal meanings attached to migration experiences shape collective pursuits of integration and belonging in *Pinays'* own communities – be they real, constructed, or imagined. I pose the following question: In what ways do personal accounts of negotiating identities within the Filipino cultural matrix in Canada enable Filipino women to participate in the local and transnational community? This question touches on epistemological and methodological issues in feminist scholarship, or what Sook Kim (2007, 107) refers to as "how feminists speak about, frame, and engage across multiple divides and putative borders without privileging the interests of dominant groups." A non-Western feminist positioning of a Western-based racialized group of Filipino (im)migrant women from the developing world in Asia who are highly exposed to Western values provides another means of understanding complex gendered lives in migration.

Pinayism provides a knowledge source for the silenced voices of racialized immigrant Filipino women as they seek out avenues of inclusion and spaces of resistance in their host communities. Using *Pinay peminism* as my approach to Filipino women's own narratives of migration in the Prairies, this book connects with feminist transnational perspectives in understanding identities, culture, community, and practices of citizenship or belonging across time, place, and space (Nagar 2002; Pratt and Yeoh 2003). In this manner, the "politics of scale" popularized by feminist geographers (Staeheli, Kofman, and Peake 2004) appear useful in analyzing the scales of intersectionality in *Pinay* lives: global, national, and local. Spatiality also determines the possible differences among immigrants in the western and eastern provinces of Canada, and the urban and rural nodes in metropolitan and regional cities. Gender further interlaces the ways in which space and place construct meanings (Massey 1994), and how women and men in places of migration subvert gender regimes – or not. According to Silvey (2004, 492), "feminist migration research investigates the construction and operation of scales – including the body, the household, the region, the nation and supranational organizations – as processes tied to the politics of gender and difference." Broadly speaking, scalar analysis is an important referent in researching Filipino women in diaspora; their international mobility is itself a product of global/national capitalist enterprise strengthened by a politicized development process. Social constructions of scale also emphasize the tensions of the politics of space traversing private and public power (England 2003) that give rise to identities and experiences of Filipino women. Pratt (1999) uses the notion of "geographies of power" to analyze Filipino domestic workers in Vancouver, where inequities spatially intersect and shape their positionality and negotiation in the global marketplace. Pratt (2004) further explores the "relational constructs" of identities between a Filipino live-in caregiver and a Canadian citizen; a Filipino housekeeper/domestic worker compared with a person from Europe doing the same work; and a nanny/immigrant within the Filipino community. These categories are laden with "complex geographies" (Pratt 2004, 40) with differing effects regarding access to certain rights and privileges. Like Bourdieu's symbolic power (1991), Filipino foreign migrant workers, Filipino immigrants, Filipino naturalized citizens, and Canadian citizens have allocated rights (in social and legal spaces) that are quite different from each other (Swartz 1997).

In Canada, I use another dimension of multi-sited power relations traversing local and transnational spaces, one that enables racialized groups of immigrant women to endure and contest aspects of inequality – *culture*. How immigrant women manage the challenges of migration, deal with the problems of settlement, and find ways to belong is a product of the complex interplay between experience and culture. This situates *Pinay peminism* in an holistic schema for understanding Filipino women's migration to Canada. Because migration is a highly personalized experience, it cuts deep into one's own culture – into one's understanding of how sets of ingrained values and practices become useful, or not, in another place. *Pinay peminism* in Canada is rooted in Filipino women's own narratives of making a difference based on negotiated "cultural script[s]" (Tapales 1992b, 114), not only for themselves but also for others in communities they now call home, in ways often overlooked by conventional scholarly discourses.

The topic of culture and feminism in immigration is both fairly substantial and also contentious (Mahalingam and Leu 2005; Kyungwon Hong 2006). More often than not, studies tend to emphasize the relative tensions between culture and feminism among immigrant women from non-Western societies (Volpp 2001; Mohanty 2003). In the case of Filipino women, the Philippines' Western colonial ties appear to be an "advantage" to their destination countries in the West. There seems to be an acceptance of Filipinos as the post–Second World War "ideal immigrants" (Barber 2008) or preferred foreign migrant workers due to their sheer number around the world, but an understanding of culture beyond its impact on the "victim" typology among racialized immigrant women is still lacking in Canadian migration studies (Langevin and Belleau 2000; Valiani 2009).

Non-Western feminists like Narayan (2004, 214) caution us to "balance the assertion of the value of a different culture or experience against the dangers of romanticizing it to the extent that the limitations and oppressions it confers on its subjects are ignored." Narayan further proposes that Western and non-Western feminists alike "understand the complexities of the oppression involved in different historical and cultural settings" (216) and be less concerned about making comparisons. In response to meta-narratives of women based on Western points of view, Rich (1986) theorizes a "politics of location" that requires that differences between and among women be recognized. The "politics of location" has shifted, according to Davis (2006, 478), and now incorporates the location of different actors in the "global hierarchies of power and explores how these hierarchies shape all encounters, both locally and globally." Filipino women occupy different "politics of location" that bear on their migration trajectories and experiences.

The "differences within women" (De Lauretis 1987, 2) across social milieus certainly holds true among Filipino women in Canada, who belong to diverse ethnolinguistic groups and whose personal narratives of migration can quite differ from one another. It is unfair to assume that "immigrant women" from the Philippines, based on popular constructs about them, arrive in Canada as caregivers. This obscures the differences in their lives and the political and economic contexts of their migration histories. "Immigrant women" is a hegemonic term applied by state policies to all women of colour regardless of their migration status. It is an effective political and social classification that divides people into "us" and "them." In a symposium I attended in Edmonton in 2008, a group of so-called immigrant women vehemently challenged the label, as it did not recognize that they had become Canadian citizens. Were they "immigrants" forever? No one could answer this question, and the silence in the room reflected the continuing struggles of non-white women in Canada.

Since Filipino (im)migrants are closely tied with cultural, economic, social, and political processes in the Philippines, their country of origin, and in their host countries, feminist transnational perspectives provide a dynamic lens for examining women's global/local connectivity. Spivak (1989, 219) underscores the condition of women in transnational cultures whose lives are "fractured by the international division of labor." The gendered labour migration, notes Barber (1997, 40), has "transformed Philippine ethnoscapes" with imagined futures in "different social and geographic locations." Transnational border crossings between "home" (country of origin) and "other home" (host community) for permanent residents and citizens make the notions of identity, citizenship, and community appear fluid and unbounded by a specified territory. Filipinos in diaspora, especially women, create and recreate semblances of what it is to be "at home."

Feminist Objectivity

How objective is research about *Pinays*? This question has stayed with me from the outset of this project. Objectivity, or what is known as value-neutrality, is the banner label of scientific investigation and is often the main criticism against feminist research. Procedures measurable by preset variables are generally considered the only valid basis for any knowledge claims or declared truths. Women have been perceived for centuries as "incapable of having knowledge of the best and most rational kind" (Code 1991, x), since the "ideal objectivity is the *masculine* epistemological stance that a knower must adopt if this project is to be carried out successfully" (51). The search for an objective process in knowledge construction in the social sciences has been heavily criticized by feminist scholars (Harding 1987; Stanley 1990; Jaggar 2007). In fact, according to Stanley and Wise (1983), there is "no such objective reality: there is only my reality, or yours, or ours continually negotiated and managed by us, either separately or collectively" (cited in Code 1991, 43). I am more inclined to accept this proposition as it applies to *Pinays* in the Prairies, whose realities frame my discourse of *Pinayism* or *peminist* praxis as it applies to Filipino women as racialized subjects in Canada.

A feminist research process encompasses various methods, positionalities, and frameworks to account for the complexity of women's lives in different places and contexts. According to Haraway (2004, 86), objectivity in feminist research is "quite simply situated knowledges" – a construct of understanding the social realities of embodied subjects. Or, in the words of Hesse-Biber, Leavy, and Yaiser (2004, 12-13), "the nature of knowledge and truth is that it is partial, situated, subjective, power imbued, and relational." From the standpoint of feminist epistemology, the actual and real-life experiences of women become the lens in "building new knowledge" (Brooks 2007, 55). From the personal narratives of *Pinays* in Alberta, Manitoba, and Saskatchewan, I draw on experiential knowledge of migration and the challenges of integration based on gender, race, ethnicity, class, and other social indicators of identity and belonging.

By and large, feminist research is "connected in principle to feminist struggles" (Brooks and Hesse-Biber 2007, 4). Reinharz (1992) identifies some features of what constitutes feminist research that touch on my positionality, or politics of location, as a Filipino, an immigrant, and a scholar. These include: (1) "feminist research aims to create social change," (2) "feminist research strives to represent human diversity," and (3) "feminist research frequently includes the researcher as a person" (ibid., 240). Because Filipino women embody the intersecting realities of a globalized world, their struggles and aspirations in host communities are an important dimension of advocacy for change in regulatory policies and practices in both the Philippines and Canada. The voices of Filipino women – including my personal sojourn from the Asia-Pacific to North America – are integrated in the following chapters to weave a different migration story. Reflexivity is a key aspect of the feminist research process and my "situatedness as a researcher" (Ackerly and True 2010, 36) permits a comparison of my own values and attitudes (Hesse-Biber 2007, 129), as both an "insider" in the Filipino community and an "outsider" (139) from the migration-for-carework trajectory and other distinct realities of immigrant women and migrant workers, with those of the participants in this study, a comparison that is reflective of our shared experiences. The narratives of *Pinays* in the Prairies create a rich tapestry for an alternative vision of their lives.

Searching for *Pinay*

The collection of primary data in the field seems a daunting task, and in many cases indeed it is. Travelling the Prairies was arduous, thanks to endless stretches of highways and flights delayed by unpredictable weather. In the end, however, the task was completed and each place evoked fond memories of the interviews conducted with *Pinays* who live there.

Searching for *Pinay* respondents required a multi-pronged approach. In 2007, I conducted focus-group discussions with thirty Filipino live-in caregivers in southern Alberta through a grant from the Prairie Metropolis Centre.

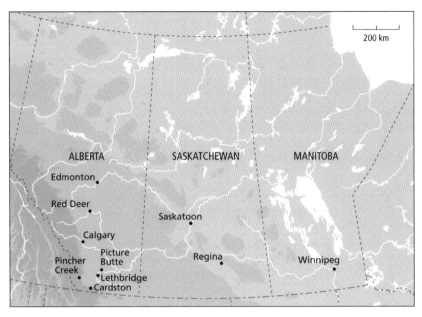

1   Research map.

In 2009, over a period of about four months of intermittent road travel, I interviewed forty Filipino women in different cities and towns in Alberta, Manitoba, and Saskatchewan, using start-up research funds from the Faculty of Arts and Science at the University of Lethbridge (see Figure 1). Including informal interviews, about eighty Filipino women in all were consulted for the various topics presented in this book. Some of them preferred informal conversations about life in Canada to signing consent forms for formal taped interviews, in which case my notes on their insights relevant to the project constitute the only record.

In 2009, I sent out letters of invitation by mail and email to Filipino organizations listed in telephone directories, Philippine consulate websites, and immigration portals in the three provinces, requesting contact with Filipino women who were active members in the organizations. Some of the mailed letters were returned because of outdated addresses. Alternative email addresses, whenever available, proved effective for following up on my requests for contacts in the community. One contact was generally sufficient to identify who was who in the community – that is, which women were actively engaged in community activities. The choice of these women was purposive and consistent with the aim of this book: to highlight Filipino women beyond the victim stereotype and present the many ways in which they make a difference, not only in their own lives but also in the lives of others, regardless of their migration status. By recruiting Filipino women of this calibre, I hoped to construct an alternative identity of Filipino immigrant women as active participants in local communities, contrary to their stereotypical representation as abused and disempowered women in Canada. Filipino women who were already involved in the community provided a complement study group of Filipino live-in caregivers who had been involved in the focus-group discussions in 2007; they provided a sufficient base for exploring the themes in this book but not for considering their experiences representative of those of the wider Filipino-Canadian population in the Prairies.

Personal introductions and referrals were the preferred means of facilitating interviews. Certainly, coming from the same culture as the participants in the study had its advantages. Being Filipino gave me access to a rich pool of potential respondents during the course of my fieldwork, whether in the cities of Calgary, Edmonton, Lethbridge, Saskatoon, and Winnipeg or in small towns throughout southern Alberta. Although my Waray-accented pronunciation of Tagalog was quite distinct from that of native speakers of the dominant dialect, it did not preclude warm hospitality from Filipino women across the Prairies, most of whom came from Tagalog-speaking regions.[12] *Kumusta* was an excellent introductory greeting, followed by jovial conversations about where we came from, how long we had been in Canada, or whether our families were with us. In many cases, a sumptuous meal even preceded the "research" conversation. Having been away from my country for about ten years, I was surprised that little seemed to change in the company of these women – a reminder that in the Philippines work and pleasure have no rigid boundaries.

Profile of Participants

Filipino women who find their way to Canada come from a wide variety of backgrounds. While most hail from Luzon, others come from as far away as Davao in Mindanao and remote islands in the Visayas. Since the 1960s, they have been following different routes to Canada: some live in the United States or Europe prior to coming to this country, whereas others come here directly. Some speak or are conversant in languages such as French, in addition to English and their own Filipino dialect. Among nurses and caregivers, Canada is the second or third country of destination; they have worked in one or two other countries before coming to this country. The extent of their mobility reflects the global spread of Filipinos discussed in Chapter 2.

The decision to migrate is strongly informed by personal aspirations and notions of success. Age appears to be no deterrent to dreaming about a better future for oneself and loved ones. At the time of their arrival in Canada, participants in this study ranged in age from nineteen to fifty-five years.

The women interviewed in Alberta, Manitoba, and Saskatchewan came at either the start or the peak of their labour productivity – as fresh college graduates, middle-career professionals, or executives of government agencies. With the exception of two women with college-level educational attainment, all of those in the study group had completed university degrees. Four women had doctoral degrees obtained in Canada, the Philippines, and the United States, and one had been awarded an honorary doctorate by an educational institution in Alberta for her exemplary contribution to the community. Three women had master's degrees from the University of the Philippines. The most common professions were accounting, engineering, midwifery, nursing, and teaching. However, despite their varying professional qualifications and work experience in the Philippines, they all started at entry-level positions in Canada.

Their educational profile, particularly those with postgraduate degrees, may appear "un-Filipino," "abnormal," or "against the grain" of the construct of Filipino immigrants in Canada. Like other immigrant groups, however, this group of highly educated Filipino women is not an aberration. The women are similar to any other immigrant woman, for example, someone with a medical degree who is initially employed as a factory worker in Canada but who upgrades her skills to become a licensed practitioner in due time. Based on the point system for eligibility to immigrate to Canada, Filipino college or university graduates cap their qualifications with a postgraduate degree, usually at the master's level, to be consistent with Canadian standards. Many Filipino women with university degrees such as nursing augment such education with another caregiver certificate for entry into Canada under the Live-in Caregiver Program, with its tempting promise of permanent residency. Kelly and colleagues (2011, 1) note the "very high" educational qualifications of LCP participants, mostly Filipino women – about 63 percent of whom had "bachelor degrees or higher (a much higher proportion than for other immigration categories)" in 2009. Ironically, the caregiver certificate constructs their identity and qualifications in Canada, whereas all other previous higher educational attainments tend to be ignored.

After many years of permanent residency in Canada, most of these women now own their homes and have found job security here. A few have risen from the ranks to become supervisors or corporate executives, but most remain content with the benefits of stable employment in jobs they learned to appreciate as their "bagel and butter" in Canada. In 2007, one of the participants in Winnipeg became the first Filipino woman ever elected to the legislative assembly: Flor Marcelino, MLA for Wellington under the New Democratic Party. For others, however, finding work similar to what they were trained for in the Philippines is more than satisfactory, and they appear to have a deep appreciation for the hurdles they overcame to do so. Whether they are newly arrived temporary foreign workers employed as live-in caregivers or chambermaids in hotels, or they are sponsored spouses or dependents, the journeys of these women were certainly rife with bumps along the way.

Besides the Vatican City, the Philippines is the only country in the world that does not recognize divorce; it does, however, have alternative arrangements when relationships break down, such as legal separation and annulment (Rodis 2009). Nine participants in this study were separated from their husbands without going through the legal process. De facto separation appears to be the norm in the Philippines, while an expensive legal separation procedure is usually invoked only when division of property is involved. In case of marital breakdown, children are usually left in the care of the mother. The 1987 Family Code of the Philippines requires legal support for the child, and the Anti-Violence against Women and Their Children Act of 2004 provides criminal sanctions for withholding support in certain cases, but there is no mechanism to enforce these provisions in the Philippines. Neither is there any legal mechanism for compelling Overseas Filipino Worker (OFW) fathers who may have found new partners during their stint abroad to provide support to their abandoned children in the Philippines (Señeres 2010). In this and other similar cases, women generally take on the responsibility of supporting their children. Five of the nine participants mentioned above were single mothers with children left behind in the Philippines. Thirty-seven women were married, twenty-two were single, and two were divorced in Canada.

The Filipino women in this study represent two main groups of Filipinos in Canada based on migration status: temporary migrants and permanent residents. Thirty live-in caregivers in southern Alberta held temporary work permits at the time of the focus-group discussions in 2007, while forty Filipino women of different professions and occupations in the Prairies were permanent residents or citizens at the time of their interviews in 2009. These two sample groups can be considered to fairly represent the wider Filipino community in the Prairies based on migration status. However, because of the differences in their status and corresponding rights and access to services and welfare, these two groups of Filipino women cannot capture the diversity of experiences and the complex subject positioning of Filipinos in Canada. I therefore do not claim that they provide a generic representation of *Pinay* lives, but their voices – integrated in the following chapters with assigned pseudonyms – offer possibilities of new meanings of negotiated identities and spaces of inclusion for *Pinays* in diaspora.

2
Pinay Migration

The Philippines is known as the "Pearl of the Orient Seas." An archipelago of more than seven thousand islands and islets, the Philippines is divided into three major island groupings: Luzon, Visayas, and Mindanao. Many of its white sandy beaches, such as Boracay, have been transformed into foreign tourist havens, with coconut trees along the shores forming indelible images for Filipinos both at home and abroad. In an archipelago where services are centralized in major islands and cities, the flow of human traffic and internal migration are constant and commonplace.

En route to the Spice Islands, Ferdinand Magellan was the first European to claim the islands in 1521 in the name of Spain (Arcilla 1998). For over 350 years, until the Philippine Revolution in 1896, the country stood at the crossroads of Western colonialism and imperialism. It became the "secure base" of the Spanish galleon trade "from Southeast Asia to Manila, across the Pacific to Mexico and across the Atlantic to the waiting markets of Europe" (Cushner 1971, 2). The lives of native residents, called *Indios* by the Spaniards, became intertwined with the international market long before our modern-day understanding of the word "globalization." Gunn (2003) considers this Philippine experience part of the "first globalization" in the Eurasian context, from 1500 to 1800. Many *Indios* became seafarers, known even then as the "best sailors in the world," while other able-bodied natives laboured in the Spanish shipyards where the Manila galleons were built (Mercene 2007, 142). Under the *polo y servicios* (forced labour) system of the Spanish colonial government, Filipino males from ages sixteen to sixty were required to work without pay in the shipyards in Albay, Cavite, Marinduque, Masbate, Mindoro, and Pangasinan (Mercene 2007; Tucker 2009, 487). The term *Filipino,* previously reserved for Spaniards born in the Philippines (Quilop 2006, 4), came to be applied to the *Indios* "only during the last years of Spanish regime in the late 1890s." The new *ilustrado* (elite) class, with property and political clout, sent their children to universities in Spain, further facilitating connections with the Western world.

Except in the southern areas, with their solid Muslim base, the Spaniards used religion as a force to colonize most of the lowland peoples of the islands, aiming to integrate the divided pre-Hispanic *barangays* (villages) headed by *datus* (local chieftains) into their "hierarchical yet centralized" (Quilop 2006, 5) spheres of influence. Christianity became the "cement of Spanish rule" (Karnow 1989, 49). Consequently, the effects of "friarocracy" (Seekins 1983, 12), or rule of Spanish friars, were evident not only in civil administration but also throughout many aspects of social life. As agents of Catholicism, for example, the friars vigorously promoted ideal roles of women in society.

While the revolution against the oppressive rule of Spain raged, the Philippines was ceded to the United States in 1899 as part of the Treaty of Paris, which ended the Spanish-American War. The American entry in the Pacific against Spain was, according to Karnow (1989, 79), "a pious endeavor to liberate Cuba" and turned "in a confused series of events, into a conflict to crush the Filipino independence movement." An ironic twist of fate made America, a former colony, the colonizer of its first territory – what Karnow (ibid.) describes as "America goes global." Colonial ties with the United States began at this time, but the Philippines remained part of the global nexus of cash-crop markets started by Spain.

An effective new colonial tool for moulding the minds of the people was introduced by the American administrators: education. Unlike the Spanish educational system, which was controlled by Catholic priests and participated in mostly by upper-class families, the American system initiated a nationwide school program with "more efficient organizational machinery" (Israel-Sobritchea 1996, 85). Like religion, education was instrumental in shaping gender roles and women's participation in society. Popular education, first facilitated by the Thomasites in 1901 and 1902 (Edgerton 1984), did not, however, alter the religion-based Spanish curricular dogma affecting women and men. According to Israel-Sobritchea (1996), the promotion of sexual division of roles in colonial American education failed to achieve gender parity. Instead, the "miseducation of the Filipino people" (Constantino 1982) to place Western values above their own was systematically developed in schools (Salamanca 1968). Over time, Western models have inevitably come to shape Filipino children, their values, and their daily lives.

Independence is usually a product of bloodbath, a hard-won fight for freedom. Independence from the United States, however, was "drafted" (Karnow 1989, 253) legislatively between the US House of Representatives and the Philippines before and after the Second World War. Independence in 1946 was a "gift" granted by the benevolent colonial master, which was seemingly ready to hand over to the control of Filipinos their "white-man's burden" (Clymer 1976). This was an anomaly in political struggles, but the

Philippines' status as a neocolony has come to define the "dependent independence" (Karnow 1989, 323) of Philippine-American relations.

Philippine democracy is an evolving experiment. It may have, in principle, adopted the fundamental precepts of representative democracy, judicial due process, and primacy of the rule of law, among others, yet it remains unable to ensure its citizens optimal freedom to exercise rights and promote social security. For instance, it is well documented that persistent poverty has rendered millions of Filipinos willing to sell their votes during elections, a practice that has been both widely acknowledged and constant through the years (Hutchcroft 2008). The long political drama with the West and its insistence on creating from scratch a democracy in the Far East is a sure experiment in what Wurfel (1988) calls the "development and decay" of modernization.

The tenth president of the Philippines, Ferdinand Marcos, came to power in 1965 and, for the first time in the country's history of electoral democracy, won a second term in 1969. In 1972 he declared martial law, which lasted until 1986. Marcos introduced the idea of a "constitutional authoritarianism" (Hedman and Sidel 2000) that follows patterns of "Asian style democracy" (Neher 1994). As with the "guided democracy" of Sukarno in Indonesia (Vickers 2005) and the "paternalistic democracy" of Lee Kuan Yew in Singapore (Kim 1997), a tight grip on political power was wed to the economics of privilege, leading to the widespread practice of "crony capitalism" (Kang 2002) that the Philippines has had a hard time shaking off in the post-Marcos period.

The return to democracy after years of the Marcos dictatorship came after the assassination of opposition leader Senator Benigno "Ninoy" Aquino in 1983 was followed by the first-ever "people power" uprising in 1986 at EDSA (Epifanio de los Santos Avenue) (Hedman 2006).[1] Sadly, the euphoria and the recasting of politics as a harbinger of hope for all under the presidency of Corazon Cojuangco Aquino, Ninoy's widow and the first woman to hold the position, eventually faded away as her administration was besieged by attempted coups d'état (Fernandez 2006).

In this chapter, the migration of Filipino women is described in the context of economic, political, and socio-cultural developments in the Philippines; the characteristics and trajectories of the global labour diaspora; and the women's arrival and settlement in the Prairie provinces of Canada.

Philippines: Goodbye for Now

The population of the Philippines reached 94.85 million in 2011 (World Bank 2012), about three times larger than Canada's. Of the sixteen regions in the Philippines, the seven regions in Luzon account for more than half of the total population. In contrast to Canada's aging demographics, half of the people in the Philippines were younger than twenty-one years in 2000; the gender ratio of the total population was 101.43 males to 100 females (National Statistics Office [NSO] 2002). With an annual growth rate of over 2 percent in the most recent census, in 2007 (NSO 2008), or roughly 1.7 million newborns each year (Meinardus 2003), it is estimated that the Philippine population will reach 150 million in 2050. This will make it one of the ten most populous countries in the world (Population Reference Bureau 2007) and is certain to pose significant challenges to development and policy planning alike. Although many factors contribute to the migration trend, I have selected three to investigate more closely here: education, economy and politics, and gender roles in Philippine society.

Education

Filipinos believe that there is gold in education, that it acts as an equalizer among those of different social classes and status. Parents invest in their children's education, and it is a common practice in many households to prominently display any evidence of their accomplishments. Professional titles usually become the colloquial names and identities for sons and daughters in the community. Attainment of an educational degree accords respect and dignity not only to the individual but also to the whole family.

With free compulsory public elementary education and non-compulsory secondary education, Filipinos ten years and older had 93.4 percent basic literacy rate in 2003 – 94.3 percent for females and 92.6 percent for males (NSO 2006) – considered one of the highest rates in any developing country (Bureau of East Asian and Pacific Affairs 2009). Adult literacy stood at 93.6 percent in 2009 (Asian Development Bank [ADB] 2011). English has been the language of instruction in classrooms and textbooks since the American period. Pilipino/Filipino is used alternatively in instruction related mostly to the teaching of the "national" language and related subject areas, although the "metamorphosis" from its Tagalog base is itself riddled with controversy (Esman 1990; Rubrico 1998). Filipino was designated the national language in the 1987 Philippine Constitution and is considered important for instilling nationalism, as reflected in a popular adage, *ang hindi magmahal sa sariling wika ay mas masahol pa sa hayop at malansang isda* (those who do not love their own language are worse than animals and smelly fish). English remains the official language in business, courts, and national newspapers, however. The Philippines is even becoming the cheap alternative hub for Asians wishing to study English, notably South Koreans (Hicap 2009). Its educational system is known as the "human resource training institute of the Far East" (Gross 1999), with graduates dispersed throughout the world.

Based on the 2008 Functional Literacy, Education and Mass Media Survey (FLEMMS) in the Philippines, female literacy rate was at 96.1 percent, compared with 95.1 percent for male literacy (PCW 2012a). Despite the system of free public education, dropout rates remain high and are considered alarming (Ubac 2009). About 1.4 million Filipino school-aged children were not enrolled at the elementary level in 2003. The highest dropout rates were recorded in 2005-6, with 10.57 percent for elementary schools and 15.81 percent for secondary schools (Remollino 2009). Figures from 2009 indicate that 36 out of every 100 new entrants drop out of elementary school, and 65 from high school (Committee on the Rights of the Child [CRC] 2009). College students have an even higher dropout rate of 73 percent. Kabataan Party List Representative Mong Palatino (2009) calls this abandonment of education a tragedy.

Poverty, increasing tuition costs, and government neglect have all contributed to the current state of Philippine education. About 25.2 million Filipinos live below the poverty line (CRC 2009), and parents spend their meagre incomes on basic necessities rather than on auxiliary school fees. Many students who do complete high school are compelled to attend private colleges and universities, mainly due to the lack of space for them in publicly funded institutions (James 1991). In fact, seven out of ten students prefer to enroll in private institutions of higher education rather than public schools (PCW 2012a). Rare among universities, the University of the Philippines adopts a "socialized tuition" plan whereby students from higher family income brackets pay more than students from families with lower incomes; the latter are eligible for tuition waivers and cash subsidies for books and living expenses. This premier state university is also known for its history of nationalist student activism, and many rich families prefer to send their children to less politically symbolic private schools.

For many high school graduates, access to tertiary schools is another problem as these are located mainly in cities; transportation and accommodation are prohibitive expenses for those living in distant towns. Development and infrastructure programs remain urban-centred, which contributes to congestion in cities while peripheral towns remain unchanged. Budget allocation for education has fallen significantly as well, from 17.4 percent in 2001 to 12 percent in 2008 (Kwok 2008). Education spending is a measly 2.5 percent of the GDP (Digal 2009), and poorly paid, worn-out public school teachers leave their jobs to find work overseas. Instead of being a right for all, education is now a privilege of the few: the wealthy and those supported by dollar remittances who are able to hang on.

Nowhere in the world are gender and education so intrinsically tied to global labour demands than in the Philippines. The number of nursing schools increased by about 200 percent from 2003 to 2006, and 70 percent of graduates work abroad (Health Alliance for Democracy 2006). The Philippines is the only country in the world with an "explicit nurse export policy" (Brush 2007, 37). Even medical doctors have turned to nursing for such opportunities abroad (Comerford 2005a). According to Tullao and

Rivera (2008), the increased demand for education as a result of temporary labour migration has been met mainly by private institutions. The high cost of nursing education did not deter 453,890 new students from enrolling in 2006 (*Sun Star* 2008). Six private tertiary schools offering health science courses even made it to the top one thousand corporations in the country in 2003 (Marquez 2005).

Caregiving is now professionalized in the Philippines, with certified programs by the Technical Education and Skills Development Authority (TESDA), mainly allied to the needs of receiving countries, especially Canada. The proliferation of private schools offering caregiver courses throughout the country is unprecedented, providing second-year college students the opportunity to tailor their education to a specific work category in Canada and enticing unemployed college graduates to re-enroll in a six-month course to seek opportunities overseas. I surmise that the high dropout rates at the college level are somehow linked to the proliferation of short-term education-for-migration courses that promise better job opportunities than a college degree.

Hotel, restaurant, or hospitality management courses have become mainstream in colleges and universities. At Enderun College, one of the "biggest hospitality schools in the world" (Salcedo 2007), local students pay a hefty sum of at least 300,000 pesos each year for a program related to international hospitality management and business administration.[2] Among the vocational courses, Housekeeping and Guestroom Maintenance had the highest numbers of women enrollees and graduates from July 2005 to August 2006 (13.27 percent and 14.07 percent, respectively) (PCW 2012a). About 120,000 students nationwide complete related courses each year for possible employment in foreign countries (Milan 2009).

In a country where class divisions are stark, education is the hope of millions of Filipinos. Education of children is the most important factor motivating many parents to seek work overseas. Filipino temporary foreign workers across the Canadian Prairies point out that many families in their native land are unable to meet the increasing needs of their children at the college or university level. Lack of government action to solve the crisis in public education (Meinardus 2003) and the inability to find better employment opportunities in the Philippines have made migration an attractive option for many. Asked Nita, a live-in caregiver in Calgary, "*Para ano pa itong paghihirap ko kung hindi para sa mga anak ko, makatapos ng pag-aaral* [what are my sacrifices for but for my children, for them to finish school]?"

Children of overseas Filipino workers (OFWs) are often advised by their parents to pursue courses that will ultimately enable them to secure jobs in the countries where the parents themselves are located.[3] Certificates or degrees in designated courses are viewed almost as passports to reunification.

Similarly, for many poor families in the Philippines, investing in education-for-migration has a dollar value and is perceived to be a ticket out of poverty. Giant billboards advertising jobs overseas and the tangible effects of *katas ng Saudi* (sweat of Saudi) hang from jeepney dashboards and in *sari-sari* (variety) stores and strongly push migration as a route to modern comfort – sans reports of abuse and exploitation.

I would argue that, unfortunately, education-for-migration in contemporary Philippines is a misguided and unsustainable development venture. The youth, or so-called *pag-asa ng bayan* (hope of the nation), are leaving in droves, to the detriment of the country's future. So far the Philippine government has supported this warped educational practice, which has effectively funnelled its human resources to foreign lands. By doing so, it shares the benefits of the OFWs' hard-earned dollars, which support an ailing economy and help prevent political catastrophe resulting from massive domestic unemployment.

Economy and Politics

The Philippines retains vestiges of a colonial economy circumscribed by feudal relations between haves and have-nots. Since the introduction of private property ownership by Spanish colonizers and the resulting appropriation of communal lands into the hands of the few, particularly the Roman Catholic Church and provincial elites, attempts at land redistribution as an engine of growth have been a political dream (Borras 2005). Even today, a majority of Filipinos are beholden to landed elites, who also hold political power. According to Putzel (1992, 27), a mere 5 percent of landed families own 83 percent of all agricultural lands in the country. Despite significant developments in manufacturing and the service industries since the 1950s, land reform is a "major obstacle to ... economic development" (Suter 2007, 54). From 1993 to 2002, about 1.4 million hectares of agricultural land were distributed to 751,900 farmers through the Comprehensive Agrarian Reform Program (NSO 2005), but as of 2009, the Department of Agrarian Reform had a "backlog of at least 1.2 million of hectares [sic]" for distribution (Asian Legal Resource Centre 2009). The high cost of fertilizer and lack of government subsidies to small farmers have resulted in many of the latter losing their land. In many areas of the country, conversion of farmland to housing projects has reduced the amount of arable land and sustainability of resources (Remo and Avendaño 2008).

The Philippine economy has also been in a perennial state of recovery since the 1976 world economic recession that led to the country's "worst balance of payments crisis" ever (Villegas 1986, 145). Foreign debt soared from US$599 million in 1966 to US$28 billion in 1986. Most was borrowed by the Marcos regime during martial law, mainly from the International

Monetary Fund and World Bank (IMF-WB), at an annual rate of 27 percent from 1973 to 1982 (Escobar 2004). By the end of 2008, the country's foreign debt had reached US$53.9 billion or 31.9 percent of GDP (*Straits Times* 2009). The 2009 debt/GDP ratio of 56.3 percent was higher than the Asian regional average of 30.6 percent. Besides other fiscal problems, such as weak tax collection, the Arroyo administration ran up a budget deficit of 199.2 billion pesos during the same year (ABS-CBN Global 2009). Foreign debt servicing and systemic corruption, among other factors, contribute to the inability of the government to deliver effective basic services to all (Bello et al. 2005).

Income disparity between rich and poor is still high, but OFW families have cushioned the emerging middle class. GDP per capita in 2007 was US$3,406, but a more accurate measurement of quality of life, the United Nations Human Development Index, ranks the Philippines 105th out of 182 countries (Ordinario 2009). Although GDP grew by an average of 4.6 percent annually during 2006-9, the poverty rate grew by 26.5 percent in 2009 (World Bank 2011). With current levels of performance in education, economy, and health, it will take the Philippines at least 175 years to reach parity with the living standards of industrialized countries (*Manila Mail* 2009).

A highly educated young population ready to chart its own life course is unable to find suitable employment in the Philippines. Only 5-10 percent of the 1 million graduates each year find work in their field of study (Milan 2009). The July 2009 Labor Force Survey of the National Statistics Office estimated the number of unemployed at 2.9 million people (7.6 percent), and the percentage of total underemployment at 19.8 percent (NSO 2009c). The national unemployment rate as of January 2011 was 7.4 percent (NSO 2012). Based on the results of the January 2013 Labor Force Survey, Filipino males comprise 63.6 percent of those unemployed (Taborda 2013).

The domestic economy has been beset by a "disastrous oversupply of unemployable graduates" (Milan 2009). About 40 percent of the 100,000 new nursing graduates each year pass the licensure examination; of these, only 5,000 find work in local hospitals. With an oversupply of nursing graduates waiting for their clinical experience in order to comply with eligibility requirements in foreign hospitals, many either allegedly pay for jobs to gain the required experience or work in the booming outsourced call centre industry (Lopez 2009).

Those who have made it into the labour force are generally dissatisfied with the remuneration scales (Higham 2007). The pace of merit promotion is slow in government agencies, and the prevailing belief is that political patronage is the only way to the top of the bureaucracy (Hodder 2009). Salaried employees are heavily taxed through a mandatory system of payroll deductions, compared with entrepreneurs, lawyers, or doctors, who allegedly are able to avoid paying full income tax or find ways to reduce it, at times even bribing government tax collectors to reduce their tax liabilities (Yang

2008; McCoy 2009). The non-agriculture minimum daily wage of 426 pesos, or about US$10 (US$1 = 41 pesos as of March 2013), in the National Capital Region (NCR) as of July 2011 (Department of Labor and Employment 2011) is insufficient to meet the cost of living (Balisacan and Pernia 2002). This combination of workplace dissatisfaction and lack of social benefits impels many new and middle-career employees to migrate and start anew in foreign lands (Ball 2004; Rothausen, Gonzalez, and Griffin 2009).

Data on employment by major occupation in 2006 break down the workforce as follows: 31.9 percent unskilled labourers; 18.9 percent farmers, forestry workers, and fishermen; 11.7 percent executives, managers, supervisors, and government officials; 9.6 percent service workers, shop workers, and market sales workers; 8 percent traders and related workers; and 7.6 percent plant machine operators and assemblers (Domingo 2008). In 2010, about 51.8 percent of the estimated 36.0 million employed persons were in services – the majority in wholesale, retail, motor vehicle repair, and personal and household goods – and 33.2 percent in agriculture (NSO 2011). Over 50 percent of the labour force worked in occupations related to agriculture that do not require university degrees, and courses offering agriculture-related topics are not popular among students.

Clearly, there is no match between available employment and the type of graduates produced each year, and the needs of the developing economy are not being met by the educational system (Gonzalez 1992). Since the domestic economy cannot absorb the ultra-high number of graduates each year, an ever-growing proportion of the educated labour force is expected to work overseas through the labour export program.

Export of human resources was initiated by the Marcos administration in the 1970s to accumulate foreign capital for economic growth. The labour export program was outlined in the Philippine Development Plan (1978-82): "The export of manpower will be allowed only as a temporary measure to ease underemployment and will increasingly be restrained as productive employment opportunities are created" (cited in Catholic Institute for International Relations 1987, 17). What was meant to be a temporary measure has since become permanent, as the much-awaited creation of "productive employment opportunities" has been stalled by a combination of economic mismanagement and political instability. In fact, successive governments have become so dependent on OFW dollar remittances that human export is now a fixture of development planning (Gonzalez 1998; Mellyn 2003; Opiniano 2004a; Bagasao 2005), and the Philippine OFW program has recently been considered as the "global model for labor export" (Center for Migrant Advocacy and Friedrich Ebert Stiftung 2009, 15). Foreign labour deployment accounted for a substantial share of the GDP, with a record of US$20.1 billion in remittances in 2011 (Remo 2012). With declining exports and remittances from OFWs amid a cataclysmic global recession, the

Philippine economy was projected to grow by only 3.7 percent in 2009 (ASEAN Affairs 2009). However, another boom in remittances reached US$17.0 billion as of November 2010, much higher than the US$15.78 billion at the same point in 2009 (Wilson 2011). In 2011, remittances grew by 7.2 percent, or to US$20.1 billion (Remo 2012). Thus, remittances are the lifeblood of OFW families, communities, and the nation, providing a social safety net and much-needed support in education, health care, and other essential areas.

The "politics of plunder" (Aquino 1987) during the Marcos regime remains an issue among present-day *politikos* (politicians). Public coffers are in a dismal state, and the American legacy of pork barrel funds for members of Congress has led to the circulation of money in favoured hands (Coronel 1998; Hutchcroft 2008). In many provinces, road construction is a common public works project, and the completion of long gravel roads often depends on disbursements made after elections. Construction projects have signs with the names of sponsoring politicians prominently displayed for passing motorists to see.

A political system subject to the tight grip of dynastic elected officials who reward their most loyal supporters contributes to social divisions and lingering unrest in the Philippines (Quimpo 2008). Local and national governance appear to be in a state of permanent crisis of confidence, adversely affecting peace and order in many parts of the country (Bello et al. 2005), which also results in the displacement and migration of residents. Communist insurgency in the countryside and Muslim separatism in Mindanao, for example, are continuing realities that only hamper genuine efforts at change (Dictaan-Bang-oa 2004). Politically motivated violence abounds, and known culprits with powerful ties to ruling families and parties are rarely brought to justice (Kreuzer 2005).

The dollar frenzy created by bilateral labour agreements (Bacungan and Ofreneo 2002) has somehow made migrant workers out of potential insurgents. The material benefits of migration are demonstrated by new palatial houses lining former farmlands and the frequency of OFW families' visits to gigantic shopping malls. These are obvious enticements given the rough mountain lives of rebels, although many continue to find hope in the leftist movement. It is plausible that aggressive recruitment of Filipinos for overseas employment is preferable to producing a new generation of discontented masses. As the political economy balances between development and maldevelopment, Filipinos as individuals have to take direct responsibility for their own welfare in the absence of sufficient government-funded programs. As diasporic citizens, they form part of a national *bayanihan* (community spirit) (Alzona 2007) that somehow supersedes state responsibility. With the feminization of migration, this responsibility rests more than ever on the shoulders of Filipino women.

Gender Roles

Women's mobility is circumscribed in many traditional cultures in Asia. In the Philippines, the "cultural script" (Tapales 1992b, 114) defining women's movement tended to be confined to upper-class families with ties to Spanish colonial authorities. Although there was no written account, the *mujer indigena* (indigenous woman) (Mananzan 1987b) prior to colonization was presumably uninhibited in undertaking common economic and social activities. Women's vital role in the household economy necessitated her free movement.

In this section, the gender roles of Filipino women and men in the modern period are discussed relative to the "culture of migration" (Asis 2006). I argue that culture is not an impediment to Filipino women's migration; instead, cultural mores actually encourage them to sustain the household economy and the nation. Culture, together with the realities of geography and economy, shapes the fluid crossing of borders that defines migration as a fact of life among Filipinos.

Filipino women enjoy a relatively privileged position at home and in society compared with their counterparts in other Asian cultures (Chant and McIlwaine 1995; Feliciano 1996). Female births are celebrated with the same joy that marks male births. While boys are still considered the source of patrilineal heritage, girls are nonetheless viewed with importance. At home, Filipino families assign roles to male and female children based on their levels of productivity (Eviota 1992). In farming communities, for example, girls take on different tasks from boys, but the distinctions are not particularly rigid (Santiago 1996; Winzeler 1996). Rice cultivation, mostly using traditional methods of brawn and carabao, is a collective enterprise, and children are valued as assets in tilling the soil and harvesting crops each season. In fishing villages, men venture out to sea while women prepare the catch for daily consumption and marketing, a parity of contribution that fosters equitable relations between husband and wife (Eder 2006). Wives are generally perceived to be the managers of household finances, the ones in charge of family assets and in control of their disbursement. Women from low-income families face the added burden of finding supplementary income (Roces 2000). Examples such as these demonstrate how gender roles tend to focus on collective goals without limiting individual participation.

However, the apparent equality enjoyed by Filipino women in the home stands in contrast to the constraints of social and political structures institutionalized by Spanish and American colonial practices, specifically in education, religion, and political life. In each of these spheres, women's roles are marked by inferiority and subordination. Education shapes the career paths of women and men, and the selection of courses throughout much of colonial history and to the present day has been gender-based (Quezada-Reyes 2003), for example, teaching for women and engineering for men.

Changes in society have encouraged both genders to pursue courses based more on personal interest and aptitude. Although teaching is female-dominated, the administrative leadership in the schools remains a male domain (Esplanada 2009). Among the 80 percent of Filipinos who are Catholics, religion remains the overarching guide to proper gender roles, resulting in a not particularly nuanced moral dichotomy of what defines a good woman versus a bad woman at home and in society. In keeping with both Spanish tradition and the dictum that a woman's place is in the home, political life remains male-dominated, but the significant and visible presence of Filipino women in politics has made them among the most active in Asia (Edwards and Roces 2004; Iwanaga 2008).

There are a number of triggers for women's migration, from the failed attempts at meaningful development across the country, to the uneven pace of modernization, to the lack of local employment opportunities. Although women's work helps sustain farming households, the physical labour required by agriculture is often better supplied by male siblings. Daughters tend to seek other opportunities in towns and cities. Poor families often send their daughters to work as domestic helpers with their own relatives and associates in exchange for education or a monthly wage. Of the 1 million child domestics in the Philippines, about 90 percent are girls (Anti-Slavery International n.d.), a disturbing figure that does not even take into account those who are trafficked for sexual purposes.

Females have higher retention rates in school, and it is possible that their completion of secondary and tertiary education enables them to migrate more readily than the males in their families. In most cases, female migration is a survival strategy of the household (Trager 1984; Lauby and Stark 1988). The well-being of siblings and parents is ensured by regular remittances to support their continued education, medical expenses, and pursuit of alternative livelihood. Maria, a government employee in Saskatchewan, emigrated and never married in order to support her widowed mother and five siblings in the Philippines, but, she says, "*Kulang pa sa kanila ang kita ko* [my income is not even enough for them]."

I contend that the "culture of obligation" rests heavily on Filipino women. Daughters are culturally oriented and religiously inculcated with the values of caring, self-sacrifice, patience, humility, and forbearance. Female children embrace maternal responsibilities of caring for younger siblings in the absence of parents. Early on, the *ate* (oldest sister) becomes a surrogate mother and lives out the value of *anak muna bago ang sarili* (child first before self) in the family. The *kuya* (older brother) also takes on paternal roles. Amid perennial poverty and desperation, gender-based cultural conditioning of sacrifice contributes significantly to the "culture of migration" in the Philippines.

In a particularly appropriate metaphor, the Philippine state becomes a kind of "meta-child" of female OFWs (Bonifacio 2009, 168), and the "work of women keeps the economy afloat" (Parreñas 2008b, 183). *Inang Bayan* (Motherland) needs the sacrifice of its female citizens in order to ensure the survival of an entire generation mostly deprived of basic services. The popular euphemism for OFWs, *bagong bayani* (new heroes), takes on a different meaning in the lives of women. An entire "motherless generation" (Mahr 2008) demonstrates how the self-sacrifice of female OFWs vis-à-vis their own children and families translates into the general welfare of the nation-state.

Marketing Filipino women as the "top choice of household helpers" (Sy 2009) or even "so wanted" wives (Patterson 2006) is a reductive move that essentializes Filipino womanhood. The conventional belief among recruitment agents that Filipina nannies "know their place" is a reflection of their cultural positioning in the family and the national collective (Pratt 1997). Popular representations of Filipino women as embodying certain qualities desirable to foreign employers is, I would argue, a persistent reproduction of women's domesticity. As women in industrializing and developed countries enter the professional labour force, women from developing states such as the Philippines take on paid domestic work in what Parreñas (2000) calls the "international division of reproductive labor." A gender shift or gender balance in modern societies is far from real since women simply pass on their domestic burdens to other women.

The Philippine government also reinforces cultural traits through its mandatory fee-based pre-departure orientation seminar for OFWs. Outbound female migrant workers are advised, among other things, to behave appropriately in host countries. The embodied Filipina becomes the unofficial "goodwill ambassador" of the Philippine labour export program. Filipino domestic workers in Hong Kong use the "Maria Clara stereotype" (i.e., a woman of virtue) to guide their behaviour and sexual reputation (Ignacio 2005, 90; Chang and Groves 1997).

As a people moulded in "our [American] image" (Karnow 1989), Filipino women are regarded in Western societies as a ready workforce conversant in the English language and familiar with modern lifestyles. As I will discuss in the following section, however, the trajectory of their work in occupations characterized by the three "D's" (dirty, dangerous, and degrading) (Ellerman 2005) demonstrates the complicated interplay of race, gender, citizenship status, and immigration regulation.

Global Labour Diaspora

While "home may be where the heart is," over 11 million Filipinos, or about 11 percent of the total population, have left the Philippines since the 1970s (Pinoy Overseas 2008). Based on the 2008 Survey on Overseas Filipinos by the National Statistics Office, about 2 million OFWs were deployed in one six-month period alone (April to September 2008), or a 14.6 percent increase from the preceding year (NSO 2009b). In 2010, about 1.5 million OFWs were deployed overseas (Philippine Overseas Employment Administration [POEA] 2010). Deployment of female OFWs in 2006 was 2 percent higher than for their male counterparts; although the sex ratio of OFWs was 104 males to 100 females, the latter increased from 764,000 in 2006 to 857,000 in 2007 (NSO 2009a). In 2007, about 63 percent of female OFWs were younger than 35 years, compared with 48 percent of male OFWs; the median age was 31 years and 35 years for females and males, respectively (ibid.). In 2011, female OFWs were still younger at 63.1 percent compared with male OFWs at 48.5 percent in the 15- to 34-year-old category (Philippine Commission on Women 2012). About 43 percent of the Filipino diaspora are permanent immigrants, while the rest are contract workers (Center for People Empowerment in Governance [CenPEG] 2008). They are scattered across more than 193 countries and territories, from the burning hot sun of the Middle East to the frigid climate of the Canadian West, which Fay (2005) describes as "from the tropics to the freezer."

Two interrelated aspects of the dispersal of Filipinos are presented in this section: characteristics of labour flows and trajectories of migration. Based on the posted labour needs of host countries, I argue that gender is a deciding factor in the deployment of OFWs. Race is another consideration in shaping the "ideal" or preferred migrant workers in certain categories. Thus, race and gender are the two main determinants of the construction of the global labour force (Gonzalez et al. 2004); these, along with Filipino workers' relatively marginal status as citizens from a developing state are intrinsically linked to their large-scale recruitment around the world.

Table 1 shows the latest official global "stock" estimates of Filipinos overseas as of December 2010. These are grouped according to the nature of residency in foreign countries. Permanent residents have acquired residency or citizenship status in their host countries; temporary residents have contracted work visas and are expected to return to the Philippines; and

Table 1

"Stock" estimates of overseas Filipinos, 2010

Region	Permanent	Temporary	Irregular	Total
World	4,423,680	4,324,388	704,916	9,452,984
Africa	4,669	62,738	7,076	74,483
Asia (East/South)	288,597	644,446	299,672	1,232,715
Asia (West)	5,645	2,717,046	127,900	2,850,591
Europe	314,710	253,870	95,309	663,889
Americas/Trust Territories	3,481,263	235,135	166,958	3,883,356
Oceania	328,796	64,003	8,001	400,800
Sea-based workers	–	347,150	–	347,150

Source: Commission on Filipinos Overseas 2012.

"irregular" residents are those without proper documents or with expired work visas, or those who are considered overstaying in their host countries (POEA 2009). "Stock" refers to the estimate of people who have changed their country of usual residence in a given period. It is a problematic term applied to Filipinos overseas, as it alludes to the commodification of Filipino labour in capitalist exchange now mediated by the Philippines as a "labor brokerage state" (Magalit Rodriguez 2010, 141), which dehumanizes the labour they engage in for their families, communities, home country, and receiving states.

The Americas and Trust Territories – including Canada and the United States, both of which are favoured destinations for permanent immigrants – have the greatest number of Filipinos, totalling over 3.8 million in 2010 (Commission on Filipinos Overseas [CFO] 2012). Of this number, there were 581,095 permanent residents, 80,444 temporary residents, and 6,135 irregular residents in Canada.[4] Different regions in Asia, particularly West Asia, which includes the Middle East, were next with over 2.8 million Filipinos, mainly temporary workers. Over half a million Filipinos abroad are "irregular" migrants; in the Americas and Trust Territories, the majority – 156,000 – were in the United States, the largest such group among the 214 listed countries (Villadiego 2002). Undocumented or "overstaying" Filipinos are euphemistically referred to as "TNT" (*tago ng tago,* or "in hiding"), and the official estimates worldwide are no doubt conservative. About 2 percent of all undocumented immigrants in the United States came from the Philippines in 2006 (Terrazas 2008). In 2008, about 300,000 Filipino TNTs were in the United States and 113,000 in Europe (*Manila Mail* 2008b; Olea 2008).

A recent compendium of OFW statistics (see Table 2) indicates that more females than males were newly hired in the top ten occupational categories

Table 2

Newly hired OFWs by top occupational categories by gender, 2010

Occupational category	Male	Female	Total
1 Household service workers	1,703	94,880	96,583
2 Charworkers/cleaners/etc.	2,612	9,521	12,133
3 Nurses, professional	1,828	10,254	12,082
4 Caregivers/caretakers	543	8,750	9,293
5 Waiters/bartenders/etc.	4,393	4,396	8,789
6 Wiremen/electrical	8,576	30	8,606
7 Plumbers/pipefitters	8,391	16	8,407
8 Welders/flame cutters	5,037	22	5,059
9 Housekeeping/related service workers	701	4,098	4,799
10 Bricklayers/stonemasons/tile setters	4,478	29	4,507
Total deployed	154,677	185,602	340,279

Source: Philippine Overseas Employment Administration 2010.

Figure 2

Newly hired female OFWs by top occupation, 2010

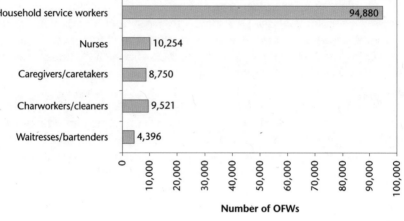

Source: Philippine Overseas Employment Administration 2010.

in 2010. Household service workers, popularly known as DH (domestic helpers) ranked first, with 94,880 women, followed by professional nurses with 10,254 (Figure 2). OFWs working as household service workers may fill the lowest occupation in host countries, but their skill levels are far above those expected from the host countries' own nationals. This means that whereas housework may be performed by uneducated or poorly educated local women, when it is opened to foreign women under a regulated mechanism of entry and exit, it becomes "professionalized" and undertaken by college or university-educated OFWs, many of whom are former public school teachers.

Female OFWs are concentrated in particular occupations that define their identities in host societies (Constable 1997; Cheng 2006). Desired skills are country-specific and highly regulated by each state. The majority of Filipino nurses overseas, mostly women, wind up in the Middle East, where the number of newly hired has remained consistently high compared with the rest of the world. Outbound nurses to the United Kingdom recorded a declining trend, from 5,388 in 2001, to 800 in 2004, to a low of 28 in 2008 – evidence of the increasing replacement of foreign-trained nurses with domestic graduates.

With more stringent requirements for permanent residency, Filipino nurses in the United Kingdom return to the Philippines after the expiration of their contracts or find other country-routes for settlement (Buchan 2006). Filipino nurses on temporary work permits in the Middle East use their foreign work experience as a second springboard to the United States and Canada, where permanent migration is possible. Six respondents in this study had worked for years in hospitals in Saudi Arabia before coming to Canada under the Live-in Caregiver Program (LCP).

Caregivers tend to the young, the old, the sick, and the physically or mentally challenged. They live with their employers and are normally given other tasks; hence, there is a thin line between care work and domestic work. Newly hired Filipino caregivers, overwhelmingly women, were bound mainly for Taiwan (6,184), Israel (1,456), and Canada (1,452) in 2010 (POEA 2010). Erratic deployment to the Middle East is partly explained by war and concerns for the security of OFWs. Repatriation of OFWs during crises is a major challenge faced by the Philippine government (Tan and Concha 2009).

Canada hosts the Live-in Caregiver Program, which replaced the Foreign Domestic Movement Program (1981-92). The LCP is dominated by Filipino women, who have accounted for 95 percent of the total number of participants since the program's inception in 1992 (Bakan and Stasiulis 1997; McKay 2003; Pablo 2008). According to the rules in effect on 1 April 2011, it offers eligibility for permanent residency on completion of twenty-four months of live-in work within four years of arrival in Canada. Canada receives more newly hired caregivers than any country in the West; the number rose from 2,152 in 2002 to 4,170 in 2007, decreasing thereafter to 1,452 in 2010 (POEA 2008, 2010). About 52,493 people entered Canada under the LCP between 1993 and 2009; the Philippines was the number one source of caregivers, with a total of 43,907, followed by India, Slovakia, the United Kingdom, and Jamaica (Kelly et al. 2011, 5, 10). Filipino arrivals under the LCP peaked in 1994 then gradually declined until 1997; numbers were relatively steady from 1998 to 2002 and increased steadily from 2003 to 2007 (ibid.).

The number of applications for caregivers submitted at the Canadian Embassy in Manila far exceeds the number of visas issued in the Philippines, however. Filipino live-in caregivers in Alberta who participated in this study agree that the processing time for caregiver applications submitted in the Philippines is longer than for those submitted in Hong Kong or elsewhere. According to Nora in Calgary, *"Patay na ang alaga mo wala ka pang visa* [your ward will already be dead and you still have no visa]." For Humena in Cardston, a small town in Alberta, *"Nakalakad na ang bata wala pa rin visa* [the child is now able to walk and still no visa]." Many caregivers who have recently entered Canada came from a country other than the Philippines. To fill expedited requests from would-be employers, recruitment agents in Canada prefer to recruit Filipino nurses and domestic workers who are already abroad.

Filipino domestic workers head primarily to Hong Kong and the Middle East, particularly Saudi Arabia and Kuwait. Between 2004 and 2006, Kuwait replaced Hong Kong as their top destination. Hong Kong regained the top spot in 2010, hiring 28,602 new household service workers, followed by Kuwait with 21,554. Italy was the only Western country belonging to the top destination countries of Filipino domestic workers, with 1,223 deployments that year. Domestic workers have also been known as domestic helpers (DH) and, since 2007, have been recorded as "household service workers" (HSW) by POEA under Governing Board Resolution No. 13.

Domestic workers and caregivers are closely related occupational categories and their job descriptions appear blurred. The Philippine Overseas Employment Administration (2009) uses different typologies that overlap; in 2009, for example, it listed "maids and related housekeeping service workers" as a category with 41 new deployments; "domestic helpers and related household workers" with 71,557 total new hires; and "caregivers and caretakers" with 9,228 new hires. These categories appear fluid and tend to use labels prescribed by host countries – caregivers in Canada or domestic workers in Hong Kong – and Philippine government directives somehow glamorize these types of occupations. For example, POEA Governing Board Resolution No. 08 (Series of 2006) requires domestic helpers bound for overseas employment to secure a National Certificate for Household Service Workers and attend a country-specific language and culture orientation (POEA 2007).

Because of the large number of application files received by the Canadian Embassy in the Philippines and the consequent long wait times for issuance of visas, employment agencies outside the Philippines tend to recruit from those who have already left the country. Filipino domestic workers in Hong Kong or elsewhere are eligible to apply as caregivers under the LCP in Canada. They take on a different job title in Canada but use their experience as domestic workers to become caregivers, since the LCP accepts a year of such experience outside the Philippines in lieu of certification from a six-month accredited caregiver course in the Philippines. According to Maria in Edmonton, "*Nagtiis ako ng sampung taon sa Hong Kong, kaya ko ang dalawang taon trabaho ng live-in caregiver sa Canada para maging residente* [I endured ten years in Hong Kong; I can bear two years of work as a live-in caregiver in Canada to become a permanent resident]."

Focus-group discussions with Filipino caregivers reveal an apparent distinction between those who came directly from the Philippines and those who arrived in Canada by way of another country. According to Lita in Calgary, "*Hindi marunong makipaglaban ng kanilang karapatan ang galing sa Hong Kong; sanay sila sa trabaho ng katulong doon na iba sa trabaho ng caregiver dito sa Canada* [those who came from Hong Kong do not know how to fight for their rights; they are used to the work of domestic helpers there, which is different from the work of caregivers in Canada]." Lita, a former accountant in the Philippines, was directly hired to care for an elderly woman. When she was asked to do more work in the home than was stipulated in the contract, she phoned the hotline number provided by Citizenship Immigration Canada (CIC). She was able to negotiate overtime pay and establish more equitable working relations with her employer, the elderly woman's daughter. She said: "*Parang pantay na kami* [it is as if we are now equal]."

Working as entertainers is another gender-specific and country-defined migration trajectory of OFWs. Overseas Performing Artists (OPAs) possess certain talents and skills, such as singing and dancing. Filipino OPAs are overwhelmingly female. For example, of the 73,246 OPAs in 2002, about 95 percent or 69,986 were women (Masaaki 2008, 121). Japan was the destination country for 99 percent of OPAs from 2001 to 2004, but numbers declined after it tightened its visa rules to curb human trafficking (*Asian Political News* 2004). In line with the "enlightened policy" on immigration, the Japanese Justice Ministry announced a dramatic cut in Filipino entertainer visas from 80,000 to 8,000 annually (McNeill 2005). According to the Japanese Embassy in Manila, the number of such visas issued decreased from 9,199 in 2008 to 7,465 in 2009 (Zenkoku Ippan Tokyo General Union 2011). Female entertainers in Japan are popularly called *Japayuki-san* (Ms. Go to Japan), and Filipino women are seen as entertainers, hostesses, and barmaids (Ballescas 1992; Anderson 1999) often associated with sex work in clubs allegedly operated by the *yakuza* (Japanese Mafia).[5] Despite stricter rules, Japan remained the top destination country of OPAs in 2008, with 2,380, followed by Korea with 1,020 (POEA 2008). Many Filipino *Japayukis* enter into romantic liaisons with their Japanese patrons, some of which end in marriage (Suzuki 2008); others return home with a love child and wait for the promised financial support of already married Japanese partners. There are about 200,000 Japanese-Filipino children in the Philippines (Nuqui 2008).

Based on these data on specific country destinations of particular types of female OFW occupations, it appears that some countries have socially constructed particular labour market niches for foreign workers based on gender, race, and nationality, a reality that raises many questions. Why, for example, are there so many Filipino domestic workers in Hong Kong, Filipino entertainers in Japan, Filipino nurses in Saudi Arabia, or Filipino live-in caregivers in Canada? Why are Filipinos, especially women, mostly singled out for certain types of work? Is the Filipina the epitome of the "global woman" (Ehrenreich and Hochschild 2002)? Or is it because Filipinos are said to be good, from another perspective, "at home in the world" (Aguilar 2002)?

The global positioning of Filipinos in general and Filipino women in particular is marked by a complex, interlayered modernization process involving history, international political economy, culture, and reproductive labour in both sending and receiving states (Magalit Rodriguez 2008). The fate of the Philippines has long been tied to its history and convoluted path to modernization. Its international competitive advantage is its people. Western countries, some through colonization, depend to varying degrees on the resources of other countries to keep their economies competitive. With an aging population in places like Canada, human capital is sourced from other countries under a system of selection and regulation. As societies modernize and labour skills become specialized, there is a perceived need for foreign workers who will take on low-paying jobs and provide services that are in short supply in the domestic economy. Foreign workers such as Filipinos have become what I call the saviours of many marketplaces because of their unrecognized contribution to maintaining economic stability and ensuring a level of comfort in wealthy and industrialized societies. Nurses, for example, are essential to the health and well-being of citizens, and the management of health care is one of the critical gauges of modern society; without their services, the very effectiveness of governance is seriously compromised (Thomas 2003). Thus, societies with aging populations, such as Canada, need to hire foreign-trained health workers to fill the labour shortage. I contend that Filipinos are not only "new heroes" in the Philippines for their dollar remittances but, together with other foreign workers, are also modern-day "heroes of the global economy" for accepting jobs very few local residents of wealthier countries are willing to take. In innumerable ways they serve the needs of families, businesses, and governments in both their native and host countries.

I would argue that this idea of "global economic heroism" applies even more to women. Women bear the unrecognized burden of domestic work and traditionally feminine or maternal tasks in the community (Hom 2008). Newly industrialized countries in East Asia have accumulated enough material wealth that foreign women's labour is now a commodity available to many middle-class families. Women in Hong Kong, for instance, have joined the productive public sector as employees or entrepreneurs, and their domestic tasks are being transferred to foreign domestic workers, mainly Filipinas (Chang and Ling 2000). Following Hondagneu-Sotelo's "new world domestic order" (2001, xix) and Parreñas's "international division of reproductive labor" (2008a, 41), the domestic labour of migrant domestic workers embodied by women from poor countries such as the Philippines replaces that expected of women in host countries.

On another front, female entertainers in Japan perform in the public sphere for the consumption of mostly male clients. Japanese male culture demands entertainment provided by *Japayukis*, a respite from their work as *sarariman* (salaried man) (Karan 2005). *Japayukis* have assumed the role of the traditional geisha, which far fewer local women now choose to fill (Kelsky 2001). Interestingly, culture is the primary reason for the proliferation of foreign nurses in Saudi Arabia; strict codes for Muslim women prohibit both their employment on night shifts and contact with men in public places.

So, why the Filipina? Women from other nationalities are also found in select occupational categories, but the sheer number of Filipino women makes them stand out. In Hong Kong, there were 123,000 Filipino domestic helpers in 2007 compared with 115,000 Indonesians, the second most numerous group. The latter are gradually gaining a foothold because of cheaper wages and their ability to speak Cantonese (Human Trafficking Project 2008), but Filipinos comprised the majority of the 251,360 foreign domestic helpers in Hong Kong as of May 2008 (Migrant Rights 2009). As of September 2012, there were 152,807 Filipino domestic workers in Hong Kong, compared with 151,382 from Indonesia (Roncesvalles and Sto. Domingo 2012). About 60 percent of entertainers in Japan are Filipino women, followed by other Asian women, particularly Thais, and many are trafficked (Fujimoto 2006). A total "stock" estimate of 210,617 Filipinos were in Japan in 2009 (POEA 2009). As of December 2011, there was a total "stock" estimate of over 1.5 million Filipinos in Saudi Arabia, where Filipino women comprised over 80 percent of the foreign nursing workforce in hospitals (*TransWorld News* 2009; CFO 2013b).

I acknowledge the professionalism and highly competitive qualifications of Filipino nurses and college-trained domestic workers, along with those of men and women in numerous other skilled occupations around the world. I argue, however, that gender, race, and nationality are factors that contribute to the predominance of Filipino women in certain types of work. There is not simply a direct relationship between supply and demand. Rather, facilitative mechanisms such as advertising, marketing (both private and government-sponsored) (Magalit Rodriguez 2008), and recruitment create the demand for an existing supply of labour. Such promotion plays heavily on the so-called desirable attributes of Filipino women and their suitability for certain types of work. The cultural-values orientation of Filipino women is hyped by recruitment agencies that tout the cost advantage of hiring them as workers compared with others; being hardworking, for example, is one of their many selling points that employers are familiar with.

Race and body are intricately connected in constructing the "ideal" worker. In Hong Kong, Filipino women with their light brown skin are desirable as they do not "scare the children" like the darker-skinned Sri Lankan and Bangladeshi women (Saptari 2008, 507). However, the identification of housework with brown-skinned Filipino women has become part of Cantonese "disdainful" lingo as *ban-mui* (Philippine girl) (Margold 2004, 53). The association of "Filipina" with domestic work is also observed in Italy and Greece (Chell 2000, 109; Lazaridis 2000). In Japan, the petite bodies of Filipina *Japayukis* make them agile performers and entertainers, and their workplaces offer opportunities for intimate engagement with Japanese men. Other Filipinas are brought in as foreign brides in Japanese farming communities (Sellek 2001), with the Japanese government even facilitating policies to allow their entry (Sassen 2004). Filipina bodies are eroticized frontiers in the West, too (Bernstein 2009). In all its manifestations, the racialized body of the Filipino woman is extremely favoured in the global service industry.

I further assert that the apparent acceptance of the Filipino's "brown" race as the "ideal" worker phenotype in the international economy perpetuates the perceived hierarchy of races, in which Filipinos become subjects of the "white" people in Asia (i.e., Chinese and Japanese), Canada, the United States, and elsewhere. According to England and Stiell (1997, 198), source country origins also reflect national identities that "highlight the various cultural, economic, political, and social constructs which divide people into difficult collectivities, based on exclusionary-inclusionary boundaries which focus on biological, cultural or historical claims in common." The hierarchy of states is reproduced in the superior-to-inferior relations among different groups of people. As Yuval-Davis (1997, 91) puts it, "people are not positioned equally within their collectivities and states, collectivities are not positioned equally with the state and internationally, and states are not positioned equally to other states." The value of Philippine citizenship and the lack of sustained proactive Philippine government intervention on their behalf in host societies make Filipino workers easy targets for unscrupulous recruitment agencies and vulnerable to discriminatory practices. Although the 1995 Magna Carta for Migrant Workers and Overseas Filipinos (Migrant Workers and Overseas Filipinos Act) provided measures for the protection and welfare of OFWs, these are not effectively implemented by Philippine agencies due to lack of resources and corruption.[6] Filipino workers form a lucrative mass serving the needs of employers for cheap labour and generating profits for the international recruitment chain, including many Filipino agents.

The trajectories of the global Filipino worker also demonstrate how state structures and practices can lead to the prevalence of particular nationalities in some occupations. Labour migration and immigration policies reflect domestic economic realities, and in most countries, such as Canada, such policies are often seen as a strategy for growth (Reitz 2004). Sovereign acts of the state foster a highly selective foreign labour entry program for industries and services in dire need of workers. The LCP, for example, sponsors the admission of Filipino women as potential citizens after they meet certain conditions as lowly paid live-in caregivers, an arrangement that remains attractive despite the potential for abuse and exploitation. Likewise, the Japanese labour code sets the criteria for types of work for which foreigners are accepted. What is clear is that state policies and practices profile the "ideal" worker who will benefit their domestic economies.

A shared cultural view is another plausible reason why Canadian employers prefer Filipino live-in caregivers. Filipino women are known to come from a predominantly Christian country in Asia, and many Christian Canadian families may find comfort in living with and entrusting the care of their children or aged parents to them (Bonifacio 2009). Because religion is not an official criterion for live-in work, or for any work in Canada except those expressly related to religious affairs, I cannot substantiate this claim with numbers of Christian/Catholic Filipinos working privately with Christian Canadian families. However, the general profile of religious affinity with Christianity among Filipinos and Canadians points to such a possibility.

Another significant contributor to the global Filipino labour diaspora is the informal process by which Filipinos themselves cope with the challenges in host societies: many workers bring with them a network of family, friends, and associates (Lott 2006). Personal and social networks, both within and outside the Philippines, facilitate chain migration, which contributes to the formation of "a sense of community that alleviates loneliness and longing to be home" (Pagaduan 2006, 78). Referrals to employers or placement agencies are a norm. "Graduates" of the LCP often submit names of family members or friends to replace them. In Cardston, a small town in Alberta, Beth extended her employment as a caregiver to await the arrival of her cousin, who is applying for a visa in the Philippines. The collectivist nature of Filipinos extends in diaspora and finds its value in seeking normalcy in lives disrupted by migration – a feat of ingenuity that transcends families and borders. Groups and even communities away from home are created from individual efforts.

Filipinos in Canada

Chilly Canada and tropical Philippines are separated by 11,144.5 kilometres (6,924.87 miles), but this distance nowadays is bridged by modern technology. The first two Filipinos arrived in Canada before 1931 (Aranas 1983), but the subsequent large-scale immigration is considered a post-1960s phenomenon facilitated by the introduction of so-called nondiscriminatory, universal, points-based immigration policies (Kelley and Trebilcock 2010). Canada's Immigration Act of 1967 abandoned the preferential treatment for "whites only" (Pendakur 2000, 12) and established a point system of desirable qualifications for selection and admission of newcomers. Subsequent changes, notably the Immigration Act of 1976 and the Immigration and Refugee Protection Act of 2001, have since made Canada apparently the "most welcoming country in the world" for Filipinos and others (CIC News 2008).[7] Furthermore, special immigration programs designed to compensate for labour shortages, such as the LCP and the more recent Provincial Nominee Program (PNP), have offered Filipinos and other immigrants an intermediate step of permanent residency status in Canada; that is, entering as a temporary foreign worker and graduating to a more

Table 3

Top source countries of permanent residents in Canada, 2004-10

Country	2004	2005	2006	2007	2008	2009	2010
China	36,429	42,292	33,079	27,013	29,336	29,051	30,197
India	25,573	33,146	30,754	26,052	24,549	26,117	30,252
Philippines	13,303	17,525	17,718	19,066	23,724	27,277	36,578
United States	7,507	9,263	10,943	10,449	11,216	9,723	9,243
United Kingdom	6,062	5,864	6,542	8,129	9,243	9,565	9,499
Pakistan	12,794	13,575	12,329	9,545	8,052	6,213	4,986
South Korea	5,337	5,819	6,178	5,866	7,245	5,864	5,539
France	5,028	5,430	4,915	5,526	6,384	7,299	6,934
Iran	6,063	5,502	7,073	6,663	6,010	6,066	6,815
Colombia	4,438	6,031	5,813	4,833	4,995	4,240	4,796

Source: Citizenship and Immigration Canada 2011.

permanent immigration status after complying with eligibility requirements for residency.

This section presents a demographic profile of the Filipino community in Canada based on census data from Statistics Canada and an immigration overview from Citizenship and Immigration Canada. The following presentation focuses on immigration status, period of arrival, gender composition, age distribution, marital status, education and occupation, residence, and mobility status from a national perspective as well as Filipinos' demographic characteristics in the Prairie provinces.

Immigration Status

The Philippines has been among the top five source countries of immigrants to Canada since the 1980s. Figures from CIC show that the Philippines consistently ranked third as a source of permanent residents from 2004 to 2008, with China and India as first and second, respectively (see Table 3). However, with the exception in 2002, the number of immigrants from the Philippines increased consistently thereafter until 2009, unlike those from China or India, which tended to fluctuate. In 2011, the Philippines was the number one source country of permanent residents in Canada, with 34,991 recorded arrivals (CIC 2011a).

In 2007, Filipinos for the first time comprised the number one group of immigrants and foreign workers in Canada, with 19,066 permanent residents and 15,254 temporary foreign workers (*Asian Pacific Post* 2009). Based on the 2009 CIC Immigration Overview, the Philippines came in second after China in that year, with 27,277 new permanent residents. It remained one of the top sources for permanent and temporary residents, with total entries of 41,761 in 2009 (Citizenship and Immigration Canada [CIC] 2009) and

46,315 in 2010 (CIC 2011a). The rapid growth of Asian immigration to Canada in general, and Filipinos in particular, is partly related to the different categories of immigrants admitted to Canada – family class, refugees, investors, independent skilled workers, and professionals. As with many other groups of immigrants, Filipinos use chain migration to sponsor family members to Canada; they tend to be heavily concentrated under independent skilled workers, professionals, and, lately, temporary foreign workers (TFWs). TFWs from the Philippines have recorded significant increases since 2000: from 6,385 that year to 51,325 as of 1 December 2009 (CIC 2009). In 2011, the Philippines ranked fourth among the top source countries for TFWs in Canada, with 7,654 arrivals (CIC 2011b).

Period of Arrival
Kelly (2006) outlines the historical trends in Filipino arrivals in Canada since 1961. Filipino immigrants numbered 215 before 1961 and increased radically every decade thereafter until 1990: 9,080 from 1961 to 1970; 42,875 from 1971 to 1980; and 52,515 from 1981 to 1990 (ibid., 7). In 1967, the Philippines was listed as a separate category in the immigration statistics published by the Canadian Department of Manpower and Immigration; the year before, China, India, Japan, and Pakistan were the only Asian countries identified (CIC 2005). But Lacquian (2012) cites 1965 as the first time "Filipinos" was listed as a category in Canadian immigration statistics, with 1,467 arrivals. In 1967, there were 2,994 immigrants who listed the Philippines as their last country of permanent residence prior to arriving in Canada.

The peak year for Filipino immigration to Canada before 1980 was 1974 (see Figure 3), but numbers declined after regulations imposed restrictions on family reunification and reduced points from applicants without prearranged employment in the mid-1970s (Kelly 2006, 5-6). Filipino arrivals again grew apace beginning in the late 1980s, with a total of 118,355 from 1991 to 2001, which was more than twice the figure of 52,515 from 1981 to 1990.

Based on the 2006 Census of Canada, most Filipino immigrants in Canada arrived prior to 2000. Those years corresponded with the height of emigration from the Philippines due to a combination of political and economic factors, especially escape from the repressive Marcos rule, a failing economy, and the state-directed export of labour from the Philippines. In addition, immigration to the United States became more difficult, and Canada became an alternative North American destination. The annual flows of Filipinos to Canada have been increasing since 2000. From 2000 to 2009, there were 164,659 Filipino arrivals in Canada. The greatest increase in Filipino arrivals was the 20 percent jump between 2007 (19,066) and 2008 (23,724). It was in 2008 that three Canadian provincial governments signed a memorandum of understanding on human resource deployment with the Philippines'

Figure 3

Immigration of Filipinos to Canada, pre-1950 to 2006

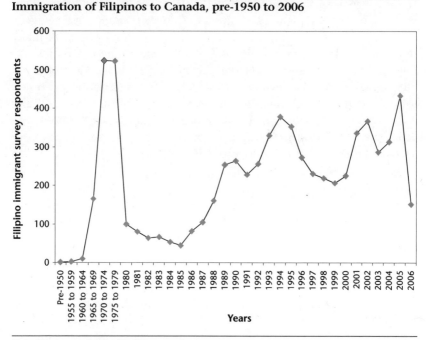

Note: This survey featured 8,553 respondents.
Source: Statistics Canada 2006.

Department of Labor and Employment: British Columbia (29 January 2008), Manitoba (8 February 2008), and Alberta (1 October 2008).

Data from the Commission on Filipinos Overseas (2009) indicates that the number of registered emigrants from the Philippines to Canada reached 237,394 in the period from 1981 to 2008. The United States was the top destination during that period, with over 67 percent of total flows from the Philippines; Canada was second, with 15 percent. Immigration to Canada exceeded 10,000 entrants annually from 1993 to 1996 and every year since 2004. In fact, the number of Filipinos arriving as landed immigrants directly from the Philippines increased steadily from 8,795 in 2002 to 16,443 in 2008 (CFO 2013a). CIC posted 11,011 and 23,724 during the same years, respectively, possibly demonstrating that a significant number of Filipinos became permanent residents while already in Canada or secured landed immigrant status by applying from another country.

Gender Composition
Most Filipinos in Canada are women. In 2001, women accounted for 62-65 percent of the total Filipino population aged 25-65 years (Lindsay

Figure 4

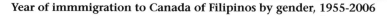

Year of immmigration to Canada of Filipinos by gender, 1955-2006

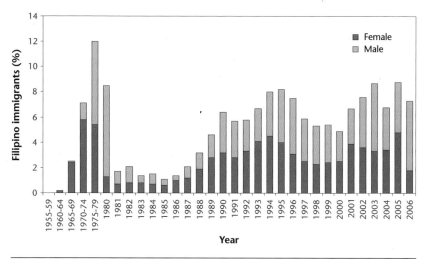

Source: Statistics Canada 2006.

2007). This is significantly higher than the proportion of women in the overall Canadian population, which was 50-56 percent during the same year. One of the major factors in the feminization of Filipino migration to Canada since the 1990s has been the LCP, as live-in caregivers are 95 percent female. In 2009, an increasing number of Filipino women are being recruited to work as hotel cleaners, chambermaids, and service personnel in fast food chains around the country. The public and private sectors in different provinces also engage in direct recruitment of Filipino nurses under the PNP. In the 2006 census, Filipinos in Canada were still predominantly female: 60 percent, compared with 40 percent males. About 7 percent of Filipino women in Canada were not permanent residents, compared with 1.9 percent of Filipino men.[8]

About 5.8 percent of Filipino females immigrated to Canada from 1970 to 1974, and 5.4 percent between 1975 and 1979 – the highest percentages of female immigration recorded from 1960 to 2005 (see Figure 4). In comparison, more Filipino males immigrated during the period 1975-79, in 1980 and 1991, from 1995 to 1999, and in 2003 and 2006.

Age Distribution

Most Filipinos in Canada were between the ages of 35 and 49 in the 2006 census, for a total percentage of 36.4 percent: 35-39 years at 12 percent, 40-44 years at 12.7 percent, and 45-49 years at 11.7 percent. Those 0-14 years

Figure 5

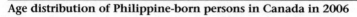

Age distribution of Philippine-born persons in Canada in 2006

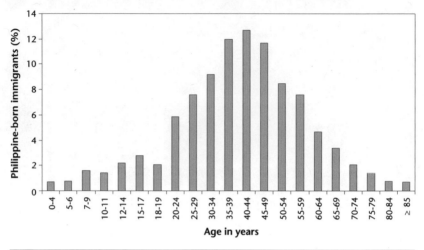

Source: Statistics Canada 2006.

old accounted for 6.7 percent, 15-24 years old for 10.8 percent, and 25-34 years old for 16.8 percent. The total percentage of those 0-34 years old was 34.3 percent. Those from 60 to over 85 years old accounted for 13.1 percent in total. These figures indicate that over 70 percent of Filipinos in Canada are younger than 49 years.

Filipinos comprised 4.7 percent (288,515) of the total ethnic population of 6,124,560 in Canada who were fifteen years and older in the 2006 census (Chui, Tran, and Maheux 2008). This group is also primarily composed of first-generation immigrants, or those who came directly from the Philippines as children and adults. The age distribution indicates that the Filipino community in Canada is relatively young and able to contribute to the economy.

In 2006, Philippine-born females in Canada outnumbered males between the ages of 35 to 49 years (see Figure 6). There were 197,940 such females over the age of 15 years, compared with 134,365 males (Statistic Canada 2006).

The 2006 census found that most Filipinos (151,000) immigrated to Canada between the ages of 25 and 44 years (see Figure 7). Filipinos who immigrated between the ages of 25 and 34 years old comprised 29.3 percent of Filipino immigrants to Canada. Del Rio-Laquian and Laquian (2008, 6) note that Filipinos in Canada have arrived during their "prime reproductive years."

More Filipino females in Canada immigrated between the ages of 25 and 39 years, a total of 42.4 percent compared with a total of 36.5 percent for their male counterparts (see Figure 8). Filipino women who immigrated at

Figure 6

Age distribution of Philippine-born males and females in Canada in 2006

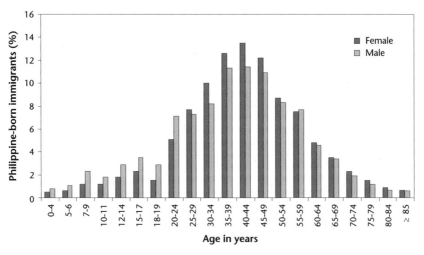

Source: Statistics Canada 2006.

Figure 7

Age distribution of Filipinos at the time they immigrated to Canada, 2006

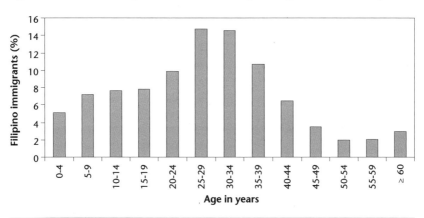

Source: Statistics Canada 2006.

25-29 years old formed the single largest group, with 16.2 percent based on the 2006 census. Males who immigrated at ages 0-19 years and 40-49 years outnumbered the females belonging to the same age groups. The younger cohort were most probably the children of first-generation Filipino immigrants. Interestingly, more Filipino women than men immigrated to Canada

Figure 8

Age distribution of Filipino males and females at the time they immigrated to Canada, 2006

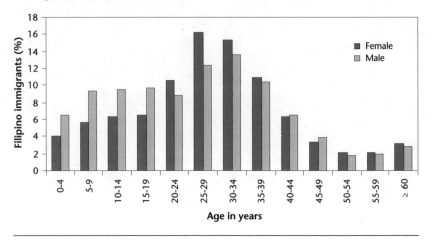

Source: Statistics Canada 2006.

over the age of 60 years. It is likely that a female parent is often sponsored to come to Canada to help care for grandchildren.

Marital Status

As of the 2006 census, 56.4 percent of Filipinos in Canada were legally married and not separated, about 33.8 percent were single or had never been legally married, and 4 percent were widowed. Those who were divorced and those who were separated each accounted for 2.9 percent. More Filipino men than women in Canada were legally married and not separated (60.8 percent versus 53.5 percent). Both men and women who were single and had never been legally married accounted for 33.8 percent each (see Figure 9).

Education and Occupation

Like the rest of the visible-minority population in Canada, Filipinos have higher educational attainment than the overall Canadian population. With regard to university education, there is a 20-point gap between visible minorities and the white population in the 35-44-year age group (Thompson 2008). The proportion of Filipinos with university degrees is 59 percent, second only to Koreans, and Filipinos ranked first for Grade 13 equivalencies. In 2001, about 31 percent of Filipinos aged 15 years and over obtained undergraduate degrees, compared with 14 percent and 24 percent of whites and visible minorities, respectively (Human Resources and Skills Development

Figure 9

Marital status of Filipinos in Canada by gender, 2006

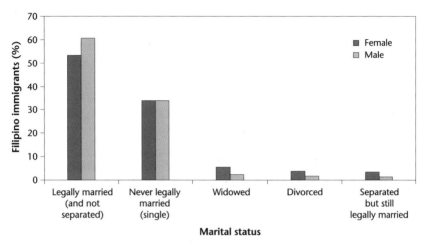

Source: Statistics Canada 2006.

Canada [HRSDC] 2012). Consistent with the trend in the Philippines, more Filipino women than Filipino men in Canada have university degrees.

As of 2012, Filipinos were the fourth-largest visible-minority population in the Canadian labour force (Catalyst 2012). According to HRSDC (2012), Filipinos had the highest labour participation rate at 76 percent, and an exceptionally low unemployment rate at 5.6 percent, compared with the rest of the visible-minority and white populations in 2001. The latest immigrant labour force market analysis in 2006 showed that Filipinos still have the "strongest labour market performance of all immigrants" (Gilmore 2008, 6), regardless of their year of arrival in Canada. Their labour force participation rate that year was 76.6 percent, and their unemployment rate, 5 percent, was slightly better than in 2001. Bramadat (2009, 231) also notes the below-average unemployment rate of Filipino-Canadians in Manitoba (5 percent), "while all other groups [visible minorities] exceeded it," and their high employment rate of 73 percent. In Saskatchewan, Filipino-Canadians had a lower provincial average unemployment rate (6.3 percent) than the rest of the visible-minority population (Bramadat 2009, 232).

Although Filipinos have high levels of educational qualifications, only 12 percent are in professional occupations, while 59 percent are in four occupational groups that earn lower incomes: intermediate sales and service personnel (19 percent), other sales and service personnel (14 percent), clerical personnel (13 percent), and semi-skilled manual workers (13 percent) (HRSDC

Figure 10

Occupations of Filipinos in Canada by gender, 2006

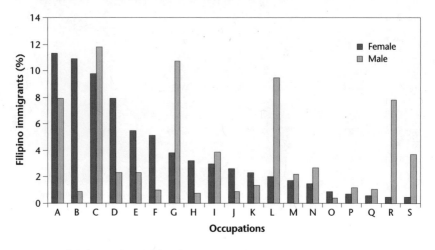

A   Clerical occupations and clerical supervisors (B4, B5)
B   Childcare and home support workers (G8)
C   Service supervisors, occupations in travel and accommodation, attendants in recreation and sport and sales and service
D   Technical, assisting and related occupations in health (D2, D3)
E   Retail trade supervisors, salespersons, sales clerks and cashiers (G2, G3, G011)
F   Professional occupations in health, registered nurses and supervisors (D0, D1)
G   Supervisors, machine operators and assemblers in manufacturing (J0, J1, J2)
H   Financial, secretarial and administrative occupations (B1, B2, B3)
I   Other management occupations (A1, A2, A3)
J   Occupations in social science, government services and religion (E0, E2)
K   Professional occupations in business and finance (B0)
L   Occupations in natural and applied sciences (C0, C1)
M   Chefs and cooks, supervisors, and other occupations in food and beverage service (G4, G5, G012)
N   Labourers in processing, manufacturing and utilities (J3)
O   Teachers and professors (E1)
P   Occupations in art, culture, recreation and sport (F0, F1)
Q   Wholesale, technical, insurance, real estate sales specialists, and retail, wholesale and grain buyers (G1)
R   Other trades occupations (H2, H3, H4, H5)
S   Trades helpers, construction, and transportation labourers and related occupations (H8)

Source: 2006 National Occupation Classification for Statistics (NOC-S) (Statistics Canada 2006).

2012). In fact, Filipinos received the second-lowest average income among visible-minority groups in 2000. In 2001, they earned only 74 percent and 86 percent of the earnings of white and total visible-minority populations, respectively (HRSDC 2012). Ironically, the high educational attainment of Filipinos in Canada, like that of other visible-minority groups, does not appear to improve their low employment income compared with whites.

Pratt (2004, 38) notes that the "educational capital" of Filipino women in Vancouver is less than that of women of British background.

Based on the 2002 North American Industry Classification System (NAICS), more Filipino women (20.7 percent) than men were employed in the health care and social assistance industry sector, while 21.9 percent of Filipino men were concentrated in manufacturing in Canada. The 2006 National Occupation Classification for Statistics (NOC-S) in Canada showed that Filipino women were mostly employed in clerical occupations (11.3 percent) and in childcare and home support (10.9 percent) (see Figure 10). Filipino men, however, were service supervisors and machine operators (11.8 percent and 10.7 percent, respectively).

Based on immigrant status, Filipino non-permanent residents in Canada are found mainly in the childcare and home support category, where they accounted for 41 percent of all Filipinos in that category in 2006, about five times greater than the next highest category of occupations in primary industries. Among these non-permanent residents, 64 percent of women and 21 percent of men were in childcare and home support in 2006, the largest occupational category for both, although men were more widely distributed in other industries (see Figure 11). The predominance of Filipino non-permanent resident women in childcare and home support is obviously related to immigration programs such as the LCP; however, the large number of Filipino men also in this occupation suggests an increasing demand for male caregivers to serve a specific clientele (Pratt 2004, 67).

Generally, the high rate of labour force participation, even if mostly in non-professional employment, is indicative of the tenacity of Filipinos in working not only to survive in Canada but also to provide for families left behind in the Philippines. The motivation behind this work ethic benefits the economy and society, as their employment translates into more tax dollars and less dependence on social assistance. Such labour force participation by Filipinos in their prime challenges the popular notion that immigrants drain Canadian public coffers. Indeed, the contribution of Filipinos, who now constitute the top group of immigrants and temporary foreign workers in Canada, is unrecognized. In particular, TFWs, like Canadian citizens, contribute to employment insurance (EI) and pension plans, and pay taxes (Pratt 2004, 46). At the expiration of their contract or on termination, TFWs are not assured of getting their contributions back or are faced with complications resulting from having an "open" work permit. Bauder (2006, 233) notes that TFWs in Canada contribute $11 million annually to EI but are denied its benefits.

Residence

The 2006 census recorded 410,700 Filipinos in Canada. About 50 percent were located in Ontario (203,220), 22.4 percent in British Columbia (88,075),

Figure 11

Occupations of Filipino non–permanent residents in Canada by gender, 2006

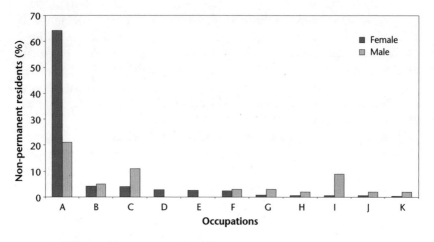

A   Childcare and home support workers (G8)
B   Service supervisors, occupations in travel and accommodation, attendants in recreation and sport and sales and services
C   Technical, assisting and related occupations in health (D2, D3)
D   Retail trade supervisors, salespersons, sales clerks and cashiers (G2, G3, G011)
E   Professional occupations in business and finance (B0)
F   Financial, secretarial and administrative occupations (B1, B2, B3)
G   Occupations in social science, government services and religion (E0, E2)
H   Chefs and cooks, supervisors, and other occupations in food and beverage service (G4, G5, G012)
I   Labourers in processing, manufacturing and utilities (J3)
J   Supervisors, machine operators and assemblers in manufacturing (J0, J1, J2)
K   Occupations in natural and applied sciences (C0, C1)

Source: 2006 National Occupation Classification for Statistics (NOC-S) (Statistics Canada 2006).

12.9 percent in Alberta (51,090), 7.9 percent in Manitoba (37,785), 6 percent in Quebec (24,200), and 1 percent in Saskatchewan (3,770) (see Table 4). Filipinos have even braved the frigid North, with 980 of them in Nunavut, the Northwest Territories, and Yukon. Filipinos have settled everywhere in Canada, and their numbers are projected to reach 540,000 by 2017 (Bélanger and Caron Malenfant 2005).

More Filipino men than women claimed Ontario (50.5 percent), British Columbia (22.7 percent), and Manitoba (9.1 percent) as their provinces of residence (see Figure 12). In contrast, more Filipino women claimed Alberta (12.4 percent), Quebec (7 percent), and Saskatchewan (1 percent) as their provinces of residence (Statistics Canada 2006).

Table 4

Filipinos in Canada by province and territory, 2006

Province/territory	Total population	Number of Filipinos
Canada	31,241,030	410,700
Alberta	3,256,355	51,090
British Columbia	4,074,380	88,075
Manitoba	1,133,515	37,785
Newfoundland and Labrador	500,605	305
New Brunswick	719,650	530
Northwest Territories	41,055	690
Nova Scotia	903,090	700
Nunavut	29,325	80
Ontario	12,028,895	203,220
Prince Edward Island	134,205	30
Quebec	7,435,900	24,200
Saskatchewan	953,850	3,770
Yukon	30,195	210

Source: Statistics Canada 2006.

Figure 12

Province/region of residence of Filipinos by gender, 2006

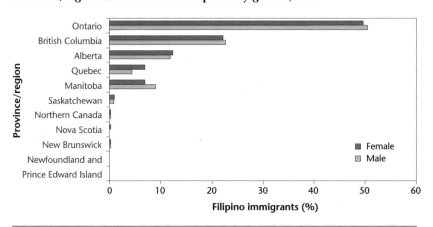

Source: Statistics Canada 2006.

Mobility Status

"Mobility status" refers to the census statistical variable of Canadians who moved from their place of residence within the past year and within the last five years. Two basic groups are tracked: non-movers and movers. Movers are further divided into non-migrants (movement in the same census subdivision)

Figure 13

Mobility status within the last five years: non-mover Filipinos by province/region, 2006

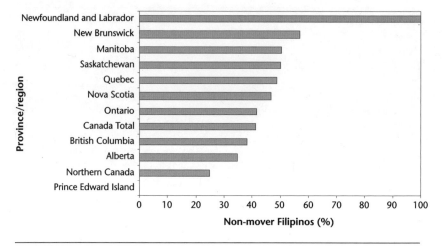

Source: Statistics Canada 2006.

and migrants (movement to a different census subdivision); migrants are also classified as internal or external, depending on whether they lived in Canada during the census (Statistics Canada 2009). In this section, "interprovincial migration" refers to the movement of Filipinos among different provinces.

According to the 2006 census, no Filipinos moved from their census subdivision within the past year in Newfoundland and Labrador (NFL) and Prince Edward Island (PEI). In New Brunswick, about 93 percent were non-movers, followed by Ontario (83 percent), Quebec (81 percent), and Alberta (75 percent). In terms of interprovincial migrants, Alberta had the highest number of Filipinos who had moved from another province within the past year, followed by Quebec, British Columbia, and Ontario. No Filipinos in Manitoba and Saskatchewan had moved there from another province. It is likely that Filipinos are moving from another province to Alberta, Quebec, British Columbia, and Ontario. In terms of mobility status in the last five years, 35 percent of Filipinos in Alberta were non-movers, compared with 38 percent in British Columbia, and 42 percent in Ontario (see Figure 13).

The five-year period shows a stark difference from the one-year period. During the five-year period, Saskatchewan (6.1 percent), Alberta (4.0 percent), and British Columbia (1.9 percent) had more interprovincial Filipino migrants compared with the national average (1.6 percent) in the 2006 census. Although the rate of interprovincial migration of Filipinos is less than the national average of 2 percent, it is indicative of the attraction of Filipinos to the western provinces, perhaps drawn by economic opportunities.

Pinays in the Prairies

The Canadian Prairies are a picturesque stretch of rolling coulees, plains, and farmlands rich with flora and fauna. Compared with the high-rise buildings of bustling cities, the Prairies offer a wondrous appreciation of the "big sky." The projected provincial populations for 1 July 2012 were over 3.8 million for Alberta, 1.2 million for Manitoba, and 1.1 million for Saskatchewan (Statistics Canada 2012). Thousands of Filipinos have made their way to the Prairie provinces, but the significance of their westward journey is rarely recognized since most immigration flows are directed towards Vancouver, Montreal, and Toronto. In 2006, however, Calgary welcomed 57,900 new immigrants (5.2 percent of the total), making it the fourth-ranked CMA (census metropolitan area) (Alberta Finance 2007), with the highest number of immigrants among all cities in the oil-rich province of Alberta.

This section presents a Prairie-specific profile of Filipino migration. An overview of the immigrant and visible-minority populations in the Prairies contextualizes the situation of Filipinos as an ethnic group. The gendered distribution of Filipino immigrants in the Prairies since 1967 is presented to show changes and patterns in Western Canada.

The majority of the immigrant population in the Prairies arrived before 1991: 295,390 in Alberta, 92,535 in Manitoba, and 30,615 in Saskatchewan (see Table 5). These figures include Canadian-born members of immigrant populations but exclude non-permanent residents. The decade of 1991-2000 showed growing immigration to Alberta and Saskatchewan, with populations of 127,960 and 9,450, respectively, but the dramatic increase has been in Manitoba where the number of immigrant arrivals grew from 27,505 in 1991-2000 to 31,190 in 2002-6. As for non-permanent residents, Alberta had 69 percent (27,095) of the total number in these provinces.

About three out of four recent immigrants since 1996 have settled in cities such as Calgary, Edmonton, Regina, Saskatoon, and Winnipeg (Mulder and Korenic 2005). Immigrants such as Filipinos tend to settle in urban areas rather than rural communities. Table 6 shows the numbers of the six largest visible-minority groups in 2006 (excluding Aboriginal peoples): South Asian, Chinese, Black, Filipino, Latin American, and Southeast Asian (Statistics Canada 2008). The table includes immigrants, the Canadian-born from immigrant communities, and temporary foreign workers. Of the total visible-minority population in Canada in 2006, 9 percent (454, 200) were in Alberta, 2 percent (109,095) in Manitoba, and 0.7 percent (33,900) in Saskatchewan (Table 6). In Alberta, Tagalog has been the number one spoken language of new immigrants since 2009 (Government of Alberta 2011).

Table 5

Immigrant and non–permanent resident population in the Prairies by gender and period of immigration, pre-1991 to 2006

	Alberta			Manitoba			Saskatchewan		
	Total	Male	Female	Total	Male	Female	Total	Male	Female
Population	3,256,355	1,630,865	1,625,485	1,133,510	556,920	576,590	953,850	469,405	484,445
Immigrants	527,030	255,355	271,675	51,230	72,960	78,270	48,155	22,690	25,465
Pre-1991	295,390	144,550	150,835	92,535	44,600	47,930	30,615	14,320	16,295
1991-2000	127,960	60,790	67,170	27,505	12,950	14,555	9,450	4,385	5,060
2001-6	103,680	50,015	53,670	31,190	15,415	15,780	8,095	3,985	4,105
Non-permanent residents	27,095	13,255	13,840	7,545	3,945	3,605	4,615	2,505	2,105

Source: Statistics Canada 2006.

Table 6

Visible-minority populations in Canada and the Prairies, 2006

	Canada	Alberta	Manitoba	Saskatchewan
Total visible minorities	5,068,090	454,200	109,095	33,900
South Asian (e.g., East Indian, Pakistani)	1,262,865	103,885	16,560	5,130
Chinese	1,216,570	120,275	13,705	9,505
Black	783,795	47,075	15,660	5,090
Filipino	410,695	51,090	37,790	3,770
Latin American	304,245	27,265	6,275	2,520
Southeast Asian (e.g., Vietnamese, Laotian)	239,935	28,605	5,665	2,555

Source: Statistics Canada 2006.

Distribution of Filipinos

Figure 14 shows that the distribution of Filipino immigrants by intended destination in the Prairies shifted from Manitoba during the period 1967-80 to Alberta in 1981-90 and continued thereafter. The number of Filipinos in Alberta grew from 5,543 in 1967-80 to 9,790 in 1991-96. By the time of the 2001 census, Filipinos in Alberta comprised more than 11 percent of the total Filipino population in Canada, while Manitoba and Saskatchewan accounted for 10 percent and 1 percent, respectively. Alberta retained its lead with the most number of Filipinos (51,090) during the 2006 census, followed by Manitoba with 37,790 and Saskatchewan with 3,770.

Figure 14

Filipino immigrants by intended destination in the Prairies, 1967-96

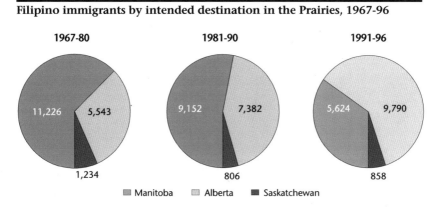

Source: Citizenship and Immigration Canada 2005.

Figure 15

Filipino immigrants by intended destination in the Prairies by gender, 1980-96 (excluding 1988, as the data were not gender-segregated)

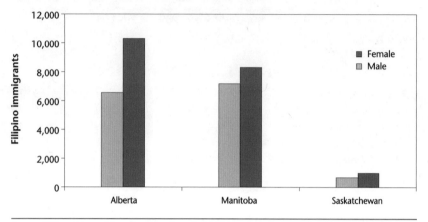

Source: Citizenship and Immigration Canada 2005.

Figure 16

Filipino population in the Prairies by gender, 2006

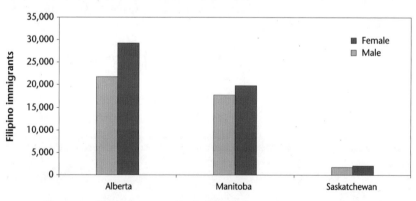

Source: Statistics Canada 2006.

Using 1980-96 aggregated immigration statistics, Figure 15 shows the distribution of Filipino immigrants by intended destination by gender in the Prairie provinces from 1986 to 1996. There were consistently more female immigrants in all three provinces during this period. The same pattern was observed during the 2006 census (see Figure 16), where Filipino women comprised over 50 percent of the total Filipino population in the three provinces.

Figure 17

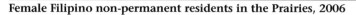

Female Filipino non-permanent residents in the Prairies, 2006

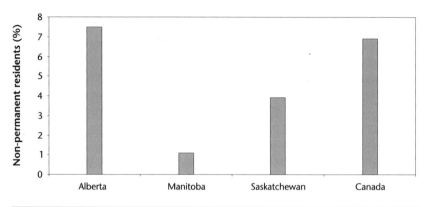

Source: Statistics Canada 2006.

In terms of immigrant status, about 99 percent of Filipinos in Manitoba and 97.6 percent in Saskatchewan were immigrants in the 2006 census. These percentages were higher than the national average of 94.9 percent. In contrast, Alberta had a slightly lower proportion of Filipino immigrants at 93.3 percent, with 0.2 percent non-immigrants. Inversely, Saskatchewan with 2.4 percent and Manitoba with 1.0 percent had the lowest proportions of non-permanent resident Filipinos, whereas Alberta had a higher proportion of this group at 6.5 percent, which was above the national average of 4.9 percent.

Among Filipinos in Canada, Manitoba and Saskatchewan showed higher rates of immigrant status than the national average: 99 percent for both genders in Manitoba; and 100 percent for males and 96 percent for females in Saskatchewan, compared with national averages of 98 percent and 93 percent for males and females, respectively. In contrast, Alberta had lower than the national rates, with 95 percent for males and 92 percent for females. Following the national trend, male Filipino immigrants were more numerous than female Filipino immigrants in Alberta and Saskatchewan.

In terms of non-permanent residents, Alberta had higher rates for both Filipino males (4.9 percent) and females (7.5 percent) than the national rates of 1.9 percent and 6.9 percent, respectively (see Figure 17), whereas Saskatchewan and Manitoba had lower rates. The situation in all Prairie provinces, however, resembled the national situation, with women comprising a greater proportion of the population of Filipino non-permanent residents.

In Alberta, the peak years of Filipino female immigration, with over 4 percent of total Filipino female arrivals for all years from 1965 to 2006, occurred during the 1970-74 period and in 1992, 2001, and 2003 (see

Figure 18

Gender distribution of Filipino immigrants to Alberta, 1965-2006

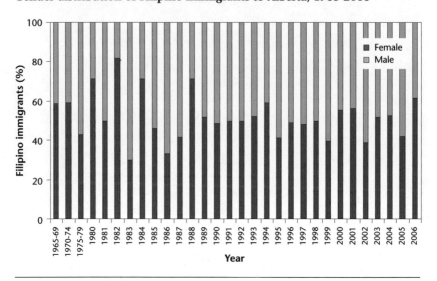

Source: Statistics Canada 2006.

Figure 18). Similarly, Filipino men recorded over 4 percent of arrivals in Alberta from the total Filipino male arrivals during the same period in 1992, 2002, 2003, and 2005. It was in 2005 that Filipino male immigration to Alberta reached 5.2 percent of the total Filipino male arrivals for all years, the highest for both genders since 1965.

In Manitoba, the peak years of Filipino female immigration, with 11 percent of total Filipino female arrivals for all years from 1965 to 2006, occurred during the 1970-74 period (see Figure 19). From 2000 to 2006, Filipino female immigration fluctuated. Filipino male immigration, on the other hand, reached its peak at 8 percent of total male arrivals for all years during 1970-74, and recorded a drop from 5.8 percent of the total male arrivals for all years in 2005 to 2.3 percent in 2006.

In Saskatchewan, more Filipino men than women immigrated during 1965-69 and 1975-79, with 12.9 percent and 16.1 percent, respectively, for the two periods. Filipino women recorded 5.9 percent and 9.8 percent, respectively, during the same periods (see Figure 20). Calculating the total percentage of Filipino arrivals, 29 percent of Filipino men and 16 percent of Filipino women immigrated during 1965-79; from 1992 to 2006, about 13 percent of Filipino men and 12 percent of Filipino women did so. In 2004, male immigration reached about 10 percent, whereas female immigration was nil. In 2006, however, female immigration was 4 percent, compared with 3 percent for male immigration.

Figure 19

Gender distribution of Filipino immigrants to Manitoba, 1955-2006

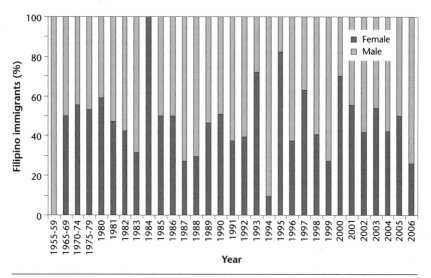

Source: Statistics Canada 2006.

Figure 20

Gender distribution of Filipino immigrants to Saskatchewan, 1965-2006

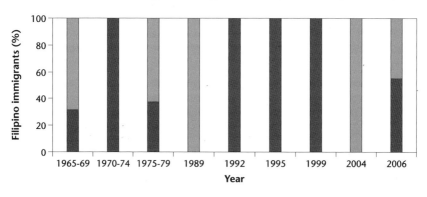

Source: Statistics Canada 2006.

Although Saskatchewan has the smallest number of Filipinos, it was the first Canadian province to sign a memorandum of understanding on nursing with the Philippines in 2008, which facilitated the hiring of eight hundred Filipino nurses and prescribed their professional treatment; it also established a procedure for recognizing overseas qualifications, instituted a $5,000 relocation allowance for each hiree, and covered the cost of air fare to Saskatchewan, housing for the first month, and a three-day course to prepare Filipino nurses to write their licensing exam (*Star Phoenix* 2008a, 2008b). Although Alberta and Manitoba have their own Provincial Nominee Programs with Filipinos as the major participating ethnic group, no similar benefits are given to foreign-trained nurses.[9] Unlike in Saskatchewan, where foreign-trained nurses are given an immediate opportunity to become a licensed registered nurse (RN) after passing the examinations, Alberta requires them to undergo a graduated scale of recognition of their credentials, moving from licensed practical nurse (LPN) to RN after a series of competency requirements. The Saskatchewan model for hiring foreign-trained nurses would likely facilitate increased Filipino migration to Saskatchewan compared with Alberta. Petra, Margarita, and Rosalinda were registered nurses in the Philippines who were directly recruited by the Saskatoon Health Region in 2008-9. Before migrating to Saskatchewan, Margarita had worked as a nurse for ten years in Saudi Arabia and for another two years in the United Kingdom before returning to the Philippines, where a massive advertising campaign in national newspapers attracted her to Canada. Petra and Rosalinda were registered nurses working in Philippine hospitals before they were recruited to work in Saskatchewan.

As is the trend with the total immigrant population in Canada, Filipinos in the Prairies are highly gendered, and the feminization of non-permanent migration is clearly indicated by the data from those provinces. Among Filipinos, women predominate as temporary foreign workers in all service-related occupations in the Prairies and in Canada as a whole. Filipino men, in contrast, tend to have more paths towards permanent residency in Alberta, Manitoba, and Saskatchewan. This suggests that female racialized bodies tend to predominate in precarious occupations such as live-in caregivers and hotel cleaners, whose labour is not much recognized as important in the Canadian economy – their "disposable bodies" (Bales 1999, 57) traded for temporary work.

The following profiles and narratives of selected *Pinays* in the Prairies illustrate their entry as dependent wives, principal applicants, and temporary foreign workers. Theirs was a westward journey that made for different starting points in the creation of common ground among themselves and other immigrant women in Canada. Their stories of migration and settlement show the depth of their lived experiences – their struggles, challenges, and triumphs.

Dependent spouses enter Canada as sponsored family members, either at the same time as their husbands or later. Rowena, Dalisay, Luningning, Josefina, and Bella arrived in Winnipeg with their spouses and children. Rowena came to Canada via the United States when her Filipino husband accepted a lucrative job offer in Manitoba in 1994; she left behind a career in one of the leading media companies in Los Angeles as well as the support of her family. Bella, a nurse, also came from the United States, joining her Filipino husband when his medical doctor's exchange program American visa expired more than twenty years ago. Dalisay, Luningning, and Josefina left the Philippines and their established careers to build a new life in Winnipeg. Because of limited opportunities at their initial settlement, all of these women accepted entry-level jobs while making their roles as wives and mothers a priority. According to Dalisay, migration to Canada is a "life of compromise." Meanwhile, in Saskatoon, Norma is married to a Filipino academic whose career has spanned three continents, following him wherever new scholarships and opportunities awaited.

Many Filipino women entered Canada as independent skilled professionals, scoring high on the point system based on their education and work experience. As principal applicants, they may have been the primary initiators of permanent migration and, ultimately, the main breadwinners of their families. The stories of such Filipino women in the global labour diaspora are often obscured by stories of abuse and exploitation of live-in caregivers and OFWs or TFWs. Dulce, a teacher in Calgary, has a PhD in education and served as dean at one of the top private universities in Manila. Carolina, a retired professor in Winnipeg, was a Fulbright scholar in the United States in the 1960s before migrating to Canada. Marilou, a social activist in Calgary, completed a master's degree in industrial relations from the University of the Philippines. They represent the selective process of immigration eligibility in Canada, with preference given to highly qualified and trained individuals. With the exception of Carolina, however, their impressive professional qualifications did not translate into comparable jobs during their first few years of settlement, and they took steps to gain recognition of their credentials in Canada.

A large number of Filipino women arrived in the Prairie provinces as temporary foreign workers under various labour migration schemes, such as the LCP and PNP. There appears to be a historical continuity of Filipinos as a preferred group of workers in certain sectors of the Canadian labour force since the 1990s, particularly live-in caregivers. Salvacion, a home care worker in Winnipeg, arrived from Hong Kong as a live-in caregiver in 1989. Rosie, a sales agent in Manitoba, came from the Philippines in 1975; her live-in work employment was arranged by her sister, who is married to a Canadian national. Maria, a registered nurse in Edmonton, applied to be a live-in caregiver in 2000 when prospects for US hospital employment dimmed. Trinidad, a single mother, part-time caregiver, and full-time employee at a manufacturing plant in Lethbridge, Alberta, left her children in the Philippines in 2002.

Finally, a significant group of *Pinay* workers can be found in the industrial and service sectors. In the late 1960s, many Filipino women were recruited for work in the garment industry. Ligaya, a retired sales associate, was twenty-three when she joined twenty-nine other Filipino women working as seamstresses in a clothing factory in Winnipeg. Dahlia and Sharon, both government employees in Saskatoon, also worked initially as seamstresses in a garment factory around 1975. Both were young and single at the time, Dahlia twenty-five years old and Sharon just nineteen. Between 2006 and 2009, many Filipino women were recruited to be service workers, such as fast food personnel or hotel cleaners in Alberta. Loida, a chambermaid in Edmonton, and Megan, a service person at Tim Hortons in Calgary, left their stable but low-paying professional jobs in the Philippines in 2007. Both were nominated by their Canadian employers for permanent residency status under the PNP. According to Loida, "*Mahirap ang trabaho sa hotel pero kakayanin ko para sa aking pamilya* [work at the hotel is difficult, but I will bear it for the sake of my family]."

Pinay migration in the Prairies is characterized by diversity in terms of roles, types of entry, and nature of work. Despite these differing experiences of migration, however, most women are convinced that they will find a better life here than in the Philippines. How they negotiate the difficulties of settlement and make meaning of their new lives in Canada is discussed in subsequent chapters.

3
Welcoming Prairies

Migration is a life-altering experience. We leave behind all that is familiar and embrace an uncertain future in a new country. Often confidence in our own abilities can be shaken to the core in a host culture with different values and measures of achievement. The landscape and the people with whom newcomers interact and engage pose additional challenges in the settlement and adjustment period. Cold temperatures in Canada may restrict socialization for many newcomers accustomed to living in warm places where people hustle around. But to start a new life in a strange country is far more challenging than simply adjusting to the cold climate. Finding normalcy and significance in the daily lives of Filipino women who are immigrants or migrant workers is thus an unfolding process; experience varies and is unique in the context of particular migration histories.

In this chapter, I explore the degree to which Canada is a welcoming society based on the initial experiences of settlement – labour market participation, housing, and social interactions – of *Pinays* outside the "big three" metropolitan centres, or MTV (Montreal, Toronto, Vancouver). Some of their narratives are observably similar to already-published voices of racialized (im)migrant women (and even men) in Canada in general and may not be uniquely Filipino (Man 2004; Zaman 2006; Agnew 2009; Tastsoglou and Jaya 2011). What is important, however, is to draw out their experiences in the Prairies that have not been given much attention and to provide a more nuanced representation of the "general." In this way, the *place-specific* voices of *Pinays* offer a glimpse – from a cultural lens using *peminist* perspectives – into how such initial experiences of settlement were negotiated.

According to Masson (2010, 47), "place matters for framing processes." Experiences are shaped by place, and spatiality is, according to Massey (1994, 4), "constructed out of the multiplicity of social relations across all spatial scales, from the global reach of finance and telecommunications, through the geography of the tentacles of national political power, to the social relations within the town, the settlement and the workplace." Space and place are not static boundaries; one's experience with a place, such as Canada, is also affected by the time spent there, or what it was like when one arrived at a particular time in one's life or in the history of that country. The "simultaneous multiplicity of spaces" that situate *Pinays* in the Prairies are, following Massey (1994, 3), "cross-cutting, intersecting, aligning with one another, or existing in relations of paradox or antagonism." Filipino women in Canada traverse multiple spatial locations as the global and the transnational subjects, or as "outsiders." In their embodied lives, they occupy both subjective spaces and concrete territorial places that also change with time: racialized immigrant women in the Prairies. Their positionality in the Prairie provinces can be seen as part of a federal immigration program such as the Live-in Caregiver Program (LCP), as temporary foreign workers, and as permanent residents – or as "forever immigrants" (Waterman 2001, 377), similar to the rest of Canada. Arguably, their positionality may shift depending on their immediate social environment or direct contacts (for example, in the workplace and even among Filipinos), although change in migration status is immaterial because of the corporeal nature of racialized and gendered work. There is a pervasive, immutable social positioning of Filipino women as the archetypal nanny and caregiver in the Canadian public eye that shapes their relations and experiences.

Canada is a nation imagined with spatial particularities from coast to coast. The Prairies in the west evoke a different meaning from the Maritimes in the east. Alberta is considered a "large rural landscape" that is "infrequently punctuated by towns and cities" (Cowan 2008, 113). Saskatchewan is described as a "land of wheat farms and soy fields," where one drives through, as Shane Rhodes notes, "endless repetitions of space" (ibid). Manitoba, like Alberta and Saskatchewan, has "lands that vacillated between wet and dry" (Bower 2011, 72), with particularly "long, cold winters, and warm short summers" (Beckett 2001, 8). Diverse landscapes permeate the Prairies, such as grasslands, plains, and oil rigs with output connected to the rest of Canada and the world: "We pull potash, oil, and water from deep underground, strip coal from the surface, and mine the soil above with wheat and corn. It is a cut-and-run economy worked in reflex to the changing demands of markets far away" (Henderson 2005, 177). To the rest of Canada, for example, Alberta is an interplay of the geographic, political, and the cultural: a rich resource-based economy managed by a conservative government that imposes no provincial sales tax and is supported by equally conservative social values (Kheiriddin and Daifallah 2005; Wesley 2011).[1] Landscapes may define places but they represent only a spectre of place making. As Massey (1994, 59) reminds us, place is "porous" and conceivably the "products of other places."

The Prairies evoke a different sense of place from the gateway cities of Toronto, Montreal, and Vancouver. "Prairie" represents a different way of life, based on farming and agribusiness, situated in the west and characterized by mountains, herds, and cowboys. Such a vision is embraced by the Calgary Stampede, dubbed the "greatest outdoor show on earth," with rodeos and chuckwagon races as major events.[2] Besides these meanings associated with geography and a "western" life is another place-specific view of the Prairies: the rural/urban contrast between outlying rural communities and city centres. Access to and from these places requires more personal driving than in areas with regular public transportation services. Newcomers face this crucial issue of transportation during their initial phase of settlement: where to get a ride, how to go to a certain place and return, what times buses run, and what alternative modes of travel are economical. "Prairie" also represents "big sky" and open spaces, which immigrants coming from congested urban areas in the Philippines may find unusual in a developed country. The vastness of open spaces dotted with small communities, or huge tracts of land with rolled hay worked by machinery, contrasts with the sea of human labour tilling the soil in Philippine countryside. Some live-in caregivers who participated in this study found employment in rural communities surrounded by acres of wheat or animal farms and found the deafening silence unbearable.

What is a welcoming community? It is one that accepts newcomers and treats them with respect and dignity as human beings. According to Esses and colleagues (2010, 9), a welcoming community spatially denotes "a town, city, or region – in which newcomers feel valued and their needs are served." The degree to which a community is welcoming may be difficult to assess, but the premise rests on the community's commitment to antiracist practices. Canada's Action Plan against Racism proposes measures to "fight racism effectively" (Government of Canada 2005, ii) in key priority areas such as racism and discrimination, regional and international cooperation, and education and diversity (12). These key areas encompass various institutions and levels of governance, with wide-ranging laws, commissions, and quasi-judicial bodies to enforce nondiscrimination and to protect human rights.[3]

How welcoming did Filipino women find their host communities in Alberta, Saskatchewan, and Manitoba? This question sets the tone for this chapter and is examined from various perspectives in light of multiculturalism as both policy and practice, including entry into the labour market, housing strategies, and social interactions. The experience of starting over in another country is marked by excitement about new opportunities and, at the same time, anguish over losing established support systems and both personal and professional networks. The initial years of settlement pose the most difficult challenges, as newcomers enter the labour market, establish social relations in the community, and build capacities for their new lives in Canada. Hence, welcoming experiences are crucial not only for newcomers but also for the community as a whole, and influence whether the former decide to stay or leave.

Multicultural Spaces

Canada is one of the most diverse societies in the world. The metamorphosis from exclusion to inclusion in its immigration policies during the second half of the twentieth century shaped the Canadian cultural mosaic (Kelley and Trebilcock 2010). Ostensibly and officially, then, Canada is a welcoming society: people of different ethnicities, religious beliefs, and sexual orientations have all made the "Great White North" their home (Baldwin, Cameron, and Kobayashi 2011). Multiculturalism foregrounds the acceptance of cultural diversity as a sort of defining ethos of contemporary Canadian society (Esses and Gardner 1996; Kymlicka 2007a, 2009). Under Prime Minister Pierre Trudeau, it grew from the concept of biculturalism (i.e., French and English) to incorporate other ethnic groups in the 1970s (Brotz 1980). The Canadian Multiculturalism Act safeguards civil liberties such as racial and gender equality that, according to Kymlicka (2007a, 106) are "inspired by liberal norms."[4] Relationships between individuals and communities or the state are based on the principles of social justice, equality, and respect (Robinson 2007).

Unlike in the United States, multiculturalism in Canada is state-sponsored, enshrined in law, and supported by administrative machinery (Bannerji 2000b; Hewitt 2005). Recognition of ethnic diversity is a distinct feature of the cultural mosaic, in contrast to the American model of "melting pot" assimilation (Gordon 1964) or the Australian preference for "core values" (Stretton 2005, 75), although the Canadian "house of difference" remains contested and fragmented (Mackey 2002; Garcea 2008). The use of historical antecedents in debates on accommodation and inclusion positions some groups of people as "exalted subjects" (Thobani 2007) in the making of the Canadian nation-state. Discourses nowadays deal with "post-multiculturalism" (Alibhai-Brown 2004) and the fragmentation position in media and scholarly texts: emphasis on differences, cultural relativism, and barriers to shared citizenship and national identity, which lead to conflict, ethnic marginalization, and social disintegration (Garcea, Kirova, and Wong 2008). Immigrants and people of colour continue to be at the crux of policy debates on the management of diversity and social cohesion and its consequent backlash (Vertovec and Wessendorf 2010). While national policy tensions rage, the idea of multiculturalism as a practice takes root in local communities.

Countless activities and festivities celebrating multiculturalism occur as part of Canada's heritage. The Folklorama in Winnipeg, Folkfest in Saskatoon, and the Heritage Festivals in Edmonton and other municipalities in Alberta every first Monday of August are but a few examples of a year-long schedule of public demonstrations of cultural diversity.

This celebratory form of multiculturalism, however, has been criticized for its failure to effectively address "racism and racialism" in social institutions (Cashmore 1996, 245). Anti-racists schooled in the so-called left argument point to the "superficial celebration of multiculturalism – of exotic cuisine, popular music, or colourful festivals and rituals – disguis[ing] ongoing economic and political inequalities" (Werbner 2003, 52). In fact, many are critical of the Canadian government's funding of ethnic festivals since the 1970s, although financial support of folkloric activities has waned from the 1980s to the present and comprises "the smallest program funded under the multiculturalism policy" of the federal government (Kymlicka 1998, 45). These events are now mainly a collaborative effort of local governments and ethnic community organizations. Cultural festivities publicly affirm diversity in the community and encourage tourism, which stimulates the local economy.

Multiculturalism is an ambitious social and political project. Pluralist societies in the West still grope for a path towards achieving equality and inclusion for all, and remain skeptical of its future (Barry 2001). The notion that multiculturalism is an illusion (Bissoondath 1994) is pervasive among populists, as the practice apparently addresses only immigrants and not Aboriginals; "ethnic intermixing or the possibilities for a new multiracial society emerging from the Canadian experience" (Bumsted 2003, 331) have not been actively pursued. The histories of nation building are bounded by racial fixities that divide "us" from "them" in all facets of human interaction, whether at the personal, institutional, or societal level. Public racism or, more aptly, "street racism" still exists, however subtly (or not so subtly) expressed. Public policy is meant to shape practices (Fischer 2003), but this occurs at a snail's pace; meanwhile, exclusivist attitudes continue to erect barriers between dominant and subordinate groups, particularly racialized immigrants. After all, a "salad bowl" of cultures displaying unique qualities or "different ingredients" (Von Meien 2006, 6) may not appeal to some palates.

There is subtle racism everywhere I go because I have a Pilipino accent. I do not know if I was well understood.
    – Gabriela, a retired government employee in Winnipeg

Life in Canada was a drawback ... I still feel prejudiced after twenty-eight years in Manitoba because I am not white. They looked down at you. I have an English accent and this makes you the target.
    – Lumen, a finance officer in Winnipeg

Race is a social construct that divides people according to perceived differences that permeate social and legal institutions (Hill 2002; Haney López 2006). While "race" serves as the generic term for exclusion and inclusion in the history of immigration policy development in Western states (Marger 2006; Hier and Singh Bolaria 2007), "ethnicity" particularizes the experiences of different groups of immigrants. The existing literature on race and ethnicity often use these terms interchangeably (Kalbach and Kalbach 2000; Schaefer 2008). While being identified broadly as racially non-white, Filipinos are more marked by their ethnicity, like other immigrant groups, with particular cultural practices, social habits, and language. However, race as a defining category for difference and inequality is also interconnected with other forms of stratification, such as class, gender, and sexuality (Ore 2008). Gender, in particular, has emerged as paramount in the discourse of multiculturalism: "Is multiculturalism bad for women?" (Okin 1999). Cultural rights of immigrant groups appear to counter avowed democratic practices of gender equality. The tensions created between accommodation of diversity or group rights on the one hand and women's empowerment on the other are significant in policy making and within immigrant groups, as in, for example, the case of "faith-based arbitration" (Saeed 2010, 226). I would argue that Filipino women are not often the victims of cultural practices that are perceived to be inconsistent with liberal democratic practices or the "uneasy partners" (Stein et al. 2007), because of the Philippines' history of Western colonialism, shared democratic principles, and Christian tradition. However, the positioning of Filipino women as "women of colour" is part of the shared destiny of racialized immigrants and manifests the "dark-side of the nation" (Bannerji 2000b). Invariably immigrants in the Prairies, like members of First Nations, have been subjected to systemic racism in institutions and social practices (Driedger and Halli 2000; Walker 2008), but the recognition of fundamental rights of citizens enshrined in charters and policies provides a sense of human security and equal protection, despite prevailing social practices to the contrary.

Multiculturalism supported by the Canadian state offers spaces of inclusion (Dib, Donaldson, and Turcotte 2008) without which nothing much can be said of pluralist liberal democracies. The rights and freedoms granted to all citizens in Western democracies logically extend to newcomers. Inclusive policies and programs are now in place in small cities and metropolitan centres alike, to help newcomers settle, adapt, and become fully integrated. The Prairies are no exception. In 1974, Saskatchewan became the first province in Canada to adopt a Multiculturalism Act, and in 1997 it passed new legislation to reflect issues of social justice (Dewing 2009).[5] The province of Alberta passed the Alberta Cultural Heritage Act in 1984 but improved its provisions in the Alberta Multiculturalism Act in 1990; in

1996, it combined multiculturalism and human rights into the Human Rights, Citizenship and Multiculturalism Act (ibid.).[6] Students in Alberta have the option to undertake language immersion classes other than French. In 1992, the Manitoba Multiculturalism Act came into effect, emphasizing the province's "multicultural society from the time of its original population, the Aboriginal peoples."[7] Prior to 1992, however, Manitoba had adopted the Intercultural Council Act in 1984. Since 2001, the province of Manitoba has had a twenty-one-member advisory body, the Manitoba Ethnocultural Advisory Advocacy Council, under the Minister of Culture, Heritage and Tourism.

The Canadian Charter of Rights and Freedoms[8] contains legal affirmations of equality and protection against its violations, whether committed by individuals, groups, or state agencies (Sworden 2006). Immigrant Filipino women in Canada are oriented towards a "bill of rights" psychology, since the Philippines has a version patterned after that of the United States. The law, however, is not necessarily a pervasive social instrument in the fair treatment of individuals, citizens, and racialized peoples (Thobani 2007; Roberts, Boyington, and Kazarian 2008). Racism and discrimination are persistent social ills from which no state can claim exemption (Reilly, Kaufman, and Bodino 2003). Lund refers to Alberta as the "heartland of hate" (2006, 181), with a history of organized hatred by "red-necks" and "Bible thumpers" (W.P. Baergen, cited in Lund 2006, 183).

What trumps all criticism of multiculturalism is that "the dynamics of inter-ethnic relations actually [do] occur in a way that the behavioral aspect of multicultural theory suggests that they do" (Reitz 2009, 13). Small gestures such as handshakes between immigrants and local residents build friendships and communities, implying that multiculturalism in practice has positive effects. Grounded and localized efforts to bridge cultures are far more important than debates among theorists, although there are sure to be bumps along the way. Unfortunately, local acts of social inclusion do not receive as much media coverage as depictions of racial hatred and violence that portray immigrants in a negative light (Klaszus 2008).

A multicultural Canada looms large in the psyche of many Filipino women in the Prairies, and this perception impacts their daily lived realities. Arguably, the politics of multiculturalism are experienced and contested differently in the lives of racialized immigrant women. "Everyday multiculturalism" (Wise and Velayutham 2009) or "lived multiculturalism" (Highmore 2011, 148) appears most important in their daily lives, as their voices are muted in national policy discourses. In this everyday trope of multiculturalism, were *Pinays* welcomed in the Prairies? The answer appears to be yes, and it is clear from the following narratives that a welcoming Canada is still fresh in their memories.

In 1962 I did not experience any negative feelings about Canadians. In fact, I felt welcome in Canada. Perhaps we provide the services as a nurse or doctor due to labour shortage here.
– Bella, a retired nurse in Winnipeg

I came from the US in 1968. Doctors at the hospital treated me like other white nurses.
– Salome, a retired nurse in Winnipeg

Most people in Canada are generally welcoming; you are treated like any other Canadian.
– Norma, a housewife in Saskatoon

Norma, Salome, and Bella, who immigrated to Canada across a span of three decades, all view their Prairie communities as welcoming. Their experiences in Winnipeg and Saskatoon suggest that these cities provided such warmth and openness during their settlement that the women have felt comfortable settling there all these years. Walking in downtown Saskatoon, Norma pointed out: *"This place is cold during winter, but the people are so warm."*

The Filipino women who participated in this study all embraced multiculturalism in the Prairies. It sets the context for their feeling of being "part of the community" regardless of how others may perceive them or their initial experiences of settlement. Salome in Winnipeg has a proactive attitude: *"Don't wait for people to welcome you; you should also reach out to them."* Multiculturalism in practice appears significant in their lives, and that space for recognition of cultural differences enables them to carve out opportunities and possibilities in their new country in the face of adversity. The generally positive feeling of identification with multiculturalism is merely icing on the cake, however: degrees of inclusion or belonging as seen through policies and social practices require further examination, particularly with regard to the labour market.

Seeking Work
Coming to Canada is certainly not smooth sailing for all Filipino women. Pre-migration selection criteria highlight education, language, and work experience as the three most desirable characteristics in the labour market. Immigration policy aims to "match the human capital of immigrants with labour market conditions" (Haddow and Klassen 2006, 89). The point system measures skilled immigrants, but it is by no means a guarantee of eligibility for employment in a desired occupation. Successful applicants for immigration to Canada are often not adequately advised that their education and professional qualifications could have little bearing on their actual employability once in Canada. As Foster (2008, 129) argues, Canadian immigration

policy "is an example of an institution that features specific racialized biases. Like many other social problems, racialized immigration signals a discrepancy between the ideals and realities of Canadian society."

The inconsistency between immigration policy and labour market practices has a profound effect on the lives of immigrant women. Although Canadian immigration laws purport to be nondiscriminatory, race and gender are their obvious qualifiers (Arat-Koc 1999). The historical preferences for Anglo-Saxon and European males as constituent builders of the nation made them seemingly "natural" claimants of the state and to appear to be natural candidates for immigration. The following narratives illustrate the difficulties of gaining entry into the labour market.

> *It's hard to be an immigrant. I need to have my professional qualifications recognized and it took quite a long time.*
> – Dulce, a retired teacher in Calgary

> *Life was difficult with five children and no family support here ... When we first came in 1976, I do not even know how to ask for support. We have to survive and I became a garment worker for the first three months before I started to inquire about my teaching qualifications ... I lost my self-worth for a while ... But I put myself together and started to work ... from hell up!*
> – Dalisay, a retired teacher in Winnipeg

> *I immigrated to Canada at the time when Canada was still in an economic recession in the late 80s to mid-90s ... I realized that one needs to have a Canadian education to be able to compete in the labour market.*
> – Hosanna, a nurse in Edmonton

> *I came to Canada in 1999 and was not able to get a job in the first month. Nobody here recognized my qualifications.*
> – Marilou, a community worker in Calgary

Marilou, Dulce, Hosanna, and Dalisay share the chronic dilemma of immigrants in Canada – the non-recognition of professional qualifications. The Philippine educational system follows the 6-4 model (six years in elementary and four years in high school) pre-college, in contrast to Canada's 6-3-3 program (six years in elementary, three years in junior high school, and three years in senior high school); thus, there is a two-year schooling discrepancy between the two countries. Year 12 graduates in Canada are eligible for many entry-level positions that in the Philippines would be available only after completion of a degree. Employment gatekeepers often disregard educational qualifications obtained in developing countries like the Philippines and equate highly trained Filipinos with Year 12 graduates, unless they submit to a rigorous process of accreditation by provincial regulatory bodies.

De-skilling is a universal pattern among newcomers to Canada (McKay 2003; Man 2004; Alboim and McIsaac 2007), many of whom turn to work for which they are overqualified in order to survive. Kelly and colleagues (2009, i) emphasize the "deprofessionalization" of Filipino immigrants in Toronto, whose lack of financial resources blocks their aspirations for "educational upgrading" and ultimately leads them to work in "survival jobs." Many immigrant women perform menial jobs to earn income for their daily needs rather than invest in the expensive and time-consuming process of accreditation. A frequently heard rationale for this less-than-ideal option among Filipino mothers is *"Ito ay para sa mga bata* [this is for the children]." They tend to set aside their own personal career aspirations and work instead for the benefit of their children in Canada and their families in the Philippines. Some with postgraduate degrees even under-report their educational qualifications in order to compete for menial jobs in desperate attempts to secure paid work. In such cases, women may downplay their foreign credentials to gain entry into the Canadian labour market, resulting in what I call a double negative for women who can already expect lower returns on their foreign-acquired education. According to Alboim, Finnie, and Meng (2005, 13), foreign university degrees "on average ... have a return worth less than one-third that of a degree obtained in Canada by the native-born." The regrettable result is an inherent "earnings deficit" for the foreign-educated (Reitz 2001, 374), or what Chiswick and Miller (2010, 41) refer to as "lower pay off" to schooling for immigrants.

Aside from non-recognition of professional qualifications, a major hurdle for those seeking employment in Canada for the first time is "Canadian work experience." This means that immigrants must establish prior work experience in Canada so that prospective employers can secure referrals for conduct and other aspects of employability.

> *In the beginning I find it very ironic that when I go for interviews they ask for my Canadian experience. I just arrived!*
> – Gaviola, a private employee in Edmonton

> *I arrived in Canada in 1976 ... In presenting our credentials they ask for Canadian experience. We have to prove our worth.*
> – Pilar, a community worker in Winnipeg

Non-recognition of previous non-Canadian work experience surely limits immigrants' possibilities for advancement. To have both their education and work experience reduced to nothing on arrival in Canada shakes the fundamental self-worth of many Filipino women. Requiring Canadian work experience for entry-level positions is "often used as a means to mitigate risk when a candidate's experience is unknown or unfamiliar and it is sometimes exploited in a discriminatory fashion to exclude candidates" (Alboim and McIsaac 2007, 4). The general sentiment among many immigrant women is that discrimination is rampant in the labour market. Initial years of settlement are marred by difficulties, and immigrants who arrived between 1991 and 1996 have the lowest participation rates in the labour market compared with the Canadian-born (Informetrica Limited 2001). Research indicates that the "economic outcomes of recent immigrants [have] deteriorated since 2000," and newer arrivals face far more difficulties in the labour market (Xue 2010, 12). Such poor participation in the labour market deserves to be contextualized. Newly arrived immigrants may have the desire to enter the labour market, but exclusionary practices stifle their aspirations. Other factors, such as gender roles and language, add to their constraints. Huang (1997, 28) underscores the great impact of "initial human capital characteristics, migration patterns, household structure, communities environment, and the structural factors in the receiving society" on immigrant women's labour market participation. Age, education, and immigrant status also affect the earning potential of immigrants by gender (McDonald and Worswick 2010, 141).

However, Xue (2010, 18) demonstrates, in her work on employment experiences of recent immigrants, that the proportion of immigrants having difficulties in the labour market "decreased with time." "Six months after landing, 70 percent of newcomers who tried to find work reported having problems. Two years after landing, this proportion dropped ... to 68 percent and further decreased to 59 percent four years after landing" (ibid.). Although immigrants have made "significant progress in the labour market in terms of higher employment ratios over time" (ibid., 24), their regional origin also contributes to variations in outcomes. For example, immigrants from Asia and Africa had "lower than average employment to population ratios." However, there are also variations within regions and countries of origin; for instance, India, the Philippines, and Romania displayed "better employment ratios" (ibid.). In general, immigrants fared better in the Prairies, with their stronger local economies compared with other provinces. According to Xue (ibid., 26), 77 percent of immigrants in Alberta were employed four years after arrival in the province, compared with 59 percent in Quebec. Calgary is the only CMA in which new immigrants reported "best performance" in finding employment (ibid.).

In 2007, the federal government announced the creation of the Foreign Credentials Referral Office (FCRO), with an operating budget of $13 million over its first two years (Alboim and McIsaac 2007). However, this major policy response aimed at integrating immigrants in the labour market misses the mark because no credential assessment is conducted by the federal government. The primary task of this office is simply to provide "informa-tion, path-finding and referral services" about the Canadian labour market and the credential assessment process of provincial professional regulatory bodies.[9] This initiative did at least finally recognize the need to harness the potential of skilled immigrants into the economy and to address their current downward mobility. About 60 percent of skilled immigrants who arrived in 2000-1 are underemployed (Statistics Canada 2005). In her study of labour market outcomes for degree-qualified migrants in Canada and Australia, Hawthorne (2008, 38) concludes that "it seems essential to redress this skills wastage" among the "chronically poor immigrant" for the sake of both national development and global competency.

A clearinghouse of information on foreign credential assessment is a welcome step towards apprising potential immigrants of potential profes-sional pitfalls that they might face in Canada. Information is vital, too, in helping them to determine which provincial jurisdiction has a better, or more convenient, foreign credentials assessment process and to identify the various professional guilds that have "statutory authority" to regulate oc-cupation (Knight 2004, 58). On 18 February 2010, the Canadian government announced the expansion of foreign credentials referral in select countries of origin – Britain, China, India, and the Philippines – with $15 million worth of funding to the Canadian Immigration Integration Project (CIIP) operated by the Association of Canadian Community Colleges (*Economic Times* 2010). The Minister of Citizenship, Immigration and Multicultur-alism, Jason Kenney, stated: "We want newcomers to be able to use their skills as soon as possible in Canada. This funding will help them jumpstart the credential recognition process before they arrive in Canada. It's good for them and good for the economy" (ibid.). This is a promising initiative that enables would-be immigrants to understand the market value of their foreign education in Canada by lowering unrealistically high expectations for parallel entry positions. In Calgary, Semana, a former teacher in the Philippines, reflected on her experience: "*Mabuti sana kung alam naming noon na mahirap pala ang licensing process* [it would have been better had we known that the licensing process was difficult]." While new policy measures are slowly addressing the issue of professional recognition, the Filipino women I met in the Prairies in 2009 encountered what most immigrants before them had also experienced. They have more stories to tell than time to contemplate the possible outcomes of these policy changes in their lives today.

Filipinos are among the largest English-speaking ethnic groups from Asia in Canada. According to Filomena, a government employee in Saskatoon, "The Americans gave Filipinos the opportunity to learn English, which is the international language." Indeed, the facility of many Filipinos with one of Canada's official languages is rooted in colonialism. Even unschooled children in the Philippines pick up the language from Western-oriented popular media.

*Because there were many women from other countries ... in the factory, they
stare at us. They often discriminate. Even the "Indians" don't like us. They
just look at you as if saying "what are you doing here?" ... It was strange and
I felt uneasy ... Later on, our co-workers spoke with us because we can speak
English!*
 – Ligaya, a retired factory worker in Winnipeg

Spoken English has different twists based on ethnicity, however, even
among those who speak it as a first language. There are varieties of intona-
tion and accent, and these are often geographically specific, just as the
American, Australian, or British accents have their own distinguishable
sounds and pronunciations. When Filipino women encounter racism and
discrimination, it is often in response to their accented English. Marilena
in Edmonton and Clemencia in Winnipeg spoke of its constraining effects
both during employment interviews and in the workplace.

*There is subtle racism and discrimination in Canada. I applied for a teaching
position in ESL and was shortlisted and interviewed for forty-five minutes.
All were Caucasians ... At the end of the interview, they said, no, you have a
heavy accent. I cried and went down ... Right in front of the elevator was a
big advertisement for adult literacy. I brushed away my tears and went inside
... After thirty-minutes of interview, they said, congratulations! I was refused
upstairs but was accepted downstairs!*
 – Marilena, a community worker in Edmonton

*I came with my parents in 1971 when I was seventeen years old. I went to
school ... and improved my English accent. I don't even understand their
accent, too! As a Filipino I cannot take away my accent! Sometimes Canadians
think we are dumb and ask, what did you say? They discriminate you but
will find out later that you are not dumb.*
 – Clemencia, a nurse in Winnipeg

By and large, Filipino women, like other immigrant women, are subject
to the inequalities resulting from gender, race, class, and immigrant status
in Canada. As immigrant women, their entry into the labour market is,
according to Ng (1990, 97), "part of the process through which women from
the Third World, who have certain skills and abilities, are produced ... as
special 'commodities.'" The state and its agents, in both the public and
private sectors, reinforce the constructs that channel them into certain low-
paying segments of the labour force (Ng 1988; Zaman 2006). Ethnicity is
constituted as a social marker in organizing certain immigrant groups in
Canadian economy and politics (Ng 1981; Pendakur 2000). Immigrant
women, especially racialized women from developing states, form a class of

their own in the labour market. There are more female Asian immigrants in service industries, with lower incomes, than Canadian-born women (Verma and Chan 2000, 123). According to Sharma (2005, 5), the idea of *foreignness* extends to the "organization of national labour markets," which leads to the "subordination of all those who can be rendered 'foreign.'" Li (2008, 30) sees race as having wide-ranging effects in the labour market, where the "unequal market values attached to various racial origins" place non-whites at an income disadvantage compared with Canadians of European background. On their arrival in Canada, Filipino women navigate this limited labour market, and the costs associated with settlement often keep them permanently in what were supposed to be temporary survival jobs.

Entry-level jobs can be a starting point for these women in securing work more closely related to their own professions. They often remind themselves of the possibilities of getting better job placements in Canada and what they would be able to offer their children as a result. This view echoes the Filipino adage *pag may itinanim, may aanihin* (if you plant, you will harvest). Dalisay, a teacher in the Philippines, took on factory work in Manitoba so that she could support her five children and save enough to pursue required courses for teaching qualification. It took a toll on their family finances, her health, and the well-being of her children, who were sometimes left on their own, but Dalisay was committed to becoming a qualified teacher, which would eventually lead to better financial returns for her family.

Housing Strategies

Housing is a major concern among immigrants and migrant workers. The literature shows "little information on the housing experiences of economic and family reunification migrants" in Canada (Mendez, Hiebert, and Wyly 2006, 83). Information about housing is one of the important things that immigrants are apprised of before they make the journey to Canada (Owusu 1999). Once in Canada, their success in finding housing varies depending on income levels and eligibility criteria set by property management. Often, an employment certificate and social insurance number (SIN) are required with a rental application. Ethnic background, number of children (as well as their ages), and other factors may hurt a rental housing application as these form the bases of discrimination by landlords (Dion 2001; Hulchanski 2004).

The Longitudinal Survey of Immigrants to Canada (LSIC) since 2001 shows that during the first four years of settlement, housing ownership of immigrants has "improved remarkably over the years," although such improvement is not universally shared by Black and Middle Eastern immigrants (Hiebert 2009, 268). Home ownership among Filipino and Chinese immigrants in Canada is better than among their counterparts in the United States but still lower than among the native-born (Haan 2007). Over 50 percent of Filipino immigrants in Canada were homeowners in 1981, and this rose to 59 percent by the 2001 census (Haan 2010, 239). The initial housing experiences of Filipinos are not well recorded, however. As Haan (2010, 241) argues, "early years of residence in Canada are important" but "housing research relies on the census, which despite its strengths (comparability over a long term, large sample size, etc.), is rather limited in the information it contains." The LSIC, however, provides new sources for in-depth analysis, which, in Haan's work (2010) indicates a "home ownership hierarchy" among recently arrived immigrant visible-minority groups – Chinese, South Asian, Filipino, Black, Latin American, and Middle Eastern – relative to white immigrants. Wealth on entry and lack of credit history are two possible factors in ethno-racial home ownership (ibid., 242).

I argue that the housing experience of immigrants during the first years of settlement is an important indicator of the degree to which a community is welcoming. Finding a place to call home is a fundamental need second to none on arrival in a new country. Housing also facilitates eventual integration, although its impact varies between short- and long-term settlement and among different groups of immigrants (Organisation for Economic Co-operation and Development [OECD] 1998; Edgar, Doherty and Meert 2007). Women are particularly vulnerable. As Wekerle (1997, 170) puts it, "access to affordable housing is an integral part of social welfare, affecting women's life chances, their security, and their access to services."

Two patterns of housing emerge for Filipino women in the Prairies based on their entry status in Canada. Permanent immigrants tend to have prearranged accommodation thanks to other Filipinos in the community. These social networks perform a vital role in the migration and settlement of Filipinos (Almirol 1985; Lee 2006) as well as other immigrants (Greve and Salaff 2005; Gidengil and Stolle 2009). Temporary migrants on work permits, however, may have housing options offered by employers or recruitment agencies. I would argue that the patterns diverge in terms of interest and motivation. Those with permanent residency status are assisted mostly by the extended kinship network before they leave the Philippines. Arrangements are made for temporary housing, usually a spare room, for the entire family on their arrival in Canada. Often a short stay will enable the newcomers to apply for social insurance numbers and search for affordable housing.

Binigyan ako ng telephone number ng isang Pilipino na nakatira dito ... Siya ang naging contact namin. [I was given a telephone number of a Filipino living here ... He became our contact.]
– Sara, an employee in Lethbridge

May kamag-anak kami sa Winnipeg. Doon kami tumira sa kanila ng mga ilang araw bago kami nakahanap ng sariling apartment. [We have a

relative in Winnipeg. We stayed with them for a few days until we
found our own apartment.]
    – Lisa, an employee in Winnipeg

The custom of Filipino homestay sponsors springs from the culture of
hospitality in the Philippines. Hospitality is one of the distinctive traits of
Filipinos, a "gracious tradition of the East" (O'Boyle and Alejandro 1988)
that is "derived from the gesture of giving comfort to a stranger" (Ongsotto
and Ongsotto 2002, 20). Because of this practice, the homestay host becomes
a "quasi-settlement agency" on whom new Filipino immigrants rely for
information and guidance, rather than on government-funded settlement
agencies. The relationship between the homestay host and the Filipino
newcomer extends far beyond the period of temporary housing and is often
culturally coded as a debt of gratitude *(utang na loob)* for the latter.

Temporary foreign workers (TFWs) enter Canada with work permits tied
to one employer. They have prearranged accommodations facilitated by
either the employer or the recruitment agency. Live-in caregivers reside with
their employers under the terms of the LCP but are at risk of finding themselves homeless should they need to leave because of abuse. No shelter is
available to foreign migrant workers in Canada. Some caregivers in southern
Alberta take refuge in Filipino homes or seek temporary shelter in another
caregiver's room – if they happen to know one in the area. In most cases,
the "homeless" caregiver becomes a transient resident in different homes
until she receives a new work permit with another employer, which takes
about three months. Many live-in caregivers, however, endure the abuse
because this waiting period affects the completion of the twenty-four-month
live-in requirement of the LCP in order to apply for permanent residence. I
write about this dilemma and the absence of transitional services for live-in
caregivers in the article "I Care for You? Who Cares for Me?" (2008).

Housing and meals are included in the live-in work arrangement, deducted
from the monthly wage of the caregiver. This is quite problematic, as many
Filipino caregivers often do not eat the food prepared by their Canadian
employers. As a result, they have to buy their own food, especially rice, notwithstanding the monthly deductions for meals. A Filipino live-in caregiver
in the south of Lethbridge even goes to another caregiver's home to cook
rice, as her employer hates the smell of it. After establishing who's who
among caregivers in the community, many Filipino women arrange weekend
get-togethers during their days off to cook traditional food, share stories,
and sing out their blues in karaoke.

Housing is a contentious issue, as TFWs are at the mercy of employers and
their associates, who sometimes work in cahoots with other Filipinos, who
provide living arrangements at exorbitant rates tied to a fixed period. Rental
fees are automatically deducted from their regular pay, which amounts to

double-dipping by employers. Many TFWs in the Prairies are vulnerable to this practice engaged in by employers and landlords, with no apparent recourse to file complaints for fear of deportation. In many cases, the employer *is* the landlord who simultaneously earns rental income from TFWs and pays their meagre wages.

> *Wala kaming magagawa; nandito na kami. Tatapusin na lang namin ang*
> *kontrata bago kami maghanap ng ibang malilipatan.* [We cannot do
> anything; we are here already. We will just finish our contract before
> we look for another place to live.]
> – Anna, a fast food worker in Lethbridge

TFWs have no say in setting the terms of the rental agreement and are unaware of housing market prices before they leave the Philippines. They constitute a group ripe for exploitation by profit-seeking individuals. Although there are certainly good employers whose primary interest is to provide decent and reasonable accommodations to their workers, many TFWs have been caught in the "housetrap" set by employers motivated only by the highest possible returns.

Employers-cum-landlords may have access to the housing premises of TFWs. Janice, a TFW in Edmonton who transferred to Winnipeg, shared the predicament of migrant workers who must try to maintain privacy in this situation: "*Bigla na lang dadating ang amo namin. Pipilitin kaming mag-overtime kasi alam niya na wala kaming trabaho.* [Our employer would suddenly arrive. He would force us to work overtime since he knew we had no work.]" According to Janice, a group of female TFWs walked off their jobs and complained to the employer about his abuses. Their actions led to concessions and better treatment of incoming TFWs.

TFWs are often housed together by employers. For example, ten TFWs may be billeted in a five-bedroom house, paired off into shared rooms by gender. These co-workers likely met for the first time at the airport. Complete strangers become roommates. Since most TFWs live together in this manner, the adjustment process seems collectively shared, as described in the following narratives.

> *At first, life in Canada was hard. It's a totally different culture and values.*
> *But I live with other Filipinos, too, and it helped us a lot to adjust gradually.*
> – Sharon, a former garment worker in Saskatoon

> *Sabay sabay kaming kumain at umalis noong una. May kausap kung*
> *nalulungkot.* [We would eat and go out together at first. There is some-
> one to talk to when feeling lonely.]
> – Annabel, a fast food worker in Lethbridge

TFW housing arrangements based on gender-pairing raise a number of issues. Getty, working for a hotel chain in southern Alberta, reflected on the set-up, which promotes gendered cultural expectations:

> *Noong una, kaming mga babae ang nagluluto at naglilinis. Ang mga lalaki kontento na sila na magbigay ng kanilang parte para sa mga bilihin. Pero inisip ko na medyo sobra na ito ... Hindi kami mga katulong nila. Kanya-kanya na kami ngayon.* [At first, we women were cooking and cleaning. The men were simply content to give their share for buying groceries. But I thought this was too much ... We are not their servants. We each fend for ourselves now.]

Gender plays out strongly among Filipinos who by contract fiat share the same residence. As Getty observed, male housemates at first appeared to expect women to take care of food preparation and clean-up.

Extramarital affairs among TFW housemates whose wives or husbands are left in the Philippines is an interesting development facilitated by housing arrangements. Such observable intimacy leads to tension and unease among all persons in the house. There is a growing trend of failed marriages because of a spouse's extramarital relations, a phenomenon comparable to what Chang and Ling (2000, 27) call "globalization and its intimate other." There are no statistics available on infidelity, but it is commonly acknowledged in the local community (Somodio 2008), as are failed marriages among TFWs (Estimo 2007).

Social Interactions

Social interaction is defined as "interaction with others" (Spitzberg 2003, 95). Immigrants and migrant workers interact with the host society at various levels: personal, group, community, and institutional. Whether newcomers feel a sense of acceptance or rejection depends largely on the context of the interactions. This section examines the social interactions of Filipino women in Canada with other Filipinos and with Canadians.

The presence of other Filipinos in areas where Filipino women migrate contributes to the impression of a welcoming Canada. A strange place seems friendlier when newcomers see a *kababayan* (compatriot) settled in the local community. Shopping malls, schools, and churches are the most likely sites of initial encounters among Filipino women.

> *Masaya ako ng makita ko yung Pilipina ... Tumingin ako sa kanya. Ngumiti siya. Sabi ko, Pilipino ka?* [I was happy when I saw a Filipina ... I looked at her. She smiled. I asked, are you Filipino?]
> – Ruby, a manufacturing employee in Lethbridge

Hinatid ko ang aking alaga sa eskwelahan. Nakita ko si ... Nag-usap kami. Magkababayan pala kami; galing din siya sa Bicol! [I took my ward to school. I saw ... We talked. It turns out we came from the same place; she is also from Bicol!]
  – Ester, a caregiver in Lethbridge

Nagkita kami sa simbahan. Nag-usap kami pagkatapos ng misa. [We saw each other in the church. We talked after Mass.]
  – Lorna, a hotel worker in Edmonton

Filipinos are both hospitable and sociable people (Thompson 2003, 56), which makes it easy for a total stranger to become an instant friend. In contrast to the Western inclination to maintain one's privacy, Filipinos tend to share their phone numbers, even with other Filipinos whom they meet for the first time. Regular home visits often quickly follow, with invitations to attend family celebrations. Contacts are an important and immediate source of information and advice for newcomers just getting settled, providing the kind of guidance – from showing bus routes to providing bargain-hunting tips and other such details – that makes strange places feel familiar.

Social interactions may also involve institutions, practices, and places of settlement. Canada offers a different way of life for first-generation Filipino immigrants, whether in terms of physical, social, or political aspects of life. The cold climate, state-funded social services, and orderly public systems are noteworthy.

I entered Canada as an OFW. My experience is overwhelming. Living in Canada is not the same kind of living in the Philippines. There are many great things in Canada like abiding laws ... the majority still does. Transportation like buses is government-owned and this means that they have the same fare.
  – Rosalinda, a nurse in Saskatoon

Maayos ang daan. Maayos din ang traffic. May speed limit pa. [The roads are good. Traffic is orderly, too. There is even a speed limit.]
  – Norma, a caregiver in Lethbridge

Kahit saan ka pumunta, may pila. Walang siksikan gaya sa atin sa Pilipinas. [Wherever you go, there is a queue. There is no cramming as in the Philippines.]
  – Siony, a nurse in Calgary

Tahimik dito kumpara sa atin sa Pilipinas. Walang mga tao halos sa kalye.
[It's quiet here compared with the Philippines. There's almost no one in
the streets.]
– Aurora, a hotel worker in Pincher Creek, Alberta

Many aspects of Canadian society are appealing to Filipino women. In
stark contrast to what they are accustomed to in the Philippines, there is
almost a stillness in the streets of smaller cities, with traffic and queues all
generally flowing in an orderly manner. In the Philippines, streets are crowded
and neighbours converge on the local *sari-sari* store, using it as a *tambayan*
(meeting place); many roads and highways have no posted speed limits and
traffic lights are sometimes ignored when no police officer is in sight; and
the idea of lining up for services is still in its infancy. Underlying the apparent public disorder, however, is the strong collectivist nature of the people:
chatting with neighbours is often a way of updating them about local events
and issues; queue jumping is often done at the urging of a friend or relative
already in line who would rather pass the time with someone they know.

Institutional practices in Canada that support fairness, order, and general
concern for the well-being of residents are viewed favourably by Filipino
women. People working towards achieving this kind of society – police
officers, health practitioners, and even politicians – tend to be highly regarded, although published reports about police brutality and mismanagement of public funds sound a familiar note (CBC News 2009a). Compared
with the epidemic of corruption in the Philippines today, there are fewer
obvious cases in Canada. Promotion of the rule of law and service, notably
the mandate of public officials in Canada to serve the public interest, is
commonly understood as a form of reward for paying income tax. Filipino
women tend to have high expectations of those in the public service sector,
and when engaging directly with public servants they believe they will be
treated fairly.

Because of their proficiency in English and their social networks in Canada,
Filipinos tend not to access the services provided by immigrant-serving
organizations. Instead, they utilize their own resources in the community,
generally contacts from family, friends, church groups, and even recruitment
agencies (Bonifacio 2008). In a sense, Filipino women "welcome themselves"
to Canada without the support of established agencies. They gather information from the Internet, from brochures, or by asking around; acquaint
themselves with the culture and climate in the area; and reach out to other
Filipinos through chance meetings in churches or in shopping malls. Other
Filipino women find opportunities to mingle at work with non-Filipinos
who become their resource for adjusting to life in Canada. In all these situations, Filipino women have found ways to integrate in the host society
outside traditional channels of government-funded agencies.

Welcoming TFWs to the community is usually an employer-specific venture, with employers or their representatives meeting TFWs at the airport. At other times, local Filipino groups such as the one in Winnipeg form reception committees that assist in welcoming TFWs and provide other services along the way.

> *I was scared at first when I came to Canada in 1968. It was my first time to be separated from my family ... We were met by a group of Filipinos upon arrival ... They showed us the way.*
> – Ligaya, a retired factory worker in Winnipeg

Generally, TFWs are provided with an information package about living in Canada when they arrive in major ports of entry. The package contains important contact information for government agencies and the only materials provided to TFWs. Employers take on the remaining responsibility of orienting TFWs to Canadian culture in the workplace and beyond. Larger corporations may work with immigrant-serving agencies to assist the foreign workers. Employers sometimes invite TFWs to attend local events, or facilitate contact with other Filipinos in the community through such agencies (Bonifacio 2008). Family-owned and smaller enterprises with one or two TFWs on their payroll tend to leave the new arrivals on their own, however. In the end, TFWs end up making the most of their contacts at weekend Masses or at the malls, just by saying *kumusta*.

The Filipino extended family system serves as the initial point of contact and forms a support group for many TFWs in Canada. The choice of destination province is sometimes based on the presence of family or associates.

> *In my case it was not difficult because I have my husband and in-laws here in Canada. This condition helped me fight sadness or depression ... I must admit that it does not exempt me, especially when I hear not much good news about my family back home.*
> – Angela, a hotel worker in Edmonton

Angela's husband came to Canada as a foreign worker whose job was arranged by his own family living in Edmonton. She followed him, also as a TFW. Both found that temporary migration led to eventual reunification. Their case exemplifies the new transnational Filipino family, redefined by the global labour diaspora (Parreñas 2005a). In the case of live-in caregivers, however, it is the woman who comes to Canada first, followed by her husband and children.

Filipino women married to Canadian nationals tend to have a very different trajectory of social interactions from those married to Filipinos. They are introduced to the Canadian way of life by their husbands but also often interact with other Filipinos in the community. Intermarriage is common, but when a racialized woman is involved with a white man, the popular imagination points to "degrading stereotypes" (Gardner 2009, 350): the "exotic, dark-eyed, raven-haired, English-speaking girls" from the Philippines "who, as virgins still at the age of 25 or beyond, marry men from all over the globe" (Morgan, cited in Lee 1998, 139). Constable (2006) notes the blurred boundaries between Asian brides, maids, and sex workers. "Internet brides," or women who meet their husbands online, face a number of challenges on arrival in Canada, including but not limited to unfamiliarity and isolation. On the other hand, a Filipina "Internet bride" in Calgary was socially isolated for the first few months after arrival until she was able to find work and meet other Filipinos at bus stops; on the other hand, a number of *Pinays* in the Prairies have had long and happy marriages with Canadian men. Some female TFWs enter into relationships with Canadian men and become acquainted with their surroundings and culture through that lens.

Another dimension of social interactions among Filipino women is the effect of pre-migration attitudes about settling in Canada. Certainly, structures and practices such as professional recognition and hiring are particular to the host country and may either enhance or inhibit full integration into the labour market, but independent of these is an individual's pre-migration perspective on what lies ahead.

> *Before we left the Philippines, my husband and I told ourselves that we will be Canadian. We know that life will be difficult at first, but we take on our insecurities head on and understand that our experiences will be like others before us. I am a fighter. I do not feel let down by other people, whoever they are.*
> – Josefina, self-employed in Winnipeg

> *Alam naming kung saan kami pupunta. Naghanda kami na malamig talaga dito sa Canada. Malungkot. Pero balewala iyon kasi nandito na kami sa Canada.* [We know where we are going. We prepared for the fact that it's really cold here in Canada. Lonely. But it doesn't matter because we are already here in Canada.]
> – Apple, an employee in Calgary

Some Filipino women researched their destinations in Canada, including the unexpected realities of the brutal winter, but they have kept an open mind about what Canada offers as their "home country." They have welcomed themselves into Canadian society through their own recognition of what lies ahead. In Finland, Yijälä and Jasinskaja-Lahti (2009) examined factors such as host society expectations, cultural knowledge, self-efficacy, and social networks to demonstrate that acculturation begins at the pre-migration stage among potential ethnic migrants. In the same vein, many Filipino women have a good understanding of what to expect in Canada and prepare themselves for the worst in anticipation of starting anew in another society. They appear to be equipped with an emotional cushion for dealing with possible discrimination in a positive way, like Josefina from Winnipeg in the above narrative. Anticipating difficulties during the first few years in Canada often mitigates negative experiences.

In seeking work and housing, and in social interactions with the community, *Pinays* have valued "place-making" (Escobar 2001) in the Prairies in such a way that the positive and negative experiences shape their sense of belonging in the community. Despite the challenges of settlement in strange places beyond the glitter of the metropolis, they have come to understand the terms of inclusion as part of the Canadian workforce and use, whenever possible, their cultural capital in overcoming housing limitations. Social interactions with public institutions and the community, as well as at the personal level, have enabled *Pinays* in the Prairies to compare their lives in the Philippines with what lies ahead in Canada. The road may be rocky for many *Pinays,* but it still opens many pathways for them to draw meaning from their marginality, "finding something of value in it, and making something of value out of it" (Heald 2008, 27) for themselves and their families.

4
Making Meanings: Identities and Integration

Integration is a multidimensional process that broadly covers social, cultural, political, identity, and economic aspects (Frideres 2008, 079). Social integration centres on immigrants' participation in society through its institutions. Cultural integration refers to the "(i) processes of value orientation and beliefs of immigrants, (ii) the process of learning the cognitive abilities and knowledge of the host culture, and (iii) the internalization of values, norms, and changes in belief systems" (ibid., 81). Political integration occurs when immigrants become naturalized citizens, exercise rights, and become politically engaged (Anderson and Black 2008). Identity integration is concerned with feelings of identification and belonging. Economic integration reflects the convergence of immigrants' economic performance with that of the native-born (Hum and Simpson 2004). These dimensions of integration and their measures of engagement vary among groups of immigrants in plural societies (Organisation for Economic Co-operation and Development [OECD] 2006; Conklin Frederking 2007). Some may be integrated in one or two dimensions but not in others. Particular groups of immigrants face certain barriers inhibiting their integration, whereas others encounter no such obstacles. In the West, for example, the Muslim community is confronted with more challenges after 9/11 (the 11 September 2001 al-Qaeda terrorist attack on the United States) (D'Appollonia and Reich 2008; McGhee 2008). It is clear that identities of immigrants are now more recognized in policy and scholarly discourses than ever before.

The idea that identity is fluid has been much debated in ethnicity and migration studies (Thapan 2005; Portes and DeWind 2007). Simply put, identity is about "who we are," but understanding identity formation and how it plays out in diaspora is a complex process. Who we are is not predetermined by birth, nor is it fixed in time; instead, ongoing engagement with various influences shapes our personalities and our perspectives. Socialization and particular life histories contribute to the formation of identities. Woodward (2004, 1) states: "Our identities are shaped by social structures but we also participate in forming our own identities." Gender, class, and culture are foremost among these social structures affecting individuals and groups. Gender is a social construct mainly defined by culture, and the role of women in a society obviously differs from that of men. Family dynamics shape how daughters are reared differently from sons, determining, for example, which child is allowed to leave home for work or marriage. Feminist standpoint theories characterize the situated experiences of women based on where they stand – in terms of gender, class, race, and other qualifiers of identity (Harding 2004; Brooks 2007). The choices we make in our lives also define who we want to be. Migration is thus a challenge to make meanings of who we are, our shifting identities, our conceptions of ourselves in relation to others, and much more.

Identity is established in relationships of power and difference (Sprenger 2004). Connolly (2002, 64) claims that "identity requires difference in order to secure its own self-certainty." Gender, culture, class, and other social categories form the bases for marking difference in society. Privileged groups that sway the dominant values in society make differences central to "othering" practices (Pessar 1999, 65). Racialized immigrants such as Filipino women are certainly "othered" by their ethnicity in a predominantly white Canada. However, "othering" practices also create a powerful cultural nexus of integration or resistance among marginalized groups. In a study of Black Francophone immigrants in Canada, Madibbo (2006) explores the multiple layers of both oppression and resistance against racism in their lives. Other ethnically defined immigrant groups have their own ways of negotiating their identities within host communities. I argue that Filipino women in Western societies like Canada engage their own understanding of Filipino identity not as an encompassing label of ethnic belonging but particularized according to gendered experiences of migration and intersecting variables of identity.

Gender intersects with other identities that impact the perceived integration of immigrant women. Shields (2008, 302) notes that gender "takes its meaning as a category in relation to another category." Most investigations of intersectionality involving marginalized groups of people – including immigrants, lesbians, and the physically and mentally impaired – centre on race, class, sexuality, and age (Mahalingam, Balan, and Haritatos 2008; Lawson et al. 2008). However, certain perceived identities among Filipino women have not been fully explored in the context of their migration to Canada – age, class, ethnolinguistic origin, religion, and sexuality. In this chapter, I present the meanings attached to these identities and their impact on the integration of *Pinays* in the Prairies, including notions of belonging as Filipinos, Filipino-Canadians, and Canadian citizens.

Variables of Filipino Identity

The notion of "identities on the move" (Goldin 1999) has particular nuances when applied to the lives of Filipino women. Meanings attributed to identities may change from the home country to the host society; hence, understanding how situated identities intersect with migration experiences provides glimpses of how *Pinays* in the Prairies make their lives meaningful in Canada. A relational analysis of gender and other variables of identity as interpreted outside the Philippine cultural base offers a better appreciation of Filipino women's lives in Canada. Factors such as being young or old at the time of migration, of being of or without "class," of coming from one region or another in the Philippines, of being religious or not, and of being *tomboy* (lesbian) are examined through the narratives of Filipino women in the Prairies.

Age

Age is an important determinant in many aspects of migration and integration. The Canadian point system for assessing immigrant applications awards a maximum of ten points for those aged 21-49 years. Other age brackets have corresponding points, but those less than 16 years net zero. Age at the time of migration affects ease of integration. Younger immigrants tend to embrace the culture and habits of host societies more readily than their parents or older immigrants (Tardiff-Williams and Fisher 2009). The following narratives echo the perceived advantage of younger immigrants over older immigrants.

> *Younger ones get better acculturated, especially adolescents. They begin to get the language, mas madali* [much easier] *to acculturate.*
> – Hosanna, a nurse in Edmonton

> *Filipinos who are younger when they came to Canada have higher adaptability ... Along the way it's difficult. For older Filipinos ... it becomes more difficult for women, with about 30-40 percent adaptability, because of the cultural expectations on their shoulders.*
> – Rowena, a manager in a media company in Winnipeg

> *Young Filipino women get more chances to be integrated; they go through the educational system and become part of mainstream society. Older women stick to the old ways and culture still remains, no matter what.*
> – Pilar, a community worker in Winnipeg

Stevens (1999), in her research in the United States, reveals that age of immigration is among the social and demographic factors that strongly correlate with proficiency in acquiring English as a second language. George (2010) notes that those in Canada who cannot speak either official language, English or French, tend to be older and female. In Sweden, the age of migration of immigrants is a factor in children's educational attainment (Böhlmark 2009). Jasinska-Lahti and Liebkind (2000) show that the longer Russian-speaking immigrant adolescents live in Finland, the greater their degree of acculturation. Migration can also have detrimental effects on young members of the family, and perceived delinquency appears to be on the rise, particularly in Europe (Berry et al. 2006; Tekin 2010).

Tensions associated with "changes to expected family roles," including the "change of power relations and empowerment of women outside the household," also affect young immigrants (Suárez-Orozco and Baolian Qin 2006, 169). Conflict at home between husband and wife tremendously affects the children's well-being. Live-in caregivers in Canada are separated from their children for long periods of time, and building mother-child relations after reunification is challenging: this can have a serious impact on school performance (Philippine Women Centre 2009; McClelland 2009). *Pinays* who participated in this study, however, did not express major concerns about their children's education. They appeared satisfied with their children's performance in school relative to "Canadian kids." As they said, schoolchildren in the Philippines wake up early to be in school by 7:30 in the morning and are normally given daily assignments, whereas in Canada, assignments are given weekly or have longer due dates. *Pinay* mothers tend to worry about what their kids are learning in school when they do not bring home any assignments; more importantly, they fear that their children might become involved with gangs or drugs (cf. Kwok and Tam 2008).

Like other immigrant youth, young Filipinos face negative stereotypes about their ethnicity and experience racism in school and the larger community (Austria 2008; Rousseau et al. 2009). In Montreal, a seven-year-old Filipino boy was ridiculed and punished by a teacher for using a fork and spoon for eating; his family subsequently won their discrimination case in the Quebec Human Rights Tribunal in 2010 (CTV Montreal 2010). Philip Kelly, professor of geography at York University, leads the 2010-13 Filipino Youth Transitions in Canada project, a national study to examine the link between the dismal high school dropout rates of Filipino youth and their low rates of university graduation and the deprofessionalization of their immigrant parents on arrival in Canada. While the term "dropout" refers to a student who stops attending school completely, its meaning is also socially constructed and suggests varied perspectives when associated with race (Sefa Dei 2008). Possible appropriate terms could be "fade-out" to refer to a student who is physically attending school "but not in spirit," or "push-out" to suggest that external factors have contributed to a student's exit from school (ibid., 263). Some of those students who have officially dropped out of one school may in fact have transferred to another – but the stigma remains the same.

The performance of Filipino youth in schools and universities in the Prairies has yet to be explored and may appear to follow the pattern observed in Toronto and Vancouver, namely, leaving the school system in order to enter the labour market. Extrapolating from the national situation, where more females are in school (Statistics Canada 2007), it is likely that more female than male Filipino youth tend to stay in school. From a broader perspective, the entry of Filipino youth into the labour market after high school is similar to the practice among Canadian youth of taking a year off after graduation. The issues faced by the sons and daughters of *Pinays* in the Prairies were not specifically discussed during this study, but a few *Pinay* mothers expressed some disappointment over their children's taking a year off after graduating from high school; they appeared to console themselves by looking on it as a normal "Canadian" practice. Daughters of Filipino live-in caregivers tend to have a deeper appreciation of their mothers' sacrifices in order to give them a better life in Canada, and completing a degree is the best way to show this.

Age determines career paths and the degree of economic integration among Filipino women. Since the majority of Filipinos in Canada are between twenty-five and forty-four years old, it follows that they are economically active, with more opportunities to find work than older women.

> *Age is a big factor in the community. I have a friend who is fifty years old. Kaya daw hindi siya na-hire because of her age* [the reason why she was not hired was because of her age]. *Because I am a bit younger I have no problem. Tamang-tama daw ang age ko* [my age is just right].
> – Samantha, a government employee in Regina

> *The average Filipino immigrant is young, under fifty, especially in the Provincial Nominee Program. We also welcome the elderly who come as parents under the family class stream.*
> – Luningning, a community leader in Winnipeg

Women who migrated before they reached seventeen years of age tend to have comparable labour market participation to the native-born (Huang 1997, 28). In terms of educational attainment and therefore earning potential, Schaafsma and Sweetman (2001) argue that "age at immigration matters" in Canada. Young, unmarried Filipino women tend to upgrade their education to reach parity with Canadian standards. More of them are able to juggle work and school than older, married Filipino women.

Madami na akong natapos na certificate dito sa Canada. Medyo naka-angat ako ng konti. [I have already completed a number of certificates here in Canada. I have prospered a bit now.]
   – Leilani, a home care worker in Calgary

Nurse ako sa Pilipinas pero dumating ako sa Canada as caregiver. Nakalagay sa work permit namin na bawal mag-aral. Nag-aral ako pagkatapos ng limang taon na trabaho sa homecare. Ngayon ... nurse ulit ako. [I was a nurse in the Philippines but came to Canada as a caregiver. Our work permit stated that we could not go to school. I went to school after five years of working in home care. Now ... I am a nurse again.]
   – Patty, a nurse in Calgary

Both Leilani and Patty in Calgary are under thirty-five years old and un-married. Leilani is an unwed mother whose child is still in the Philippines. Their determination to upgrade their professional credentials may well be a factor of age and marital status. Married middle-aged women tend to focus more on finding survival jobs to meet the basic needs of their families or, if they are able, switching to new career paths to negotiate the labour market. Looking for new professional opportunities takes time, money, and commit-ment, and some Filipino women reach a point of surrender after calculating the costs and benefits of such endeavours at a certain age. Still, achievement in the labour market forms part of one's identity in the community. As in the Philippines, the value of one's work can be a source of pride for the family, and one's work can form part of one's identity in familiar modes of introduction, as in "This is X; she is a teacher."

Another view of age among Filipino women that impacts their personal and social relations in the community is length of residence. There are two main groups in Canada: the *bagong dating* (newcomer/recently arrived) and the *matagal na* (old-timer).

Parang mahiyain pa kung bagong dating [it seems like those who have recently arrived are shy]. *They are very timid regardless of age. Maybe they are not familiar with the Canadian system yet.*
   – Victoria, a private employee in Saskatoon

Personal attributes like timidity and confidence are more often understood to be a product of culture rather than of age. The perception of Canadian society as liberal and open compared with the social codes for women in the Philippines may affect how newcomers are viewed by others, but not for long. In the following narratives, Helena and Leilani explain why they believe personal attributes like shyness among newcomers are transitory.

It depends on the personality. There are young adults who are shy, they observe others first. Once they get into the environment and get to know others, they are more cooperative, more assertive compared to older women. They want to observe first.
– Helena, a nurse in Regina

Medyo mahirap sa umpisa. Parang bago lahat ang tao, ang mga gawi ... makikiramdam ka muna kung sino sila. [It's quite difficult at first. Looks like everyone is new, including their habits ... you need to first get a feeling for who they are.]
– Leilani, a home care worker in Calgary

One issue of concern that arises with age during migration is elder abuse, defined as "violence, neglect and other crimes aimed at [an] elderly person" (Fryling, Summers, and Hoffman 2006, 5). Elder abuse is not limited to physical harm but also includes a wide range of abusive behaviours, including financial exploitation and emotional mistreatment (Brandl et al. 2007). Older Filipinos who are sponsored by their children in Canada tend to experience inter-generational conflicts resulting from lifestyle changes. Some of these conflicts can lead to neglect or elder abuse (Park 2006), particularly among elderly women, who are "more vulnerable to severe physical and emotional harm compared to men" (Brozowski and Hall 2004, 70). Widespread forms of elder abuse among Filipino seniors are compelling them to perform caregiving and babysitting without remuneration, and verbal abuse from their own children. (Seniors Council, n. d., 116) Verbal abuse is especially deplorable since talking back to parents is considered gravely disrespectful in Philippine culture.

Family sponsorship in the Canadian immigration program enables many families to be together in Canada, with parents being generally sponsored by their well-settled children. Often unanticipated, however, is the pressure that the elderly may place on family finances and caregiving responsibilities. The ability of *tatay* (father) or *nanay* (mother) to exercise power and control over their children changes with dependency on them in Canada. Filipinos sixty-five years and older who are sponsored by their children have to comply with the ten-year residency requirement in Canada before they become eligible to receive the federal Old Age Security benefit. In the interim, they are financially dependent on their own children. While care of the elderly is integral to the Filipino family tradition, such an obligation is quite difficult to fulfill in Canada in the absence of the extended kinship system. Com-bining work, family, and elder care can have unintended consequences, such as isolation and potential neglect of the elderly. According to Gemma Dalayoan, president of the Manitoba Association of Filipino-Canadian Teachers, "elder abuse is like a cancer that spreads quietly and rapidly without being noticed" (cited in Crocker 2010).

Three elderly Filipino women in Winnipeg pointed out their plight in the following narratives:

Older women were not ready to be exposed ... they cannot take the bus or do grocery by themselves. Women in their fifties with children here in Canada are sponsored to babysit their children and not to be a part of the community but to serve them and their kids.
– Asuncion, a retired nurse in Winnipeg

We view people as young and middle-aged rather than old. We have an elder abuse campaign going on ... This is a problem with fifty-five-years-plus people. First, parental authority is lost in Canada. They are dependent on their children for basic needs ... In turn the younger ones are more assertive, more abusive. We have unreported cases of elder abuse. Not much is said because of the protective nature of the community. Elders expressed frustration of losing respect of their children.
– Dalisay, a retired teacher in Winnipeg

If you are older coming to Canada, at least do not sell your house in the Philippines. You still have a place to go back to. We used to be the boss in the Philippines but not anymore in Canada. We are not equal with our children.
– Carolina, a retired teacher in Winnipeg

The elderly hold a respected position in Filipino culture (Chen 1999; Bautista 2001). *Lola* (grandmother) and *lolo* (grandfather) play a vital role in the rearing of grandchildren as they stay with their families in old age. Migration to Canada has changed the dynamics of this highly regarded tradition, however. Placing the Filipino elderly in nursing homes is often seen as un-Filipino and is resisted by both children and parents (Robles 2001; *Balita* 2009). Consequently, female family members may take on more responsibilities in caring for the elderly at home. Based on the 2006 census, Filipino females spend more hours giving unpaid care or assistance to seniors compared with Filipino males during the week before the census was taken (7-13 May): less than 5 hours (7.9 percent for females and 7.3 percent for males); 5-9 hours (3.1 percent for females and 2.6 percent for males); 10-19 hours (1.6 percent for females and 1.1 percent for males); and more than 20 hours (1.9 percent for females and 1.4 percent for males). Interestingly, more females spent no hours giving unpaid care to seniors (80.3 percent, compared with 78.6 percent for males, which may suggest that these women have no parent to care for in Canada.

As a result of these difficulties, returning to the Philippines becomes an attractive option for many elderly Filipinos, the impact of which is beyond the scope of this book. Suffice it to say that age does matter in patterns of migration, and the notion of age is not limited to genealogy but also includes intergenerational relations and residence in Canada.

Class

"Class" can be thought of as a social measure of status in society, or what Bourdieu (cited in Jenkins 1992, 88) calls the "categories of people who occupy positions within a field (the political power? economic field?) which are ... similar or close to each other." In the Philippines, status is historically rooted in a rigid class structure, in which the rich have for centuries controlled the fate of Filipinos (McCoy 2009). Colonial and postcolonial policies favouring a few sectors of the population facilitated class formation in the country (Basch et al. 1994, 230), which now has a "perfectly defined class system" (Fee [1910] 2009, 104) with stark contrasts between rich and poor in choice of schools, residential options, lifestyle, and access to material benefits.

Sources of wealth in the Philippines are diverse, from the "old rich" with their landholdings to the "new rich" composed of urban-industrial, commercial, and financial elites (Billig 2003, 259). About 23 percent of the population were living below the international poverty line of US$1.25 a day in 2005 (United Nations Children's Fund [UNICEF] 2003). As of 2009, one-third of the population remained poor (Remo 2010). The gap between rich and poor remains wide as the country continues to move along the neoliberal path of economic globalization, where the landed political and economic elites reap the benefits and control the country (Krinks 2002; Clarke and Sison 2005). According to Rothenberg (2007, 11), "differences between rich and poor, which result from particular ways of structuring the economy, are socially constructed as innate differences among people ... used to rationalize or justify the unequal distribution of wealth and power that results from economic decisions made to perpetuate privilege." The attributes of *mayaman* (rich) and *mahirap* (poor) are well defined in the Philippines. A day's observation of the Metro Manila highways or major road crossings reveals who struggles to survive: a swarm of the young and the old skillfully hawk their wares to passersby, public bus passengers, and cars in traffic jams. Gated communities and posh condominiums contrast with the urban slums and shantytowns of Manila where 3.4 million people live (Comerford 2005b). The Marxist ideology of class struggle still looms large among leftist organizations like the New People's Army, which has a strong presence in rural areas (Hilhorst 1997). The "unfinished revolution" of the nineteenth-century *Katipuneros* (revolutionaries) of Andres Bonifacio (Ileto 1998, 177) to gain genuine independence for the country, which was thwarted by elitist nationalists who eventually yielded to American rule, which turned the Philippines into a neocolony, may give progressive organizations hope to continue the struggle for national liberation and social justice for all. The labour movement, for example, remains active in advocating for the rights of workers and their families.

Where lies the middle class? In the Philippines, the middle class is composed of "teachers, merchants, small [landed] farmers and professionals" (Riedinger 1995, 132), about 25 percent of whom come from "lower class background" (King 2008, 102). Conceptualizations of the expansion of the Filipino middle class vary (Kimura 2003; Villegas 2010), and so do their origins (Bautista 2001). Industrialization, modernization, and wider access to social benefits such as education and labour participation have given rise to this group. Rivera (1994) examines the consequent change in the Philippine social structure with industrialization and the growth of new entrepreneurships in manufacturing. Rivera (2000, 255) investigates the rise of the Filipino middle class through participation in national politics and its "decentralized nature" of political mobilization with no defined political agenda. Villegas (2010, 306), however, points to the "revolutionary" role of the Philippine middle class in democratic politics as viewed from the "EDSA II revolution" of 2001, which culminated in the ousting of President Joseph Estrada.

Middle-class families in the Philippines are classified in terms of either income or more general socio-economic characteristics. Such a family would have a total annual income of 251,000 to 2,045,280 pesos (in 2007) or meet all of the following criteria: "1. housing unit is made of strong roof materials; 2. own[s] a house and lot; 3. own[s] a refrigerator; 4. own[s] a radio" (Virola 2007). (With the booming communications industry, middle-class families today own much more than a radio!) Certainly, the means of private transportation – the type of car ownership – is a strong index of social class in the Philippines. Domestically assembled transportation, including the popular jeepney and jeeps, characterize the lower middle class, whereas imported cars and sport utility vehicles (SUVs) are characteristic of the upper middle class or the ultra-rich. Middle-class consumerism drives demand for "chop-chop" items (imported second-hand goods from Japan, Korea, and Hong Kong). As a whole, the Philippine middle class is "not necessarily homogeneous" (Kimura 2003, 274), with disparities in income within and across the "new, old, and marginal middle classes" (276). The unstable economy and the high cost of services have pushed the Filipino middle class to turn to migration. As a result, the number of middle-income families has been shrinking since 2000, a phenomenon called by Llorito (2007) the "vanishing middle class."

Migration has created a new type of middle class in the Philippines: the "overseas middle class" (San Juan 2006), or what I call the "transnational middle class" of immigrants and migrant workers moving between states and sustaining a flow of remittances to their families in the Philippines. Education and skills are the major tools of this group, whose migration may have averted their plunge into poverty. Millions of Filipinos belong to this new "floating middle class," who have gained a bit of material security through property ownership or by borrowing money from loan sharks at usurious rates to initially finance their travel abroad. Their dollars and sweat gain for them visible signs of class, popularly regarded as "lifestyle and tastes" (Olin Wright 2005, 1), often in the form of huge concrete houses. Families of overseas Filipino workers (OFWs) had a mean income 95 percent higher than the rest of Filipino families in 2003 (Llorito 2007), making overseas labour migration a very desirable option for climbing the social ladder. A study by the Asian Development Bank indicates that OFW families spend less on food and more on health, with "fairly stable" expenditures for education and housing since 2000 (Opiniano 2010).

However, the traditional understanding of class associated with economic wealth has evolved into a more complicated typology of "overlapping and mutually constitutive" dimensions (Kelly 2007b, 5): position, process, performance, and politics. Class as position suggests one's location in the division of labour and wealth structure; class as process signifies the nature of the relationship between different classes in the production, appropriation, and distribution of labour, which intersects with race and gender; class as performance subjectively defines "everyday understanding of class in a cultural register" (ibid., 8) in different settings, broadly consisting of two forms – consumption and embodiment; and class as politics pertains to the built solidarities arising from particular experiences of class, such as political mobilization. Kelly's conceptualization of class encompasses Filipino migration to Canada and its place in the global economy: deprofessionalized and de-skilled workers in low-paying occupations, whose labour is expropriated for Canadian employers while they finance businesses or properties in the Philippines, are consumed by the desire to purchase a house and car in Canada to demonstrate a middle-class standing in this country similar to the one they enjoyed in the Philippines. And, despite the appearance of marginalization, these workers are galvanized into community action for social justice.

Kelly and colleagues (2009) examine the importance of Filipino class origins, the class structure of Philippine society, and the country's standing in the international economy and its role in labour market integration. Filipino immigrants mostly belong to the "educated and professionally qualified middle class" but with usually "modest personal resources and assets," a huge portion of which is spent on pre-migration expenses (medical examinations, procurement of documents, consultant fees, etc.) (ibid., 16). The scarcity of their capital in Canada is compounded by pressure to support their families in the Philippines, hence the immediate push to secure employment in "survival jobs" (ibid., 14). The likelihood of deprofessionalization, or the loss or reduced value of one's professional qualifications (e.g., from mechanical engineer to machine operator), on migration to Canada can be seen among *Pinays* in the Prairies, particularly TFWs in transition to permanent residency, whose entry into the local labour market often comes about through their existing social network.

How does class as social identity in the Philippines impact the migration, settlement, and integration of Filipino women in Canada? There are two competing views about class in the lives of *Pinays* in the Prairies. One is that class is an intrinsic aspect of Filipino identity in the community; the other is that class is not noticeable, or may even be non-existent, among Filipinos in Canada. The measuring stick of "middle classness" is the perceived ability to attain what the rest of the Canadian population presumably possesses: a job, a house, and a car. Unlike in the Philippines, the middle class in Canada seems "stagnant" while the numbers of the rich and the poor increase (Cohen 2008). About 85 percent of Canadians self-identified as middle class as of 2006 (Curry-Stevens 2008, 386), and in the Prairies most Filipino women view their social status as middle class, too.

> *Filipinos are mostly in the middle class. There are some rich Filipino women here, but I haven't seen anybody who is poor because most of us are hardworking.*
> – Carmen, a community worker in Calgary

> *Wala pa akong na-encounter na mayaman* [I have not encountered a rich person] *who came to Canada just to work. In the Philippines, it's easy to identify yung mga* [those who are] *rich, class A, B or C. But in Canada ... Ang status dito pareho ... Depende nalang kung gaano sila ka-hardworking.* [The status here is the same ... It depends on how hardworking they are.]
> – Petra, a nurse in Saskatoon

> *In the Philippines, pag may connection ka, mayaman ka* [if you have connections, you are rich]. *Wala yan dito sa Canada* [it's not like that here in Canada]. *The middle class is emerging more in the Philippines because of OFWs, but the rich still control ... Middle class ang tingin ko dito* [it seems that it's the middle class here].
> – Josefina, self-employed in Winnipeg

As indicated in the foregoing narratives, employment in Canada is an important indicator of belonging in a social class. A job opens up opportunities and provides access to privileges such as a good credit standing, enabling Filipinos to purchase a house and car. Hard work makes "middle classness" possible for many Filipinos living overseas. It is common among Filipinos, both women and men, in the Prairies and elsewhere in Canada to have two or three part-time jobs in addition to their full-time employment. The same trend is seen in the United States, where two out of ten Filipinos have two jobs (Gonzalez 2009, 74). Combining wages from all these sources raises their total income level for loan purposes, travel, and other needs, including supporting families in the Philippines or sponsoring relatives to come to Canada. In 2000, about 88 percent of Filipinos in Canada received more income from earnings than from government transfers, compared with 77 percent of other Canadians; only 8 percent received more income from government transfers, compared with 12 percent of other Canadians (Lindsay 2007, 16). Income from non-government sources is well appreciated among Filipino adults; the term *pal* (from *palamunin,* literally someone who is given food) denotes dependency. However, although more work means more money, working three jobs or sixteen hours a day on average takes a toll on the body and results in absentee parents for many Filipino children in Canada.

Many Filipinos value visible symbols of status, such as living in a middle-class suburb or driving a new car. It has been observed that class among immigrant Filipinos in San Diego, California, is "ambiguous" – that is, they may work in an assembly plant but own homes in middle-class areas (Espiritu 2003b, 265). This is true of Filipinos in many Prairie communities as well. In Winnipeg, settlement patterns show "an increasing number of Filipinos skipping the 'natural' inner city settlement process entirely" and living in the upscale Fort Garry neighbourhood (Vachon and Toews 2008, 119). They are well distributed in about a third of Winnipeg's census tracts, similar to West Indian professionals (Loewen and Friesen 2009, 125).

The following narratives demonstrate how class determines residential location and forms part of Filipino identity in the community:

> *Mayroon pa rin* [there is] *[class] whether we like it or not. Class is very strong in the Filipino community. Sa* [in the] *Calgary quadrants – NE mas mababa* [much lower], *puro* [full of] *immigrants with low house value ... NE is a practical place to stay because it's close to the airport and an industrial area. After two or three years here the mode of behaviour changes with the objective to go to SW ... because walang masyadong* [not too many] *immigrants.*
> – Marilou, a community worker in Calgary

> *I see that [class] more for Filipinos here for a long time. In Saskatoon east side, the better part of the city; east side people get together especially with Canadian citizens. More upscale mas* [more] *rich ka* [you]. *But don't see much of class other than this ... The recently arrived are not really poor; they have lands in the Philippines.*
> – Victoria, a private employee in Saskatoon

Class is more where your house is located ... houses in ... cost more than
$350,000 so you need three jobs and work hard to get it. At the north end ...
below average class lives.
  – Barbara, a retired employee in Winnipeg

Another aspect of class as identity for Filipino women is established by
their type of profession or work, which strongly shapes one's social circle.

Yes, class exists. Among workers the caregivers tend to live or go together.
Having the same work allows same opportunities to be together.
  – Anita, a private company employee in Saskatoon

Professionals have their own group ... Class cut across the lines in other
groups but many are still based on perception of wealth ... The first Filipino
immigrants were good ambassadors in Manitoba. They hold good jobs as
doctors and nurses. They speak good English and mingle with other
Canadians. Later on the factory workers arrived and we see Filipinos in
group.
  – Carolina, a retired teacher in Winnipeg

Filipinos have the tendency to show their class ... Yung may sinasabi dating
mga doctor, sila ay segregated sa iba [those who are said to be former
doctors, they are segregated from others]. *Nurses, kanya-kanyang grupo*
din [have their own groups, too]. *Garment workers iba* [different] ...
Noong una ang mga garment workers umiiwas sa akin [previously the
garment workers would shy away from me] *because I work in a better*
place ... The feeling of class was there.
  – Gabriela, a retired government employee in Winnipeg

There is always a tendency, it's [class] happening here. We tend to own,
we relate to what they do, their job. We don't feel it even though we know it
exists. It's subtle.
  – Filomena, a government employee in Saskatoon

Filipino newcomers are aware that their class standing in the Philippines
may shape their status and reputation in Canada. This is reflected in their
initial reluctance to accept low-paying jobs.

Yes, class is evident. Being rich or poor medyo halata sa bagong dating. May
pera pa. After a while in Canada wala ng pera! Sa trabaho, halata ang class
din. Halata yung may edukasyon sa Pilipinas. [Being rich or poor seems
obvious among newcomers. They still have money. After a while in

Canada no more money! At work, class is obvious, too. It's obvious who
were educated in the Philippines.]
– Rosal, a nurse TFW in Winnipeg

*Class is an unspoken rule in the Philippines. Those with higher class status
and came to Canada have higher frustration levels, more heartaches. Need
accreditation to practice as a doctor and get more local experience. A very
handful of them masuwerte* [are lucky] *and get accepted right away. It
requires maturity to pass that stage.*
– Rowena, a manager in a media company in Winnipeg

How class is constructed and formed in the Philippines somehow relates
to the apparent acceptance of "survival jobs" in Canada (Kelly et al. 2009,
14). In the Philippines, the highly institutionalized practice of patronage
makes possible entry into the class strata: "Whom you know" is the basic
dictum of success, enabling those with less than stellar qualifications to
occupy positions. Nepotism is a social malady that awards merit to people
on the basis of fictive or blood relationship, thereby degrading Philippine
public services (Kang 2002). Political dynasties are widespread in the country,
and the turnover of political appointees in government services – from
municipalities, cities, and provinces to the national government – resembles
a circus. Qualifications are secondary to patronage.

In Canada, the social network acts as a sponsor for newcomers seeking
employment. I would say there is "familial or regional nepotism" among
Filipinos in certain workplaces in the Prairies and elsewhere. That is, a Filipino employee of a Canadian entity who comes from one province in the
Philippines often becomes the contact person for would-be Filipino TFWs
from the same province. For example, Filipino live-in caregivers who are in
Canada under the LCP represent a form of "ethnic nepotism," with huge
numbers compared with other immigrant groups. Many of those in the
Prairies have secured their posts through an existing social network of friends
and family members. A case in point is the *Pinay* caregiver in Calgary who
worked quite well with an aged employer, whom she persuaded to hire her
cousin in the Philippines after the expiration of her contract. In a small city
in Alberta, a private home care agency relies on a constantly replenished
pool of workers hired directly from the Philippines who are relatives or
known associates of already employed Filipino caregivers. In this way, recruitment costs are minimal and retention of Filipino employees is quite a
bit higher since they feel obligated to employers who facilitate this avenue
of family reunification. However, such practices perpetuate the status of
Filipinos in general and Filipino women in particular as the underclass in
particular sectors of the Canadian economy (Kelly 2010, 160).

Accepting employment referrals from social networks is an easy route to earning money immediately, and a practical way to recoup the costs of settlement and help migrants' families in the Philippines. As the source of information about living in Canada, the social network epitomizes a key value among Filipino immigrants: *basta may trabaho* (as long as you have a job). Hence, the opportunity to land a job right away to cover the costs of migration and deal with the structural challenges of gaining jobs comparable to what they had back in the Philippines make up for the downgrading of credentials.

Class as an element of social identity is a strong motivator for success. The idea of "making it" in Canada spurs competition among Filipinos – to be seen, to be known, and to be respected for reaping the rewards of industriousness and hard work. However, this form of competition also highlights an alleged Filipino trait known as "crab *(talangka)* mentality," which sees Filipinos "pulling each other down" and establishing "who is better than the other" (Vergara 2009, 77). There is little scholarly literature on crab mentality, but it "can be defined as the desire to outdo, outshine, or surpass another at the other's expense" (Nadal 2009, 129).

> *Pare-pareho ang tingin* [looks like we're viewed equally]. *But there is still class in Canada although with a little bit of difference ... Hindi lahat parepareho* [not everyone is the same]. *May inggitan or tsismisan* [there is jealousy or gossip]. *Having a nice house or a small house, inggit na inggit ang iba* [others are so jealous]. *Competition.*
> – Ligaya, a retired factory worker in Winnipeg

Crab mentality is decried in Philippine politics and blamed for disunity among Filipinos in achieving goals for social change and development (De la Torre 2002; Enriquez 2009); at the same time, however, the example of successful immigrants inspires intense resolve in Filipinos to live a better life in their adopted countries. In the Philippines, crab mentality is related to "leveling off" or the "desire to be on equal footing" with others socially and economically (Garzon 1999, 325). However, the negative side of crab mentality is seen when those who "strive to be better" are "put down" (Mendoza 2002, 57). Someone who is presently successful may be persecuted for previous life circumstances, such as coming from a poor background in the Philippines. There are many variations on this universal tendency to envy, and crab mentality in particular takes many forms across cultures, as seen, for example, in the use of "crabs in our midst" (Royeca 2010) to refer to those individiduals who put down others.

At the other extreme, when it comes to class discourse among Filipino women, class distinctions among Filipinos are viewed as barely noticeable, even non-existent, in Canada.

Class is not as present as before in Canada. We do not see that. Filipinos are relatively close even if they are not related to each other.
   – Clemencia, a nurse in Winnipeg

Not as much as I have seen. It's more in the Philippines where the rich have the attitude that they are better than other people. Poor? Filipino? Never seen one in Canada unless they think they are poor! But there are still those who came in as rich in Canada, but there's no classification now.
   – Helena, a nurse in Regina

There is no such thing as poor in the Filipino community.
   – Asuncion, a retired nurse in Winnipeg

Wala akong napapansin dito [I don't notice it here]. *Class, hindi ko mas-yadong ma-identify* [I cannot really identify with it]. *Pero ang nag-socialize like professional or educated class* [but those who socialize are the professional or educated class] ... *Others timid, nahiya kasi* [because they are shy].
   – Samantha, a government employee in Regina

All women in my group became successful – businesswomen, etc. When we come together for parties and other events there is no such thing as class.
   – Marilena, a community worker in Edmonton

Class is less in Canada. They don't look at status here, unlike in the Philippines where we cannot rub shoulders with the rich and famous. That's how I see it. There is so much discrimination between rich and poor in the Philippines ... Mas convenient ang buhay dito may pera ka o hindi [life is more convenient, whether or not you have money].
   – Sharon, a former garment worker in Saskatoon

Interestingly, the retreat of class from such a paramount position actually points to the upward social mobility resulting from migration to Canada: only when one reaches a certain status can she afford not to be so concerned about class. The prevailing assumption is that Filipinos have the ability to achieve the same class position as other Filipinos in Canada through diligent work and industry. Class is based on attainable material benefits in Canada – the opposite of what their situation would have been had they remained in the Philippines. Filipinos have the same low-income levels as the rest of the Canadian population (Lindsay 2007), and this "levelling off" or attainment of a middle-class lifestyle is an effect of migration.

Filipinos identify with the democratic conception of equality that presumably enables immigrants to prosper in Canada, as evidenced by the following narratives:

There is the influence of Canadian society. We are more equal in Canada, whether rich or poor. We go to the same grocery, same school, same restaurant compared to the Philippines where the poor are miserable. Maganda sa [it's beautiful in] *Canada, it's a great equalizer to some extent. I don't feel the class difference. I don't feel rich or poor.*
  – Hosanna, a nurse in Edmonton

With class system here, there is no rich or poor as long as you work. Everybody is equal.
  – Rosie, a sales agent in Winnipeg

In Canada everybody is equal. It is up to you to improve your lives. Parang ok lang ang class dito [it seems that class is okay here]. *Ano ba yung mayroon ang mayaman na hindi mo makukuha* [what do the rich have that you cannot get]? *They have more money but you can have their lifestyle, too. But in the Philippines, poor is poor.*
  – Salvacion, a home care worker in Winnipeg

Their narratives tend to obscure the class divide that marked these individuals in the Philippines. Access to material benefits in Canada through paid employment somehow "equalizes" the different classes, enabling all Filipinos to embrace the romanticized notion of the Western middle class. Acquiring the social and economic characteristics of the middle class – job, house, car – is what many working-class Filipino women aspire to. Although indicators of social class – "occupation, education, status, wealth, ownership" (McMullin 2010, 37) – persist, Filipino women strive to raise their class position through equal opportunities in the labour market, even if it means having to work three jobs in one day.

Class is an important variable of identity among *Pinays* in the Prairies. Although their views on class are still defined by the traditional measures of consumption and class markers, a number have rejected the idea of a Filipino class divide in Canada since such a divide is apparently easily crossed through hard work and perseverance. Understandably, those working in lowly paid jobs reconstruct class as a border that can be breached in time, yet in the interim they may, following Kelly (2007a), succumb to the consumption patterns of the middle class.

Not all is equal in the class spectrum, however. The ability of *Pinays* to navigate the Canadian labour market is also dependent on intersecting factors, such as migration status, especially the type of immigration program participated in, educational qualifications, professional experience in regulated and non-regulated occupations, existing support network, place of residence, and financial resources at the time of migration, including previous class background in the Philippines (Kelly 2007b). *Pinays* arriving in Canada under the LCP have to wait longer periods than those who come under the skilled independent classification before they can claim permanent resident status and access benefits and privileges. Educational attainment defines the level of applicable jobs – those with postgraduate degrees have greater chances than college graduates of being eligible for supervisory or managerial positions. Certain professions are highly regulated and the comparable years of experience required for recognition determines the likelihood of practising the same profession in Canada. The majority of those in such professions are therefore advised to take upgrading courses. Support networks play a role in facilitating mobility, in child minding, and in offering options for Filipino women. Place of residence also determines the opportunities available to *Pinays:* cities tend to offer more work than small towns, although small towns sometimes offer better jobs for those with the necessary skills, with less competition. Financial resources available at the time of migration provide an advantage to Filipino women who may decide to take upgrading courses right away instead of at some indeterminate time in the future.

Although a person's class background in the Philippines may predict better life opportunities on migration to Canada (Kelly 2007b), this is not an absolute. As conveyed by *Pinays* in the Prairies, the "do-it-all-yourself" mode of living in Canada, which contrasts with the use of hired help in the Philippines, makes determination and commitment vital for successful integration. How perceived class structures in the Philippines and Canada are "evaluated comparatively *by* migrants (rather than simply frameworks for the evaluation *of* migrants)" (Kelly 2007b, 16) provides a more nuanced understanding of their class positionality. Arguably, being of "high class" in the Philippines becomes immaterial amid similar tasks of keeping house while being gainfully employed in Canada and enjoying performatively Bourdieu's signification of class, of "being [with] class" (cited in McCracken 2001, 155).

As an immigrant group, Filipinos are a subordinated class in Canada, or an example of *"prima facie* class degradation" (Kelly 2007b, 16). Following Bourdieu's concept of *habitus,* their history of migration to Canada, including gender-stratified occupations, determines the "social space" that "corresponds to a particular set of life conditions" (Weininger 2005, 92). As the epitome of the nanny-cum-domestic worker, Filipino women exhibit far lower class position than other immigrant women, even if LCP participants represent 23 percent of total Filipino arrivals in 2008 (5,376 out of 23,724); Filipino men, however, do not have any similarly constructed class marker in Canada. It is the racialized Filipino female subject that embodies class stereotypes, and although the concept of class has evolved to incorporate complex relationships and processes of individuals and collectivities, the notion of what class a Filipino woman belongs to in Canada remains particularly etched in the social imaginary.

Ethnolinguistic Origin

The Philippines is a multi-ethnic state with nearly one hundred ethnolinguistic groups, eight of which are spoken by about 90 percent of the
population: Tagalog, Cebuano, Ilocano, Hiligaynon, Bicolano, Waray-Waray,
Pampangan, and Pangasinan (Dolan 1991). The country is divided into administrative regions and provinces reflecting the ethnolinguistic character
of the people (Abinales and Amoroso 2005, 13-14). Much of the existing
regionalism is rooted in the Spanish colonial practice of divide and conquer,
whereby a group from one area was used to suppress revolt in another area
(Espiritu 2005, 334). Today, as in the past, one's primary identity is derived
from one's birthplace, and the question most commonly asked by Filipinos
meeting for the first time is, "*Taga saan ka* [where do you come from]?"
(Lopez 2006, 47). Regionalism is reinforced by the boundaries of geographic
territory as well as by distinct language and culture. Perceived traits of Filipinos from particular regions translate into stereotypes: for example, Bicolano
= *mainitin ang ulo* (hotheaded), Ilocano = *kuripot* (stingy), Ilongo = *malambing*
(sweet), and Waray = *matapang* (brave) (Woods 2006).

Does ethnolinguistic or regional identity remain pronounced among
Filipino women on migration to Canada? How is such regional identification
observed in the community? The following narratives provide some
insights:

*Regionalism is very strong among the Filipino women. Many are members of
the various regional Filipino associations. Since we have different dialects
they prefer to be with persons who speak the same dialect.*
– Carmen, a community worker in Calgary

*Filipinos tend to be regionalistic. Ilocano tend to mingle with Ilocano and it's
the same with others.*
– Traning, a TFW in Lethbridge

During Mass sila ay nag-iipon ipon [they come together during Mass].
Regular din silang magkasama [they regularly go together] *as they came
from the same region.*
– Norma, a housewife in Saskatoon

Bisaya marami dito. Malaki silang community [There are many Visayans
here. They are a big community] ... *It's more on regionalism than class.*
Malakas ang Bisayang Dako – Bisdak [Bisayang Dako – Bisdak is strong].
– Samantha, a government employee in Regina

*Kanya-kanya. Padamihan ng angkan. Ilocano mas marami mas dominant
dito ... Pero mayroon pa din tayong kaisipan na ang Ilocano kuripot, mga*

stereotype images. [To each his own. They tend to increase their kin group. Ilocanos are many and dominant here ... But we still have our own ideas that the Ilocano is stingy, the stereotype images.]
    – Salvacion, a home care worker in Winnipeg

In Canada, Filipino women identify with their respective regional origins, as evidenced by their spoken dialects and preferred groups for religious and social activities. They participate in shared events with others from the same province, such as attending Mass or a Christmas party, and tend to enjoy closer affinity with those who share their dialect. Indeed, ethnolinguistic origin forms an integral part of their identity in diaspora. Hosanna, a nurse in Edmonton, justifies such a bond: "Regional groups are social clubs that is part of human nature and Filipino women form them because they feel comfortable." The strangeness of the new country seems to bring together people with something as fundamental as language. According to Vergara (2009, 39), a Filipino "naturally searches for the company of one's own." Communication in the same tongue permits better understanding and empathy regarding migration experiences.

Doon ko napansin sama-sama ang mga Pilipina sa regional groups sa community [I realized that the Filipinas join together in regional groups in the community]. *I don't see anything wrong about that. Language is a barrier. They are comfortable in Tagalog or their dialect.*
    – Petracia, a TFW in Saskatoon

May strong regional affiliation ang mga Pilipino dito [the Filipinos here have strong regional affiliation]. *They speak or communicate with in their own dialect. They speak English but with an accent. They feel comfortable with their own regional group.*
    – Rosal, a nurse TFW in Winnipeg

In essence, whether we like it or not, we go to where we fit. We have our own culture. It's positive ... to belong right away.
    – Marilou, a community worker in Calgary

People form their own regional groups. It's a community expression, about language and culture, whatever is unique to that region.
    – Gabriela, a retired government employee in Winnipeg

Regionalism is one of the multiple layers of Filipino identity. For example, one may be both an Ilocano and a Filipino. The interplay of these two identities, the regional and the national, is complicated and largely context-dependent. One's regional identity is primary with fellow Filipinos, while a national "Filipino" identity is assumed in interactions with non-Filipinos. Regionalism in diasporic space seems to impact the lives of Filipino women on various levels – personal, intra-group, community, and social. Aside from ease of communicating in one's own dialect, a regional identity promotes belonging in a group that reflects a collective membership in the Philippines. The tendency to identify with a group is consistent with the "collectivist nature of Filipino culture" (Tolentino 2004, 66). However, regional and national identities are not necessarily mutually exclusive for Filipinos; instead, the regional is part of one's frame of reference, like saying, "*Bisaya siya* [she's Visayan]," in a multi-regional or a multicultural group. Intra-group relations based on shared ethnolinguistic identity are not fixed but rather are flexible enough to accommodate inclusion in a larger Filipino collectivity. The following narratives show the dynamic social exchange among Filipino women in various activities in Winnipeg:

> *I am friends with anybody coming from different regions. I do not see any difference with us. We have the same blood ... Language, maybe. I am Ilocano, but some people even ask me to join their Bicol group because they are my friends ... We are still Filipinos.*
> – Bella, a retired nurse in Winnipeg

> *Every Friday, Saturday, and Sunday ... the party never ends. One association organizes one party. Manitoba is a friendly and party place! Everybody knows everybody in a small town ... It does not matter who you are if they invite you.*
> – Clemencia, a nurse in Winnipeg

> *Always gathering, fundraising for church in the Philippines ... in Canada they have more freedom to do it. They have money to spend. Kaya malimit din ang party ... Nakakalito. Minsan madami na ang pupuntahan. Magastos din.* [That's why there are often parties ... Confusing. Sometimes you go to many affairs. It's also costly.]
> – Ligaya, a retired factory worker in Winnipeg

Parties organized by Filipino women and their families are common in Canada. Special occasions are reasons to celebrate not only with family members but also with others in the community. The inclusion of other Filipinos in these social events even replicates the same communal arrangements to which its participants are accustomed, and news of the gatherings is often relayed back to hometowns in the Philippines. Each occasion is an opportunity to showcase regional foods. The "sharing of food, both in times of need and at ceremonial occasions, is very important to Filipinos" (Smith et al. 1999, 88). Particularly for Filipinos in diaspora, food symbolizes the richness of coming together among friends. In the Prairies, sumptuous

Filipino gatherings are quite distinct from the simplicity of "Canadian" treats.

Regionalism is viewed both positively and negatively by Filipino women. On the positive side, strategic alliances along the lines of "unity in diversity" (Ignacio 2005, 134) are a means of collectively meeting the challenges of immigrating to Canada. The following narratives indicate that despite their strong regional loyalties, Filipinos in Winnipeg and Edmonton, for example, are willing and able to support each other:

> *We categorize ourselves from where we came from. We identify which province we came from ... Now in Canada, we support each other ... It is easier in Canada because there are diverse people here.*
> – Rosie, a sales agent in Winnipeg

> *Malakas ang samahan ng* [there is strong camaraderie among those from] *Quezon, Bisaman, each with own strengths although they try to mingle.*
> – Gabriela, a retired government employee in Winnipeg

> *We have a big problem in Edmonton but still are one. Filipinos become united at times. But there is still the stereotype image of Filipinos. Kapampangan ay mayabang, bato* [Kapampangan are boastful, stiff], *etc. Despite regional differences Filipinos are one ... Bayanihan* [mutual assistance or cooperation][1] *spirit is very strong.*
> – Julita, a community worker in Edmonton

> *When it comes to social issues Filipinos are not anymore based on regionalism ... Everyone helps.*
> – Hosanna, a nurse in Edmonton

> *Regionalism is not a negative. It's like a barangay* [smallest political unit] *group. It does not qualify as ghettoing, saying we are different from the rest. Part of my own region [group] is to strengthen what we have back home. We talk Ilokano, but ... we deal with other regions. We are trying to cling to our own regional culture. We have independent celebrations. But all groups come to support ... we all come together.*
> – Marilena, a community worker in Edmonton

Some of the issues and concerns with pulling Filipinos together despite their ethnolinguistic diversity include, but are not limited to, financial assistance to TFWs, bereavement support, and collaboration in fighting discrimination. Shared information about a distressed live-in caregiver in one community, for instance, may bring offers of assistance from those in another. As discussed earlier, employment referrals from *kababayan* (those coming from the same place) are prized by newcomers. At the same time, regionalism among Filipino women in Canada has its drawbacks. As much as it may bring people together, regionalism can just as easily lead to disunity (Espiritu 2005). Identifying exclusively with one's ethnolinguistic cohort limits the potential of being engaged with those outside the group. Also, the positioning of one's regional identity in the Filipino hierarchy of regions may play out anew in Canada. Bisaya-speaking Filipinos, for instance, are often mocked by Tagalog-speakers for their *matigas na punto* (strong accents).

> *Regionalism does not affect Canadians but affect Filipinos ... This is not healthy. I do not like regionalism. I do not want to be known by my regional group. I want to be known as a Filipino!*
> – Carolina, a retired teacher in Winnipeg

> *Culture is tough. In regionalism people tend to clutter, stick to the same region ... Filipino culture is tough on ourselves; we have accent on our regions. It's part of being Filipino. The Bisaya accent of English ... we tend to laugh at it. So we become conscious with our accent in talking to the mainstream society.*
> – Rowena, a manager in a media company in Winnipeg

> *All organizations of provinces are represented in Manitoba. There are also splinter groups, and this is not good. Instead of helping each other, they are divided.*
> – Casandra, a nurse in Winnipeg_

Carolina voices the preference of many Filipino women to be identified in Canada as being from the Philippines rather than from a certain province. Although a regional identification may be useful for facilitating the integration of newcomers into the Filipino community here, it can also limit integration in the Canadian social landscape because "Filipinos" is considered a generic term for all those coming from the Philippines. Carolina and Casandra desire cohesiveness among Filipinos in Canada and aim for the triumph of nationalism over regionalism – of being Filipino first.

Religion
Filipinos are a deeply religious people (Dancel 2005, 121). Religion plays an important role in their socio-political lives, whether the precolonial beliefs in *Bathala* (Supreme Being) or the present-day embrace of Catholicism by lowland people, or the practice of Islam in the southern part of the archipelago (Rebullida 2006). As a consequence of Spanish colonization, over 83 percent of Filipinos profess Catholicism (Harris, Moran, and Moran 2004,

401). Coupled with the Protestant missions under American patronage, the Philippines is the only country in Asia with a Christian majority (White and Walker 2008). Contemporary Filipino religiosity is a complex mix of pagan practices, Western Catholicism/Protestantism, fundamentalism, and populist charismatic movements such as El Shaddai (Gorospe-Jamon and Mirandilla 2007). The Church of Jesus Christ of Latter-day Saints (the Mormons) is increasingly making inroads in towns and rural communities with their missionaries who speak the local dialect (Yorgason 2003). The Mormons, mainly apolitical and neatly dressed in suit and tie even in scorching heat, appear to have widespread appeal in areas where Catholic priests are absent. Iglesia ni Kristo (Church of Christ) and El Shaddai, on the other hand, are courted by politicians for their perceived practice of bloc voting during elections. One simply cannot examine the socio-political landscape in the Philippines without considering the important dimension of religion.

Religion defines the ways and mores of Filipinos. Baptism of newborns is a closely observed tradition and serves as a celebratory occasion that enhances the *kumpadre* (godfather) or *kumadre* (godmother) system of kinship network. Among Catholics, death is observed with a solemn Mass and prayers for the first nine days and the first forty days, and annual remembrances thereafter. Attending Sunday Mass is a ritual among Filipino Catholics, and many women participate as lay ministers, altar servers, and choir members. While a separation between church and state is legislated in the Philippine Constitution (Moreno 2006), religion is ingrained in the school system as well as in public affairs. The clergy and nuns certainly contributed significantly to the redemocratization of the Philippines even before the fall of the Marcos dictatorship (Claussen 2001), and to this day, politicians regularly appear side by side with members of the clergy in local festivities.

Religiosity is inherently gendered. Filipino women are practising adherents of their faith in the informal avenues of Catholic worship, but men control the formal priestly (and therefore the religious ruling) class. Still, as Mananzan (1987b, 34) notes, religion was the only mode of public access available to women and they developed "a religious fervor which would verge on fanaticism." Filipino women today are the primary agents of transmitting religion to the next generation. Their passion for venerating special saints, replete with a local organization to ensure the regimen of prayers, is passed on to their daughters and sometimes their sons as future *hermanas/ hermanos mayores* (big sisters/brothers). Public displays of devotion led by women culminate in colourful processions and typify the religious dynamism of local parishes and communities.

Religion and migration are closely linked with the Filipino global diaspora. Sharing their faith and their beliefs draws many Filipinos together and opens a Bourdieuan "sense of place" (Hillier and Rooksby 2005). Comprising the largest group of migrant workers in the world today, Filipinos promote and practise Christian evangelization and are identified by the Lausanne Committee for World Evangelization as "God's secret weapon" (cited in Bonifacio and Angeles 2010a, 265). Through their actions of faith and collectivism, Filipino (im)migrants recreate religious practices wherever they may be – from a small gathering in a house, to rented spaces in buildings, to participation in church services.

Migration is a radical uprooting of the familiar. What remains most familiar for Christian Filipino women in the West is religious identity, as the following narratives demonstrate.

> *Most Filipinos are Catholics ... I am a Baptist. I worship in the same church*
> *– Holy Spirit. Every third Sunday we're at St. Paul because of the Filipino Mass.*
> – Analisa, a community worker in Saskatoon

> *During the Holy Week ... a lot of Filipino women would participate in the*
> *procession. In the Catholic churches, there are a lot of Filipino women*
> *attending the Eucharist celebration ... I still think most of us are Catholics.*
> – Carmen, a community worker in Calgary

> *Mapapansin mo every Sunday mga babae spend time to go to church. Hindi*
> *mawawala ang religious orientation.* [You will notice that every Sunday
> the women spend time going to church. Religious orientation will not
> disappear.]
> – Petracia, a TFW in Saskatoon

> *Catholic religion pa din ang mga Pilipino dito ... Palasimba ako.* [It's still
> the Catholic religion for Filipinos here ... I often go to church.]
> – Lumen, a finance officer in Winnipeg

Religion and faith-based beliefs are often believed to facilitate the post-migration adjustment process. For Christian Filipino women, the anxiety of migration to Canada is often mitigated by the continuity of their religious social environment and their perception of democratic values and policy of multiculturalism. Sharing the same religious ethos as the host country creates spaces of inclusion and familiarity that give Filipino newcomers a ready sense of belonging (Bonifacio and Angeles 2010a). In Canada, about 81 percent of Filipinos were Catholics and 15 percent were Protestants or belonged to another Christian denomination as of 2001 (Lindsay 2007, 11). According to Fay (2005, 31), Filipinos "fit easily into Catholic parishes across Canada." These parishes represent one of the first venues of contact with other Filipinos in the community and often become welcoming places for volunteer work. In the following narratives, Gabriela, Bella, Dulce, Samantha, and Pilar describe the dynamism of Filipino religiosity in various parishes in Calgary, Regina, and Winnipeg.

> *Religion somehow facilitates integration. Maraming religious groups dito* [there are many religious groups here] ... *Filipino women are so active in the service of the Lord.*
> – Gabriela, a retired government employee in Winnipeg

> *Many Filipino women are involved in churches here as readers, choir, ministries. Every church has a Filipino choir because they like to sing. I like that. Besides being a nurse I like to sing.*
> – Bella, a retired nurse in Winnipeg

> *Many women volunteer in choir and collection during Mass. This is a good exposure for them to be involved.*
> – Dulce, a retired teacher in Calgary

> *Mas religious ako dito* [I am more religious here]. *The church is near to us. I signed up immediately in the church when I arrived. I did not do this in the Philippines. Nakita ko ang sense of belonging dito. Walang hinihintay na bayad.* [I saw the sense of belonging here. No one waiting for payment.] *I got encouraged to be like them ... We were two Filipino women who organized the multicultural choir ... this is our way of giving back to the Lord for our migration to Canada.*
> – Samantha, a government employee in Regina

> *I feel the difference in the 1970s. There are now more vibrant churches with lots of Filipinos being part of ministries. They keep the churches alive! I am part of the inter-faith group of fifteen denominations ... which exclude Iglesia ni Kristo. These are small denominations and are very close and very active. Really, this is part of the migration experience and helps in our adjustment.*
> – Pilar, a community worker in Winnipeg

Filipino women actively express their religious identities as choir members and lay volunteers in various church-related activities. Some, like Samantha, may have practised their faith only nominally in the Philippines but became more religious after migration. One possible explanation for this enhanced religious engagement may be the greater opportunity for involvement in Canada compared with the Philippines, where the sheer number of people going to church results in a surfeit of potential volunteers.

Women actively participate in Filipino religious groups in Canada, which have formed in a similar manner to those in the Philippines. They are often attached to a local parish, making the church the hub of their activities. One example is the Filipino Catholic group in Saskatoon, which organizes Filipino Masses, prayers, and novenas throughout the year. Another is Couples for Christ (CFC), a religious association that originated in the Philippines in 1991 and now has chapters around the world (Bonifacio and Angeles 2010a), with active members from different churches in the Prairies.

Religion is very strong among Filipinos ... Even though I am not involved in religious organizations it makes the Filipino community vibrant ... Big, nice choir ... Filipinos spearhead the Santa Cruzan, too. They are able to educate Calgary of the Filipino culture like Flores de Mayo and Santa Cruzan.
   – Marilou, a community worker in Calgary

The Filipino Catholic group was formed by six people about twenty-five years ago. The core group is in charge with organizing the Filipino Mass, deal with Saskatoon diocese ... Sto. Niño fiesta on the third Sunday of January is celebrated by the Bishop. May kainan [food is served] and they bring a small Sto. Niño to be blessed. There is a Christian Alliance and Filipino Community Church ... smaller groups, but they do a lot of things together. Their pastor came from the Philippines ... I like to attend the Filipino Mass ... feel na feel mo ang kanta kasi Tagalog [you really feel the songs because they're in Tagalog].
   – Filomena, a government employee in Saskatoon

Christian-oriented Filipino churches have carved a niche among immigrant Filipinos. The Christian Alliance and the Filipino Community Church in Saskatoon, established in 1987, are two examples. Filipino pastors in Saskatoon like Julius Tiangson and Danilo Fabella helped cultivate the Filipino Community Church, which has hundreds of worshippers today (The Alliance in Saskatoon 2003), many of them women. The Filipino Alliance Church also has its own groups in Calgary, Edmonton, and Winnipeg. Many Filipino women devote significant amounts of time and money to these churches.

Many pastors welcome newcomers to give invocation ... Filipino women are active usually in catechism, Bible studies. Mayroon [there is a] council outside of the Catholic church, council of pastors and I know one female pastor. The International Worship Centre is headed by Filipino pastor and uses the PCCM every Sunday. They started by a few hundred and they are now over five hundred and is moving to a bigger place, building a church now ... Pastors here are grateful many newcomers are being involved.
   – Gasela, a sales clerk in Winnipeg

More recently, the Jesus Is Lord (JIL) Church was launched on 4 April 2010 in Winnipeg. It originated in the Philippines, and its founder, Eddie Villanueva, also known as Brother Eddie, ran for president in the 2010 national elections under the *Bangon Pilipinas* (Rise up Philippines) political party. JIL churches incorporate healing in their services, and this type of ministry is popular among Filipinos (Catholic News Agency 2008). Victoria in Saskatoon observes:

> *Lots of Filipino women here are religious. Gaya ng* [like] *JIL is barely new and it started in the Philippines, it's not Catholic.*
> – Victoria, a private employee in Saskatoon .

Being religious does not always mean importing one's own practice from the Philippines wholesale. As the following narratives attest, many Catholic Filipino women converted to another denomination when they became disillusioned with Catholicism, grew annoyed with the absence of services similar to those found in the Philippines, or began seeking a more personal meaning for religion in their lives in Canada.

> *I am a former Catholic in the Philippines but now a Protestant in Canada ... Our pastor has a better way of preaching compared to the priest ... I compared the way of preaching in our church with the Catholic. The examples are from true experiences and not bookish. Our pastor crack jokes and we are not sleepy! Lively songs and music. It's so solemn in the Catholic church.*
> – Salvacion, a home care worker in Winnipeg

> *Catholic sila sa Pilipinas. Pagdating dito sa Canada many are converted to different churches kasi mahirap daw makipag-appointment sa priest.* [They are Catholics in the Philippines. Many are converted to different churches when they arrived in Canada because they say it's difficult to set an appointment with the priest.] *In other sects it is easier to see the pastor ... More women are converts to other Protestant churches.*
> – Dulce, a retired teacher in Calgary

> *In the Philippines we are so close to the church, prayerful and stuff. In Regina, there is hardly any activity in the church because of the weather. I miss the Philippines because there are lots of Masses to go to. In Regina, there is only one mass a day, not even, while in the Philippines it's all day! ... I don't think that people get more religious here. It's the lack of services here.*
> – Helena, a nurse in Regina

> *We are more independent here. We can choose our religion.*
> – Rosie, a sales agent in Winnipeg

The relationship between the individual and the Catholic Church changes on migration; indeed, Catholic Filipino women often adopt new religious affiliations in Canada. Often, priests tend to be non-Filipinos and are quite busy covering many communities because of the country's "priest shortage" (Schenk n.d.). Thus, Filipino priests are being recruited to Catholic dioceses in Canada (Fay 2005; Gonzalez 2006), and, as of 2008, there were five Filipino priests in Vancouver, twelve in Calgary, and twenty-seven in Toronto, serving both Filipino and non-Filipino parishioners (McGowan 2008, 76). As it turns out, Catholic retention among Filipinos is higher in communities with a Filipino priest. In the Philippines, priests are central figures in the community; people go to them for spiritual advice, counselling, and other forms of pastoral care, and they are in demand twenty-four hours a day, seven days a week. In contrast, priests in Canada are considered by many *Pinays* in the Prairies as "holding a job," with specified times of services.

A salient impact of the Canadian climate is the seasonal reduction in church activity among members, including Filipino women. Many struggle to bear the freezing cold during winter, and neither driving nor walking to church is a desirable option. Instead, prayer gatherings are held at home with family and friends, often in conjunction with another religious observance, such as a novena to a favourite saint in festive mode. Nevertheless, quite a number of Filipino women attend Sunday services without fail. Lita, a public health worker in Lethbridge, never misses a weekend Mass: "*Isang oras lang ang para sa kanya. Maski malamig sige pa rin ako.* [Only one hour for Him. Even if it's cold, I still go]."

Rosie, a sales agent in Winnipeg, suggested that migration results in independence and choice in religion. A number of Filipino women with whom I have spoken disclosed that some of their family members are no longer Catholics and now embrace another Christian fellowship. This has resulted in conflicts over religious services for family occasions such as death anniversaries. Some Filipino caregivers and TFWs in rural southern Alberta have ventured into non-Catholic churches simply because these are available. They view the cross as a "welcoming symbol" to practise their faith but are not necessarily converted (Bonifacio 2008, 39), a practical choice that points to a determination to sustain religiosity against all odds.

Sexuality
Sexuality is a social construction (Caplan 1987; Seidman 2009) that categorizes men and women based on certain "expressions of desire" (Mwale 2008, 88). Confining sexuality to sexual behaviour is limiting, however, because sexuality encompasses "not only the physical but the mental and spiritual as well" (DeLamater and Hyde 2004, 8). Human sexuality is a central aspect of identity (Johansson 2007), and our understanding of its processes is unsurprisingly complex. A number of cultural factors, such as socialization and religion,

affect the meanings attached to sexual identities, which, like masculinity and femininity, "vary widely along race, ethnicity, class" (Allen 1996, 268).

This section presents the perspectives of Filipino women on the effect that the sexual identity of *tomboy* has on their integration in the Prairie provinces, and on how the acceptance of non-heteronormative identity differs between the Philippines and Canada. The cultural meanings of *tomboy* (lesbian) or *bakla* (gay) in the Philippines may have very different inflections in the context of migration. The narratives of *Pinays* in the Prairies add another dimension to the scarce scholarly literature on sexuality and migration in general (Mai and King 2009; Kosnick 2011) and Asian migration in particular (Constable 2000; Manalansan 2003, 2006; Huang and Yeoh 2008; Walsh, Shen, and Willis 2008).

There are four commonly accepted gender types in the Philippines: *lalake* (boy/man), *babae* (girl/woman), *bakla*, and *tomboy* (Villareal, Tope, and Jurilla 2002). These categories are not fixed, however, and the *binabae* (effeminate) and *silahis* (bisexual) exist as additional types. Many cross-dressers, transvestites, and transsexuals participate in annual beauty pageants, such as the Ms. Amazing Philippine Beauties in Manila (Vasquez 2007), and the Philippines, like some of its neighbours in Southeast Asia, has a "long tradition of highly valued male transvestite and transgendered roles" in animist spirit and healing practices (Nanda 2000, 78-79). There are more than twenty derivative (some derogatory) labels for *tomboys* (Weegender 2009). Both *tomboy* and *bakla* have "high public visibility" in certain stereotypical occupational niches: security guards and bus conductors for the former, and beauticians and entertainers for the latter (Tan 2001, 122; Laurent 2005). Although *tomboys* are less visible than *bakla* in the mainstream media, they are by and large accepted in Philippine society. Arlene Babst writes about the *tomboy:*

> There is a relieving thought that tomboys are easier to handle than boys, less socially shattering than male homosexuals, less expensive than a pregnant daughter, and easier to live with than whores. The lesbian is saved by default, by the Filipinos' tendency to think of the worst and then thank God, bad as things are, the worst has not yet befallen them. (cited in Fleras 1997, 830)

Children play jump rope to the rhythm of "girl, boy, *tomboy, bakla*" for the four gender types in the Philippines, which somehow consciously constructs gender diversity, unlike in Western societies. Acceptance of *tomboys* and *bakla* in the Philippines is, according to Tan (2001, 123), "conditional as long as the bakla remain confined to certain occupational niches and fulfill certain stereotypes of the man with a woman's heart, of the village entertainer, of the outlet of male sexual desire." Conceptions of homosexuality differ, however: the Filipino *bakla*, in contrast to the Western gay, prefers "real men" as partners (Cannell 1999, 215). The same can be said of the Filipino *tomboy*. Both are intimately attracted to their opposites: that is, the *macho* (masculine) for the *bading* (gay) and the *seksi* (sexy) for the T-Bird. However, open expressions of sexuality between the members of the same sex are still frowned on by Christians and Muslims, similar to the heteronormative ideal "dominant paradigm in Western society" found in Canada (Ingraham 2006, 307). Being "queer" is both a signifier and a social category "produced through the intersectionality of identities, practices and institutions" (Manalansan 2006, 225). Same-sex relationships are officially not recognized in Catholic Philippines, but popular representations of openly gay celebrities make them a part, albeit still marginal, of society.

More celebrities are coming out in the open and are accepted. They are vocal about it and are paid well for their talents they bring.
– Lisa, an employee in Winnipeg

They are already out of the closet in the Philippines.
– Clemencia, a nurse in Winnipeg

What happens when a *tomboy* migrates to Canada? Does sexuality affect integration into the community? Filipino women's replies to these questions reveal three positions regarding the acceptance of sexual identities in Canada and the Philippines. The first position suggests that Philippine society may in fact be more accepting of *tomboys* than Canadian society.

They are more free in the Philippines. People in the Philippines are not so judgemental compared to Canada. People here are not much open about sexuality.
– Helena, a nurse in Regina

May hindrance din. In Saskatoon hindi pa masyado like ... or San Francisco. [There is hindrance also. In Saskatoon it's not so very much like ... or San Francisco.] *In the Philippines, bakla or tomboy is accepted ... not sure if they are ridiculed. But I have not seen anyone expressed as hard core tomboy.*
– Filomena, a government employee in Saskatoon

I guess it doesn't matter what class, colour or gender you belong or are, Albertans are very conservative "country" folks.
– Kathy, a community worker in Red Deer

Unlike in the Philippines where *tomboys* have large kinship networks, lesbians in Canada tend to have smaller families and less access to this type of support. For a long time, studies of lesbians and the family in Canada focused on "sociology of deviance" or "social problems" (Mitchell 2009, 164), which suggested their negative positioning compared with hetero-sexuals. The Prairie provinces, in comparison with Ontario and Quebec, have lower acceptance rates for homosexuals. For example, 69 percent of Quebecers consider homosexuality as personally acceptable, compared with 40 percent in Saskatchewan (Korinek 2010, 282).[2] Alberta has shown the weakest support for gay rights among the Prairie provinces, while the strong-est support can be found in Quebec, British Columbia, and the Maritimes (Gudgeon 2003, 190).[3] Attacks in the streets and bullying in Alberta and British Columbia, for example, have sent a public message of gay bashing and homophobia (Janoff 2005; Nolais 2011). In her study of sexual exploita-tion of young men in four western provinces (British Columbia, Alberta, Manitoba, and Saskatchewan) in the mid-2000s, McIntyre (2009, 29) notes that the highest rate of gay bashing occurred in British Columbia at 55 per-cent, compared with 33 percent in Saskatchewan.

Filipina *tomboys*, like other racialized women, have to navigate the chal-lenging path within the white, middle-class lesbian world in Canada, described by what Audre Lorde calls the "institutionalized rejection of difference" (cited in Dhruvarajan and Vickers 2002, 57). Lesbians of colour face the "struggle for acceptance and positive self-definition" (Silvera 1996, 175) not only within their own communities but also with the larger society. As racialized immigrants, Filipina *tomboys* confront multiple social hierarchies of ethnicity, class, and sexuality between the host and home cultures. The *tomboy* constructs an alternative representation of a "Filipino woman" – neither meek, docile, nor sweet – in the global imaginary of the "other."

However, the second position avers that Canada is actually more accepting of diverse sexualities than the Philippines. Canada is considered "post-modern" by many, not only for its multiculturalism but also for its liberal stance on homosexuality. Groups like Citizens for Public Justice have peti-tioned Parliament for legal equality of gays and lesbians (Lyon 2000, 17), and in 2005 Canada became the third country, after the Netherlands and Belgium, to officially recognize same-sex marriage (Smith 2008).

In some ways there is discrimination in the Philippines and it's not pro-nounced here in Canada, not so blatant. You are accepted for what you are in Canada.
    – Sharon, a former garment worker in Saskatoon

Canada is a free country.
    – Candy, a cleaner in Calgary

They are very free to express in Canada now that we have same-sex marriage. In the Philippines, tago pa yan [it's still hidden] ... Some Filipinos will accept homosexuals and some will not. They are not normally accepted by everybody.
    – Raymunda, a caregiver in Lethbridge

Marami na ang lumalabas, kasi hidden parati iyan [there are many now who came out because it's always hidden] *... although we are encouraged to get out of the closet because the Canadian government supports that. Canada is better off to live and to express our sexuality.*
    – Marilou, a community worker in Calgary

The walking path is wider in Canada. People have more sense of freedom.
    – Josefina, self-employed in Winnipeg

Much of the perceived acceptance of *tomboys* is based on the legal equality of homosexuals in Canada since the passage of the Civil Marriage Act in 2005.[4] The history of same-sex marriage in Canada attracted the interest of many Filipino women in the Prairies while I was conducting the interviews. The recognition of same-sex marriage in Canada contrasts with its prohibition in the Philippines, a country that many Filipinos still view as traditional and moralistic, but rapidly changing.

Mas open sa Canada. In the Philippines ... closet at tinatago pa. [It's more open in Canada. In the Philippines ... closet and still hidden.] *But the generation now is more accepting.*
    – Salvacion, a home care worker in Winnipeg

Yes, women are able to express their preferences in Canada since I see that Canadians are more broadminded compared to our counterpart in the Philippines ... I also feel that nowadays people in the Philippines are becoming more openminded with regards to this matter.
    – Minerva, a private employee in Calgary

There is less sexual harassment in this country against women.
    – Jennifer, a cleaner in Calgary

These days the community is more open to sexual orientation. We have come to terms with the third sex. I'm not very sure about this in the Philippines.
    – Luningning, a community leader in Winnipeg

Canada is very open to different sexualities. Filipino women have the courage to come out from their shell ... They are very active and not afraid to identify

as gay... because society allows it. Canadians are more accepting of sexual orientation and they feel they belong here.
– Gabriela, a retired government employee in Winnipeg

Unlike in the Philippines, Canada is not a Catholic-dominated country which sets "moral standards."
– Abby, a caregiver in Red Deer

I see some tomboys *here but not a lot. Even if gay marriage is allowed here, so far I haven't heard of any Filipino* tomboy *who is married to another lady. Yes to some extent Filipino women are able to freely express their identities and individualities here in Canada ... because they are not anymore bound by some traditional rules.*
– Carmen, a community worker in Calgary

The sexuality here is more open compared to our country. Religion is not so big deal in here ... probably because we are more busy here to work than to engage in social gathering and to entertain people's business ... and sometimes even to ourselves we don't have time, so how much more with other's business?
– Zandra, a health worker in Calgary

However, equal protection of non-normative sexualities in Canada is seemingly superficial, as the deeply rooted aversion of the Catholic Church follows some *Pinays* in the Prairies.

Lesbians are generally accepted in Canada, perhaps even more than the Filipino community. Some Filipinos are Catholic ... Catholic faith strongly condemns gays, lesbians and transgendered way of life, even in a so-called "liberal" society.
– Kathy, a community worker in Red Deer

Kathy suggests that despite the seeming acceptance of *tomboys* in Canada, Filipinos who are still largely Catholic condemn such expressions of sexuality. While Canadian society may be liberal-minded, some Filipino Catholics remain conservative when it comes to recognizing same-sex relationships. This is similar to the practice in Alberta, where same-sex marriage is legal but still socially unacceptable; the Alberta government's "historical reluctance" (CBC News 2009b) to adopt same-sex marriage seems consistent with its conservative values. By September 2008, however, 747 same-sex weddings had been recorded by provincial data in Alberta (*Edmonton Journal* 2008). In Manitoba, eleven marriage commissioners were compelled to resign as of November 2004 for their refusal to perform same-sex marriages (CTV News

2004). The Saskatchewan Court of Appeal ruled on 10 January 2011 that allowing marriage commissioners to decline same-sex marriages due to their religious beliefs was unconstitutional (Maniquet 2011). Legal precepts may have silenced conservatives in the Prairies, but social tensions remain, although local urbanites tend to be more tolerant than those in rural areas (Korinek 2010, 282).

Migration is considered a factor in "coming out" for *tomboys* in Canada. The absence of close relatives among TFWs and immigrants has enabled some *tomboys* to be who they are away from home. This follows the pattern of many homosexuals, who leave their families to achieve "some degree of anonymity" (Biery 1990, 287), and resonates with the "running away from home" model that is prevalent among LGBT (lesbian, gay, bisexual, transgender/transsexual) youth (Bozett 1989; Arnett 2009).

They can express more freely here because they are accepted here. In the Philippines madami ang closet queen/king at hindi mahayag sa family. Walang masyadong nakikilala sa kanila because they are far from home. [In the Philippines, there are many closet queens/kings and they cannot disclose to family. Nobody really knows them because they are far from home.] *Second, they can see people with different sex orientation not really discriminated as in the Philippines.*
– Petracia, a TFW in Saskatoon

Nag-migrate at lumantad na tomboy. Hindi bading sa Pilipinas pero bumigay sa Canada [They migrated and came out as *tomboys*. They were not gay in the Philippines but gave in in Canada] ... *Sa Pilipinas* [in the Philippines] *not allowed to hold hands, kiss for gays, etc. In Canada, it's okay.*
– Rosal, a nurse TFW in Winnipeg

In the Philippines, lesbian sexuality tends to be viewed as an "alternative sexual preference" of migrant workers (Roces 2012, 120), with some Filipina domestic workers freely entering into same-sex relationships (Lott 2006). For example, a Filipino caregiver in Alberta who had been married in the Philippines became openly associated with another female caregiver on migration. This poses a "sexual alternative" in the global economy called "tomboyism," which, according to Chang and Ling (2000, 40), allows Filipina domestic workers to "avoid being perceived as cheap" and "save[s] them from sexual harassment from men while offering some protection themselves to other Filipinas." A couple of Filipina *tomboys* and their Filipina partners, whose relationship began in Hong Kong a number of years before they came to Canada, pooled funds to buy their first home together in Calgary.

Finally, the third position argues that both Canada and the Philippines accept diverse sexualities and treat *tomboys* similarly. I surmise that *tomboys* are recognized as daughters first and that their sexuality is secondary in Filipino and Canadian families. In both countries, *tomboys* remain "other" to heteronormativity but are gradually emerging in their own right as citizens. On 8 April 2010, the Supreme Court of the Philippines ruled in favour of the controversial gay rights political party *Ang Ladlad* (literally, coming out), which wanted to field candidates under the party-list system for the 10 May 2010 national elections (Makosky 2010).

> *In Edmonton, they are well accepted.* Baklas *love to be a part of our group. But here I don't know if we are grouping them like that. No different from* baklas *back home or tomboy. I see them very active, not ostracized in the community. It's normal to us because back home we don't really talk about their sexuality ... but in the community they are well accepted.*
> – Marilena, a community worker in Edmonton

> *Sexual orientation, like religious orientation, is tolerated and accepted in the Philippines. I have observed it is not much different in Canada.*
> – Benilda, a retired employee in Lethbridge

> *I've never seen such openness here ...* Bakla, *gay, lesbian are well appreciated, well recognized in the Philippines as they are here ... lots of freedom for them. They feel welcome in the Filipino community.*
> – Hosanna, a nurse in Edmonton

In Canada, the occupational representation of *bakla* as beautician is similar to that in the Philippines:

> *Beauticians make more money here. In the Philippines ... become manicurist, but not in Canada. They own business in their lines of expertise, they are rich and accepted by the Filipino community. But we like* bakla *better than* tomboys. *I don't know why. But I believe that we let them be happier out of the closet.*
> – Carmelia, a private employee in Winnipeg

> *There is an open gay relationship here. Some Filipino gays open beauty parlors like in the Philippines.*
> – Asuncion, a nurse in Winnipeg

The situation is different for *tomboys*, however, as the feminized job of caregiving or domestic work in Canada contrasts with their stereotypical masculinized jobs as security guards or bus conductors in the Philippines. Their integration in the Filipino community is viewed ambivalently:

Yes they do get involved. We all have worked with lesbian, tomboy, *and they are very active. There's no difference of sexuality at all to be involved in the community.*
– Victoria, a private employee in Saskatoon

I don't really know who is a self-identified tomboy *here.*
– Analisa, a community worker in Saskatoon

I do not see them [tomboys] *as active in the community.*
– Siony, a private employee in Regina

I never look at sexuality as important identities. I separate the person from the deed.
– Bella, a retired nurse in Winnipeg

These narratives appear to underscore the ambivalent acceptance of homosexuality in the Filipino community and in the Prairie communities. Victoria attests to their presence while Analisa is not aware of them; neither has much contact with them in the community. As with many other immigrants, Filipinos tend to circulate in certain social circles, and their activities may be confined to members of those groups. Of course, there are also those like Bella in Winnipeg who interacts with anyone regardless of his or her sexual identity and places primacy on personhood. However, wherever Filipino *tomboys* interact with other Filipinos, homosociality seems accepted, and in the course of my fieldwork I have not encountered any reports of sinister acts against them. Lesbians comprise a quarter of the Filipino domestic workers in Hong Kong (Constable 2000, 238), and their significant presence mirrors a similar open homosociality among caregivers in Canada.

Indeed, sexuality contributes to the construction of meanings in diaspora and remains fluid in time and cultural context. Varying perceptions of acceptability of homosociality between home and host cultures suggest the strong influence of religion among *Pinay* Catholics in the Prairies; their views are somehow affirmed by prevailing social conservatism in these provinces compared with the more progressive outlook of urbanites in Ontario or Quebec. Identities based on sexual orientation are manifested in the integration of *Pinays* in the Prairies and, according to Kosnick (2011, 122), "struggles around sexualities contribute to place-making practices and mobilities at different scales and across different localities." There are positive indications of acceptance of Filipino sexuality away from home, of equal respect and dignity as human beings now made concrete by legislation in Canada.

Filipino Womanhood

Culture defines the roles and expectations of women in society (Sanford 2006). Gender roles may shift or be reinforced on migration, becoming complicated as new realities affect the performance of these roles (Ennaji and Sadiqi 2008). Even more important is the resulting negotiation of multiple identities as women and men face these new realities. Women may take on additional tasks and men may have diminished economic roles, as in cases where only the wife is able to find a job (Espiritu 1997; Cooke 2003). The "realignments of identity may both precede migration (and in a sense, therefore, 'cause' it), and they may also occur as a result of movement to a new location" (White 1995, 2). In this section, the central question is: "What does it mean to be a Filipino woman in Canada?" In particular, does the idea and practice of Filipino womanhood at home and in society differ outside of its cultural base, the Philippines? The responses of Filipino women in the Prairies reflect three perspectives: first, that the role of Filipino women is the same as though they were in the Philippines; second, that their roles are still based on tradition but are changing; and third, that Filipino women have individual capacities for agency unbounded by traditional gendered expectations.

Women in the Philippines are culturally oriented to their roles as daughters, wives, and mothers, but these do not impose rigid limits on their own aspirations. The absence of strict cultural proscriptions on their activities both inside and outside the home arguably makes Filipino women seemingly free to venture into both spaces. Pegiña (2009, 1) argues that "Filipino woman today is an image of strength" and attempts to demystify the "image of a docile woman under the influence of the tyrannical nature of the patriarchal society" in twenty-first-century Philippines. The realities of Filipino women as breadwinners, political leaders, and major entrepreneurs, among other roles, present alternatives to supplant – or at least challenge – the idea of women as homemakers, passive citizens, and simple consumers. Nevertheless, most feminist scholars writing about Philippine society argue that Filipino womanhood continues to be subject to a patriarchal script (Israel-Sobritchea 1990; Eviota 1992; Parreñas 2008b). Roces (2000, 133) writes that "Filipino femininity has altered little despite the major breakthroughs made by women throughout the entire twentieth century." The notion of a Filipina is "interchangeable with her role as wife and mother" (Roces 2000, 134); accordingly, marriage remains the ultimate goal of womanhood.

The first category of responses about Filipino womanhood in Canada suggests that migration did not alter the expected roles of women at home. A woman's identity remains connected to her culturally prescribed duties towards the family.

Walang change sa akin. Kung ano ako dapat as wife and mother, parehas lang sa Pilipinas o Canada. [There is no change for me. What I should be as a wife and mother is still the same in the Philippines and Canada.]
    – Norma, a housewife in Saskatoon

Kahit nandito na tayo sa Canada wala akong nakitang pagbabago sa ugali ng babae sa tahanan ... Kung ano ang gawi sa tahanan doon sa Pilipinas, ganoon din dito sa Canada. [Even though we are already here in Canada, I do not see any changes in women's behaviour at home ... Women's work there in the Philippines is the same as here in Canada.]
    – Ligaya, a former garment worker in Saskatoon

A Filipino woman is the same wherever she is, as in the Philippines.
    – Rosemarie, a nurse in Saskatoon

I guess everything are almost the same as in the Philippines, too, at home – doing all the woman chores like cooking, organizing stuff, cleaning, paying bills.
    – Sylvia, a health worker in Calgary

Asawa ko Pilipino. Ganoon pa din ang gawi sa bahay dito sa Canada. Ikaw ang magluluto para may baon siya. [My husband is Filipino. Practices at home are the same here in Canada.] *I have to be home when he is home. Pag nauuna siya sa bahay, maghihintay lang sa akin para ako ang magluto* [if he comes home first, he'll just wait for me to cook]. *We are still expected to do everything at home.*
    – Lumen, a finance officer in Winnipeg

Magluluto ako, maglalaba at iba pang trabaho sa bahay [I cook, do the laundry and other chores at home]. *My husband takes care of the manly work at home but helps me as well.*
    – Rowena, a manager in a media company Winnipeg

If I must add the feudal patriarchal mind set of both men and women from the Philippines are brought here.
    – Kathy, a community worker in Red Deer

What these responses intimate is that the roles of Filipino women at home remain the same even after they migrate to Canada: they are still mainly responsible for domestic tasks. Based on the 2006 census, Filipino women in Canada spent more hours than Filipino men doing unpaid housework during the week before the census was taken: 18.4 percent spent 15-29 hours, 11.4 percent spent 30-59 hours, and 6.1 percent spent 60 hours or more. The corresponding rates for men were significantly lower, almost half for longer periods of housework: 6.6 percent spent 30-59 hours, while 3.3 percent spent 60 hours or more.

Filipino women in Canada also spent longer hours than Filipino men in unpaid childcare during the week before the census was taken in 2006: 6.9 percent spent 30-59 hours and 8.3 percent spent 60 hours or more, compared with the less than 5 hours to 14 hours reported by men who cared for their children. However, a greater percentage of Filipino women (50 percent) than Filipino men (47.4 percent) spent no time at all on childcare. This suggests that a significant proportion of women were too busy with paid employment to undertake childcare at home, or they may not have had children at all in Canada. In general, the differences between men and women indicate shared time, with variations for shorter or longer periods of unpaid childcare.

While women are generally expected to undertake household chores, it is not an exclusive domain since men usually assume other domestic tasks, such as shovelling snow, mowing the lawn, and heavy lifting. Older Filipino women tend not to drive much, if at all, and depend on the men in the family to take them around. Nevertheless, the centrality of the home in the hearts and minds of Filipino women remains the same in Canada as in the Philippines.

We still have our own tradition at home. Filipino women in Canada have more responsibilities at home and in the office. We try to balance everything. In the Philippines, we have more help compared to Canada where we juggle family, children and job.
– Helena, a nurse in Regina

It is very challenging at home. My husband brings the dough, but I do the planning. He works night shift, too. I am moulded into the good mother type and has to juggle with work and family. It is exhausting and tiring.
– Rowena, a manager in a media company in Winnipeg

A Filipino woman's role starts with the family ... Woman is the heart and the man is the head in the family. How do we raise a family? Mapagkalinga ang ating ina. Pero ang modernized view ngayon ay bahala ka na sa buhay mo. [Our mothers are caring. But the modernized view now is that whatever you do with your life is up to you.]
– Dulce, a retired teacher in Calgary

As in the Philippines, the double standard that sees women as having "jobs not careers" (Parreñas 2005a, 58) is pervasive among Filipinos in Canada. The perceived success of children in school and "holding on" to husbands rests on women's ability to balance the demands of work and family life. This appears to apply to both Filipino women married to Filipino men as well as those married to men of other nationalities. In *Conversations with Feminism,* Weiss states (1998, 189): "What men do *for* women is thought of as some gift for which enough appreciation cannot be expressed. What women do *for* men is thought of as a woman's duty (for which there exists no natural limit). What men *do* to women is thought of as women's fault." Balancing work and family in Canada tends to be more stressful in the absence of the domestic servant, or *kasambahay* (household help) (Flores-Oebanda, Pacis, and Montano 2003), and the extended family network available to working mothers in the Philippines. To ensure that young children are properly cared for at home while they are at work, many Filipino women decide to sponsor their parents, particularly their mothers, to come to Canada. Parreñas (2006, 48) describes the phenomenon as an "international transfer of caretaking," wherein migrant Filipina domestic workers are sandwiched in a three-tiered hierarchy of care and commodified international division of reproductive labour: the top tier is occupied by rich or middle-class female employers, and the bottom tier by the local women who care for children left behind in the Philippines. By extension, this concept applies to the sponsorship of mothers who move to Canada to undertake a "labour of love" for their now middle-class children. Hosanna, a nurse in Edmonton, sponsored her sixty-year-old mother to come to Canada primarily to look after her young children.

The second view of Filipino womanhood in migration is that there are notable changes in attitudes, gendered roles, and expectations in Canada, and that such changes take place in three areas: as women, as wives, and as daughters. These changes are a reality for migrants in a new cultural environment who are grappling with the challenges of paid work and settlement.

We are now in Canada. We accept their standards on women. In the Philippines, women are considered second class to men. In Canada, we have a voice and the opportunity to compete and become what we want to be.
– Filomena, a government employee in Saskatoon

Very restricted ang babae sa Pilipinas. Timid tayo. [Women in the Philippines are very restricted. We are timid.] *But in Canada, we are learning to communicate how we feel. Dati kinikimkim natin ang sama ng*

loob [it used to be that we would hide our bad feelings]. *Now we are learning to do away with that.*
– Sharon, a former garment worker in Saskatoon

The liberal democratic precepts of freedom and equality in Canada impact the personal lives of Filipino women at home and at work. Filomena in Saskatoon affirms that being a Filipina in Canada means embracing the standards of women in society with the same voice, rights, and opportunities as any other woman. The new socio-political setting also affects how Filipino women relate to others, most notably by encouraging them to engage in open communication instead of keeping ill feelings to themselves.

Filipino women have reverse roles in Canada compared to the Philippines. They are domesticated and usually follow the traditional role of women ... In Canada, we have double jobs and sponsor our husbands. Filipino women are more powerful, assertive, financially independent than their husbands.
– Dalisay, a retired teacher in Winnipeg

Rich or poor, husbands are considered the "man of the house" and are expected to turn over all family income to the wife. Wives are expected to run and manage the family and the household. Here in Canada, since almost all of the Filipino women are working, equality in almost all aspects is very evident.
– Benilda, a retired employee in Lethbridge

Filipino women are expected to do everything. This has changed in Canada in my experience. Because of my work and I travel a lot my husband has to do something.
– Liberty, a private employee in Winnipeg

Changes in husband/wife relations are brought about by the demands of settlement, which result in almost all Filipino women in this study undertaking paid employment. Couples often plan work schedules around taking care of young children. Men frequently take the night shift and women the day shift. Many women learn to drive in order to transport children or go to work, which gives them significantly more day-to-day mobility. Although it is well established that Filipino wives generally hold the purse strings of the family in the Philippines (Nadal 2009), major financial decisions are still made by their husbands. Contributing to the family coffers in Canada means gaining financial independence, which enhances women's position at home and is a primary catalyst for transforming traditional husband/wife relationships from interactions of domination and subordination to more equal partnerships. However, many Filipina wives still consult their husbands on major financial decisions.

A shift in "gender power" (Duerst-Lahti and Kelly 1995) occurs when Filipino live-in caregivers and female principal applicants sponsor their husbands and children to come to Canada. Women are in a position to either make or reverse the decision to sponsor their husbands who are waiting in the Philippines. I interviewed about five Filipino women in the Prairies who excluded their husbands from their applications for migration due to infidelity, but I also encountered an interesting case of marital breakdown that occurred in the process of migration: the female applicant followed through on the sponsorship so that her husband could accompany the children to Canada; on their arrival, however, she decided to file for divorce.

Traditional expectations of their children lie at the crux of change among first-generation Filipino immigrant mothers. Filipino parents imbue their children with cultural values such as obedience, respect for authority, and deference to elders. In the Philippines, for example, young daughters are treated differently from sons to protect the former from becoming unchaste before marriage (Espiritu 2003b; Arnett 2007). How these values play out in the lives of women who migrate is constantly being negotiated.

In the Philippines, I tend to be dependent on my parents. I have a laidback lifestyle and do things lightly. But when I came to Canada I became more responsible and independent.
– Petra, a nurse in Saskatoon

My parents are very traditional and we were brought up in a very strict and disciplined household ... We show our respect by not answering back. But in Canada I am learning to be myself.
– Victoria, a private employee in Saskatoon

Natural sa Pilipina maging [it is natural for a Filipina to be] *prim and proper, soft spoken. We are easily intimidated, especially women coming from the provinces ... My parents and others always tell me that I cannot do this because I am a girl. But once exposed to Western culture, we improve. Values about equality and opportunity between men and women in Canada are good.*
– Pilar, a nurse in Saskatoon

This is Canada. At home, there is a little bit of Filipino culture and Canadian culture.
– Claribel, a hospital worker in Winnipeg

*My parents prefer that my sisters and I marry a Filipino. This expectation
gradually changes as we later on dated other men.*
– Bivia, a health worker in Regina

First-generation immigrant Filipino mothers tend to face an uphill battle
when it comes to raising their daughters in Canada with traditional Filipino
values. The different forms of expression and more liberal demonstrations
of sexuality among young girls in Canada are concerns shared by many
women. A generational gap in defining womanhood between cultures exists
between mothers and daughters (Irving 2000).

The third view of Filipino womanhood in Canada is that regardless of location, whether in the Philippines or in Canada, Filipino women exercise personal
agency in defining their lives outside the constraints of culturally gendered
expectations. Migration is but a stage in their lives, and their identities and
aspirations remain consistent throughout. Reared by liberal and progressive
parents in the Philippines, these women demonstrate that they are their
own persons and define their own roles and measures of success in Canada.

*My parents did not raise me traditionally. I have my voice. I can talk back to
them. They encouraged me to go far with no limitations or inhibitions on my
being a woman. Although my husband is Filipino, we view our marriage as a
partnership in raising our child in Canada.*
– Analisa, a community worker in Saskatoon

*I was brought up to be a strong Pilipina. Gender is not a weakness ... I force
myself to adjust even when I am lonely. Balewala sa akin kung babae o lalaki
ka. Eh, ano kung babae ako?* [It doesn't matter to me if you're a girl or a
boy. Eh, so what if I'm a woman?] ... *My father wants a boy and so I grew
up tomboyish, outgoing, madaldal* [talkative]. *Dad showed me plumbing,
plowing, everything.*
– Rosal, a nurse TFW in Winnipeg

Filipino parents who embrace a modern view of child rearing are liberal
with their sons' and daughters' choices of activities (Medina 2005). I would
maintain, however, that many of these parents tend to encourage "manly
tasks" such as plumbing or fixing cars in their daughters only in the absence
of sons; if there are sons in the household, these tasks are still relegated to
them. In terms of freedom of expression, liberal Filipino parents generally
allow their children to respond but in an appropriate and respectful manner; ultimately, self-expression does not supersede respect. The sense of
independence, autonomy, and agency of Filipinas in Canada – women who
are asserting their own "Pinay power" (de Jesus 2005) – is often rooted in
their less traditional upbringing in the Philippines.

I do not see any difference between a man and a woman. I have the same opportunities and do not see any limitations just because I am a woman or a Filipina.
  – Leticia, a housewife in Saskatoon

Filipino women are traditionally shy and unwilling to verbalize their thoughts. But I am not like that in Canada or even in the Philippines ... I am outspoken. This is how I say there are many changes in my life. I learned to adapt to any society ... I believe in women's rights.
  – Gabriela, a retired government employee in Winnipeg

They think Filipino women are weak. But if we put our profiles in one place, it's men who are weak! Masculinity is still present in Canada and the Philippines. But it does not matter to me. Filipinos and whites are the same, women and men are the same. It is now your own qualifications.
  – Clemencia, a nurse in Winnipeg

These Filipino women demonstrate a high level of confidence in their own abilities and a sophisticated understanding of women's rights in Canada. They represent a new prototype of Filipino womanhood beyond the model of victimhood and weakness. I prefer the term "womanhood" over "femininity," as the former suggests a state of being that changes by definition, whereas the latter denotes qualities of being a woman that remain culturally fixed. On both the personal and societal scales, today's *Pinays* are changing the gender dynamics in diaspora.

Am I Canadian?

Migration results in a complex fusion of ethnic, national, and political identities with fluid boundaries. A Filipino (national) may, for example, embrace a Waray (ethnic) identity and maintain dual citizenship (Filipino and Canadian). Canada's multiculturalism etches identity configurations along multiple axes of belonging. According to Luzviminda, a private employee in Calgary, "Canadian multiculturalism allows us to retain our own identity and live according to our culture as Filipinos as long as it does not interfere with the law." In a so-called privileged environment of diversity with presumed spaces for expressing ethnocultural identities, the question of identity affiliation naturally arises. Do Filipino women in Canada identify themselves as Filipinos, Filipino-Canadians, or Canadians? What does Canadian citizenship represent for Filipinos in today's transnational world? This section explores the meaning of Filipino national identity, Filipino-Canadian hyphenated or conjoined identity, and Canadian citizenship in the lives of *Pinays* in the Prairies.

Filipino identity is a conundrum rooted in the historical development of nationhood under colonial rule. As discussed in Chapter 2, the term "Filipino" was initially reserved for Spaniards born in the Philippines, and only later came to be applied to the local inhabitants, the *Indios*. Interracial marriages, the *mestizo* (mixed racial ancestry), and Chinese Filipinos add diversity to the notion of "Filipino." As a result of migration to foreign lands, a new concept of Filipino as *balikbayan* (returnee), either temporary or permanent, has emerged. The idea of a Filipino national identity is a work in progress, given intense regionalism, civil strife involving indigenous and Muslim communities, a lack of any significant role played by the state in the genuine promotion of people's welfare, and weak institutional commitment to unifying symbols of pride in the nation's history. Bankoff and Weekley (2002, 93) note that Philippine history "provides no expedient agents, no indigenous monuments, citadels or palaces, nor even a suitable naturalized creed" to use as symbols in modern nation building.

Mapping a national Filipino identity in this multi-ethnic and multiracial context is a difficult process (Abinales 2000; Ang See 2008). A national identity is an "awareness of self within a defined national context" (Sobhan 1994, 63) and it can be weak or strong. This identification is made through shared beliefs, values, and experiences; in the context of the nation, these are constituted by language and culture (Alcoff and Mendieta 2003), cultural resources mobilized to "create a representation of the nation," or "a community of which they are all members" (Poole 2003, 272), or what Anderson (1991) calls an "imagined community." The idea of being Filipino in terms of certain cultural narratives, myths of common origin, or other ethnocultural framing exists in the imagined community of the Philippines, although attachment to the country may not necessarily be strong (Gamolo 1985).

Language is the heart of our culture. We are still Filipinos in Canada. I have spent over thirty years in Manitoba and I have high expectations from Filipino newcomers to pass on culture through language.
– Dalisay, a retired teacher in Winnipeg

Mas matimbang ang pagka-Pilipino [being Filipino has more weight]. *After fifty years in the Philippines I came to Canada. It is my education which helped me adjust to the Canadian way.*
– Dulce, a retired teacher in Calgary

For Filipinos, we ... have pride in our culture. There are few of those who reject Filipino culture now that they are here in Canada. But with still a brown skin and accent, they are Filipinos!
– Marilena, a community worker in Edmonton

Interestingly, a Filipino national identity is most pronounced outside of the Philippines. Roy (2001, 709) notes that "being somewhere else" makes migrants "create a sense of a particular identity" that has not been previously "experienced or claimed as uniquely one's own" on home soil. Anderson (1998, 73) refers to this phenomenon as "long distance nationalism" with the migration of peoples and the changes in global capitalism. In this sense, Filipinos tend to embrace a more nationalist frame as Filipinos or become conscious of their national identity (Constable 2000, 223) and promote consistent values of "what it is to be Filipino" to the world.

> *I am a Filipino. I came to Canada twenty-five years ago and still considered myself as Filipino ... I am still Filipino at heart. It does not matter how long we live here in Canada or spent time in the Philippines. We have our own ways and our physical features cannot deny us.*
> – Rosie, a sales agent in Winnipeg

> *To me it still means I am a Filipino, whatever I do, that will always be my identity.*
> – Kathy, a community worker in Red Deer

> *Kasi sa akin deep inside Pilipino pa rin ako* [because for me I am still Filipino deep inside]. *I have Filipino blood and never change; Canadian yung security lang ba* [being Canadian is just for security] ... *yung feeling ko pa rin Pilipino* [my feeling is still Filipino] ... *Para yung* [it's like] *love of the country; it's who you are. I think I'm proud to be Filipino.*
> – Esther, a health worker in Cardston

> *I never really say Filipino-Canadian ... I say I am Filipino in how I look. It is about my location as I was born in the Philippines and an immigrant in Canada. But my daughter is Filipino-Canadian because she was born here.*
> – Analisa, a community worker in Saskatoon

In her book *Between the Homeland and the Diaspora*, Mendoza (2002, 57) theorizes about the politics of the Filipino and Filipino-American move to "recapture the sign 'Filipino' and wrest it from its bastardization in the colonial narratives." Using the discourse of indigenization, popularly known as *Sikolohiyang Pilipino* (Filipino psychology) based on a new Philippine historiography *(Bagong Kasaysayan)*, Mendoza writes about *pook* (location) as the "locus of determination" or the "reference point for constructing national discourse on civilization" – of the Filipino nation (ibid., 91); where a Filipino is structurally located defines his or her "Filipinoness" (92). Mendoza cites the view of Philippine-based indigenization scholars on

Filipinos in America: "Filipino Americans are no longer 'Filipino' on the basis of their differing pook or structural location. Rather, they are, more aptly, both Filipino *and* American, and their context – no matter their attempts to reclaim historical memory and their earnest desire to 'go home again' – already grounded in another pook, another location" (ibid.). Not all indigenization scholars are in agreement about this apparent boundary of Filipino identity, however. For example, Virgilio Enriquez argues that "overseas Filipinos are no less Filipino than the indigenous and tribal peoples who have opted to stay within the confines of the archipelago" (cited in Mendoza 2002, 93). His view is shared by many Filipino women in Canada.

> *Working or living in Canada does not need to change one's own culture. Because whatever we do, we are still Filipinos. We can adapt some Canadian values and cultures as long as it will not change who we are as Filipinos.*
> – Rebecca, a nurse in Saskatoon

A Filipino-Canadian identity is a transversal, multifocal, cultural-political hybrid: it speaks to both the Philippine heritage and the Canadian way of life; it addresses multiple levels of belonging – family, region, community, and nation-state – between the Philippines and Canada; and it is an ethnocultural affinity with political implications.

> *What I think by the meaning of the phrase "Filipino-Canadian" is we have our Filipino culture and with our added benefit of sharing our culture with other people. We become Filipino-Canadian when we decided to move to Canada and embraced and accepted our new life here.*
> – Babie, a private employee in Calgary

> *It is being integrated in Canadian society but still separated due to my heritage. I think my concerns are still closely linked to the Philippines.*
> – Kathy, a community worker in Red Deer

> *What I understand as a "Filipino-Canadian" is one who has been influenced by, and inherited, the Canadian women's way of life.*
> – Benilda, a retired employee in Lethbridge

> *I have a Filipino-Canadian identity. I have a non-white colour with features and accent that is Filipino. Filipinos have come to embrace Canadian culture but the Philippine connection is very much strong.*
> – Luningning, a community leader in Winnipeg

Becoming a Canadian citizen does not negate one's Filipino identity. Naturalization is perceived as a significant formal step in the settlement and integration of immigrants in adopted societies (Bueker 2006), but like the Filipino women in Australia in a related study (Bonifacio 2003), *Pinays* in the Prairies still identify as Filipinos even after obtaining Canadian citizenship.

> *Filipino-Canadian means a Filipino citizen by birth and a Canadian citizen by naturalization.*
> – Jennifer, a cleaner in Calgary

> *A Filipino who became a Canadian citizen but a real Filipino in and out, only a citizenship changes.*
> – Sylvia, a health worker in Calgary

> *I identify as Filipino-Canadian. I have been a Filipino and always will be a Filipino but I am grateful that Canada offered us a second country where colour and culture are not neglected ... I understand and know what is life in Canada.*
> – Josefina, self-employed in Winnipeg

> *More Filipinos identify as Filipino-Canadian. But I started using this identity of Filipino-Canadian as a citizen; to be proud that I am Canadian as well. At the same time to raise awareness for others that as a Filipino I am Canadian, too. Canada is part of you because we are living in Canada. We are now part of Canadian culture and we must verbalize that.*
> – Marilou, a community worker in Calgary

Embracing a Canadian identity among Filipino immigrants means respecting the rights and obligations of their new home country. These expectations of Canadian citizenship form part of their new identity as Filipino-Canadians.

> *Filipino-Canadians are Filipinos in Canada with the same rights as other Canadians.*
> – Rafaela, a nurse in Regina

> *I am Filipino first by virtue of birth and Canadian because of citizenship. I can practise being a Filipino in Canada – my traits and virtues. Multiculturalism is something that I admire in Canada. They respect who we are ... However, being Canadian is a responsibility. I chose to be Canadian and therefore must abide the law.*
> – Gabriela, a retired government employee in Winnipeg

Filipino understanding of Canadian citizenship includes subscription to such rights as voting, mobility, equality, and freedoms of expression, religion, and assembly.

> *The meaning of Canadian citizenship is that you enjoy the benefit of having to do all things as what real Canadians do without limit; except go against the law of the land.*
> – Siara, a sales clerk in Calgary

> *Canadian citizenship ... eh, di obey mo yung mga rules nila, share mo yung talent mo sa community nila; huwag kang tamad katulad ng ibang Canadian* [so you have to obey their rules, share your talent with their community; do not be lazy like other Canadians].
> – Susie, a caregiver in Calgary

In a survey conducted by Statistics Canada and the Department of Canadian Heritage in 2002, Filipinos displayed a "strong sense of belonging" both to Canada and to their ethnocultural group: 78 percent and 89 percent, respectively (Lindsay 2007, 17). These high scores, Barber (2006, 72) notes, are interesting but not surprising. Looking at the gender implications of such a positive sense of belonging in Canada, Barber describes the case of Filipino women who enter the country as live-in caregivers: "Surely women in the various stages of (im)migration, often separated from their families, sometimes hopeful for their reunification, will have differing issues and sets of experiences relative to identity and identification" (2006, 72). Indeed, citizenship is the ultimate promise of the LCP, for which the pain and misery of live-in work is endured. However, the steps for naturalization for many of these Filipino women are borne out of practicality, convenience, and survival.

Other dimensions of Filipino-Canadian identity include Canadian birthplace, dual citizenship, and transnationality. A child of Filipino parentage who is born in Canada is considered a Filipino-Canadian. So is one who retains Filipino citizenship while adopting Canadian citizenship. Dual citizenship has been permitted in Canada since 15 February 1977, and the Philippines enacted its Citizenship Retention and Reacquisition Act (Republic Act No. 9225) in 2003 to grant the same privilege (Del Rio-Laquian and Laquian 2008, 302). Being able to keep Philippine citizenship together with Canadian citizenship may be a stimulus for naturalization (Hammar 1990). Certainly, Peter Spiro argues, the "retention of former nationality will not in itself retard the process by which the new citizen deepens his [her] identification with the community of his [her] naturalized homeland" (cited in Schuck 1998a, 171). Filipino women in Canada who reacquired Philippine citizenship after 2003 are eligible to cast their votes as absentees and possess property in the Philippines without restrictions on ownership (Abinales and Amoroso 2005; Capili 2010). As a result, many of them work hard to build houses in their hometowns or secure vacation properties.

The more interesting aspect of Filipino-Canadian identity is the notion of transnationality of identity: the idea that one is a Filipino in the Philippines and Canadian in Canada.

> *I am Filipino-Canadian in Canada. But in the Philippines, I am Filipino.*
> – Dulce, a retired teacher in Calgary

However, this transnationality also shifts depending on the context of what is "Filipino." The sense of belonging in Canada is achieved in part through a rejection of perceived "bad" Filipino practices. Identifying with what is good about Canadians and what is good about Filipinos is the apparent middle road of crossing cultures.

> *I am Filipino but adapt more Canadian culture. I spent more time in Canada than in the Philippines! So, I am Filipino-Canadian. Sometimes I cannot tolerate Filipino stuff anymore like* tsismis *[gossip] ... Even our Filipino leaders in the community show this acts of backstabbing – very unprofessional and is an embarrassment to others.*
> – Clemencia, a nurse in Winnipeg

> *I already adopted the Canadian ways and rejected those Filipino ways that I don't agree.*
> – Genosa, a private employee in Winnipeg

While Canadian citizenship appears to be integrated in the notion of Filipino-Canadian identity, it has particular implications from the perspectives of *Pinays* in the Prairies. The nuances of their interpretation of Canadian citizenship today account for challenging realities such as racism, discrimination, and insecurity.

> *The only thing I feel about Canadian citizenship is we believe that Canada is the future of my children. It's like success for me when I got my citizenship. I can now compete with Canadian citizens. I am already a Canadian citizen, but I am not white but still a citizen.*
> – Leilani, a home care worker in Calgary

> *Since we decided to stay in Canada and after acquiring all the values in Canada, then that's the time you realized that, oh, I want to become a citizen,*

too ... before you become a citizen you ask what is it to be a Canadian? Who is Canadian? How to be a Canadian? That's the questions you have to know, right? ... In case something happen to you, they just can't deport you.
   – Remy, a home care worker in Edmonton

I argued in another study that citizenship is an "empowering concept in the lives of Filipino women, which contributes to their ability to negotiate for equality at work" in Australia (Bonifacio 2005, 296). Like their counterparts in Canada, Filipino women in Australia face restrictive policies regarding recognition of foreign degrees, de-skilling, underemployment, and racial discrimination. Obtaining citizenship, however, "provided women a powerful tool to negotiate these constraints" and, by extension in Canada, enables them to "construct a political space" to combat marginality (Bonifacio 2005, 318). Canadian citizenship provides salient political leverage, igniting a passion to compete and be equal in society.

For transnational Filipinos moving between borders, a Canadian passport becomes one of the "most appreciated result[s] of citizenship" (Hammar 1990, 101). According to Yuval-Davis (1997, 91), "people are not positioned equally" in their collectivities internationally and are treated differently. At the international level, a Canadian passport is perceived to be more acceptable proof of belonging to a developed state than a Philippine passport. With Canadian citizenship comes trust in the ability of the Canadian government to protect its citizens, as opposed to the weak response of developing states (Oishi 2005; Bach and Solomon 2008).

Canadian citizens are holding that Canadian passport so when you go to another country you are considered a Canadian citizen; so you have their protection as citizen of Canada.
   – Lara, a caregiver in Lethbridge

Okay maging Canadian citizen ka parang hindi ka e-treat ng different ... hindi ka palaging api [it's okay to be a Canadian citizen so that you will not be treated differently ... you will not always be mistreated]. Kahit saan ka pumunta [wherever you go] ... you can show your passport ... that you are Canadian, and it's easy to access to go to another country.
   – Libby, a home care worker in Cardston

You can travel around if you are a citizen ... more pride. Pag hindi ka [if you are not a] citizen, you feel like a secondary citizen.
   – Remy, a home care worker in Edmonton

Obtaining Canadian citizenship is not the end of the migration story, however. Flexibility is what many Filipino women most desire: to stay in

Canada as long as they choose or to go back to the Philippines in due time. Important factors to consider are the presence of family in both countries, available care for the elderly, and the possibility of living the best of both worlds.

> *Canadian citizenship depends on the person; if you enjoy it, well, good for you; if you don't enjoy, nasa sarili na rin naman yun, eh* [it's really up to you, eh] ... *Kung hindi ka satisfied, bakit ka mag-citizen pa, di ba?* [If you are not satisfied, why would you still become a citizen, isn't it?] *You can always go back.*
> – Mayra, a health worker in Edmonton

Filipino-Canadian identity appears to be "shifting" or "constantly variable and renegotiable" (Bhavnani and Phoenix 1994, 5) along multiple cross-cutting axes of reference: cultural, economic, political, and social. Identities, then, are in an endless state of flux where *Pinays* navigate and negotiate an ongoing process of becoming and being.

Pinays in the Prairies embody multiple identities with varying social significations between the Philippines and Canada. The meanings attached to age, class, ethnolinguistic origin, religion, and sexuality, including notions of Filipino womanhood and Canadian identity, demonstrate the cultural context and place-specific particularities of constructing and reframing identities in the Prairies. When we look at the intersections and fluidity of *Pinay* identities in migration – culturally bounded yet changing – we connect with a human story that may be similar to or different from others.

5
Building Bridges: Activism and Community Engagement

Immigrant and migrant women act as agents of change in negotiating personal empowerment and are engaged in their adopted communities in many ways (Pojmann 2006). In Canada, Ng (1991, 184) asserts that immigrant women have "beg[u]n to make their needs and concerns known" and are not "passive victims of a purportedly democratic system." Together with other marginalized groups, they have found ways to participate in various activities to make their lives meaningful. Tastsoglou (2006), in her study of immigrant women in the Maritime provinces, emphasizes the "claiming of an ethno-cultural 'voice'" (213) and "getting involved in organizations that fight against racism and for equality and social justice," as well as belonging to "all kinds of voluntary social service organizations" (214). In the same vein, Filipino immigrant women and migrant workers strive towards a common set of aspirations – respect for human dignity, pursuit of happiness, equal opportunity, safe neighbourhoods, well-being, and protection of rights (Choy 2003b; Gonzalez 2009). These newcomers share with other women in Canada these aspirations and the desire to pursue better lives. For example, immigrant women as mothers are no different from Canadian-born mothers in their concern for safe communities for their children. Or migrant female workers may struggle to earn a decent wage to support their families, just like their Canadian counterparts. Their aims and ambitions find different pathways and are quite complex to discern. In this chapter, I explore an often unrecognized aspect of the lives of Filipino immigrant and migrant women: volunteerism and community engagement. Based on the narratives of *Pinays* in the Prairies, I develop a construct contrasting with the "nanny" that has shaped popular and scholarly discourse of Filipino women in Canada (Pratt 1999; Stasiulis and Bakan 2005) – the "activist *Pinay*" who makes a difference in her own life and those of others.

Volunteerism is a complex field of study in the social sciences and is "defined, in part, by its motivation" of unselfish interests (Musick and Wilson 2008, 12). Volunteer work is a form of unpaid labour rendered by free choice towards others and the community (Tilly and Tilly 1994; Anheier et al. 2003). There are many dimensions of volunteer work with no defined boundaries: altruistic and unaltruistic, commodified and uncommodified, and informal and formal characteristics (Voicu and Voicu 2003, 144). The idea that "good works" are inspired by the virtues of "generosity, love, grati-tude, loyalty, courage, compassion, and a desire for justice" somehow makes volunteers distinct from other people (Musick and Wilson 2008, 17). Women are generally involved in more volunteer work than men, but men are more likely than women to occupy leadership roles (Rotolo and Wilson 2007).

Scholars have long distinguished volunteerism from social activism; the former focuses mainly on voluntary associations and non-profit organiza-tions, whereas the latter deals mostly with social movements (Musick and Wilson 2008, 18). Since volunteer groups in civil society tend to comprise the membership of social movements as well, I endeavour to combine the two concepts of volunteerism and activism in the lives of *Pinays* in the Prairies. The prevailing assumption among this population is that both refer to the same act: volunteering is becoming active; becoming active in the community is achieved through volunteering – in short, volunteerism is activism. Filipino women's volunteerism is infused with what I call "multiple activism," involving a synthesis of personal, professional, spiritual, and ethnocultural dimensions, although not necessarily all at once. At the per-sonal level, volunteer work that is directed towards others reflects the motives and desires of the individual as a member of a community. For example, volunteer work may be motivated by a desire to find a space to belong and to nurture bonds of friendship; alternatively, becoming involved in the community promotes recognition of Filipinos as immigrants. Voluntary actions are also seen as consistent with faith: the belief in working for the common good (Howard Ecklund and Park 2007; Wuthnow 2009). "Making the world a better place" based on values and beliefs provides psychic benefits resulting from volunteer work (Wilson and Musick 2003, 433).

Multiple activism intersects with different aspects of integration, from the personal to the public. It is essentially grounded in volunteerism and sug-gests a holistic approach to understanding the complexity of motives or aspirations in the lives of Filipino women. This chapter builds on the position that Filipino women's multiple activism provides the means of developing lasting connections in their communities. It examines the forms of volun-teerism undertaken by *Pinays* in the Prairies as mothers, workers, and mem-bers of organizations, under the headings of personal politics and feminism, grounded volunteerism, and Filipino communities.

Engagement with the community is often premised on personal politics, which translate subconsciously into feminist practice. I reframe the term "grounded volunteerism" (Eckstein 2001) to denote the fundamental inter-relationship between volunteer work and the lives of Filipino women, in contrast to the conventional idea of volunteer work in which the individual simply puts in time. Profiles of selected *Pinay* community leaders in Alberta, Saskatchewan, and Manitoba are integrated in the discussion to demonstrate an alternative vision of Filipino women in Canada – as "movers and shakers" in building links among Filipinos and with the larger community. This time, Filipino women are not hapless victims of social and structural inequalities but are agents of change. I do not imply, however, that their engagement in the community necessarily depicts the larger *Pinay* community in the Prairies or in Canada. My motivation in focusing on this aspect of their lives is rather to highlight this unrecognized dimension, often perceived to be the space of "Canadian (i.e., white) women." We cannot all be leaders or volunteers, but those who are in the face of challenges that normally push many into a home/work routine are worthy of inclusion in migration discourse, which may herald a possible reframing of the "Filipino woman" in Canada. The last section examines the role of Filipino women in Filipino community organizations, the impact of Filipino values on their community involvement, and the changing gendered perceptions of leadership and community building.

Personal Politics and Feminism
"Man is a political animal," said Aristotle (Young 2005, 74). So is a woman. History attests to male control of state building and "big" politics through holding public office, running for elections, campaigning for political parties, and the like (Dickerson, Flanagan, and O'Neill 2010). The apparent and actual exclusion of women from the art of state enterprise remains almost a universal phenomenon, despite steps towards gender political parity in some countries (United Nations Development Programme [UNDP] 2005; Gelb and Palley 2009). The "small" politics of women's activism in communities has not been as widely accepted as "real" politics. In fact, many community activists in the United States are "hesitant to identify themselves as political" or engaged in politics due to negative connotations arising from the "violent and corrupt public sphere of male politics" (Ackelsberg 2005, 74). Farrell (1999, 202), describing her experience at Oxfam, concludes that "volunteering, in whatever capacity, in whatever role, is a political act." Regardless of its connotations, I use the term "politics" broadly as a process and an action that affect our lives. As Faulks (2003, 3) claims: "Politics should matter to us all because it is concerned with fundamental questions that are of profound relevance to human beings, whenever or wherever they may live ... What rights should I be entitled to? How can I make my voice heard?"

Politics aims to channel particular interests and views into bringing about change. The conventional model of politics refers to acts towards state structures by and for citizens, the process of policy or law making, allocation of resources, and the like. The politics I am concerned with here, however, is multidirectional, involving informal (e.g., organizations), formal (e.g., state structures), and personal avenues. Recognizing the limited participation of racialized immigrant women in the formal political process in Canada, I see their politics as a transformative process – of voicing concerns and of acting on the motivations and aspirations within their communities as volunteers. A number of Filipino women participate in community organizations that may have direct or indirect connections with representatives of the Canadian state. In a way, the multidirectional trajectory of volunteerism facilitates a relationship in which visible minorities in Canada, although power may generally appear to tilt away from them, gain some leverage in certain political situations, as when candidates solicit their support during elections (Bilodeau and Kanji 2010).

Migration facilitates a kind of personal politics that translates into feminist praxis. That is, the experiences of marginalization, discrimination, exploitation, oppression, and related forms of "othering" practices in host societies lead immigrant and migrant women to act on such challenges in their own ways. The narratives of Filipino women in previous chapters show that suffering from racism and discrimination raise their awareness about inequalities in a Western society. A new consciousness about the realities of living in Canada enables them to recognize their social position, and thus marks the beginning of personal politics. "Personal politics" refers to a set of beliefs and actions that form the cornerstone of feminist practice. According to Whelehan (1995, 65), radical feminism suggests that "personal politics warrant closer materialist analysis" in the private/public dichotomy founded on male dominance. Materiality is inscribed by patriarchal values that delegitimize care work and women's "double burden" (Mellner, Krantz, and Lundberg 2006). Despite the increasing acceptance of shared domestic responsibilities in Western societies, women still bear "disproportionate responsibility" for home and care work (Satz 2010, 72). While Filipino women's personal politics may not necessarily be directed towards male control in their lives, lived material conditions in Canada serve as their benchmark for action and resistance.

Sister Mary John Mananzan, founder of the feminist organization PILIPINA in the Philippines, states in her critique of Western feminism: "We [PILIPINA] make it a point to distinguish ourselves from some Western feminists *kasi* [because] sometimes they trivialize the whole thing; they make it a man-against-woman thing which we don't believe in. With us, it's a matter of how you get a woman to really maximize her whole potential" (cited in Roces 2005, 150). The majority of *Pinays* in this study direct their personal politics for change and empowerment not specifically against their husbands or men in general but towards their own subject positionality as immigrants and towards supporting groups through community activism. *Positionality* is the point of reference for these women, "where values are interpreted and

constructed" (Naples 2003, 22). While Mananzan's critique of Western
feminism seems valid, patriarchy and its myriad manifestations through
religion and politics, for example, shape the rights and privileges of women
and men in the Philippines. *Pinays* in the Prairies have not expressed "man-
against-woman thing" or claimed that men embody the roots of their oppression, as in the Western context (LeGates 2001), although concerns about
their "Filipino ways" (what men are supposed to do, or not) have come up
in passing in the discussions. I contend, however, that participation in the
community is a challenge to a patriarchal culture's public/private divide,
and *Pinays* can claim an active role in traversing both spaces. An indirect
challenge to such structures and practices becomes a direct negation of
their limitations in personal lives. The "public" (i.e., community) has become
a space for personal politics.

The feminist dictum "the personal is political," or the term "personal
politics" in this section, acknowledges that the individual chooses her own
politics and spaces of engagement based on realities and experiences. Code
(1991, 44) notes that the "author of an experience is uniquely and solely in
a position to manage and negotiate *that* 'reality:' only she can get it right."
Hence, civic engagement differs according to the context and meaning of
such personal experiences. For instance, workplace discrimination may
encourage workers to seek support from labour unions, or immigrant mothers
may reassure themselves about their children's well-being by participating
in school activities and seeing first-hand how the Canadian educational
system works.

First-generation Filipino immigrant women presumably know their
politics. Politics of, by, and with the people are deeply entrenched in daily
life in the Philippines (Kerkvliet 1995; Roces 1998; De Castro 2007). Young
Filipinos are politically integrated as members of youth councils now known
as *Sangguniang Kabataan* (SK), the successor of *Kabataang Barangay* (KB) in
the Marcos era (Bessell 2009; United Nations Children's Fund [UNICEF]
2011, 48).[1] The politicization of Filipino youth stands in stark contrast to
the political passivity of their Canadian counterparts (Hooghe and Stolle
2005, 44; Wiseman 2007, 56). Many *Pinays* in the Prairies have, at some point
during their time in the Philippines, participated in local youth assemblies
and community activities (Arcenas 2006; Veneracion-Rallonza 2008).

Filipino women are particularly active in local community politics and
organizing, and their dynamism is commonplace in the Philippines (Roces
1998; Tapales 2005; Iwanaga 2008). Such visibility in public spaces carries
over to their lives in Canada. For example, the National Alliance of Philippine
Women in Canada (NAPWC) held a research conference at the University
of Toronto in November 2008 and addressed four major concerns: Filipino
women's equality and human rights, Filipino youth in communities, racism,

and economic marginalization. In 2009, the Philippine Women Centre of British Columbia presented a quilt exhibit on Filipino women's empowerment, and in 2010 conducted a multimedia presentation and public dialogue about the (in)visibility of the Filipino-Canadian community in Vancouver. Many other activities have been organized in Montreal, Toronto, and Vancouver by other Filipino community groups, and almost all core activities involving Filipino women, youth, and migrant workers appear to be highly visible in these major cities. In the Prairies, the Philippine Women Centre in Manitoba (PWC-M) and Damayan Manitoba are the most active and progressive community organizations.[2]

My interviews with Filipino women in the Prairies indicate that personal politics arise from two reference points: the Philippines and Canada. As first-generation immigrants, Filipino women have formed values and beliefs about their place in a democracy. These ideas are entrenched despite their sojourn overseas, remaining part of who they are. In Canada, life's many unexpected twists and turns put these long-held ideas to the test. Experiences of discrimination, direct or subtle, or perceived inequalities in a liberal democratic country create opportunities for this population to act on its beliefs. Personal politics thus become part of a continuum of ideas and action extending from the Philippines to Canada.

> *In the Philippines, this is what we did. We organize the youth choir ... out of school youth, encourage education and participate in computer classes with the initiative of my husband ... My background of activism was in the university where poverty is all around you, abuses. Manipulation by may-kaya, at mga nakakataas* [manipulation by the rich, and those in high places].
> – Josefina, self-employed in Winnipeg

Josefina's account demonstrates how her activism in Winnipeg is not new but stems from her experiences in the Philippines, first as a student, and then as a resident of the Roxas district advocating for the displaced poor. Poverty in Metro Manila and other major cities is prevalent, and many students have witnessed the demolition of squatter areas by the government to build gigantic shopping malls or other projects without an effective relocation plan (Sidel 1998; Mahlum 2009). In Winnipeg, Josefina is motivated not by poverty per se but by a need to give back to the community to help the homeless. She volunteers in soup kitchens and confides that "volunteering when I can is the only way for me to say 'Thank you' [to Canada]."

Even in its developing state, the Philippines promotes the rights of citizenship and democratic principles such as equality and social justice. This knowledge infuses the personal activism of women migrants, motivating them to improve the status of Filipino women in Canada. Salvacion, a founding member of the Filipino Domestic Workers Association of Manitoba (FIDWAM), states:

> *Why did we form this organization? First, few members talked about it ... we have no relatives here, walang tumutulong* [nobody helps]. *We like to look after the welfare and protection of domestic workers. Now, we have over one hundred members ... About two to three years ago I met new DHs with no relatives ... They stay every weekend. I want them to help others who are new once they landed here.*
> – Salvacion, a home care worker in Winnipeg

FIDWAM was founded by thirteen Filipino live-in caregivers in 1988 and now has a membership of about one hundred (*Filipino Journal* 2009a). For eighteen years, these women have been advocates for the rights and welfare of domestic workers and their families in Manitoba. In Salvacion's narrative, having experienced the sense of vulnerability common to live-in workers inspires her to provide shelter to other domestic workers even today. Her house has become a temporary sanctuary for displaced Filipino migrant workers. Once these women obtain permanent residency and normalcy in their work, Salvacion hopes they will extend the same empathy and compassion to other live-in caregivers in need of company and support.

A recent and more progressive advocacy organization for migrant Filipino workers in Manitoba is Damayan Manitoba (*damayan* means "caring for another"), currently under the leadership of Secretary-General Jomay Amora-Mercado.[3] Born of its members' experiences as temporary foreign workers (TFWs), the organization has been an advocate for workers' rights and benefits since its founding in April 2008. While working in a fast food outlet in Edmonton, Jomay realized that abuses in the workplace occur even in Canada. She commented: *"Hindi pala naiiba ang Canada ... akala mo advanced sila pero* [Canada is not really different ... you think they are advanced, but] *oppression and abuses exist."*

In Calgary, the BABAE Council of Filipina-Canadian Women was organized in 2003 by Maribel Javier, Dolly Castillo, Marichu Antonia, Connie Raz, and Joann Zulueta. BABAE (woman) is a growing organization and a member of the Ethno-Cultural Council of Calgary (ECCC) (Kriaski 2009). According to Maribel Javier, its basic mission is to "lift the status of Filipino women in Canadian society." BABAE now has more than thirty-five active members from all types of professions. Maribel comments: "The name *babae* will have an impact on Filipino women. We hope that the idea that '*babae ka lang*' [you're only a woman] will diminish." Such a stance acknowledges the gender inequalities rooted in culture and tradition yet at the same time considers the possibilities of Filipino women's own empowerment in Canada.

Encounters with other nationalities in the course of employment, or with members of the public, have motivated some Filipino women to prove their own abilities in the community.

> *Alam ko mas mabuti dito sa Canada. Pero minsan makakatagpo ka ng ibang tao ... nakakainis. Pero pag-hindi nila alam kung sino ka, ganoon pa din ang pagtingin sa iyo. So, pinakita ko sila kung sino ako.* [I know it's better here in Canada. But sometimes you meet people ... it's annoying. But if they do not know who you are, then they will continue to look at you in the same way. So, I showed them who I am.]
> – Apple, an employee in Calgary

Apple's response to how she was perceived at work was to get involved. She is single and without a family in Canada, and belonging to a group provides her with opportunities to utilize her skills.

Some Filipino women may shy away from the label "feminist," but when the term is defined as working against oppressive structures and practices that devalue women's contributions and their equal worth as human beings, they tend to agree with this aim. This consensus cuts across class, profession, education, and regional origin. The context from which the label "feminist" is derived in the West differs from that shaped by *Pinays'* historicity and place in the global social hierarchy. According to Grewal and Kaplan (1994, 20), there are "different forms that feminism takes and different practices that can be seen as feminist movements." Many Filipino women in the Prairies embrace certain ideals, political or otherwise, about living in Canada. Working these out in various community activities serves as "feminist practice" without necessarily being defined as such. It responds to the Filipino activist cry for action captured in the slogan *"Kung hindi tayo kikilos, sino pa, kung hindi ngayon, kailan pa* [if we do not act, who will; if not now, when else]?" (Roces 2005, 136). Activist Filipino women tend to be emboldened by ideals of justice that cut across race, class, and status – practising *Pinay peminism* in their daily lives to counter minimal spaces of engagement as racialized immigrants.

Grounded Volunteerism

Volunteers are the forerunners of change. They have been a driving force in many social movements throughout history (Henderson 1984). The same can be said of their impact on the restoration of democracy in the Philippines (Hedman 2006) or on changing social policies in Canada (Clément 2008). Volunteers are motivated by a range of interests – "personal, humanitarian, and social justice" (Messias, DeJong, and McLoughlin 2005, 27) – to contribute unpaid work for a cause.

Grounded volunteerism is rooted in the experiences of individuals – in this case, racialized Filipino women. I argue that grounded volunteerism differs from the populist idea of volunteerism as simply a generous act of unpaid work. *Pinays* engage in volunteer work that directly affects their lives as immigrants or migrant workers in Canada. It is a multi-faceted activism that touches various dimensions of their lives, from the personal, to the professional, to the ethnocultural collective. Embedded in their activities as volunteers is the idea that "what we give, we get back," whether through learning about the Canadian socio-political system, working to integrate other Filipinos, or building the Filipino community in Canada.

Most studies characterize volunteers as people belonging to the middle or upper class, mainly middle-aged or older women (Wilson and Musick 1997; Warburton and McLaughlin 2006). This archetype ignores the contribution of poor or marginalized women who work as volunteers in the community. Iacovetta (1995) notes that in postwar Canada volunteer work was undertaken not only by middle-class women but also by many immigrant women, who contributed mostly to the development of ethnic organizations. Tastsoglou and Miedema (2003, 204) argue that the contributions of immigrant women in community development in the Canadian Maritimes are "largely overlooked." Unlike the well-documented activities of Latin American immigrant women in the United States (Hondagneu-Sotelo and Cranford 1999; Shapiro 2005), the numerous examples of Filipino women involved in various charitable, political, and social activities in host societies remain unrecognized in migration studies (Roces 2003; Padilla 2007; Posadas and Guyotte 2008).

The altruistic work of Filipino women in the Prairies challenges the classic volunteer model: most are not of the middle class, and not all are middle-aged or older. In Chapter 3, I explored the meaning of class for Filipino women and their self-positioning in Canada as part of the economic middle class. In the psyche of the Canadian public, however, an immigrant is of "low class." Some Filipino women's volunteerism began early in their settlement in Canada, and being of "low class" was not a deterrent to community participation. Depending on whose perspective is being considered, economic status or social standing seems insignificant in many Filipino women's volunteerism in Canada; the young and old tend to be as active as the middle-aged in the community.

> *Regardless of age, as first timer, adjustment is the problem. Regardless of age women can volunteer and engage in the community.*
> – Dulce, a retired teacher in Calgary

Age does determine the type and level of community involvement among the *Pinays* in the Prairies, however. Although the boundaries between them are quite fluid, there are different types of involvement for young, middle-aged, and older immigrant Filipino women. Categorization of these ages varies from one person to another, although the official Canadian definition of a senior citizen is sixty-five years old. Studies indicate that age and volunteerism are directly related: "As age increases, volunteerism increases until middle age, then decreases as the individual gets older" (Wymer and Self 1999, 153). Those between thirty-five and forty-four years old are said to have the highest rate of volunteer activity (ibid.). In the case of *Pinays* in the Prairies, especially first-generation immigrants, this assumption may not hold, as this age group corresponds with their age of arrival in Canada. The realities of settlement may not permit them to pursue volunteer work immediately. However, a number of them do eventually engage in volunteer work to secure Canadian references while looking for a job. For example, some Filipino live-in caregivers in southern Alberta volunteered in non-profit organizations to improve their job profile and prospects after completing the Live-in Caregiver Program (LCP) requirements.

The roles of young, middle-aged, and older Filipino women in the community vary: young women are likely to engage intermittently in sports or social activities, while middle-aged and older women tend to engage in service-related activities.

Young women in sports, social activities. Middle-aged women are more of services type, or in volunteer events and form part of cultural group.
– Filomena, a government employee in Saskatoon

Older Filipino women tend to be more involved. Not really old or elderly but more mature in their thirties to forties ... some young people take part in cultural shows.
– Analisa, a community worker in Saskatoon

Older ones arrived earlier. I see the seniors as active in participating in organizations, both Filipino and mainstream, because I am one of them. Young people tend to follow what we've done in the past.
– Gabriela, a retired government employee in Winnipeg

The middle-aged are more active, working together long time within the Filipino community, not outside.
– Sharon, a former garment worker in Saskatoon

Maramimg matanda sa community service organizations. Ang mga bata busy sa activities nila na hindi masyadong nag-engage sa community. [There are many older women in community service organizations. Young people are busy with their own activities and do not engage much in the community.]
– Samantha, a government employee in Regina

Age at the time of migration and the level of development of community
organizations have an impact on the participation of *Pinays* in the Prairies.
Those arriving in areas with fairly established Filipino organizations may
pre-select certain activities to engage in, while those moving to areas with
no or new ethnic community associations are more likely to be involved in
organizing and soliciting support for community building. Other studies
suggest that "volunteer activity is highest in the most heterogenous regions
of Canada and the lowest in the most homogenous regions" (Wymer and
Self 1999, 153). Most volunteer activities of *Pinays* in the Prairies occur in
cities rather than small towns. The presence of other Filipinos in the community tends to facilitate the building of social networks that also determine
choice of volunteer activity.

> *I was very young at that time in our group, early twenties. We all volunteered.*
> *We have so much energy ... We were young and active then. We became leaders*
> *... we did not wait to be, not being asked. Mahirap ang mga bago ngayon [it's*
> difficult for newcomers now]. *They socialize too much ... Why not volunteer?*
> *... More older women are active in the community ... Who will succeed us?*
> *Organizations are run by people my age – sixties, seventies. Young ones don't*
> *see it necessary to get themselves in the community anymore.*
> – Marilena, a community worker in Edmonton

Different priorities define the arrival of different groups of women in Canada. Middle-aged newcomers tend to focus more on their settlement and
on finding new career paths, becoming involved in community activities
only later on.

> *Older women, thirty-plus, on their first few years of migration, the tendency is*
> *to get settled ... not unless they are volunteer conscious. The willingness to get*
> *engaged comes with age. I don't have much young Filipino women coming to*
> *volunteer orientation.*
> – Marilou, a community worker in Calgary

> *Mahirap pag bago. Kailangan matuto muna sa mga pasikot-sikot dito. Wala*
> *tayong panahon para sa iba.* [It's difficult for newcomers. They have to
> learn the ins and outs here. We have no time for others.]
> – Susan, a caregiver in Edmonton

When Filipino women do get engaged in their communities, it is through
grounded volunteerism. What they do for others in unpaid services reflect
their personal lives – their hopes and aspirations in Canada. Based on the
narratives collected for this study, I would argue for the following categories

of *Pinay* grounded volunteerism: (1) volunteerism motivated by faith, (2) volunteerism as an extension of work, (3) volunteerism to improve professions, (4) volunteerism in schools, (5) volunteerism for community building, (6) volunteerism for social justice, and (7) volunteerism motivated by circumstances. Some of these may overlap, but these motivations and activities all speak to women's work, which, according to Messias, DeJong, and McLoughlin (2005, 26), "transpires within complex and dynamic social, cultural, emotional, economic, political and geographic contexts."

Volunteerism Motivated by Faith
All of the Filipino women who participated in this study embrace a religion; almost all are Catholics. Tropman (2002, 2) writes about the "Catholic ethic," which is rooted in community, "strong connections with others, a sense of 'we are all in the same boat' and norms of helping, supporting and cooperating with others." Filipino culture is highly community-oriented, from the family network to loose relations built by the *padrino* (sponsorship) system (Gripaldo 2005). This dovetails easily with the Catholic ethic and its ideal virtues of charity and kindness; in the Prairies, Filipino Catholic women have found churches to be appropriate channels for their volunteer activities.

> *We accept that grace is not only for us but to share with others. We form part of independent apolitical group. We help others not for self-interest ... because of religion? I think so.*
> – Josefina, self-employed in Winnipeg

> *Faith for me. Other things follow. How can you say na tumutulong ka ng mahirap kung wala kang gagawin?* [How can you say that you help the poor if you don't do anything?]
> – Trinidad, a migrant worker in Calgary

It is generally claimed that religiosity facilitates volunteerism in the community (O'Neill 2005); in fact, some find a strong connection between faith and volunteerism (Koenig, Lawson, and McConnell 2004, 128). Gonzalez (2009, 181) writes about the "strong, faith-centered, civic-oriented religious life" of Filipino immigrants in the United States. Similarly, Josefina in Winnipeg describes the idea of grace, of living a new life in Canada, and a sense that such a blessing ought to be shared with others through volunteer work. In Trinidad's account, her Catholic faith serves as the foundation for her involvement in community activities in Calgary.

Many Filipino women participate in church-related activities, as readers, altar servers, and choir members, and in committee work and governance. In fact, women's volunteer work has "sustained religious practice" (Andersen and Taylor 2006, 471). The Catholic Church offers a familiar space of worship where many Filipino women first find public recognition as members of their community. During my fieldwork in Winnipeg and Saskatoon, I attended a Sunday Mass where a number of Filipino women acted as ushers, readers, or members of the choir along with other Canadian women.

> *I volunteer as trustee of St. Peter's church ... I have everyday involvement in church ... Now, we're looking for a building, a new church. I am chair of the building committee ... of eight and I'm the only woman ... I work every day ... There's so much going on. Am also in charge of readers ... for Mass. As one of the two trustees, we do counts every weekend in church. I do the financial statement and report.*
> – Lumen, a finance officer in Winnipeg

> *At church, I have been a teacher in catechism for St. Mary's for fifteen years ... I feel blessed so much in Canada ... Volunteer comes from the heart because I have time.*
> – Rosie, a sales agent in Winnipeg

> *I proclaim the word as lay minister ... This is where I go to since I came to Canada ... Volunteered at bingo or Knights of Columbus to raise funds ... Once a month or every last Sunday of the month ... in church – hospitality, serve food, wash dishes ... they call me when needed.*
> – Samantha, a government employee in Regina

> *Noon palagi akong dumadaan sa simbahan. Nadadaanan ko pagsakay ng bus. Sabi ko, bakit hindi pumasok naman para magdasal. So, ngayon araw-araw akong dumadaan sa simbahan. Yung mga tao sa simbahan nagtanong kung ok daw na sumali ako sa kanila. Anyway, nandoon naman ako. Sa madaling salita, kasama nila ako hanggang ngayon. Dito ako palagi.*
> [I used to pass by the church before. I passed by it whenever I would take the bus. I told myself, why not enter the church to pray? So, I now go to church every day. The people in church asked me if it would be okay for me to join them. Anyway, I'm there already. In short, I am with them until now. I'm always here.]
> – Maria, a government employee in Saskatoon

These women in Winnipeg, Regina, and Saskatoon find fulfillment in sharing their skills and abilities in the context of their Catholicism. Lumen is an accountant and has used her skills to gain a respected leadership position in various church projects and activities; Rosie, a former teacher in the Philippines, has found her classroom management experience useful in catechism classes; and Samantha is an active churchgoer who volunteers to be on call for various activities. Maria arrived in Saskatoon as a garment worker and found the welcoming atmosphere in church a means of belonging. In their work on the intersections of gender, religion, and migration, Bonifacio and Angeles (2010, 263) examine the activism of Filipino women in recreating Filipino Catholic practices in Philadelphia, forming a "huge group of devotees whose faith keeps the tradition alive in their adopted country."

Filipino women have found ways to show community spirit in church, and their strategies for negotiating spaces in patriarchal institutions are significant in settlement and integration (Ebaugh and Chafetz 2000; Eclarin Azada 2006). Participation in church activities provides continuity of the familiar and a sense of normalcy in lives altered by migration. Shared religious expressions between the homeland and the host society offer comfort and a sense of belonging.

Even as the Catholic churches in Canada, the United States, and Europe witness a shrinking base of volunteers drawn from their own nationals, immigrants to these countries, largely women, have infused church activities with a new energy (Long Marler 2008). Church engagement is a safe venture, spiritually enhancing and also personally uplifting for its "double recognition" of work – from God and from others. Filipino Catholics can turn to the church for acceptance, and their involvement creates an alternative representation of Filipinos in the community. A Filipino woman may work as a live-in caregiver five days of the week in the private domain, but she becomes an accepted member of the "church public" on weekends. Service-oriented volunteerism in religious organizations is instrumental in facilitating women's entry into the public sphere (Bojar 1998). In a society where migrant workers' work defines their life, religious volunteerism provides a sense of relief and release; in the church and in the eyes of God, the Filipino caregiver-cum-domestic worker and her Canadian employer stand as equals.

Volunteerism as Extension of Work
Paid work and unpaid work are usually separate from one another, and it is generally assumed that volunteer work takes place in the absence of paid work (Erlinghagen and Hank 2006). There are instances, however, when these two may coincide in one job. For example, corporate employee volunteering has been a growing phenomenon among companies in Japan and the United States: employees are given time off to participate in community programs (Chelladurai 2006). According to Verba and colleagues (2002, 39), in their study of American civic volunteerism the "border between voluntary participation and paid employment is blurry." Often the reasons for extending work into the voluntary realm complement personal and organizational

objectives such as learning more about one's company, developing rapport or camaraderie with colleagues, or building a name for the organization in the community, among others.

Some of the participants in this study are employed in non-profit organizations working with different ethnic groups; a few hold managerial positions that have direct contact with the community; many others are nurses working in hospitals, home care, and retirement homes. Paid employment provides opportunities for community engagement in these instances.

> *I work for the local non-profit organization ... That in itself is a form of civic engagement ... I do a lot of volunteer work for my organization above and beyond my job description which is the case in most non-profit anyway.*
> – Julita, a community worker in Edmonton

> *I work with immigrant sector, with much broader community participation ... My main interest is to foster citizenship engagement, organize coalition of immigrant communities to advocate issues. I am not really a member of the Filipino organizations but ensure that Filipinos get engaged in the wider community ... a bouncing consultant of all Filipino organizations, help them find resources ... we advance the engagement of Filipinos ... now they are going out of their shell in solidarity with other groups.*
> – Hosanna, a nurse in Edmonton

Julita and Hosanna in Edmonton both work for non-profit organizations whose clientele consists mainly of immigrants to Canada. Julita views volunteerism as part of her work in this sector. This so-called volunteering on the job is prevalent among non-profit organizations (Bojar 1998, 42). Immigrant women working in the settlement sector perform extra unremunerated hours of work to ensure the continuity of programs, or even undertake fundraising activities for their organizations (Lee 2008, 106). By doing both paid and unpaid work in the settlement sector, for instance, immigrant employees are caught in a double bind. Funds raised sustain programs directed towards immigrants, and with recent federal cuts in immigrant services made by Prime Minister Stephen Harper's government, the work/volunteer scheme is most likely to expand (Pagliaro and Mahoney 2010). As a consequence, immigrant-serving agencies, with their mostly gendered workforce, need to intensify their demands to obtain a share of public resources, and women-specific programs could take a back seat. Under neoliberalism, autonomous citizens are expected to act on their own with less government intervention, and their advocacy work for social justice is reduced to "private mobilizations to gain public resources" (Hawkesworth 2006, 22).

Julita understands the social realities of Filipinos and other immigrants in Edmonton and aspires to organize the Albertan chapter of MIGRANTE, an advocacy group for migrant workers. Hosanna, on the other hand, works for a multicultural non-profit organization and serves as an unpaid consultant to many Filipino organizations seeking government funding for their projects. Through her paid work, Hosanna ensures that these organizations join with other ethnic-community groups in becoming engaged citizens.

Being an employee of a company that serves the public provides opportunities for volunteering in the community. These activities are corporate-sponsored but do not provide time off from work in exchange for volunteering. In many such events held on weekends, Filipino women like Victoria also involve their families.

I work in a credit union and generally involved in the community during the Credit Union Days, have barbecue for the community ... my kids come along, too.
– Victoria, a private employee in Saskatoon

Community involvement is with mainstream and job-related activities where we volunteer. I get involved in lots of causes, with partners in the community. There are many opportunities to work.
– Rowena, a manager in a media company in Winnipeg

Rowena works in a media company in Winnipeg, and her position is instrumental in creating lasting community projects and partnerships.

A number of Filipino nurses are involved in medical missions and community health initiatives. Some live-in caregivers in Canada who were registered nurses in the Philippines volunteer at the Red Cross or in hospitals on their days off. Many consider this involvement an important step towards becoming acquainted with Canadian practices and establishing connections in the community.

Wala naman kaming pupuntahan na iba kung hindi sa mall o simbahan. Nag-volunteer ako sa hospital. Maganda iyon kasi nakita ko kung papaano magtrabaho ang mga Canadian. [We have nowhere else to go except the mall or church. I volunteered at the hospital. It was a good experience since I saw how Canadians work.]
– Siony, a nurse in Calgary

Volunteerism to Improve Professions
This section focuses primarily on the circumstances affecting Filipinos in the nursing profession. As discussed in Chapter 3, foreign-trained nurses

have difficulty getting recognized by provincial regulatory bodies such as the College and Association of Registered Nurses of Alberta (CARNA). Nurses from the Philippines tend to be marginalized by their profession, and as a result, many have found alternative immigration entry points as live-in caregivers or migrant workers to secure immediate employment. In Alberta, Philippine-trained registered nurses (RN) are equated with licensed practical nurses (LPN) and are required to take additional courses of study in recognized institutions (De la Cruz 2009). While the Prairie provinces have different approaches to dealing with foreign-trained nurses, Filipino nurses have formed their own associations to work jointly for their interests across borders, such as the Filipino Nurses Association in Alberta (FNAA) and the Philippine Nurses' Association of Manitoba.

Teresita "Tessie" Oliva, who was a registered nurse in the Philippines and now lives in Edmonton, is considered a pioneer in advocating for Filipino nurses in Alberta as the founder, past president, and adviser of the FNAA since 1973.[4] Tessie recalls: "I was the first Filipino nurse to ask for accreditation in Alberta and opened the doors for other nurses here. I took three courses in the University of Alberta in the 1970s. I took specialized courses in cardiology in the United States, but Canada did not recognize my qualifications." Through her initiative, the FNAA began a partnership with Capital Health Region in Alberta in 2006 to improve the recruitment and integration of Filipino nurses in the community. She developed course materials to assist foreign-trained nurses in preparing for their Canadian Registered Nurse Examination (CRNE), helped improve the practice of an interdisciplinary approach to patient care delivery, and developed effective protocols and a quality assurance program for the Capital Care Group in Edmonton.

> *In Manitoba, a group of practising and non-practising nurses and students are members of the Philippine Nurses' Association of Manitoba ... we tie up with some colleges in Manila.*
> – Rosal, a nurse TFW in Winnipeg

Tessie and Rosal are examples of Filipino nurses working tirelessly to improve their profession in the Prairies. Collective gains have slowly come about as they make their voices heard, particularly with regard to the recruitment of Filipino nurses; for example, in Saskatchewan, Filipino nurses arrive as migrant workers with relocation allowances and with contracts contingent on their passing the CRNE (*Philippine Asian News Today* 2008). Those involved with ethnic nursing associations develop individual and institutional linkages with the Philippines to raise awareness of the process of registration with provincial regulatory bodies in Canada. These women have learned to work "outside the power structure" (Okamoto and Ebert 2010, 530) and have created a way for Philippine-trained nurses to collectively address the issue of non-recognition, employment equity, integration, and culturally sensitive health care delivery.

Volunteerism in Schools

Most participants in this study extend their nurturing roles as volunteers in their children's schools. They undertake various tasks such as canteen convenor, field trip guide, driver, and classroom or library assistant.

In school, I was convenor at the canteen for four years. I spend more money there because you use your money first and they paid back later. During graduation, I drive kids home after the party.
   – Clemencia, a nurse in Winnipeg

Most of our community involvement is related with our children's activities ... being a scout leader, chaperoning field trips, volunteering in the classroom or school library and sports activities ... We lend extra hand, manual labour or volunteer.
   – Norma, a housewife in Saskatoon

Parent volunteers have been common since the rise of the modern schooling system. Mothers are more likely to volunteer in school than fathers (O'Donnell and Stueve 1985), with the exception of some activities such as coaching in sports (Hall 2003). A number of *Pinays* in the Prairies have volunteered at some point in their children's pre-university life. Besides helping with various school activities, Filipino women are able to build their own social networks. Those without employment have used school volunteer work as a transition to paid work. Samantha in Regina, for example, first started as a library volunteer on arrival in Canada, offering her services when job prospects appeared dim.

First, I enrolled the kids in school three months before I work. I have no job then. Tumulong ako sa school [I helped in school] ... I said, I am a librarian and teacher by profession in the Philippines. Maybe I can help you at the library. They said, okay, two to three hours a day before I get the job.
   – Samantha, a government employee in Regina

Feminists consider women's volunteerism in school to be an extension of domestic roles. Shelton (1999, 386), in her essay "Gender and Unpaid Work," notes: "If women's participation includes parent-teacher organizations, organizing children's recreational activities, or other activities related to children it can be counted as additional childcare." Women's voluntary activities are essentially "domestic" or "expressive" (ibid.), grounded in care work. While school-based volunteerism is gendered, I argue that immigrant

Filipino mothers who give time, money, and effort in assisting with school activities are "empowered mothers" in their own right – mothers who shape the experiences of their children outside the home, which consequently translates into extending care to other children. Although it is not in the same political spectrum as empowered mothering in feminist practice,[5] I push for the inclusion of this type of volunteerism among racialized immigrant mothers in the context of their limited spaces for political engagement. Given that the avenues of socio-political activism are not the same among women of diverse backgrounds, volunteerism in schools qualifies racialized immigrant mothers like *Pinays* as empowered mothers whose interactions with school administrators, teachers, parents, and even children contribute to the general welfare of a micro-community in their midst.

Mothers' volunteerism in school follows the interests of maternal practice – "preservation, growth, and acceptability" of children (Ruddick 2007, 99). Mothers preserve the life of a child through care and nurture into adulthood. A child's growth has many dimensions, from the physical, intellectual, and psychological to the spiritual. Schools provide space for the growth and development of the child that is consistent with the acceptable social norms and values of society. For immigrant mothers, these norms may be different from the ones they were oriented to in their countries of origin. I would surmise that "empowered immigrant mothers" also negotiate these value differences in the school when they are able to. "Mother activism" (Osnes 2008, 280) is directed towards not only changing policies that affect children's welfare in society writ large but also being involved in little ways at school. Involvement in school activities is not measured by how many parent-teacher council meetings one attends or how many times one assists in sports activities. Simply sharing what one is able to at the moment is enough for a number of *Pinay* mothers; this includes even one-time acts, regular acts within a period, or selective acts, depending on availability of time. However, many, too, face particular challenges that may inhibit their participation as volunteers in school: lack of time due to multiple jobs, shift work, and domestic burdens; lack of financial means to pay for travel and other expenses in doing volunteer work; and physical and psychological health conditions that impede volunteering (cf. Behnia 2009), including feelings of exclusion in a white-dominated school environment (Tastsoglou 2006).

Maria Doris Collantes was an accomplished teacher educator in the Philippines.[6] She migrated to Canada in 1990 and in 2005 founded the Pilipino Educators Advocated Council (PEAC)[7] in Calgary. PEAC promotes Filipino heritage and Filipino as a Second Language (FSL) in schools. In our interview on 4 July 2009, Maria Doris reflected on her community involvement: "I like others to have the same opportunity to promote our heritage."

Volunteerism for Community Building

As newcomers in search of belonging and the familiarity of shared practices, a number of *Pinays* in the Prairies volunteered their time and resources to establish or sustain Filipino associations as well as build relationships with the wider community.

Towards the Filipino Community

"Pioneer" Filipino women in the area often become the link in the formation of informal or formal ethnic associations. Josephine "Josie" Enero Pallard is one of them.[8] In 1967, she joined the Philippine Bayanihan Association (PBA) in Edmonton. *Bayanihan* is translated as "community spirit" or "mutual aid" and is emblematic of Filipinos helping one another (Lawsin 1998). According to Josephine, "initially there were very few members. Later on, people from Calgary and out of town came to Edmonton and joined us. Culture is the biggest barrier and we have no family to support us here." She believes that by creating a nucleus they can form a group and eventually a community in Edmonton. Josephine also founded the Saranay Youth and Adult Rondalla Ensemble, which uses traditional Philippine instruments and travels every two years for concert tours in the Philippines and Europe (Gonzalez 2007). Her experience reflects the activism and community-building efforts of immigrants who remember and preserve their culture and histories through collective interactions (Gabbacia and Ruiz, 2006, 10).

Virginia "Jean" Gonzales Guiang arrived in Manitoba in 1969 via Brussels and quickly became active in the Filipino community.[9] In 1970, she formed a small dance group of four members for the International Centre of the Citizenship Council of Manitoba. She said: "I was challenged by the Council's Executive Director ... who I guess saw my potential. I bought myself a Philippine Dance book and learned *Pandanggo sa Ilaw* [fandango with light]. Our performance of this dance later on became the symbol of the International Centre of annual sponsorship for newcomers. Our *Pandanggo sa Ilaw* symbolized light for them." In 1971, Jean Guiang became the first cultural director of the Philippine Dance Ensemble (now the Kayumanggi Philippine Performing Arts in Winnipeg) of the Philippine Association of Manitoba (PAM), and for the next eight years the group participated in the famous Folklorama festival. She was instrumental in bringing Philippine culture into mainstream activities in Manitoba and was elected president of PAM from 1988 to 1991. During her presidency, she initiated the relocation of the old Philippine Centre on Juno Street to its new site on Keewatin Street, where it is now the Philippine Canadian Centre of Manitoba (PCCM). Since its inauguration in 2004, the PCCM has been a hub for Filipinos in Winnipeg.

Perla Javate arrived in Canada in 1976 via the Netherlands.[10] She was hired in the Philippines by Berghause BV, a Dutch company, as the social worker responsible for a group of young Filipino women garment workers bound for Holland. The initial contract for three years in Holland was cut short when the Berghause garment factories closed down. Perla facilitated the immigration of 92 of the 120 garment workers to Canada by inviting Silpit Industries, which had several garment factories in Winnipeg, to visit and interview the women for possible jobs so they could enter Canada as permanent residents; the rest of the workers were allowed to stay in the Netherlands. Perla initially planned to move to Toronto but went first to Winnipeg to visit the garment workers for four months; she ended up staying for over thirty years. As president of the Philippine Heritage Council of Manitoba (PHCM) for a number of years,[11] she is respected for her leadership and management skills. Remarkably, she has united the large Filipino community in Winnipeg and drawn ever-increasing participation in their activities from Canadians.[12] As she puts it, "My volunteer work is more demanding than my full-time job."

Gemma Dalayoan was a teacher in the Philippines who migrated to Canada with her family in 1976. She was one of the founders of the Bicol Association of Manitoba in 1983 and the Manitoba Filipino Writers' Guild in 1998.[13] She served as president of the Manitoba Association of Filipino Teachers thrice, between 1988 and 2011. She started as a teacher's assistant in Manitoba, then became a classroom teacher before becoming the vice-principal in three schools until her retirement in 2004. She is a prolific writer and a poet, and has co-authored a work on the first Filipino immigrants in Manitoba (Dalayoan, Enverga-Magsino, and Bailon 2008). In 2010, she was appointed to the board of directors of the Winnipeg Regional Health Authority (WHRA) by the Manitoba Minister of Health.

Estrella "Estrel" Dato arrived in Saskatoon in 1970.[14] She has volunteered in various multicultural organizations in Saskatchewan. In 1975, with thirty-nine Filipinos in the area, Estrel was instrumental in founding the Filipino-Canadian Association of Saskatoon (FILCAS). She started the first dance group with a few pioneering nurses and teachers and, with the federal multiculturalism policy still in its infancy, received a grant to stage Filipiniana performances, travelling with the dance group to different small towns in Saskatchewan and showcasing Filipino culture. From these modest beginnings evolved the Kumintang Folk Ensemble (KFE), which for over thirty years has presented dances at the Philippine Pavilion during the annual Saskatoon Folkfest. Philippine folk dances as a medium of cultural exchange in Canada led to the KFE's two SEVEC (Society for Educational Visits and Exchanges in Canada) youth exchanges.[15] According to Estrel, "youth leadership is being honed and developed through these youth exchanges. I consider it a personal achievement that through involvement in folk dancing and Filipino ethnic instrumentation, they learn something about themselves, their culture, and become proud of their unique identity." She has helped to fuse Philippine arts and culture into a rich tapestry in the lives of many Filipinos, young and old. She says: "My biggest achievement is personal: Knowing that I had a small hand in having a strong Filipino community in Saskatoon ... contributed in educating and sharing my culture ... through which tolerance, understanding, and happy co-existence is achieved." Another person who has been active in FILCAS is Felicitas "Fay" Santos-Vargas, who served as president in 2004-5 and secretary in 2008-9; she is also a columnist in the organization's newsletter, *BALITA*, and has been involved in other ways since her arrival in Saskatoon in 1980, including with the Filipino Heritage School.[16] She volunteers as an assistant for Dr. Carlos Maningas, the Philippine Honorary Consul for the province of Saskatchewan.

The efforts of these exemplars of *Pinay* activism to build a strong network of Filipinos follow similar efforts of earlier cohorts of immigrant women in Canada. For example, Latvian-born Rita Gerse in Ontario became involved in her ethnic organization not only for the value of charitable work but also as "a tool for ensuring that her children, whom she enrolled in heritage classes and folk dancing, did not lose their culture" (Parr 1995, 151). Culture foregrounds national identity and belonging, evokes pride in one's heritage in diaspora. Many of these *Pinay* community leaders in the Prairies are engaged in promoting Philippine heritage through folkloric arts, crafts, dances, and food – a general pattern among other ethnic communities in Canada and Australia (Stratton 2005; Pietrobruno 2006; Bottomley 2010).

In her study of Greek folk dancing in Canada, Caterina Pizania reveals that "government funding was plentiful if the group was involved in folkloric activities – such as dance – but there was almost no funding for contemporary poetry/or Greek theater" (cited in Kamboureli 2009, 107). She adds that "when we go public, so to speak, as Greeks in multicultural Canada, we are expected to perform a heritage that in many ways is as awkward, foreign, and exotic to us as it is to our audiences" (ibid.). Greek folkloric dancing demonstrates how a "heritage is pruned and tended before it is performed for the audience of the host country" (ibid.). Critics of multiculturalism point to the containment of ethnic-minority groups whose rich cultural traditions become the "other" to Canadians (Pietrobruno 2006, 98). Peter Li reveals the two-tiered system of funding for arts and culture between American/European and visible minorities: the former, with its orchestral music and ballet, is supported by the Canada Council; the latter, with its folk arts, by federal multicultural programs, primarily to "celebrate Canadian diversity" and their "ethnic exoticism" (cited in Pietrobruno 2006, 98).

Although the promotion of Philippine culture and heritage is but one area of activity among Filipino associations and is mostly directed by women, it appears to be the hub for community organizing and liasing. Filipino folk arts are one of many patches in the Canadian multicultural mosaic and visibly mark Filipinos as the "ethnic other" from a "white gaze" (Fanon [1952]

2008, 95). Claiming a limited space in a Western society that constructs the "other" as "exotic" can be read from another perspective. Multiculturalism as a practice derived from a policy that places the creativity of ethnic artists on a predetermined agenda for Canada Day is akin to a "performance on demand," where the "other" performs that part of their culture that defines their identity – a form of cultural consumerism. The space and place for a public performance of the presence of Filipinos in the community is, however, merely one aspect of their story. While the outcomes of such public cultural displays are the focal point of critics of multiculturalism, I am particularly interested in the processes involved in bringing together for a particular exhibition a community led by women, and in how these processes transcend the individual *Pinay*. I acknowledge the good intentions of these women who are involved in organizing children and adults to create a dance/arts synergy and the unpaid hours spent in completing a task, negotiating schedules that are next to impossible, and relying on their own creativity and their recollection of the skills required to put on the performance. They start with what is familiar through the only public opportunity to show their pride in their heritage, regardless of whether it produces an aura of exoticism. Viewing their contribution as simply part of the exotic fold prioritizes the senses of the "Canadian public" who may also be "exotic," not the immigrant women and men with their children and friends who may gain something from the experience. In a way, folk arts become the festive avenue of all that is, from the vantage point of the "other," what makes the Canadian imaginary of multiculturalism meaningful.

The narratives of individual *Pinays* in the Prairies indicate the importance of engagement with heritage activities. All of the community exemplars mentioned in this section are also involved with other causes or issues affecting the Filipino community. I surmise that participation in these initial activities developed their self-confidence and enabled them to connect with their communities. Celebratory multiculturalism provides them with the space to hone their leadership skills before moving on to other interests, and to mentor newcomers who will replenish the pool of community leaders. Messias (2011, 156) relates community engagement to immigrant women's health and well-being in urban areas, which parallels the experiences of *Pinays* in the Prairies. Their participation in ethnic-inspired events may be downplayed in political and scholarly discourses of multiculturalism, but what is missing from such discourses are the positive effects of this kind of participation on the development of the personal and social well-being of immigrant women, particularly racialized Filipinos, who may embrace the opportunity to promote their own happiness, by meeting with friends, going out of the house, sharing stories, and so on.

The opportunity to network in a family-friendly atmosphere also enhances the value to Filipino women of imparting their cultural heritage to their children. Dewey (1938) argues that the new modalities of education and democracy should recognize the maintenance of "cultural balance" "between the ethnic heritage of immigrants and societal harmony" (cited in Stuckart and Glanz 2010, 29). In the absence of a culturally rooted curriculum in formal school settings for diverse immigrants in Canada, heritage activities for public exhibition provide the space for immigrant youth to learn about and understand their own heritage. Following the Filipino saying *ang ina ay ang unang guro* (the mother is the first teacher), first-generation *Pinay* moms in the Prairies appear to use community events as an informal method of giving their children a glimpse of Philippine culture and nurturing a love of their traditions, although these are interpreted in various artistic forms.

Towards a Multicultural Community
Pinay leaders also engage the wider multicultural community in the Prairies. Their voluntary involvement demonstrates initiative in building bridges with other women and organizations, although most of these opportunities result from their being considered representatives of the Filipino community. Some have made a name for themselves and are likely sought for their contribution to programs and services affecting residents in the province. Gemma Dalayoan, for example, is an active volunteer not only with Filipino associations (see "Towards the Filipino Community," above) but also with government and non-governmental organizations in Manitoba. She has served in notable positions, most recently being appointed by the provincial Minister of Health to the board of the Winnipeg Regional Health Authority from 2010 to 2013.[17]

In addition to her involvement with the Filipino community (see "Towards the Filipino Community," above), Jean Guiang was one of the board members of the Folk Arts Council of Winnipeg and led the Queens and Mayors, representatives of the Folklorama's forty-four pavilions for three years. She also acted as mayor, ambassador, coordinator, chairperson, and volunteer in many aspects of Folklorama. In 1972, she was leader of the group that assisted new immigrants at the International Centre of Winnipeg. She was a co-founder of the Immigrant Women's Association of Manitoba (IWAM) in 1983 and its executive secretary for six years, as well as co-founder of the National Organization of Immigrant and Visible Minority Women of Canada in 1986 and Manitoba's first delegate for three years. Jean has held numerous appointments with government and non-governmental agencies. As a result of her significant contributions and civic work, she has received many awards, the most prestigious of which was the Order of Manitoba, presented by the Lieutenant-Governor of Manitoba in 2004.[18]

In Alberta, Tessie Oliva's volunteerism extends to the wider community as well. A nurse who has worked tirelessly to improve her own profession (see "Volunteerism to Improve Professions," above), she was also the first president of the non-profit Multicultural Coalition Society for Equity in Health and Well Being; an advisory board member of the Edmonton Multicultural Association; a member of the leadership team for Capacity Canada and of the advisory committee of Capacity Alberta, the national and provincial associations working to recognize and accredit internationally trained professionals; a board member of the Alberta Multicultural Commission from 1990 to 1994; and a member of the board of directors of the Edmonton Heritage Association since 2006. In recognition of her community involvement, Tessie received the RISE (Recognizing Immigrant Success and Endeavors) Award – Community Service Category in 2005 and the Stars of Alberta Volunteer Award in 2009 from the government of Alberta.

Lucenia M. Ortiz understands the struggles of many newcomers to Canada. Since her arrival in Edmonton in the 1990s, she has worked extensively with immigrant and refugee communities at the Multicultural Health Brokers' Cooperative, where she served as co-executive director from 2000 to 2008. As a multicultural educator and practitioner, Lucenia engages in numerous voluntary community activities in Alberta.[19]

Through the years, Josephine Pallard has been a staunch advocate and organizer for Filipinos and other immigrants (see also "Towards the Filipino Community," above). As a teacher of English as a Second Language (ESL), she was instrumental in creating the Alberta Ethnic Language Teachers Association, now the International and Heritage Languages Association, in 1978. She first began teaching English to Lebanese women in her kitchen and later extended this voluntary initiative to international students. She has also assisted immigrant women in upgrading their professional qualifications. In 1984, Josephine became one of the founding leaders of Changing Together, a Centre for Immigrant Women, whose brochure describes it as "the only organization in Edmonton that focuses exclusively on the needs of all immigrant women." She served on its board of directors for six years and, after retiring from her teaching post in 2005, became its executive director, a position that she occupied until June 2012. Josephine is passionate about empowering immigrant women in Edmonton and believes that breaking barriers to integration is the key to their success. According to Alice Colak, director of immigration and settlement services at Alberta's Catholic Social Services, "she is an amazing leader who is excellent at building relationships in the community and meeting people's needs" (cited in Gonzalez 2007).

In Saskatchewan, Estrel Dato has served as director and secretary of Saskatoon Folkfest Inc., as well as secretary and newsletter editor of the Multicultural Council of Saskatoon, now the Saskachewan Intercultural Association. Fay Vargas-Santos, interviewed on 31 July 2009, expressed her enthusiasm for teaching heritage languages, saying that "we need to contribute to the community not only for the benefit of the Filipinos but to the general community as well." Cognizant of the importance of race relations in Canada, she has advocated for many activities encouraging cross-cultural harmony. According to her, "everybody is welcome in Canada. There is a sense of feeling good of what we do. When we accomplish something you're part of the group." Her commitment to creating a welcoming community for all in Saskatoon has inspired her to volunteer in various organizations, and she has served on the board of directors of both the Saskatchewan Intercultural Association and the Saskatchewan Organization for Heritage Languages. For her contributions to the community, Fay received the Saskatchewan Centennial Medal for cultural volunteerism in 2005. She declares: "There are so many things we could do in both cultures." (For details of Estrel and Fay's involvement with the Filipino community in Saskatchewan, see "Towards the Filipino Community," above.)

These *Pinays* in the Prairies have all built lasting cross-cultural linkages that serve as a foundation for future Filipino immigrant women, and possibly other racialized immigrant women, in their communities. Theirs is a collective story of overcoming difficulties in a new country, of using their talents and abilities to create a niche for Filipinos and other marginalized groups, of empowering themselves to empower others. Such cross-cultural engagements of immigrant women, particularly racialized women, have not received much scholarly attention in migration discourse, however (Bonifacio 2012). The focus remains on difficulties in their economic and social integration in host communities and not on how they are able to forge cross-cultural alliances as part of the larger society.

Volunteerism for Social Justice
Striving for social justice includes

> developing an understanding of distributive principles (fair allocation of rewards) and retributive principles (appropriate responses to harm); how they relate to political economy and historical conditions; their local and global manifestations; the struggle for their institutionalization; how human well-being and development at the social and individual levels is enhanced by their institutionalization; and developing evaluative criteria or processes by which we may measure their effects. (Capeheart and Milovanovic 2007, 2)

The ideals of social justice, albeit complex and context-based, perhaps provide the major inspiration for grounded volunteerism among Filipino women in Canada. As a whole, the activist *Pinay* organizations embrace social justice, for instance, to promote the rights and welfare of TFWs subject to unfair practices and legislation, many of whom belong, or previously belonged, to these same organizations or occupational groups. Clearly, what is just for the Canadian state as expressed through policies set by governments may not be just after all to those affected by those policies. The bases for calling for social justice may differ; for example, TFWs may refer to international law and not domestic law in Canada in the absence of legislative protection. Social justice forms part of the strand of inspiration for those working against racism and discrimination in all facets of human life.

In our interview on 21 August 2009, Jomay Amora-Mercado, secretary-general of Damayan Manitoba, a group of around twenty members, mostly immigrant Filipino women, recalled the many instances of discrimination and workplace exploitation that ignited her passion for activism as a student in the Philippines and as a TFW in Canada: *"Hindi pala naiiba ang Canada* [Canada is not really different] ... *akala mo advanced sila pero* [you think they are advanced but] *oppression and abuses exist. Hindi nagbabago* [nothing changes]."* While working in Edmonton, she realized that even Canadians suffer abuse at the hands of their employers. Jomay was one of the founding members of Damayan Manitoba. Her background at the University of the Philippines, with its activist slogan *"Kung hindi ikaw, sino?* [if not you, who?]," inspired her to help create Damayan Manitoba in 2008 in response to local, national, and international issues.

Maria Bella "Maribel" Javier arrived in Calgary with her family in 1999.[20] In our interview on 4 July 2009, she said that she decided to get involved in the community while looking for a job: "I have no job then so I volunteered a lot. I do not want my skills to stagnate. I am a social activist back home." She eventually became one of the co-founders of BABAE Council of Filipina-Canadian Women in 2003 (see "Personal Politics and Feminism," above). Together with five other women, Maribel aims to empower Filipino women in Canadian society, especially those who find themselves in crisis situations.

From these examples of *Pinay* leaders in the Prairies, it is clear that volunteerism for social justice means engagement for change and for recognition. Fraser (2003, 7) argues that social justice takes two major forms today: redistributive claims and recognition. Redistributive claims "seek a more just distribution of resources and wealth" and recognition for the "distinctive perspectives of ethnic, 'racial,' and sexual minorities, as well as gender difference" (ibid.). While Fraser (2003) is concerned with identity politics and the politics of recognition, her argument can be applied to the case of *Pinays* in the Prairies who are advocating for the rights and interests of TFWs and women. Subordinate groups such as immigrants form an "alternative public" or "subaltern counterpublics," which, according to Fraser (1995, 291-92), provide the "awareness in which to undertake communicative processes" and "deliberate on their needs, objectives and strategies." Their grounded work to change policies that exploit migrant labour in Canada seems consistent with the "politics of recognition" (Fraser 2003, 7) – of recognition of their human rights. In the Prairies, activist *Pinay* leaders run public campaigns similar to those found in Toronto, Vancouver, and Montreal, especially during commemorative days and events. No matter how small these activities may seem, these *Pinay* leaders create ripple effects in raising public awareness of, and solidarity with, the plight of TFWs in their communities.

Volunteerism Motivated by Circumstances

Grounded volunteerism is experiential. Sometimes it may be a product of choice, at other times a result of circumstance. Helena and her family in Regina became active volunteers in their community, helping at-risk Aboriginal youth, after unknowingly violating a city ordinance prohibiting signage in lawns of private property.

> *We volunteer at ... Family Centre, centre for Aboriginal people ... we help kids*
> *... There is a drop-in centre after school ... In evening they go swimming ...*
> *My husband and me volunteer ... after a long story. The City fined us with*
> *a sign on our lawn, "Young Athletes for Saskatchewan" signage on the lawn*
> *without our knowledge. It's not allowed by the city by-law and we paid the*
> *fine. In the second year, this group put up the sign again while we were on*
> *holiday. So, a fine again, about $900-$1,000 and then went to court ... Even*
> *if we are not there it's our property. It's our responsibility to take off the sign.*
> *Instead of paying fine we chose to work in the community.*
> – Helena, a nurse in Regina

Helena's family opted to render community service instead of paying the hefty fine. That was about five years ago. They are still volunteers at North Central, working "the toughest neighborhood in the whole country." Helena adds: "Most of them are criminals, but these people have lots of problems in their life. Since my husband organized the marathon team, no more car theft among the kids." Helena's family may have become involved by court fiat, but their continuing volunteerism not only provides support to marginalized Aboriginal youths but also testifies to their belief in promoting healthier lifestyles and safer communities.

These forms of grounded volunteerism illustrate different kinds of community engagement among the *Pinays* in the Prairies: as leaders, supporters, and members. Although commendable in its purposes and motivations, volunteerism is not for every *Pinay* in the Prairies. As gleaned from the life experiences of live-in caregivers, this may be due to a number of factors, including: no spare time to volunteer, multiple jobs or shift work, lack of knowledge of volunteer opportunities, limited access to places of volunteer work, distance between residence and place of volunteer work, lack of transportation, and exclusion. Mothers with young children or with other care responsibilities at home tend not to prioritize volunteer work. The absence of a support network makes all these familial tasks, coupled with paid work, seem daunting. However, those *Pinays* who make the effort to participate in community activities and engage with issues that affect their lives and those of others in similar situations demonstrate grounded volunteerism, not invisibility. Dobrowolsky (2008, 446) notes that racialized immigrant women in Canada "continue to exert their agency, and despite formidable constraints, interrogate such processes that serve to limit the terms and scope of citizenship in Canada." *Pinays* in the Prairies thus interact within their own communities and with the larger society in expected and unexpected ways.

Filipino Communities

The concept of community is highly contested in different disciplines because of its ambiguity and generic usage (Mannarini and Fedi 2009). In political theory, Little (2002, 1) notes the "lack of conceptual clarity around community" and the impossibility of "provid[ing] an acceptable definition of community to everyone." What is apparent is the generic view of community as a form of collectivity with shared values in which individuals find "rootedness, cohesion and belonging" (Little 2002, 2). Sociological conceptions of the community based on structure encompass the following: "(1) the nature of social bonds and relations; (2) group membership and size; (3) organizational structure and social hierarchy; and (4) the role and form of community institutions and organizing" (Campbell 2000, 25-26). An important consideration for members of a community is the "network of connections" (Campbell 2000, 28) configured as a "web of individual *nodes* (people, groups, institutions, states, or other collectives) interconnected through a series of *ties* (friendship, kinships, resource exchanges, or other forms of formal and informal relations)" (29).

Another aspect of the community that fits well in this section is the issue of "power and influence" (Campbell 2000, 30) that impacts relations between and among members. How power is demonstrated, either directly or indirectly, reflects the distinctive histories, culture, and process of community formation. Beyond the spatial, institutional, and structural interplay of bonds and relations is the succinct notion of community as *sentiment* – in other words, what Campbell (2000, 43) refers to as "community as felt, experienced, conceived (imagined) or communicated entity."

Studies on Filipinos in diaspora highlight the dynamic community associations in areas of settlement (Okamura 1998; Espiritu 2003a; Buell et al. 2008). Filipino community formation in diaspora represents, according to Cruz (1994, 235), a distinct survival strategy in response to hostile environments. He adds (244):

> Communities provide avenues for people to establish networks ... with whom they identify and ... reflect on shared circumstances; they make possible a

supportive social milieu that promotes ... collective meanings and interests ... foster opportunities to define ... needs; and they facilitate the mobilization of resources ... including the strengthening and maintenance of emotional and psychic bonds, the pooling of economic assets, the organization of cultural activities ... promote the community's well-being.

Living away from the comfort and familiarity of the home country often leads to migrants' finding of the same in ethnic-based community groups. While there is a rich literature on Filipino associations in the United States, particularly on the establishment of regional associations and cultural activities (Lau 2007; Tyner 2007; Lim and Pangan-Specht 2010), its Canadian counterpart remains sparse (Lusis n.d.; Chen 1998; Silva 2006; Del Rio-Laquian and Laquian 2008). In both countries, however, a gendered analysis of their role in Filipino women's lives is still lacking.

Compared with men, women tend to socialize more and are more other-centred. They are "typically more expressive in public or social settings" and "show more social responsivity and affiliativeness" than men (Burgoon and Bacue 2008, 184). This translates into their participation in community activities through volunteer work. Esteves (2002, 230) notes that "volunteering is largely the work of women, both in terms of its symbolic construction and material performance." Filipino women in Canada have been actively involved in community organizations – as leaders, volunteers, members, and even simply as sympathizers. However, this type of civic engagement has not received much scholarly interest in Canadian migration discourse. This section presents *Pinay* perspectives on Filipino organizations, the impact of Filipino values on their community engagement, and notions of women's leadership.

Filipino Community Organizations

The formation of organizations or quasi-groups is common among Filipinos. The diversity of groups reflects varied interests and goals – cultural, political, religious, social, and athletic, to name a few. Their existence demonstrates groupism and collective orientation among Filipinos wherever they may be. It is often said that "whenever Filipinos get together, they form a club" (Tyner 2007, 264). In Canada, formal, informal, and even casual groupings of Filipinos contribute to their visibility in community public spaces. Filipino community organizations, according to Tyner (2007, 264), "serve as social spaces that promote group solidarity and cohesiveness." Migration gives Filipinos the opportunity to share stories, discuss settlement concerns, build friendships, preserve cultural traditions, or work out plans to help others. The network of friends and associates forms part of the social capital that Filipino newcomers rely on "to meet various needs and interests" in the course of their settlement and adjustment (Vissandjée, Apale, and Wieringa

2009, 186). Filipino community organizations, like many other immigrant associations, are a "source of cultural survival" where memories of the homeland bloom afresh in the various cultural activities (Perez 1999, 76). Almirol (1985), in his study of a Filipino community in Salinas, California, notes that Filipinos engage in social and recreational activities such as dances, potluck lunches, ticket raffles, beauty contests, sightseeing trips, and parties. These activities characterize many Filipino community associations in diaspora.

In contrast to the individualist orientation of Western societies, Filipinos tend to find a group that makes adaptation easier. Del Rio-Laquian and Laquian (2008, 174) report that a survey of Filipinos in Canada conducted in 2006 found that 67.1 percent were members of at least one organization; for those who arrived in Canada before 1981, that figure was 85.7 percent. Being other-centred may contribute to making Filipinos the "second happiest people in Asia," according to the Axa Asia Outlook Index (Arcibal 2007). Migration for many is a lonely venture and belonging to a group is therapeutic. A number of live-in caregivers in southern Alberta find casual groupings on weekends a way to enjoy a karaoke blast. It is also common practice among Filipino live-in caregivers who are still under the terms of the LCP to share room rental expenses so that they can be together on weekends, when they can cook Filipino dishes, share stories of home, and enjoy simple together-ness. (Many of them claim that the distinctive smell of Filipino dishes offends their employers.) Such "rooming groups" become like family to these migrant women.

As discussed in Chapter 3, Filipino community associations contribute significantly towards resolving the initial settlement difficulties of new-comers, particularly those who do not access services provided by conventional immigrant-serving agencies. Chen (1999) highlights the role of these associations in linking Filipinos with Canadian society.

> It's very cold here, but people are warm in Saskatoon. Filipinos who come here are very self-sufficient ... Do not need government or immigrant services. Mas madali tayong mag-adjust [we adjust quite easily] ... Filipinos are considered ideal immigrants. There is more support for the Filipino community that they do not need outside help ... we are more independent ... more Westernized, we have a language, easier for us to be adjusted than other cultures.
> – Sharon, a former garment worker in Saskatoon

The ready network of Filipinos in the community aids in the process of adaptation and transition. Filipino groups tend to form along the lines of particular interests or shared experiences, mostly regional in origin, in the Philippines. Newcomers from the same region find ethno-specific groups a medium for facilitating transition to a Canadian lifestyle. Within major associations, there may be further subgroups based on common interests, which can be useful in addressing specific concerns not addressed by the larger group (Bonifacio 2003).

In Alberta, the Filipino business directory (CalgaryFilipino.com) lists nine associations and clubs. Other Filipino groups include the Fil-Nannies Foundation, Cavite Association of Calgary, Filipino Calgarian Seniors Club, and the Filipino Canadian Nurses Network. An umbrella organization of Filipino associations is the Calgary Federation of Filipino Associations, formed in 1989. In Edmonton, the Council of Edmonton Filipino Associations was founded in 1988 with eight Filipino associations. It now has a strong base of about twenty-six associations. Women's associations in Edmonton include the Filipino Canadian Women's Barangay Association of Alberta, Filipino Women's Association of Alberta, the Karilagan Dance Society, and informal groups of Filipino caregivers in Alberta.

May mga [there are about] *forty-three Filipino organizations in Edmonton, lots are social clubs and not social-development organizations.*
    – Julita, a community worker in Edmonton

In Manitoba, Filipino community organizations have been the most active of all immigrant groups for the past fifty years. As the largest visible-minority population in Manitoba, Filipinos appear to have crafted an image of themselves as "ideal immigrants" (Barber 2008). Their high levels of participation in mainstream-sponsored activities produced the first Filipino Member of Parliament, Dr. Rey Pagtakhan (1988-2004), who also became the first Filipino cabinet minister in Canada (2001-4) in the Liberal governments of Jean Chrétien and Paul Martin; the first Filipino elected to the Legislative Assembly of Manitoba in 1981, Dr. Conrad Santos; and, in 2007, the first Filipino woman elected to the Legislative Assembly, Flor Marcelino, MLA for Wellington. The emergence of elected Filipino officials in Manitoba can also be attributed to the degree of residential concentration among Filipinos in Winnipeg, as opposed to the wide dispersal of their counterparts in Toronto and Vancouver (Kelly 2010, 161). Winnipeg has the highest concentration of Filipinos, at 5.9 percent of the total population of the City of Winnipeg based on the 2006 census (City of Winnipeg 2006). They are overconcentrated in the city itself, with 6.7 percent and 32.5 percent of them living in 50 and 90 percent of the 2001 census tracts, respectively (Balakrishnan, Ravanera, and Abada 2005). These concentrations prove significant in contesting electoral seats (Hill 2002, 353). In the 2011 provincial election, three Filipinos vied for the seat in Tyndall Park, ensuring Filipino representation of this constituency (Alcuitas 2011). Filipinos in Manitoba have achieved political representation at the municipal, provincial, and federal levels, a feat not replicated in Saskatchewan or even Ontario as of 2011.[21]

In 1962, the first Filipino association to be organized in Manitoba was composed mainly of nurses and doctors (Dalayoan, Enverga-Magsino, and Bailon 2008), by 2009, the Philippine Heritage Council of Manitoba was listing thirty-six member organizations (PHCM 2009).

> *The main purpose of the Philippine Heritage Council is to make it work as a unified body, this is always a challenge ... The events continue to flow because more people are getting ownership.*
> – Pilar, a community worker in Winnipeg

The Manitoba Council of Filipino Associations was organized in late 2008, with seven founding, mostly regional, organizations. It envisions uniting more than fifty Filipino organizations and planned for the first convention of Filipino associations in Western Canada in 2010 (*Filipino Journal* 2009b).

> *Malakas ang mga Filipino dito* [Filipinos are strong here] ... *strong regionalism. Luckily there are many people working to bridge that gap ... It's healthy to have many organizations so long as you don't put others down.*
> – Josefina, self-employed in Winnipeg

> *I cannot say much. They come from all over the place ... There are over thirty regional Filipino associations here. It's good to have different organizations. An umbrella organization also exists; it's a big community. Filipinos are regionalistic.*
> – Luningning, a community leader in Winnipeg

At a time when no immigrant services were available, Filipino associations in Manitoba "played a great role in assisting the almost simultaneous arrivals in the '60s of five batches of garment workers straight from the Philippines and from Holland" (Dalayoan, Enverga-Magsino, and Bailon 2008, 80). The tradition of warmly welcoming newcomers to Winnipeg has continued through the years. Today, Filipinos in Manitoba take pride in the renaming of Keewatin Street north of Santa Fe as Dr. Jose Rizal Way in 2008 (*Filipino Journal* 2008a).[22]

In Saskatchewan, the Philippine Association of Saskatchewan (PAS) in Regina and the Filipino-Canadian Association of Saskatoon are the two mainstay Filipino groups. Although diversity appears to be the norm among Filipino organizations, only a few formally organized Filipino associations have thrived in the province since the 1970s. Eusebio Koh, mathematics professor emeritus at the University of Regina, was the co-founder of PAS and served as its first president from 1971 to 1972. FILCAS was founded in 1973, with Dr. Lino Pabello as its first president (Dato 2004). Dr. Carlos Maningas, former president of FILCAS and now honorary consul for the Philippines in the province of Saskatchewan, writes (2004, 11):

> FILCAS is a lighthouse that show and guide them [new immigrants] all the way into the new world. To the few, it provides a safe haven to protect them from abusive employers. It consoles those who are grieving for departed relatives. In rare instances, it provides help for disillusioned compatriots who couldn't make a go here and decide to go back. These are but a few of the things the association is able to do, and [has] done in the past.

Like other Filipino associations, FILCAS held meetings in the homes of officers. In 1998, it moved into its first rented office, in Regent Plaza. In recognition of the Filipino contribution to the city of Saskatoon, 12 June – which also marks the anniversary of the declaration of Philippine independence from Spain – was designated Filipino-Canadian Day in 2004. Some of the notable projects undertaken by FILCAS since 2008 include the Saskatchewan Immigrant Nominee Program (SINP) Community Capacity Building Fund, which assists newcomers, as well as fundraisers such as bingo, camping at Glenburn Regional Park, the Saskatoon Folkfest, Christmas parties, sports, and a seniors' social club (*Balita* 2008). Through the years, it has collaborated with the Filipino council of Knights of Columbus (San Lorenzo Ruiz Council), Filipino Senior's Social Group, Santo Niño core group, Saskatoon Filipino Community Church, and the Filipino Heritage School (Dato 2004).

> *There is only one Filipino organization, FILCAS. Seniors used to be with FILCAS but are now doing things on their own ... Regional groups socialize together but go as one; we are proud of the Filipino community. The structure is already there. People come in and join.*
> – Filomena, a government employee in Saskatoon

> *There are different groups but they have not set up their own organization ... But they tend to group together. Out of 5,000 Filipinos in Saskatoon only about 500 are members in Filipino-Canadian Association. Regional groups do not contribute yet, don't get involved.*
> – Victoria, a private employee in Saskatoon

For *Pinays* in the Prairies, the existence of many Filipino community associations is both positive and negative. Although, they offer a sure way to belong to a group and to promote Filipino culture in many respects they also suffer from a duplication of activities, can be time-consuming, and often foster divisiveness.

> *Very positive groupings. Mga* [these are] *support groups for specific regions. They are thriving and play a major role. The setback is one country and is not a unified group. The Philippine Heritage Council of Manitoba efforts to unify action despite differences ... unify them for a cause.*
> – Pilar, a community worker in Winnipeg

> *Regional groupings are strong in fundraising. But with so many groups it is difficult to unify them.*
> – Asuncion, a nurse in Winnipeg

> *This is evident [sic] by almost fifty regional organizations here. I was one of the few community leaders who opposed the use of exclusive banners ... puro kanya-kanya* [almost to each their own] *... The first effect of regionalism is to create division rather than unity. But I have no objection ... On one side it divides but on the other hand it enhances, help people outside the Philippines appreciate our culture ... Like Indians, the mountain people in the Philippines have been oppressed by white people or others. We are proud to be called Ifugaos, etc. This really demonstrates the uniqueness of our culture.*
> – Gabriela, a retired government employee in Winnipeg

Some Filipino organizations collaborate with other community organizations that complement their activities. At times they rely on the expertise of a different group to conduct a particular activity for the benefit of their own members. In supporting other groups, organizations hope for the same positive response – a kind of trade-off to ensure the success of their own activities.

> *It helps, too. Nalalaman ko may mga program sila* [I learned that they have programs]. *May dancing* [there is dancing]. *May lectures sa seniors* [there are lectures for seniors]. *Nag-represent din kami* [we also represent (our group)]. *We collaborate with them and [they] return the favour as well.*
> – Dulce, a retired teacher in Calgary

One of the measures of success for a Filipino community activity is the number of participants; the more people who attend, the better for the sponsoring organization. Hence, it is important for community leaders to personally attend events in anticipation of receiving the same level of support for their own activities in the future. Filipino women usually outnumber men at these various activities and are the undeclared ambassadors of goodwill between organizations.

Another indicator of a successful event is the participation of key political figures and celebrities. It is standard practice among Filipino organizations to invite politicians and known personalities to their activities (Bonifacio 2003). I would argue that the strength of the New Democratic Party in Manitoba electoral politics is partly due to the political culture of immigrant Filipinos, long oriented towards this form of civic participation. Filipinos, together with the Sikh community, are the "strongest of all visible minority groups" in their "influence in civic, political and federal politics" in Manitoba (Wesley and Summerlee 2011, 13). The presence of politicians at Filipino community affairs symbolizes the value they place on immigrants or their eagerness to court their support; either way, it is significant that such relations translate into actual votes through Filipino cultural values such as *pakikisama* (smooth interpersonal relations) or *utang na loob* (debt of gratitude) (Hedman and Sidel 2000, 6). These concepts will be discussed in the next section.

One of the oft-cited negative aspects of Filipino groups is internal politics, usually politics of personalities. Filipinos tend to form cliques, with certain leaders influencing a group of followers or members following a certain leader. Contention among leaders divides organizations, with the stronger group winning the right to control the group's activities. These forms of "*barangay* politics" (village politics) are reminiscent of Philippine party politics, wherein dissatisfied leaders form their own political groups (Rocamora 2007; Esguerra 2011). Unfortunately, in-group politics discourages many younger Filipinos in Canada from getting involved.

> *There are different organizations in Manitoba ... most spend politics on fighting. We need a little bit more of solidarity to become stronger. Impossible to ask for – to stop infighting, mistreatment ... It's harder to be mean when being mean is being right. Sometimes culture makes us weaker. Young people are passionate and interested but don't want the politics.*
> – Vivian, a public health worker in Winnipeg

> *We need more youths to be elected to the Board of PCCM ... they are our future. But what happens is that the youths are turned off by the matatanda* [older folks] *because of the way ... mga palakad nila ... mga away* [how they implement ... the infighting]. *Nag-quit din sila* [they also quit].
> – Lumen, a finance officer in Winnipeg

In the 1980s, Aranas's study (1983, 116) of Filipino immigrants in Canada noted that "associational life is disrupted by internal squabbles and petty bickering." The same holds true today among Filipino organizations, although smaller associations tend to have limited resources and are often organized for specific purposes, thereby reducing the intensity of such infighting.

In general, Filipino community organizations contribute significantly to the settlement, adaptation, and integration of newcomers in the Prairies. Filipino immigrants' postwar history of community engagement shows their resiliency in working with each other to make their lives meaningful and to be productive in their adopted country. Statistics Canada notes that Filipinos actively participate in Canadian society; in fact, the 2002 Ethnic Diversity Survey revealed that 78 percent of Filipinos had a strong sense of belonging to Canada, and almost 90 percent had strong affiliations with the Filipino community (Lindsay 2007).

Both Filipinos and non-Filipinos may view the personality politics and in-group bickering as a negative that mimics Philippine-style politics (Vergara 2009), and express a desire for an all-inclusive Filipino association in their community. Although this pan-Filipino view is perhaps a sensible approach in order to effectively utilize limited resources in diaspora, I find the existence of internal politics a healthy aspect of human social interaction – of trying to win support for a particular cause, of expressing varied interests, and of encouraging diverse opinions and beliefs, especially in those uprooted from their homeland. In fact, this is democracy on the ground. A community group or association is a microcosm of society in which individual aspirations merge with collective pursuits. Groups embracing a liberal democratic framework usually resort to voting by majority to achieve a consensus. As we all know, however, this is not simply a mere casting of the ballot; it entails a far more rigorous process of lobbying to shape its outcome. The same process occurs in Filipino community associations, where members come face to face with the messy world of politics. Recognition of interests, after all, is a "fundamental, overarching moral category" (Fraser and Honneth 2003, 2-3).

To resolve personal and other concerns, Filipinos seek out groups that manifest their collectivist culture and socialization (Selmer and de Leon 2003). Filipinos find essence in a group that embraces their social identity, unlike the individualist in Western societies, who finds "self" at the core (Espiritu 2003a; Nie 2007). Filipino culture somehow encourages volunteering as an expression of community spirit (Skinner et al. 1995), where men and women of varying ages endeavour to get involved when time, occasion, and opportunity permit.

Filipino Values and Community Participation

Culture and community are intrinsically linked; culture is an "integral part of community" (Campbell 2000, 47). Organizations are forms of communities in which gender relations reinforce the patriarchal culture and values of a society (Chisanga 2003). Members hold particular cultural beliefs that may impact the way organizations are managed. As well, an organization may develop its own culture that shapes the participation of its members (Pauleen 2007). For both members and organizations, culture is a mutually constitutive element directing participation.

Community involvement is usually a matter of making choices – what to engage in, which activities to attend, and with whom. These are but a few personal considerations to weigh along with other factors (e.g., political and social) motivating such involvement. I would argue, however, that there are certain cultural values among Filipinos in diaspora that potentially contribute to why and how they become involved in community activities.

Big Filipino beliefs in the community ... For example, we welcome newcomers, feed them, embrace them, give clothing ... It's our culture, giving to the community.
– Clemencia, a nurse in Winnipeg

I identify with Filipino values, which a lot of cultures don't have.
– Vivian, a public health worker in Winnipeg

Filipino values in the community that is still very strong among us. Hindi ata maalis iyan [don't think we can do away with it]. *Ang values natin* [our values] *are still there. Malakas ang values natin. It's almost nakakagayuma* [Our values are strong. It's almost like a love spell.]
– Gabriela, a retired government employee in Winnipeg

Yes, there are relationships between values and participation in the community. I am always proud to be Filipino and wherever I am, I would like to be recognized as one. Because of our inherent hospitality, I do exercise that value especially to newcomers. Out of hiya [shame] *and pakikisama* [smooth interpersonal relations] *to a Filipino ... I do have high respect for the elders ... I normally go out my way to assist them even beyond what I can give. I do not expect utang na loob* [debt of gratitude] *from all the people I helped, but in a way I see that in them.*
– Carmen, a community worker in Calgary

Filipino cultural values play a major role in our activities everywhere and Filipinos are well liked and loved by people, especially our hospitality.
– Connie, a cleaner in Calgary

Based on these narratives, perceived Filipino normative cultural values somehow encourage community participation and facilitate or sustain volunteerism. These cultural values include *pakikisama* (smooth interpersonal relations), *utang na loob* (debt of gratitude), and respect for elders or authority. In his study on esteem values in the Philippines, Manlove (2004, 399) emphasizes that concepts such as *amor propio* (self-esteem), *hiya* (shame), *pakikisama*, and *utang na loob* "are not independently defined or independently operative" among Filipinos. The reiteration of these normative values in the socialization of Filipinos and development of their identity serves to educate them regarding their place in the social order. While seemingly part of the construction of a Filipino psychology *(Sikolohiyang Pilipino)* (Panopio and Rolda 2007; Pe-Pua and Perfecto 2012), these normative values essentialize Filipinos; contrary actions or behaviours, however, do not make them un-Filipino. Essentialism serves to romanticize certain aspects of a culture seen as unchanging and static (Fuchs 2001), but it is of scholarly interest to refer to these normative values and their role in Filipino women's community participation in diaspora. These expected norms act as a gauge of responsiveness and social identity among first-generation Filipinos in Canada. Like Penner (2000), who argues that orientation towards certain cultural values may influence how a person becomes involved in prosocial actions such as volunteerism, I include examples of Filipino value concepts in describing the community participation of *Pinays* in the Prairies.

Feminist scholars have focused their attention on women as "culture-bearers" (Shachar 2009, 152). I argue that the active presence of Filipino women in local organizations fosters the transmission of cultural values in Canada, reproducing them in the process of sustaining community life. Bourdieu and Lévi-Strauss view "women as bearers in their persons of embodied cultural capital" but also see them as "key functionaries and agents in the capital holding strategies of families, kin, ethnic group" among others (cited in Lovell 2004, 50). In the same manner, the volunteerism of Filipino women is both cultivated and sustained by socialized cultural values that contribute to maintaining group norms and expectations in Canada. This section looks at the impact of these values in the participation of *Pinays* in their communities. The discussion does not cover all Filipino values; rather, it demonstrates the use of a cultural lens to gain an understanding of their community engagement in diaspora.

Pakikisama

Kapwa (shared identity) is considered a core Filipino value that Gingrich (2002, 16) says "leads to heightened awareness and sensitivity to the feelings of another." Because of this strong moral ethic, *kapwa* is the determining factor without which "one ceases to be a Filipino and a human" (Enriquez 1993, cited in Tolentino 2004, 66). One manifestation of *kapwa* is *pakikisama*. *Pakikisama* (going along with others in order to maintain a good relationship) is a Filipino value aimed at sustaining smooth interpersonal relations. Lynch (1973, 10) suggests that *pakikisama* is interchangeable with "good public relations" and could mean in its "more restricted sense 'giving in'" or "following the lead or suggestion of another"; in other words, "concession." Some might describe this concept as "harmony" (Manlove 2004, 425). Filipinos hold this value in high regard, especially in achieving group goals or gaining social acceptance. In organizational practice, *pakikisama* is a "lauded practice of yielding to the will of the leaders or majority so as to make the group decision unanimous" (Lynch 1973, 10). Although there is no standard for defining *pakikisama*, whether as a trait, a norm, or a value (Enriquez 1992; Leoncini 2005), *pakikisama* is essentially an outward-looking process that positions the individual in a collective; the self assumes a secondary role in relation to the group, cause, or goal. Leoncini (2005, 172) notes that *pakikisama* "can, indeed, make the Filipino good whether we consider it a trait or norm towards a value, a part of a larger value, or a value itself." Hence, the expression of *pakikisama* tends to have positive impact in community relations.

> *Yes,* pakikisama *sometimes play a good part. People get involved, they do good ...* Pakikisama *is a very positive Filipino trait.*
> – Rowena, a manager in a media company in Winnipeg

> *All Filipino values come to play in relationship with community members within an organization.* Pakikisama *especially for first-generation immigrants and not for the second generation ... Kids now tend to be more independent, more self-centered ... we were taught to think of others and not just for ourselves but for families and extended families.*
> – Luningning, a community leader in Winnipeg

Philippine values are generally underlain by concepts of "selflessness and relatedness" (Lee Guy 2005, 136). Since the primacy of the group to which one belongs can supersede individual interests, Filipinos use culture-based interpersonal skills to negotiate tensions between the self and the collective. For example, Filipinos in diaspora have tended to sacrifice their personal wants in response to incessant requests for help. Life changes in migration, however, and this traditional normative value appears to be waning in younger generations. In Canada, Filipino immigrants like Luningning describe the lack of *pakikisama* among second-generation Filipino youth, who are now more familiar with a nuclear family model and exercise increasing autonomy in decision making. In my fieldwork, almost all of the Filipino associations were composed of first-generation immigrants, among whom explicit demonstrations of *pakikisama* remain strong.

Filipinos care. During surgery, I was down and depressed. They provided support ... Others do prayer. Pakikisama ... *even if we're tired we do it ... In the Philippines, we are very good to our neighbours. We have to know our community ... As Filipinos we are proud.* Pakikisama *is an individual thing.*
– Carolina, a retired teacher in Winnipeg

The reason we do not have a hard time here is because of our special relationship. Not utang na loob, *but more on respect. More on the relationship we build up with them. Scratch yours, scratch mine in business affiliations ... It's more of* pakikisama. *Relationship counts more ...* Pakikisama *is still practised, but people sometimes abuse it ...* Mayroon tayong [we have a] *close-knit Filipino community in Winnipeg.*
– Rosie, a sales agent in Winnipeg

Yes we never lose the Filipino values. We still have pakikisama. *New Filipinos who arrived help them settle whatever we can.*
– Helena, a nurse in Regina

Migration is a personal journey that becomes less isolating with group or community support. Filipino associations make considerable efforts to express *pakikisama,* and better yet *pakikipagkapwa-tao* (concern or regard for others), to newcomers, making them feel welcome through a sense of hospitality and of belonging to a group. The operation of this cultural value explains why Filipino immigrants tend to rely on their compatriots rather than established immigrant-serving agencies. Filipinos in the area often become the first point of contact for needed information, direction, referrals, and other concerns of newcomers.

Filipino values do not operate independently of one another, and *pakikisama* is closely tied to the concept of *bayanihan* (community spirit). Traditionally, *bayanihan* described rural people "press[ing] their shoulders together to transfer a neighbor's bamboo house for free" (Zialcita 2000, 177). In migration, *pakikisama* and *bayanihan* demonstrate community engagement. Filipinos lend a supporting arm to newcomers, many of whom they meet by chance in shopping malls and churches. This "other-orientedness" facilitates the development of positive perspectives on settlement and adaptation. Practising *pakikisama* also builds a ready social network that wards off isolation, initiates community engagement, and offers newcomers opportunities to learn about Canadian culture.

Pakikisama sa maraming Filipino [have good relations with many Filipinos]. *We do bayanihan ... Nakikiramay sa pamilya* [share grief with family], *hospitable or invite them [newcomers] sa bahay* [to our homes].
– Ligaya, a retired factory worker in Winnipeg

Bayanihan *spirit is innate in the Filipino community. They are there for you.*
– Julita, a community worker in Edmonton

Yes, definitely ... Values influence a lot in community participation.
Pakikisama *is positive ... Even though we require many volunteers some Filipinos do not actually sign up but show up ...* bayanihan *spirit. This usually happens and it's good.*
– Victoria, a private employee in Saskatoon

Pakikisama among *Pinays* in the Prairies is comprehensive in scope – personal, group, and larger community. At the personal level, and depending on the context of the relationship, *pakikisama* primarily benefits the recipient. Since this social relationship is reciprocal, the doer of the act of *pakikisama* may in turn become its recipient. Such a relationship is open to abuse, however (Leoncini 2005). *Pakikisama* demonstrates one's "belongingness and loyalty to one's in-group" (162) in order to maintain social harmony; one has to abide by the group consensus. Achievement of group goals seems easy when members focus on expected contributions. On a broader scale, *pakikisama* promotes good citizenship, as seen, for example, in the positive actions through which Filipinos demonstrate their belonging to the polity, such as their high labour force participation and acquisition of Canadian citizenship.

Pakikisama *is good if we work for the good of the community.*
– Bella, a retired nurse in Winnipeg

My emphasis is tama na pakikisama [my emphasis is on the correct *pakikisama*] *... We keep the best of the Filipino culture but also Canada to become better Filipinos and Canadians.*
– Josefina, self-employed in Winnipeg

Empathy or compassion for others are elements of *pakikisama* or *bayanihan* and translate into community involvement in many instances. Women like Julita in Edmonton, for example, have taken up the cause of Filipino domestic workers who suffer abuse from their employers. Those sharing common experiences band together to find a voice in Canada, like Damayan Manitoba in Winnipeg. In terms of community participation, leaders of Filipino associations show camaraderie or *pakikisama* with regard to the activities of another organization. Members of organizations do likewise towards those who belong to other organizations, whether or not it is a personal concern. In this case, one's *pakikisama* leads to *utang na loob* on the part of another person.

Utang na Loob

Utang na loob, or debt of gratitude, is a dominant Filipino value of reciprocity – a form of repaying favours received. Non-repayment causes *hiya* (shame), and being branded as *walang hiya* (showing no shame) is a great dishonour (Panopio and Rolda 2007). *Utang na loob* relates to the concept of *loob* (inner self) that defines Filipino moral character: "*Loob* is the inner self, the core of one's personhood and where the true worth of a person lies" (Andres 2002, 51). *Loob* provides a frame of reference for ethical conduct; the feminine version is *kagandahang loob* (goodwill) (De Castro 2000). Observance of these values ensures group harmony and unity.

Migration involves numerous interlocking personal dynamics of exchange. Pooling the resources required to emigrate to Canada from the Philippines is a monumental undertaking. The cost, although prohibitive for an individual, is often shared by relatives and friends, who contribute to making the goal of migration a reality. Although financial capital may be limited, social capital is boundless, connecting one person to another beyond national borders. For Filipinos in diaspora, the chain for "repayment" can be a long one, obligating them to return the kindness they have been shown, by good deeds or services or in kind. As Barbara in Winnipeg explains, *utang na loob* is a fundamental aspect of human nature, "like a part of a golden rule."

The concept of *utang na loob* figures prominently in community volunteerism among *Pinays:*

> Utang na loob – *we have a doctor here since 1960s and he is the rock of the organization ... It's because of him, his help to others ... We think of him highly. People can't say no to him ... To tell you I was about to quit two years ago, but he called me. Say, we need you. I can't say no to him.*
> – Victoria, a private employee in Saskatoon

> *My wanting to be part of the International Women of Saskatoon is I'm passionate about women* – utang na loob, *pay back for the warmth I experienced. I was warmly embraced. So I wanted to work with this organization. I know now how it feels to give back.*
> – Analisa, a community worker in Saskatoon

Analisa in Saskatoon extends *utang na loob* to the larger Canadian society. By becoming involved, she shares her gratitude not only with Filipinos but also with other immigrant women. While *utang na loob* is mostly confined to interpersonal relations, particularly between family members and close relations, it has wider implications for individuals as members of organizations and ultimately as citizens. As Salcedo and colleagues (1999, 46) have posited, *utang na loob* is "a complicated system of mutual obligation" with different degrees of observance. Some Filipino scholars attest to its potential to instill "solid cooperation" in communities (Bustos et al. 1999).

Utang na loob, *yes it's still there ... People that you help try to help, want to give back something ... Because of that you make friends, even if you don't know the person. You have bonding as Filipinos. Canadians, they help once, but I don't think they'll be there, unlike Filipinos.*
– Betsy, a nurse in Regina

We have no family here in Regina. Wala kaming kamag-anak [we have no relatives]. *PAS [Philippine Association of Saskatchewan] when they learn about it, the next day gave us microwave, clothes. I was touched by them. Mga Pilipino ito* [these are Filipinos]. *Ang pag-treat sa amin maganda ... yes, tutulong ako kasi maganda ang pag-treat sa akin.* [They treated us well ... yes, I will help because they treated me well.]
– Solis, a government employee in Regina

Like other values, *utang na loob* can have its downside. Many Filipinos find that the obligation of indebtedness to another person limits their own freedom of choice (Gorospe 1994; Yengoyan and Makil 2004). And the repayment of favours, large or small, may seem endless. Dancel (2005, 127) asks, "How much gratitude is enough?"

Utang na loob *is good, an appreciation to one's debt but it is also negative – a lifelong gratitude!* Utang na loob *is source of conflict in Filipino families ... many expects something.*
– Dalisay, a retired teacher in Winnipeg

Utang na loob, *sometimes we do a little bit too much. People always feel, mayroon kang utang na loob! Families break up because of* utang na loob. *Forever na tatanawin mo yun* [you have to repay it forever]. *That's bad.*
– Lumen, a finance officer in Winnipeg

Utang na loob *– mali ang connotation. Kasi ang utang na loob, forever ka na may utang na loob ... sunod-sunod na lang?* [*Utang na loob* – the connotation is wrong. Because of *utang na loob* [debt of gratitude], you are forever indebted ... do you just keep on following?]
– Siony, a nurse in Calgary

The implications of migration for notions of repayment and non-repayment of *utang na loob*, especially among families, are profound. However, my respondents' general assessment of this value relative to their community volunteerism is by and large positive. One may have a sense of obligation to an individual member of an organization, but volunteer work transcends this and extends to others. Ethno-specific groups are important social contacts for Filipino newcomers; they facilitate understanding of the Canadian system and act as a quasi extended family away from home. When a *kababayan* (compatriot) extends help, invitations to attend social events usually follow. Filipino women tend to show their gratitude for help received by volunteering with an organization.

Respect for Elders or for Authority

The value of respect is highly esteemed in Filipino culture. It is typically based on hierarchical relations – age, class, status, or position – within a group or in society. Filipinos demonstrate respect through language, actions, and deeds. Words like *opo, oho,* and *po* are used to address people of higher social standing; in the same way, there are different forms of titles for elders: *kuya* (older brother), *ate* (older sister), *lolo* (grandfather), *lola* (grandmother), *tita* (aunt), *tito* (uncle). The physical gesture of *mano po* – a younger person greeting an elder by touching the latter's right hand to his or her (the younger person's) forehead – is still expected. These expressions of respect are not limited to family members but apply to all Filipino elders. In Canada and elsewhere, younger Filipinos address older persons as *tito* or *tita*, creating the sense of a quasi family system as part of a larger framework of reference for Filipinos in diaspora.

By-products of respect are, among others, conformity and loyalty. Filial obligations call for respect towards parents and elders, but the same deference is shown to people of comparable standing outside the family structure. Persons of authority (i.e., moral, political, economic) are also revered in Filipino society. In fact, as a sign of respect, Filipinos, according to Lassiter (1998, 81), "seldom express disagreement."

> *Absolutely, Filipino values facilitate community involvement ... With Dr. Carlos Maningas you can never say NO. He has not even asked, you say yes already.*
> – Filomena, a government employee in Saskatoon

Filomena in Saskatoon disclosed that she always granted any request made by Dr. Carlos Maningas, an esteemed Filipino physician and leader. One of the founding fathers of the Filipino community in Saskatoon, Dr. Maningas still exerts a strong influence in the lives of many Filipinos in the area. Western feminists may explain this as constitutive of patriarchal and class relations, where subordinates accede to a male elder. However, Filipino culture, like other non-Western cultures, has its own complexities. In the case of Filomena, contributing to the community at the request of a respected male leader is not viewed as blind subordination. She is fully aware that this distinguished person has also given much of himself to others, and by helping him in the course of many projects, she is in effect combining respect with volunteerism.

Amid Western influences concerning equality, freedom of expression, and tolerance of opinions, *Pinays* in the Prairies remain firm in instilling the value of respect towards elders and authority in their children. All the participants in this study affirm its beneficial impact on desired goals, whether personal or group-oriented. For them, respect begins with their own good examples.

> *Set parents according to the values ... worst thing ever is for parents who do not set the example, we are in Canada ... the continuity of moral tradition ... learning culture and doing it. See how old people interact and provide example to our youth. This is one of the challenges as an emerging community ... Filipino values enriches or strengthens community participation.*
> – Marilena, a community worker in Edmonton

For first-generation Filipino migrants, settlement includes the process of reproducing value structures. Since many Filipino women have left their elderly parents in the Philippines, Filipino seniors often become pseudo-parents in Canada to whom they show affection, trust, and respect.

> *Respeto sa matanda. Tatay-tatayan, nanay-nanayan ... Ganoon ang Pilipino ... Tulong-tulong tayo. Tuwang-tuwa sila* [Respect for the elderly. Fatherlike, motherlike ... Filipinos are like that ... We help each other. They are very happy] ... *doing something for newcomers. I'm just paying forward.*
> – Samantha, a government employee in Regina

> *Yes, you have that respect all the time for older Filipinos.*
> – Sara, an employee in Lethbridge

It is common for older Filipinos to assume leadership positions. Even if they are not officially at the helm, there exists an "unspoken hierarchy and authority, regardless of actual leadership positions" (Nadal 2009, 119). Filipino men tend to play these roles, but the idea of women assuming such positions is gaining wide acceptance. In Canada, many Filipino women have made remarkable strides in their professions and are accorded the same opportunity to lead. These women in turn encourage other Filipino women to become involved in the community in substantive and meaningful ways. Associating with a known personality in the organization or community also raises the social status of members.

In the community I know it's more on respect. Because I work with ... sige
punta tayo doon kasi nandoon ka [let's go there because you are there,
too]. *Respect for position, a good engagement really.*
– Marilou, a community worker in Calgary

Marilou in Calgary reiterates the concept of respect based not on age but
on status or position in Canadian society. I argue that those who have "made
it" as the equal of Canadians by passing through the social merit system
command respect in the Filipino community or group circles. Other aspects
of respect include, but are not limited to, moral authority, professional in-
tegrity, and trustworthiness; those viewed with respect also have the obligation to live up to high expectations (Tolentino 2004). Persons accorded such
recognition form a class of their own distinct from the economic classes
based on material wealth. Broadly, the hierarchical and class-based Philippine society operates in varied categories, depending on the persons who
are accorded respect at the community or organizational level.

Philippine cultural values and traits such as *pakikisama, utang na loob,*
and respect for elders provide a nuanced understanding of certain aspects
of Filipino women's participation in the community. These values not only
lend context to interpersonal relations but also shape their community
engagement.

Values work on the positive side, but there are idiosyncrasies ... we see it in
action very strongly, we see its negative impact, too. Pero [but] *making it*
work in specific projects like pakikisama *or* utang na loob *predominates.*
– Pilar, a community worker in Winnipeg

Maganda ang sama-sama ng Pilipino ... peace-loving people ang Filipino.
Pakikisama doon tayo natututo. [The camaraderie of Filipinos is beautiful
... Filipinos are a peace-loving people. We learn from *pakikisama.*]
Respect for authority in organizations, yes. No negative comments so far.
– Dulce, a retired teacher in Calgary

Since Filipinos are considered sociable people, their self-identities become
particularly meaningful in relation to one another. Lynch's contested operational framework (1973, 18-19) of the Philippine value system includes
equivalence, solidarity, reciprocity, and compassion *(awa)* (Yengoyan and
Makil 2004). Equivalence refers to views outside the group; solidarity focuses
on views from inside the group; reciprocity points to a moral system of
exchange; and *awa* is assistance to those in need. These operational dimensions all make their mark on the various manifestations of Filipino normative values in community volunteerism among *Pinays* in the Prairies. In my

opinion, they contribute in part to Filipinos' highly adaptive capacity in their host countries.

From a feminist perspective, Philippine cultural values reproduce relations of power based on gender, age, and class. Filipino men still hold the sceptre as "head" and women are followers. Male authority is further enhanced with age and a distinguished professional career. Undoubtedly, *Pinays* in the Prairies adhere to these cultural scripts and to their prescribed role in shaping their involvement in the community. They embody the reproductive and productive labour, albeit in a voluntary capacity, to reify an "imagined" (Anderson 1991) national community akin to a "spatiotemporal performative" act (Alarcon, Kaplan, and Moallem 1999, 7). The space of *Pinays*, following Alarcon, Kaplan, and Moallem (1999, 6), is "between woman and nation," which "intersect in specific ways" to produce a subject. The culture-nation/community dynamics between *Pinays* and Filipino associations do not appear so rigid as to stifle expressions of agency; women appear to exercise their own judgment and construct meaning out of their engagement.

Pinay Views: Gender and Leadership

At the risk of igniting debate, I argue that women are born leaders. If a leader is one who leads to accomplish common goals or objectives, one might reasonably wonder when a person can be considered a leader. A leader is known by association and other forms of social interaction in which the individual has demonstrated leadership skills – for example, someone who can articulate and work for the interests of a group, or even a type of personality (Northouse 2010). I argue, however, that women's socialization and roles at home make them leaders in their own right: women manage households, coordinate multiple tasks, ensure cooperation among members, and much more. These are qualities demanded of leaders in formalized leadership structures. Women's marginalization in these public spheres of leadership has drawn considerable criticism from feminist scholars (Blackmore 2002; Chin et al. 2007).

Gilligan (2000, 273) emphasizes women's perspectives "in a different voice" from men with "different judgements" or "different ways of imagining the human conditions, different notions of what is of value in life." Women's leadership shows remarkable efficacy, employing collaborative skills as well as building consensus (Alston 2005). This alternative leadership approach combines unique personal and organizational strategies to create harmony and deliver results. Women's ways of doing things are, in terms of leadership, their "female advantage" (Helgesen 1995).

The idea of *Pinay* leadership has not yet gained wide recognition in the scholarly literature (Zontini 2010), although there have been two democratically elected female presidents in modern Philippine history.[23] In Western societies, research on gender and diversity in leadership continues to lag behind in leadership studies (Parker 2005; Fine 2009). In fact, studies on all visible-minority women leaders in immigrant-receiving countries are scarce (Tastsoglou and Miedema 2003; Kawahara 2007). A *Pinay* leader in Canada challenges assumptions of immigrant women. According to Kawahara, "the racialization of Asian womanhood blends racism and sexism by presenting Asian and Asian American women as stereotypically feminine, thus upholding white superiority" (2007, 18). Filipino stereotypes in Canada do not include the image of a leader, let alone a woman leader. Those of the caregiver, domestic worker, nanny, or nurse are the traditional images of a Filipino migrant. Based on the conventional model of appointed or elected executives among organizations, however, *Pinay* leaders in the Prairies are actually fairly common. Notable examples have included Linda Cantiveros in Manitoba, Ellen Sacoco in Saskatchewan, and Rhoda Abada[24] in Alberta. Although the development of Filipino women's public persona as political leaders (for example, Flor Marcelino as MLA in Manitoba in 2007 and Mable Elmore as MLA in British Columbia in 2009) is a recent phenomenon, *Pinay* leaders in communities have in fact long been the backbone of their organizations and unrecognized grassroots leaders.

Nevertheless, leadership remains largely a male domain. Top elected positions in the history of local Filipino associations tend to be held by men. For example, in Saskatoon, only five women were elected presidents of FILCAS from 1973 to 2004: Beth Dickhoff in 1987; Joan Cruerer in 1988; Estrella Dato in 1998, 1999, 2002, and 2003; Cora Dario in 2000 and 2001; and Felicitas Santos in 2004 (FILCAS 2004). Henrietta Maquiling was identified as president of the Filipino Canadian Women's Barangay Association of Alberta in the List of Women's Organizations produced by Alberta Community Development (2002). Rosalinda Natividad-Cantiveros was elected president of the Winnipeg-based Philippine Canadian Centre of Manitoba in 2007 (*Filipino Journal* 2007). Although women have contested leadership positions, there is still a significant gap between the number of female and male leaders elected to executive positions. I was not able to gain access to the documents of any Filipino association in Alberta, Saskatchewan, and Manitoba regarding the history of its elections for this study. It is possible that fewer women put their names forward, or that a number of organizations originally began as a "boys' club." The idea that leadership is a male preserve is reflected in various narratives.

In general, it's a men's world.
– Sharon, a former garment worker in Saskatoon

Organizations are predominantly run by men, but women gradually coming out and assuming that role. Women are just busy with kids ... while working

*full-time. Men have more time to be involved outside because women take
more on tasks at home ... But women have the skills and the ability to run
organizations. Filipino women also excel in larger Canadian community
as equals with men. Canada has a positive view of us, unlike other cultures
where women are more secondary in roles.*
  – Pilar, a community worker in Winnipeg

*There's leadership already among women ... more prominent now ... It will
never come to the point for women on top of men especially, among Filipinos
... A huge percentage of Filipino women are more on secondary roles.*
  – Lumen, a finance officer in Winnipeg

As Sharon, Pilar, and Lumen all observed, Filipino women perform secondary leadership roles in Filipino associations. Men occupy the position of
president more often than women. The achievement-conscious leadership
framework among Filipinos is highly gendered, with men taking on the
public tasks of becoming heads of organizations while women juggle multiple
burdens at home, at work, and in the community. Filipino women address
the issues of income security and well-being of children before seeking
leadership roles in community associations.

*In the local Filipino association, I would say that there are enough number of
women in the leadership. Since I first moved here, the president has always
been a man ... Although having said that, women do play active leadership
roles within the organization, not necessarily the "head" of the organization.*
  – Mayra, a health worker in Edmonton

Male leadership is a dominant prototype. Fine (2009, 181) notes that the
"male ideology of leadership is visible in two critical ways: (1) the lack of
representation of women in leadership" and "(2) the construction of leadership as comprising masculine characteristics." Men and masculinity permeate our understanding of power, leadership, and governance in society
(O'Connor 2010). Although the number of women pushing against the
glass ceiling is increasing, their successes are still attributed to being "masculine" – assertive, forceful, and direct (Wajcman 2000; Coleman 2003;
Tosone 2009).
  Times are changing, however. The Filipino male ideology of leadership is
being increasingly contested by *Pinays* in the Prairies. Salome and Bella,
retired nurses in Winnipeg, challenge the male-centred practices of the
Knights of Rizal.[25]

*The male is always the leader ... Men think highly and women cannot say
anything ... Women can do things like men, we have brains, too. Don't tell*

*me what to do ... start empowering women. We are not in the Philippines
anymore. This is the twenty-first century!*
– Salome, a retired nurse in Winnipeg

See less gender expectations of what we can do. Filipino women can do more.
– Bella, a retired nurse in Winnipeg

Salome and Bella reflected on the traditional norms of leadership and management in their own associations that they find unsuitable now that they are in Canada. Many *Pinays* do not consider being a woman a deterrent, but, like Jamie in Edmonton, they reflect on its impact.

*For me, there is no difference in gender for leadership roles. Eh, ano kung
babae?* [Eh, so what if one is a woman?] *... But to move it to the broader
world ... medyo* [maybe] *something is missing. Perhaps no resources to run
for office.*
– Jamie, a nurse in Edmonton

*As a woman, it doesn't matter. We get involved in many organizations not
only in women's organizations. Don't have feeling of less or more because I
am a woman.*
– Salome, a retired nurse in Winnipeg

Salome declares that Filipino women are no less qualified than men to become leaders. In practice, however, they are at a disadvantage. Men may have the networks and resources to effectively fund campaigns for elected positions in particular. In her study of Filipina business leaders in the Philippines in the 1990s, Roffey (1999, 401) concludes that the lack of financial resources hinders Filipinas from reaching managerial positions "even though the role models are already visible." In fact, according to research by Grant Thornton International a decade later, the Philippines has the highest proportion of women in senior management positions in privately owned businesses: 47 percent, compared with the global average of 24 percent in 2009. Ultimately, gender seems to be less significant than the qualifications of the leader, whether man or woman. According to Rosalinda in Saskatoon, what matters is what one brings to the position: the ability to lead and be committed to the role for the greater good of the organization.

*Both men and women are active in the community. Women even take more
active roles ... We have two women presidents already and gender is never an
issue. Mas importante yung kung ano ang madadala mo sa position* [what
you can bring to the position is more important].
– Rosalinda, a nurse in Saskatoon

We have lots of Filipino women leaders ... They are equal to men ... If you have the talent to do the job, why not? Personally, gender is irrelevant.
– Claribel, a hospital worker in Winnipeg

No division between man/woman in Filipino community. Kung kaya mo, ok ... Kaya ba natin? [If you can do it, okay. Can we do it?] *Always a push ... maybe there's a limit not everyone can be assertive, aggressive in order to be well known in the community.*
– Mayra, a health worker in Edmonton

There are several Filipino women leaders now. Filipina MLA won. Gender is not much an issue – Kitaham has a lady president, Bisaman has a lady president, and the honorary consul is a lady, too.
– Asuncion, a nurse in Winnipeg

Pinay leaders exist in the Filipino community. Their numbers may be small compared with their male counterparts, but they have made their voices heard. Among my respondents in the Prairies, gender per se is not considered as much an obstacle to leadership as other factors, such as resources, social capital, and the qualities that define a leader. Gender is but one factor in a complicated mix of dynamics that determines leadership. Ethnicity, for instance, is certainly more prominent than the issue of gender in many cases, as seen in the rise of federated Filipino councils composed of different member organizations with regional cliques vying for the top leadership post.

I think in this local Filipino organization that I am pertaining [sic] to, the discrepancy lies more in the ethnic "cliques" more than gender. I am not entirely sure of the reason, but that seems to be the reality.
– Jamie, a nurse in Edmonton

Pinay leaders are not imagined constructs among Filipinos in the Prairies. They may have developed a distinctive leadership style to address specific purposes, as discussed below, but they are women leaders in community organizations nonetheless.

Leadership Is Important
Pinay leadership is an important offshoot of community life in an agricultural society now modernized with liberal democratic precepts. Farming and other collective means of livelihood acknowledge women's contribution to society (Shaver Hughes and Hughes 2001). In the Philippines, there are three dominant views of women's leadership at home: first, the mother exercises authority in decision making but the father has the final say; second, the husband has a nominal position in a matriarchal society; and third, there

is a shared leadership at home that is not male- or female-dominated (Nam 2006, 73). Unlike other traditional societies in Asia, Filipino women are less restricted by religion and social codes from becoming leaders. In 2009, Republic Act No. 9710, known as the Magna Carta of Women, was signed into law; it bans discrimination against women and mandates their equal rights and welfare. Women have higher voter turnout than men during elections, and they occupy important leadership positions in government, education, and business in the Philippines (Roces 2000). Today in Canada, Filipino women believe that they can be – and in fact are – leaders.

> *Women leaders are just them, not behind anybody. They lead. Women can do what men can, it does not matter. Women excel, too.*
> – Salvacion, a home care worker in Winnipeg

Salvacion reiterates the notion of gender equality in leadership. This perspective has been put into practice by many Filipino community organizations in the Prairies. Some Filipino women have vied for the top posts or have been recruited to fill them. Their active participation tracks the history of women's inclusion in public spaces in a democratic state, and underscores the importance of women being in leadership roles today (Åseskog 2008).

> *In Filipino organizations, Filipino women tend to hold top leadership positions. They are also recognized in their professions ... my position comes with responsibility ... I take upon myself as a good role model. A lot more women will follow suit hopefully in my footsteps.*
> – Luningning, a community leader in Winnipeg

Filipino women are no different from men in demonstrating that leadership means responsibility and that a leader is a model to emulate. Luningning in Winnipeg underlines the relationship between assuming a leadership position and its implications for future women leaders.

> *I was co-founder of FILCAN – Filipino Canadian Association, first organization in Winnipeg in 1962 ... We need to connect with people. That's why I go to this group or organization ... to connect is my reason to be part of the group.*
> – Bella, a retired nurse in Winnipeg

Pinay leaders build bridges to connect with other women. Becoming the central figure in an organization gives them many opportunities to network, not only during their period of leadership but also afterwards. The organizational and social aspects of community building are integrated into the fabric of their lives in Canada. Huffington (2004, 59) discusses women's leadership as grounded in the "person-role system model of looking at the way an individual negotiates his/her position in the organization." This leadership modality appears important in Bella's perspective on her experience in Winnipeg – her goal is to build lasting relationships.

Pinay leaders are visible in the Filipino community and, to some extent, a few have made a name for themselves in the larger host society. Hosanna and Marilena point to the active engagement of *Pinay* leaders in Edmonton. Although there are many male leaders in the Filipino community, women tend to be more involved in activities involving non-Filipinos, usually in multicultural groups. They become cross-cultural collaborators for change, particularly on the local government's health and well-being initiatives.

A very important role of Filipino women is community building ... In Alberta, Filipino women are able to create or carve leadership role within the community and outside ... it's always been females. Within the Filipino community, there are many male leaders. But women do both within and outside the Filipino community.
– Hosanna, a nurse in Edmonton

In different volunteer groups here it's always the Filipino women who lead ... all these women are part of the community. In any community, when meeting in the mainstream – Filipino women lead in many ways. Yes, they are recognized, some even urging us to become political ... In our new generation, lots of them are leaders, teachers in their own way lead others.
– Marilena, a community worker in Edmonton

Leadership is not limited to officers of organizations but also includes other roles in the community – teachers, nurses, and professionals. Any position that entails service to the public is considered a site of leadership.

And a factor here is that women work more than one job. In the Philippines, whoever earns more has the power or voice. So, here women who are earning more in the sense regain their voice against the feudal practice.
– Angela, a hotel worker in Red Deer

The economic windfall of migration lends itself well to women's leadership in the Filipino community. As Angela has observed in Red Deer, Alberta, most Filipino women become leaders because of their equivalent or higher incomes compared with Filipino men in Canada. *Pinay* leadership appears to give women a voice to articulate their issues and interests. In communities where Filipino live-in caregivers abound, a *Pinay* leader's voice comes across as more authoritative and genuinely sympathetic than that of a male leader in another occupation.

Pinay Leadership Style

Women experience leadership differently from men, and as leaders they naturally demonstrate divergent approaches or management styles. Coleman (2003, 333), in her study of women secondary school head teachers in England and Wales, notes the stereotypical male and female leadership styles: "Women are thought to be caring, tolerant, emotional, intuitive, gentle and predisposed towards collaboration, empowerment and teamwork. Men are supposed to be aggressive, assertive, analytical and more inclined to act independently." As the study showed, however, a combination of both leadership styles is in fact found in women leaders. This interplay of masculine/feminine leadership styles depending on situational contexts is what makes women effective leaders.

Philippine society has its own stereotypes of female leaders (e.g., *mahina ang loob*, or weak-willed) enshrined in patriarchal culture, but an increasing number of women have become prominent in the political scene, the corporate world, non-governmental organizations, and even rebel groups that dispel these gendered constructs. In Canada, *Pinays* in the Prairies craft their own leadership style: an integrative humanist paradigm consisting of women's caring or nurturing qualities, intelligence, relational skills, responsibility, accountability, and morality. Earlier in this section, I argued that women's socialization draws on the leadership qualities of management, cooperation, and the like. These leadership skills may be implicitly honed, becoming useful when the time comes for women to occupy leadership positions.

Clemencia in Winnipeg has observed the dynamics of some Filipino organizations where women tend to lead while men follow. In her view, *Pinay* leaders accomplish tasks quite well, gain more popular support from members, and are articulate. It seems that even when males are nominal leaders, the real strength of many organizations lies in women's ability to coordinate tasks.

> *Women lead and men just follow. Without the help of women nothing will happen in organizations ... sometimes women are the brains. They are more articulate than men. Women get more positive feedback from members. They can explain more to men. That is how I observe many Filipino organizations here.*
> – Clemencia, a nurse in Winnipeg

Women's capacity to care and nurture distinguishes them from men. Care for the welfare of the organization in general, and that of its members in particular, are vividly demonstrated by *Pinay* leaders.

Women play an important leadership role ... With our "motherly nature" women tend to be the shakers and movers in the organization. Filipino women are making names both in the Filipino community and outside.
– Rowena, a manager in a media company in Winnipeg

Filipino women's role is to calm everyone down ... be more nurturing.
– Lisa, an employee in Winnipeg

Women are good leaders and are easily more focused and hardworking. Actually, women are stronger leaders than men ... can relate more because we are more emotional, passionate than men, and good listeners.
– Rosie, a sales agent in Winnipeg

Comparative studies of male and female leaders indicate that the latter utilize nurturing and caring skills that form part of a transformational leadership style (Fine 2007). Women's "motherly nature" applied in leadership practice suggests that women leaders tend to emphasize inclusivity, participation, and more interpersonal communication in the process of dealing with members and in completing tasks. A *Pinay* leader of an organization takes time to build harmony among members, resolve conflicts, and avert confrontation. Rosie in Winnipeg cites women's emotional nature, their passion about the work to be done, and their ability to be "good listeners," all so-called people skills relevant in organizations (Broussine 2009, 268). In this way, relational leadership transforms attitudes and relationships among individual members towards the attainment of goals.

In an echo of dominant/subordinate relations in the Philippines and as an alternative to the traditional model of letting others do the work, *Pinay* leaders tend to lead by example. Following an authoritarian leadership style is, according to Salmer and de Leon (2003, 162), "permissible within Filipino context, as subordinates prefer to avoid conflict with superiors and to ensure their social acceptance within the work group." This is what Rosal in Winnipeg refers to as *lumang system* (old system), where leaders simply sit down while members do the hard work. In Canada, however, Rosal alludes to a hands-on approach that is progressive and promotes effective results since leader and members work together.

As a child hindi ko kinalakihan ang values na iyan [I did not grow up with those values as a child] ... *My leadership is progressive. Do something, say something, and commit to it. Ang lumang system, upo lang* [in the old system, they just sit down] *because they like the title ... Don't talk but demonstrate ... Mulat na mulat na ako* [I'm fully aware] *that Filipino women are more in the front. Gender is not a weakness ... Women are not for the*

background ... Make your voice be heard. Kung lagi kang nasa action [if you
are always where the action is], *they can't deny you.*
– Rosal, a nurse TFW in Winnipeg

Since first-generation immigrant Filipinos comprise the majority, if not
all, of the membership in Filipino associations, the traditional leadership
stereotype of "title and not action" somehow sticks to male leaders. That is,
Filipino male leaders are perceived to be more interested in title and status
than in being doers. However, migration to Canada provides another context
in which these allegedly "title-savvy" leaders operate. More often than not,
leadership among Filipinos in Canada appears to require more time, more
commitment, and the ability to forge in-group harmony for the completion
of tasks, especially if those leaders are also employed full-time. Wise leaders
delegate tasks and provide general guidance for everyone. Filipino associations are formally structured, with various committees to oversee different
aspects of running the organization. In Canada, where there is less of a
support system to assist leaders in meeting the requirements of the position,
the "title-only" Filipino leadership stereotype is contested, although the
male bias persists.

*Leadership by example in meetings ... Self-discipline like observing schedules
... Ikalat* [spread it] *so they can learn, matututunan nila* [they will learn].
Word of honour, if I say it, I do it.
– Dulce, a retired teacher in Calgary

Leadership by example is viewed as a form of discipline. Dulce in Calgary
mentioned the habit of tardiness when attending meetings; that is, Filipinos
tend to arrive late for meetings (Lim and Makani-Lim 2006). In its cultural
context, though, one recognizes that in the Philippines activities often start
with a number of preliminary protocols, such as socializing, which delays
important matters. Likewise, political leaders and dignitaries are used to
being waited on, "meeting and greeting" en route to an event. "Tardy leaders" create a spinoff effect, making others late for their appointments.
Correcting this habit of being late for meetings is an area where *Pinays*
demonstrate leadership by example in Canada, as Dulce points out. Change
from the top, by the leadership, means change at the bottom, but the latter
has been quite slow in coming for people in the Philippines.

Other important aspects of leadership are responsibility, accountability,
and morality. Responsibility is seen through actions: *Pinay* leaders are perceived to follow through in projects, even in the smallest details, especially
compared with male leaders.

Filipino women are capable of everything. Mas responsable ang babae. Ang babae palagi ang kumikilos. Umaasa sa babae minsan ang mga lalaki. Ang lalaki lagi daw mali ang ginagawa nila. [Women are more responsible. It's the women who are always active. Men sometimes depend on women. It is said that men always make mistakes.]
    – Dahlia, a private employee in Saskatoon

Palabra de honor (word of honour) is particularly valued by Filipino women. Doing what one says he or she will do is highly regarded in the completion of tasks. Keeping one's word is emblematic of the moral leadership that resonates in local and national governance in the Philippines (Institute of Philippine Culture 2005). Consistency between word and action shows accountability both to the position and to the organization. In feminist practice, accountability is a principle that operates in the sharing of goals, process, and results (Chin et al. 2007).

Patriarchal societies position men as leaders and women as their followers. After outlining the project or the "intellectual domain" of organizations, male leaders tend to leave in the hands of women the tasks to be completed. Dahlia in Saskatoon notes this practice and finds it ironic that, in her view, *Pinay* leaders actually run organizations, from top to bottom. Often their skills in organization and administration eventually make them leaders.

Filipino women have leadership roles. They lead by example. But their contributions are downplayed. Filipino women tend to be humble, modest, don't want to mention their achievements, their contributions ... Filipino women do lots in the community. We keep on giving and expected nothing in return ... parang [it's as though] being Catholic is part of it. It's a bit of obligation, duty positively reinforced in social life. A way of feeling for the community. Part of Filipino culture is giving ... We do a lot more than what we get credit for it.
    – Vivian, a public health worker in Winnipeg

Vivian in Winnipeg claims that *Pinay* leaders downplay their contributions in community organizations. Unlike some male leaders, *Pinay* leaders show modesty and humility in what they do. In this, they reflect the socialized values of Filipino womanhood in Philippine Catholicism, primarily self-sacrifice. Doing more than what is expected seems to be the mantra of a Catholic-minded *Pinay* leader. Their existence is a continuum of "giving and more giving" in kindness, service, and monetary support. Applying this to a community organization, a *Pinay* leader becomes a selfless person, one who sacrifices for the sake of the group or, in Vivian's words, who has "a way of feeling for the community." *Pinay* leaders in this mould give a lot of themselves to achieve group goals.

The "culture of giving" is very much part of the Filipino tradition (Opiniano 2004b). Giving occurs for the benefit of families, communities, and the nation, but it can be exploited. In his speech at the Consultation on Lausanne Diasporas Leadership in Manila on 5 May 2009, David Kilgour (2009), MP for Edmonton-Beaumont, stated that Filipinos "do far more for Canadians than we do for them." Filipino workers tend the sick, the elderly, and children as live-in caregivers or nurses, they work in fast food outlets and hotels to make the lives of Canadians comfortable, and more. In community associations, *Pinay* leaders demonstrate to the larger Canadian society their acts of giving through volunteerism so that Filipinos are recognized as new Canadians.

Leadership as Purpose

Pinay leaders in the Prairies are characterized by their purpose: to serve and to raise awareness. Many of them have occupied leadership positions not because they want to but in response to a need. In other words, they tend not seek the positions but feel compelled to lead and serve.

> *Leadership doesn't have to be with organization, but when need arises and somebody needs help you can spearhead something. Filipino women direct presentation to help the church ... Filipino women in the community serve the community and Canada as a whole, not ... self-gratification.*
> – Asuncion, a nurse in Winnipeg

For Asuncion, leadership does not have to be with a Filipino organization but can be exercised as a member of any community, such as a congregation or church that benefits Canadian parishioners. Filipino women often lead various church-related activities, as choir directors, parish council members, and lay ministers. Many of them have taken up the challenge of being at the forefront in these church communities. As the parishioner base ages in Canada, younger Filipino women are changing the demographics of those assisting the parish priests. Western feminist scholars may challenge my inclusion of the church as a space for women to exercise their leadership skills, but this is a popular place for many Catholic Filipino women to begin their community engagement – a good fit in Christian Canada.

> *Linda Cantiveros has done a lot to PCCM [Philippine Canadian Centre of Manitoba] ... It's just built in her to lead. Some have ulterior motives not from the goodness of their heart ... Women are starting to know their strength. Men know that ladies are even stronger sometimes.*
> – Carolina, a retired teacher in Winnipeg

Service is one of the chief expressions of leadership. *Pinay* leaders are generally viewed in terms of their service to others in the Prairies. In community associations, they usually consider their involvement to be a form of service without expectation of any return. Carolina in Winnipeg referred to the leadership of Linda Cantiveros as "from the goodness of [her] heart." While first-generation Filipino immigrants still have cultural baggage about who leads, the freedom to choose which organizations and activities to take part in enables potential *Pinay* leaders to find their niche in the community.

> *Some Filipino women have the mentality that class relates to leadership. My view of leadership is to serve others. But with Filipinos, spoiled brat ... sila ang sinisilbihan* [they are being served]. *It's human nature, though ... but we have more freedom of expression here ... I was one of the fundraising coordinators and am glad to be of service, not for self-gratitfication but satisfaction that I was able to help and did something for the community and for others.*
> – Josefina, self-employed in Winnipeg

Some *Pinay* leaders, however, have found their place outside of Filipino community associations. In Edmonton, a number of them are recognized in multicultural organizations. They find their own space to use their talents in non-exclusive Filipino associations and in fact gain acceptance on their own terms. Active participation in non-profit multicultural organizations is but one example of immigrants making a difference.

> *Women are not doing this in the community to be recognized; we want to make a difference in the lives of people.*
> – Antonia, a health worker in Edmonton

An interesting undertaking among activist *Pinay* leaders is consciousness-raising among immigrant women in general. This is, in the words of Hosanna from Edmonton, "politicalizing" women, not "politicking." The difference between politicalizing and politicking is rooted in purpose: the former aims to engage women in issues and work collectively, whereas the latter refers to partisan politics and solicitation of support. Politicalizing follows Freire's "education for critical consciousness" (2007), with its close link to feminist pedagogy based on similar theories of oppression and structures of ideological and material domination (Jackson 2004, 24).

> *Women's way, our way of doing political work is not politicking but more on politicalizing, as forum on issues ... ang* [the] *limitation of women: don't rub elbows with old boys club.*
> – Hosanna, a nurse in Edmonton

Because of their facility in the English language, *Pinay* leaders connected with multicultural organizations are able to articulate the issues and concerns of immigrants to various stakeholders. Often, these *Pinay* leaders represent immigrant women's groups in their communities.

In this chapter, we have seen how *Pinays* in the Prairies are engaged in varied forms of volunteerism or multiple activism that touch the personal, professional, and ethnocultural dimensions. In contrast to the stereotypical view of Filipino women in Canada as "nannies," this chapter portrays the "activist *Pinay*," whose personal experiences of migration, settlement, and integration are negotiated through her own culturally distinct ways of grounded volunteerism in different spaces – school, work, church, and community associations. *Pinay* community leaders continue to serve without remuneration in Filipino communities and multicultural associations while remaining unrecognized in scholarly discourses in Canada. The chapter highlights the intersections of identities with migration and culture and the social currents in the Philippines and Canada. Although the experiences of community participation described here are not representative of the general population of Filipino women, they show the diversity and rich contribution of racialized immigrant women in their adoptive communities in Canada. Invariably, their acts of volunteerism and leadership benefit the larger society. As well, migration fosters new modalities of *Pinay* leadership that challenge the construct of "immigrant women" or "visible-minority women" in Canada (Boyd and Yiu 2009, 216). Theirs is a leadership that is motivated by purpose, that integrates the woman-centred value of care into an effective relational leadership style and that combines the qualities of responsibility, accountability, and morality with modesty and humility. *Pinays* in the Prairies initiate or pursue cross-cultural linkages in their adoptive communities, despite the challenges along the way.

6
Vested Transnationalism

International migration is a radical change that uproots individuals and disrupts their sense of place. One leaves one's homeland to settle in another place, but this life-changing event is not always a permanent separation, as immigrants continue to participate in activities that connect them to their countries of origin. In their seminal work *Nations Unbound*, Basch, Glick Schiller, and Szanton Blanc (1994, 6) define transnationalism as "the processes by which immigrants forge and sustain multi-stranded social relations that link together their societies of origin and settlement." In this view, immigrants are "transmigrants" who establish linkages in multiple spatial locations and "take actions, make decisions, and develop subjectivities and identities embedded in networks of relationships that connect them simultaneously to two or more nation-states" (ibid., 7), also referred to as "social fields" (Mahler and Pessar 2001, 444). Networks of relations spanning borders include a complex interlocking web of personal, institutional, and organizational activities in various realms – economic, cultural, political, religious, and social (Guarnizo 1997). Portes, Guarnizo, and Landolt (1999) refer to these realms as comprising the sectors of transnationalism (economic, political, and socio-cultural) that occur in the process of immigrant adaptation. Participation in these transnational spaces does not occur, according to Levitt (2001, 7), in "isolation from the transnational social fields in which they are embedded." Individuals, organizations, and communities become integrated in these dimensions.

The intersection of transnationalism and gender is the site of a fairly new discourse and has "rarely been a principal focus" in migration studies (Mahler and Pessar 2001, 441). The male prejudice in migration literature obscures gender relations in transnational practices (Salih 2001; Pessar and Mahler 2003). Even scholars dealing with women's experiences fail to integrate gendered perspectives of migration and are often biased towards their relations with the host country (Simoes 2006). The mainstreaming of feminist scholarship in transnational migration is occurring slowly in a small yet significant body of work (Bauer and Thompson 2004). There is a growing consensus that transnational practices and relationships occur in gendered spaces, including other dimensions of identity, shaping the experiences of women and men alike (Itzigsohn and Giorguli-Saucedo 2005; Dreby 2009). Mahler and Pessar (2001, 445) have developed a conceptual framework of "gendered geographies of power," underscoring that "gender operates simultaneously on multiple *spatial and social scales* (e.g., the body, the family, the state) across transnational terrains." This framework is useful in analyzing women's agency in the context of their own social location across "multiple hierarchies of power" (Mahler and Pessar 2001, 447) and can be constructively applied to the position of Filipino women in Canada as temporary foreign workers (TFWs) and immigrants. TFWs traverse the power hierarchies of states as they move from a developing country to a developed one, and these state spatialities shape the rights and level of protection accorded to them and their interactions with non-state entities such as labour unions and organizations. Like other women, *Pinays* in the Prairies form parts of families embedded in patriarchal relations of power and culture-based role expectations that influence decisions to migrate. Their social location in the segmented global labour market employed in marginal work simultaneously cuts across race, ethnicity, and class relations. In each of these multi-sited power relations, Filipino women negotiate their identities, countering hegemonic representations in social space or, in particular, what Pratt and Yeoh (2003) refer to as "transnational (counter) topographies."

I use the term "vested transnationalism" to suggest that cross-border movements and interactions between spaces of belonging among Filipino women, between the Philippines and Canada (or any country of residence), provide some form of benefit both to individuals and to the people or communities they associate with. I hold the view that migrants have a vested interest in continuous participation in transnational ventures, especially between home country and host country, for the good of the families they have left behind or for other purposes. For the many *Pinays* in the Prairies who are cognizant of "home" and its needs, transnationalism is fostered by gendered role expectations and familial obligations, and transnational activities are almost always undertaken with these in mind. The personal satisfaction derived from such activities lies at the core of the women's attachments as Filipinos or Filipino-Canadians. How these vested interests operate in transnational spaces is facilitated by multiple agents – individuals, non-profit organizations, business, media, the state, and so on. This chapter explores the dynamism of Filipino transnationalism and *Pinay* transnational practices and the forms these take place in the lives of *Pinays* in the Prairies. Because there are apparent similarities with observable patterns among Filipinos in diaspora, the narratives of these women can serve as a lens in understanding how transnational practices operate in Canada. I do not claim that these practices are universal, but the particularities demonstrate the variant modes that occur from the personal to the institutional. Measuring the actual extent to which these practices are found in the Filipino community in Canada is a subject for future research, however.

Filipino Transnationalism

Over 8 million documented Filipinos traverse global spaces, reaching more countries than any other group of people in the world today. Multitudes leave the Philippines to seek better economic opportunities overseas in almost all sectors of the market economy, but thousands return as *balikbayan* (Filipino returnee).[1] Busy and crowded airports with long queues at customs and departure areas attest to the daily realities of transnational flows of people, goods, and services.

Kelly and Lusis (2006, 835) applied Bourdieu's concept of habitus, or the socialized norms guiding one's behaviour or thinking, to how "various forms of Filipino capital [economic, social, and cultural] are evaluated, exchanged, and accumulated across transnational space." The economic capital of Filipinos in transnational habitus comprises the value of financial resources they bring to Canada, the ability to accumulate properties or wealth after migration, and the value of their remittances back to the Philippines. The social capital of Filipino immigrants in Canada consists of the co-ethnic ties that facilitate job hunting, and continuous connection with home through technologies such as the Internet and cellular phones, among others. Cultural capital comprises the *institutional* and *embodied* aspects of Filipinos in transnational space (Kelly and Lusis 2006, 843). Regarding institutional cultural capital, for example, the educational attainment obtained in the Philippines, such as nursing, is generally devalued in Canada and other Western countries, but the social network resulting from studying in the same school could contribute to finding employment overseas. Embodied cultural capital points to the facility of Filipinos in the English language and their exposure to Western cultural norms, which consequently "eases entry into new workplaces in the Canadian context" (ibid.). Other forms of capital in Filipino-Canadian transnational habitus include "being Filipino," with "Filipino-ness" imbued with stereotypical attributes such as "caring and nurturing" (ibid.) that appear to normalize their entry into lowly paid occupations in Canada; and overseas travel or living abroad, which is equated with success in the Philippines (ibid., 844). In another work, Kelly (2007a, 216) also notes the Filipino transnational "connections and obligations" that hamper their "potential for collective political engagement in Canada." These works indicate the varied aspects and dimensions of Filipino transnationalism, which this chapter attempts to elucidate.

In the Philippines, where almost everyone is connected to an OFW or immigrant, and many dream of following suit, transnational crossings mark family reunions, alumni homecomings, and town fiestas. Coming home is always a celebration and goodbyes are but promises of future returns. Filipino transnationalism touches families, groups, communities, and the state in numerous ways. In this section, I discuss forms of transnationalism represented by transnational families, cash remittances and *balikbayan* goods, media and popular culture, dual citizenship, and absentee voting. These forms are among the recognizable examples of transnationalism facilitated by states, institutions, and organizations integrated in international systems in which *Pinays* in the Prairies participate.

Transnational Families

One of the social realities brought about by migration is the changing structure of Filipino families. When one or both parents are overseas and the children are left behind in the Philippines, a transnational family is born. Transnational families are defined by Bryceson and Vuorela (2002, 3) as "families that live some or most of the time separated from each other, yet hold together and create something that can be seen as feeling of collective welfare and unity, namely 'familyhood' even across the national borders." Transnational families are variously described by scholars as "astronaut families" (Chiang 2008), "flexible families" (Waters 2002), and "split-households" (Yamanaka 2005). Parreñas (2005a, 10) discusses the creation of transnational families from "the macroprocess of *care resource extraction*" occurring through "two mechanisms – (1) the labor migration of women as domestics and nurses and (2) structural adjustment policies that enforce the reduction of state welfare provisions in lieu of servicing the foreign debt." Notably, labour migration of Filipino husbands also results in transnational familial relations. Millions of Filipino parents opt to leave the country to secure the material well-being of their families amid rising living costs and fewer, if any, state subsidies for education and health.

> *Noong una ang asawa ko ang umalis papunta sa Saudi at naiwan kami*
> [at first, my husband left for Saudi Arabia and we were left behind].
> – Ester, a caregiver in Lethbridge

> *Medyo nakakalakad na ang anak ko at ako ay nag-apply papunta sa Hong Kong* [when my child started to walk, I applied to go to Hong Kong].
> – Leilani, a home care worker in Calgary

> *Palagi akong umiiyak pag gabi pagkatapos ng trabaho. Naaalala ko ang mga bata sa Pilipinas. Kailangan naman gawin ko ito para sa kinabukasan nila.*
> [I always cry at night after work. I remember my children in the Philippines. I have to do this for the sake of their future.]
> – Rosal, a nurse TFW in Winnipeg

The absence of Filipino mothers due to migration has stirred much public debate about the stability of the traditional family in the Philippines (Arellano-Carandang, Sison, and Carandang 2007; Rodriguez 2008). Gendered outmigration challenges the ideology of female domesticity and women's primary role as mothers above all else (Parreñas 2008b). The phenomenon of "househusbands" is becoming increasingly widespread (Castro, Dado, and Tubesa 2006; Advincula 2009), with the perceived social impact of demasculinization of Filipino men and reports of increasing cases of incest (Uy 2007). The effect of transnational families on children's long-term welfare remains a major concern for advocates and policy makers. In a patriarchal society, caring for children falls to mothers, now breadwinners, who are, however, too far away to remain *ilaw ng tahanan* (light of the home). Mothers may be miles apart from their children, but, ironically, "maternal thinking is much a part, if not the *raison d'etre*, of the[ir] decision to migrate" (Bonifacio 2009, 162).

Certainly, physical separation from the children does not spell the end of mothering practices. Nowadays, in the era of global telecommunication, various technologies have strengthened cross-border links. Physical distances are bridged by information and communication technologies that enable Filipino women to practise alternative forms of mothering. Migrant mothers demonstrate "cyber mothering" through webcam, Skype, or Facebook. "Cellphone moms" set aside a portion of their wages to pay for long distance calls, and "text moms" send regular text messages to the Philippines, the "SMS [short message service] capital of the world" (Singh Roy 2006).[2]

Halos araw-araw ka-text ko ang anak ko [my child and I exchange texts almost every day].
– Aurora, a hotel worker in Pincher Creek

Filipino live-in caregivers rely on these new media to stay updated on their children's progress in school or to keep track of the whereabouts of their spouses and other family members. A home computer, Internet subscription, and cellphone are essential tools for communicating with loved ones and bridging the distance with what Wilding (2006) calls "virtual intimacies." Connectivity may not alleviate a mother's anxieties about her children growing up in the care of others (Parreñas 2005b; Larsen and Urry 2008), but maintaining as much communication as possible is vital to virtual parenting.

Maligaya ako pag nakikita ko ang mga bata sa webcam o Skype [I am happy when I see my children on webcam or Skype].
– Angela, a hotel worker in Edmonton

In rural areas of Alberta, where there is less access to the Internet, the Filipino live-in caregiver relies on the kindness of the employer for use of the computer or telephone. Dionisia in southern Alberta stayed at a ranch for nine months before finally deciding to return to the Philippines and forgoing the remaining months of the Live-in Caregiver Program (LCP); she left because she was denied access to the telephone and computer by her female employer.

Transnational mothering offers an alternative paradigm to traditional on-site mothering practices. Transnational motherhood is described by Hondagneu-Sotelo and Avila (1997, 548) as "a variation of organizational arrangements, meanings, and priorities of motherhood" separating the mother and child. These mothers who are spatially separated from their children "reconfigure their representations of motherhood in a variety of ways" (Mahalingam, Balan, and Molina 2009, 74). Many studies have focused on Filipino mothers whose migration shapes diverse transnational mothering practices (Asis, Huang, and Yeoh 2004; Fresnoza-Flot 2009). Parreñas (2001b, 371) describes three ways in which transnational mothers deal with emotional strains of separation: "Commodification of love; the repression of emotional strains; and the rationalization of distance" through communication. Filipino children are often on the receiving end of a periodic showering of gifts by distant mothers, now physically replaced by other female kin at home; materialism and economic security substitute for other expectations. Transnational mothers "relativize" the different ways in which they "establish, maintain or curtail relational ties" and the "modes of materializing the family as an imagined community," depending on their feelings of belonging and obligation, either through "active pursuit" or "passive negligence" (Bryceson and Vuorela 2002, 14). To compensate for their absence, Filipino transnational mothers often engage in giving of material goods and other distant acts of nurturing in what Bryceson and Vuorela (2002) call "active relativizing." Although immigration policies in different countries are complicit in the separation of families of migrant workers, mothers reconstruct their roles in transnational spaces and negotiate "long distance intimacy" in the best way possible (Parreñas 2005b).

> *Nag-uusap kami palagi ng mga anak ko sa Skype ... Nag-iipon din ako para makabili ng laptop sa kanila. Dadalhin ko ito sa susunod na bakasyon ko.*
> [I am always talking with my kids through Skype ... I am also saving money to buy a laptop for them. I will bring it on my next vacation.]
> – Salvacion, a home care worker in Winnipeg

The extended nature of the Filipino family makes transnationalism a continuing social process. A trip back to the Philippines means not only seeing immediate family members but also reconnecting with cousins, aunts, uncles, and other relatives. A week-long trip to one's hometown is hardly long enough to accommodate the many invitations to various *salu-salo* (parties). People also expect to receive *pasalubong* (souvenirs or gifts) from abroad. Many *balikbayans* give gifts in appreciation for past favours or for the care of their children, especially by female kin.

Second-generation Filipino-Canadian youth also express their displacement and isolation "between homes" – between the Philippines and Canada (Pratt 2003/04). In various accounts of this youth group in Vancouver, identification with the Filipino culture becomes a strategy to fight "isolation/ alienation" (ibid., 53). The youth, too, are engulfed in "emotional transnationalism," particularly when they visit the Philippines or encounter its national symbols (Wolf 2002, cited in Pratt 2003/04, 55). Much of their experiences between two cultures have been translated into creative advocacy campaigns.[3]

Another visible marker of transnational Filipinos is the construction boom in modern houses in hometowns. Many *balikbayans* engage in "return-home" projects such as building new residences for their eventual retirement in the Philippines. Others have vacation houses for their holidays. Large real estate development corporations even have international agencies that target *balikbayans*. These property acquisitions are often made by middle-aged individuals with a stable income or permanent job. Architecturally designed houses or newly renovated homes equipped with the latest technology are often looked after by relatives until the *balikbayan* comes back for a few weeks or months.

Marami akong kaibigan na bumili ng condo sa Manila o nagpatayo ng retirement house sa kanilang bayan [I have many friends who bought a condo in Manila or built a retirement house in their hometowns].
    – Helena, a nurse in Regina

Kahit konti [even if a little], *I save up to repair our house. Sana pag-uwi ko maayos na. Gusto ko pa din sa atin kahit papaano.* [I hope that when I go home it's already fixed. I would still like to go home, no matter what.]
    – Rosal, a nurse TFW in Winnipeg

When older Filipino-Canadians become "snowbirds," they tend to spend only about five months a year in the Philippines in order to be able to claim their pensions and health benefits in Canada. They can enjoy the comfort of their own homes with *katulong* (domestic helpers) in the Philippines, whereas in Canada their pensions are barely adequate to cover living expenses. Living in the Philippines with a dollar exchange rate of 1:40 works well for those who pursue this retirement option. These "Filipino snowbirds" are similar to those Canadians who flock to popular sunny spots in the

United States (Chappell, McDonald, and Stones 2008). The decision to divide parts of the year between the Philippines and Canada presumably eases the domestic burden of senior women, who are able to hire live-in domestic helpers in the Philippines and are usually surrounded by relatives willing to share household tasks. However, this exacerbates the class divide in the Philippines: the *balikbayans* occupy a higher class than local women, and their "*balikbayan* living" or Western style of comfort accentuates class consciousness, especially in rural towns where the contrast is stark.

> *Hanggang kaya ng katawan ko ang mag-travel uuwi ako ng Pilipinas.*
> *Maganda ang buhay doon kung may pera ka. Pag malamig na dito sa*
> *Canada, uwi na ako sa atin.* [As long as my body is able to travel, I will
> go home to the Philippines. Life is good there if you have money.
> When it gets cold here in Canada, I am going home.]
> – Bella, a retired nurse in Winnipeg

The extent of Filipino snowbird practices among the community in the Prairies is not part of this study. In fact, scholarly literature on the state of Filipino seniors' lives in Canada is scarce (Alama 2009). Many have expressed the desire to return home, but the resources to do so on a regular basis pose particular challenges. So far, there are no available statistics on the number of Filipinos in Canada who want to be buried in the Philippines.

> *Halos patay na lahat ang mga kamag-anak ko sa Pilipinas. Nandito sa*
> *Canada ang mga anak ko. Baka dito na rin ako mamatay at ilibing sa*
> *Canada.* [Almost all my relatives in the Philippines are dead. My
> children are all here in Canada. I might also die and be buried in
> Canada.]
> – Rubia, employee in Lethbridge

To be sure, the saying "there is no place like home" resonates in everyone who desires to return to his or her native land when opportunity arises. Happy memories come alive on every return trip, no matter how brief it may be, and the longing to return is always there. Being a Filipino snowbird may be a one-time or short-term venture, and usually Filipino seniors end up staying permanently where they have the most family members to care for them. In addition, the issue of health care costs in the Philippines becomes a major deterrent for some to continue as Filipino snowbirds. There is no universal health care in the Philippines comparable to that in Canada, and medical expenses are mainly borne by individuals. Filipino snowbirds with health problems may pay more for required medical services in the Philippines.

The rapid increase in the number of Filipino transnational families may be a new development in the West, but I would argue that such a phenomenon, although it now extends beyond national borders, is actually a common practice among island peoples, with their regular, circuitous paths of leaving and returning. This means that, in general, Filipino families have their hometown base and the children move out to continue their education and ultimately find work in capital cities, returning home for visits during fiestas, *pista ng patay* (All Souls' Day), *Pasko* (Christmas), and anniversaries. With the advent of internationalization, moving out now occurs at greater distances – between countries instead of between regional towns. Philippine development has often been city-focused, with post-secondary schools, administrative offices, and banks all converging in urban centres, requiring local townsfolk to make periodic *siyudad* (city) trips. By extension, the Philippines is now the analogous peripheral country in the global system, with overseas Filipinos making return trips as transnationals. For many "wired parents" (Jackson 2005, 140), the trip need not be taken too often because of the increasing reliance on new technologies to nurture children from afar. A parting quote among *balikbayans* in a small rural town in Leyte now includes "see you on Facebook," or "*i-text mo na lang ako* [just send me a text]." These relationships are, in the words of Vertovec (2009, 3), "globally intensified and now take place paradoxically in a planet-spanning yet common – however virtual – arena of activity."

Cash Remittances and *Balikbayan* Goods

Perhaps the most studied aspect of Filipino transnationalism is the multi-billion-dollar yearly remittances to the Philippines (Burgess and Haksar 2005). The US$7 billion in remittances from January to May 2009 surprisingly "save[d] the Philippines" from the global economic recession during this time (Adriano 2009). The Philippines, according to the World Bank report on remittances, was the fourth-largest remittance recipient in the world in 2010, after India, China, and Mexico (Torres 2011). Figures from the Bangko Sentral ng Pilipinas (Central Bank of the Philippines n.d.) demonstrate the increasing value of remittances, the top sources of which in 2008 were the United States, Saudi Arabia, and Canada. Remittances from Canada more than doubled during these years. Remittance figures from the United States may be overstated, since remittances from other countries are channelled through US banks as well (Medalla 2007, 219). Canada and the United States are countries of permanent settlement for Filipinos, whereas those in Saudi Arabia are mainly overseas Filipino workers (OFWs). In 2006, there were 1.6 million Filipinos in the United States and 436,190 in Canada. Cash remittances of overseas Filipinos from Canada totalled US$1,962,663 in 2012 (Bangko Sentral ng Pilipinas n.d.).

The flow of remittances is gendered (Peterson 2010; Kunz 2011). The ratio of Filipino women to Filipino men is 1.81 (64.5 women to 35.4 men) in Canada, and 1.39 (58.7 women to 42.1 men) in the United States (Darden 2009). Immigrant Filipino women and female OFWs tend to be more conscientious than men in sending money and goods back to the Philippines. In a study of gender, remittances, and development involving Filipinos in Italy, Filipino women demonstrated consistency in monthly remittances to pay for health, education, and other basic needs of their families, with a generally positive impact on local development (Ribas-Mateos 2008). Filipino women appear to be meticulous in assessing what needs are to be met on a regular basis and are more likely to anticipate future necessities. Mothers pay particular attention to their children's school requirements.

> *Palagay ko mas malambot ang puso ng ina kaysa sa ama; kaya madalas akong magpadala ng pera sa mga bata.* [I think a mother has a softer heart than a father; that's why I often send money to my children.]
> – Susie, a caregiver in Calgary

Remittances totalling US$17.3 billion accounted for 10.8 percent of the Philippine GDP in 2009, an increase of 4 percent from the previous year (*AsiaOne News* 2010) and equivalent to a quarter of the country's merchandise exports (Medeiros et al. 2008, 107). In 2011, total remittances from overseas Filipinos reached US$22.5 billion, which contributed mainly to the country's "surprisingly strong growth" (Ko 2012). Records of remittances are, however, often based on documented money transfers to the Philippines from regulated banks and do not include unofficial channels such as mail enclosures, person-to-person *pakiusap* (request), and private agencies. Women tend to utilize their social network, especially other women returning home to the same province, for personal delivery of funds. A more common practice of *balikbayans* is to give cash to siblings, parents, and relatives on returning home. To capture this lucrative business market, innovative ways of remitting money, such as the Smart Communications phone-based system have cropped up (International Bank for Reconstruction and Development and World Bank 2006). Smart cellphone subscribers use a SMART Money Card to withdraw money from automated teller machines and businesses such as McDonald's, SM (Shoemart), 7-Eleven, and Tambunting Pawnshop.

> *Doon ako pumupunta sa Asian store sa northside. Isip ko mas malaki ang exchange rate nila kaysa sa Western Union.* [I go to the Asian store in the north side. I think their exchange rate is higher than Western Union's.]
> – Annabel, a fast food worker in Lethbridge

Philippine money transfer services operate globally. Offices and agents are found in every Filipino community around the world. Even television networks have joined in the remittance business (e.g., ABS-CBN EasyRemit). Remittance agents in Calgary, for example, include Forex Alberta, iRemit Global Remittance, Acumen Allied Services Ltd., and Reliable Peso Remit. Filipinos in Canada also utilize the MoneyGram money transfer service available in post offices, as well as Western Union branches commonly found in Walmart stores. Transaction fees and the setting of different exchange rates make international money transfer services a profitable business. On the one hand, migrant workers bear the burden of extra costs in sending money back to their home countries (International Organization for Migration [IOM] 2006). On the other hand, the money transfer business also provides additional income to many enterprising Filipino immigrants. Becoming a sub-agent of Philippine remittance companies requires only a computer and a small cash bond. Filipino and other Asian stores often serve as money transfer sub-agents. About three Filipino women in southern Alberta work as home-based sub-agents of remittance agencies and earn a commission with each transaction.

Migrants have also used remittances as leverage in organizing trans-national protests against exploitation, force migration, and the failure of governments to protect their rights and welfare. About 112 migrant organizations, including Migrante International, the International Alliance of Filipino Migrant Organizations, declared 29 October as Zero Remittance Day in 2008, coinciding with the opening of the Global Forum on Migrant Development in Manila (GMA News 2008). Damayan Manitoba joined Bayan Canada and Migrante International in a campaign for a "no-remittance day" in July 2009 to oppose the convening of the House of Representatives as a constituent assembly to amend the Philippine Constitution and allegedly ensure the political hold of President Gloria Macapagal-Arroyo beyond 2010. Provincial remittance figures in Canada are not known. The amounts from Alberta, Saskatchewan, and Manitoba need to be extracted from national reports.

Aside from cash remittances, Filipino transnationalism is marked by the constant shipment of goods in *balikbayan* boxes. Shipping, receiving, and door-to-door deliveries involve transnational Filipino business partnerships at both ends of the market, usually operated by small enterprises. Maas (2008, 135), in her study of the Philippine door-to-door industry, describes "how basically simple and small business ventures, initiated at grassroots level, can actively stimulate transnationalization beyond the narrow kinship systems that migration usually engender, as they expand these pre-existing social relations into a dense and varied web of cross-bordering ties." The transnational flow of these boxes also enables many Filipinos, both in the Philippines and overseas, to become what I call "on/off entrepreneurs" or petty businesspersons. That is, Filipinos engage in small-scale buy-and-sell operations of imported goods for their own social networks – officemates, relatives, and friends. Profits from petty selling are not reported as income for tax purposes, and *balikbayan* boxes are potential sources of additional revenue for many households in the Philippines. Many of these undertakings are initiated by women in the family who take pains, while abroad, to select the items for resale and to facilitate the shipment of goods across borders.

Sending a *balikbayan* box at least once a year is a laborious process for Filipinos in diaspora. In Alberta, TFWs scour thrift stores and garage sales. *Balikbayan* boxes typically contain non-perishable items, including flat-screen televisions, but contents differ based on their point of origin and the particular needs of the recipients. Filipino women engage in a selective process of finding items that best suit a specific child or member of the family, and *balikbayan* boxes often show "how mothering from afar occurs" (Tung 2003, 308). According to McKay (2004, 19), the *balikbayan* box represents "a kind of transnational grocery shopping that reproduces [women's] domestic identity in their family at home." Filipino women perform a ritualized act of transferring care to a purchased commodity, assuming that when the item reaches the intended person, the love will be requited.

Interestingly, it is often cheaper to send money so that these items can be purchased in the Philippines than it is to buy and ship them from Canada. Imported goods are readily available in local supermarkets. As well, the shipment process is not entirely smooth, with cases of abandonment, delays, fraud, and mishandling of packages en route to the Philippines (Espinosa 2010). In the Prairies, *balikbayan* cargo agencies are usually located in big cities, and transporting cargo boxes from outlying communities takes time. Filipinos in Lethbridge, for example, have to drive about two hours to the nearest cargo depot in Calgary. From there, the boxes are transported to Vancouver and transferred to Manila-bound ships. Sub-agents in smaller communities are known to only a few people and do not advertise their services. Because cargo boxes sent through sub-agents are picked up on designated dates, delivery can be quite delayed. And yet, it is not surprising that the *balikbayan* box is an institutionalized transnational cultural icon in Filipino migration, as values, filial expectations, and identities become entrenched in the material moorings of global displacement. Alburo (2005, 138) uses the *balikbayan* box as a metaphor for the (dis)location of Filipino-Americans and describes its preparation as an "allegory of bonds" between those away and those at home. The *balikbayan* box represents a material symbol of Filipinos' attachment to their homeland and conveys the message that one still connects – and possibly may be home too, one day.

Media and Popular Culture

Migration of people is accompanied by different ways of reproducing their cultures through mass media. Following Appadurai's concept (2003, 25) of "global cultural flows," Filipino lives in diaspora are intricately woven in "globalscapes" (Bretell 2000, 97) of media networks that culturally reinforce a sense of belonging to an imagined nation (Anderson 1991).[4] In this section, I draw on the use of Philippine global television networks, the popularity of *Pinoy* celebrity concerts and appearances in Canada, and the use of beauty and fashion as avenues of Filipino transnationalism.

The Filipino Channel (TFC) has been the "undisputed all-Filipino network in the world" since 1994 (ICON Group International 2008, 65). It is owned by ABS-CBN Corporation, the largest multimedia company in the Philippines. Overseas Filipinos can watch the latest Philippine news, entertainment, and other broadcast genres all day. There are over 1 million Filipino TFC subscribers in the United States alone. In Canada, ABS-CBN signed an agreement with Rogers Communications to make TFC available on Rogers Cable, beginning on 26 April 2010, to subscribers in Eastern Canada, which includes the provinces of Ontario, New Brunswick, and Quebec (*Visayan Daily Star* 2010). In Western Canada, TFC has aired on Shaw Cable's Channel 509 since 2011. The number of Filipino household subscribers to Shaw TFC, Rogers TFC, or satellite TFC is unknown, but it is safe to say that TFC is becoming a popular channel among Shaw's Filipino subscribers in Alberta, although the selection of programs is limited compared with TFC box (i.e., a digital converter box that is connected to the Internet via modem to access TFC). The Filipino Channel Canada ULC has three dealers based in Winnipeg, Montreal, and Richmond, British Columbia. There are also central dealers in Alberta, Manitoba, and Saskatchewan.[5] Alberta was the best Canadian province in TFC sales performance in 2009. Top dealers receive a warm welcome to the Philippines, with tickets to shows and vacation tours.

A rival media company, GMA (Global Media Arts) Network Inc., currently operates two international Filipino channels: GMA Pinoy TV and GMA Life TV, launched in 2005 and 2008, respectively. GMA Pinoy TV is available in the Asia Pacific region, Diego Garcia in the British Indian Ocean Territory, Canada, Europe, the Middle East, North Africa, and the United States (Hawkes 2012). In Canada, GMA Pinoy TV was made available through Bell ExpressVu (now Bell TV) in December 2007 and Rogers Cable in August 2008.

Paragas (2006, iii) in his doctoral thesis on OFWs and communication, describes the mass media networks as "direct link[s] with the homeland" and, at times, a "surrogate venue for interacting with the host country." Tagalog (or Pilipino) programming is a worldwide phenomenon that connects Filipinos overseas to the homeland every second of the day. In many social gatherings in Filipino homes in Canada, gossiping about celebrities or critiquing Philippine politics is common among those with Pinoy channels. Multicultural programs showcasing Filipinos in Canada also provide updates on issues, events, lifestyle, and tours to the Philippines, among other topics.

> *Gusto ko yung mga drama sa TFC. Medyo malungkot at masaya rin ako.*
> *Marami silang episode tungkol sa mga OFW.* [I like the dramas on TFC. I feel sad and happy, too. They have many episodes about OFWs.]
> – Lorna, a hotel worker in Edmonton

> *Nanood ako ng TV Patrol palagi. Malalaman mo kung ano ang nangyayari sa atin. Parang ganoon pa din ng umalis ako.* [I always watch TV Patrol. You will learn about what's happening in our country. It seems the same as when I left.]
> – Rosalinda, a nurse in Saskatoon

Philippine international television networks mediate transnational connectivity among Filipinos in diaspora right in their own homes. Schein (2008, 188) argues that the media create "transnational subjectification," wherein "people develop social imaginaries and senses of community and identity" without even being mobile. The increasing popularity of *Pinoy* channels now carried by mainstream media networks in Canada represents the institutionalization of multicultural mediascapes (cf. Appadurai 2003), which fuel nostalgic notions of home and at the same time reinforce perceptions of Canada as the better place to be, particularly when reports of, for instance, natural disasters, poverty, and corruption are broadcast from the Philippines.

Philippine media networks have successfully branded themselves as belonging with the Filipino people wherever they may be. GMA is known as the *Kapuso* (one heart) network; its new slogan is *Kapuso ng Pamilyang Pilipino* (One Heart with the Filipino Family), whereas before 2002 it had been "Where You Belong." ABS-CBN, however, has been referred to as the *Kapamilya* (member of the family) network since 2003. Both embrace the idea of the Filipino family as the locus of belonging, and their reach to millions of Filipinos around the world indicates success. The media have increasingly been instrumental in mediating projects of nationalism and national identity since the last century (McCourt 2008). Through global television networks like TFC, Filipinos identify with an "imagined community" (Anderson 1991) by creating "constructs and images of what the nation is, what it means to belong to the nation" (McCourt 2008, 283).

Centring on the family in Philippine international television has far-reaching implications, however. Ideals of women's roles at home and in society are main themes in drama skits, telenovelas, and *teleserye* (television series), perpetuating a gendered ideology (Eviota 1994). According to Tyner (2004, 117), Philippine shows "reinforce images of motherhood, beauty, docility, and subservience in the portrayal of women" as "dutiful housekeepers and loyal wives and mothers." Alternatively, Philippine cinema tends to depict women as "sufferers" (Manalansan 2003, 179). The plight of women abroad reinforces gendered representations of Filipino women, with filial obligation being the core justification for suffering and separation. Of course, seeing their lives portrayed on the silver screen by popular actors affirms for many that, despite the difficulties, they made the right decision. Migration is not only a personal choice but a choice validated by gendered expectations; the pain and suffering of female OFWs becomes normalized in popular television. Filipinos affected by migration have the world viewers on their side, and their story is shared with all of them – personal pain becomes transnational pain.

Philippine media networks and entertainment companies, in partnership with Filipino local businesses and organizations, sponsor live concerts of Philippine-based entertainers around the world (Bonus 2000; Vergara 2009). In Canada, the lineup of Philippine artists in 2009 and 2010 indicates the popularity of these events among Filipinos and their Canadian friends. *Pinoy* concerts in Canada reflect the cultural exchange of the local and the national within global spaces – that is, local Filipino talent in Canadian communities participating with Philippine-based artists (Delos Reyes 2010). The ability of young Filipino-Canadians to interpret folk rhythms or follow the latest dance craze points to parallel trends in the Philippines and Canada. Cultural performativity suggests that "Filipino-ness" is reproduced through singing, dancing together with Philippine celebrities, and laughing along with comedians. The notions of "local" and "national" shifts between Filipinos in Canada and Philippine artists; this time, those in Canada are viewed as local and those coming from the Philippines are considered national. Some of the Filipino concerts held in the Prairie provinces include the Celebrity Fast Break Canadian Tour in Winnipeg and ASI in Calgary and Edmonton in 2009, and the Laughin' N' Loving Comedy Valentine Show and the One Kapamilya Go Canada in Calgary in 2010.

Moreover, Philippine talents today have gone global in mainstream pop culture, with artists such as Charice Pempengco, Arnel Pineda, and Lea Salonga leading the way.[6] Many Filipinos in Canada and the United States, for example, share Internet links to these entertainers' concert dates. It seems that Filipinos patronizing and participating in *Pinoy* concerts become "cultural citizens" of the Philippines based on an extended application of what Ong (2004, 157) calls "a dual process of self-making and being made." *Pinoy* concerts reinforce Filipino cultural identity and community in scattered global spaces. Even international boxing sensation Manny Pacquiao appears in concerts in the United States after a successful bout in the ring, performing to large Filipino crowds as the symbol of national pride – the *pambansang kamao* (national fist). Singing is thus an act of national cultural rendition.

Philippine popular culture is also transnational in terms of sourcing of talents. Many Philippine celebrities are sons and daughters of transnational Filipino families and interracial marriages or relationships. Actress Judy Anne Santos is the daughter of a former Filipina caregiver in Toronto. GMA television soap actress Marian Rivera's mother was an OFW in Spain while she was growing up in Cavite, Philippines. Many mixed-blood young Filipinos grace contemporary television and cinema screens – Gerald Anderson (Filipino-American), Assunta de Rossi (Filipino-Italian), Anne Curtis (Filipino-Australian) Valerie Weignman and Empress Schuck (Filipino-Germans). Television, magazines, advertisements, and cinema have certainly created an opportunity for aspiring Filipino youth overseas to come home as Philippine stars. *Pinoy* pop culture has gone beyond borders through the Philippine global television network. Young Filipino talents audition for programs like ABS-CBN's *Showtime* or *Pilipinas Got Talent*.[7]

The dominance of the entertainment genre in Philippine television networks aired globally provides fun and comic relief. Poverty in the Philippines generates a pool of willing participants ready to try their luck and win cash prizes in contests sponsored by variety shows. Giving away cash prizes seems like a temporary solution to the problem of poverty: one simply needs to line up early in the morning to get inside the studio. Keeping the poor hooked on chance-in-a-lifetime TV contests potentially keeps them away from becoming involved in politics to address the root causes of poverty in the country. Philippine media with global networks somehow remind Filipinos in diaspora of the life they left behind and what the present means for the future.

Another gateway to "celebrityhood" for Filipinos is competing in beauty pageants. Recent winners of competitions have included mixed-blood Filipino women.[8] The mestiza tends to be the representative Filipina for such beauty competitions, which has wide-ranging implications not only for the beauty and fashion industries in the Philippines but also the reproduction of a certain standard of beauty.

The Philippines is a beauty-crazed society. The concept of "beautiful" is primarily based on a flawless fair complexion and sharp-contoured facial features, or the mestiza look. Gemma Araneta-Cruz, the first Filipina to win an international competition as Miss International in 1965, noted that *maputi* (white-skinned), and not the typical brown-skinned woman, defines Filipina beauty. She urged Filipinos to "send girls [to beauty pageants] whose beauty reflects our heritage" (cited in McFerson 2002, 32). *Kayumanggi* (brown-skinned) Filipino women have been finalists in the Miss Universe pageant twice: Miriam Quiambao was first runner-up in 1999 and Venus Raj was fourth runner-up in 2010 (CBS News 2010). Although these non-mestiza beauties have Malay features, they still do not represent the average-looking

Filipina because of their height. They may look *kayumanggi* or *morena* (tanned, brown), but they are tall and slender. The average height for Filipinas is five feet, two inches, or 157.48 centimetres (Galicano-Adanza et al. 1991, 306), whereas Miriam Quiambao stood at 170.18 centimetres and Venus Raj towered at 175.2 centimetres. Beauty pageant organizers set a minimum height that excludes the average Filipina. For example, the application form for Miss World Philippines 2011 required contestants to be five feet, six inches tall.[9]

The fact that tall Filipinas are considered ideal to represent the nation in international competitions probably facilitates the continued participation of *balikbayan* youth. No data are available regarding the number of *balikbayan* youth from the Prairies or from Canada who have gone back to the Philippines and participated in hometown or national beauty pageants. The important thing is not total numbers but rather the appropriation of "foreignness" as Filipino. Filipino TV programs and cinema cast *balikbayan* actors despite their tongue-twisting delivery of Pilipino lines.

Philippine show business is dominated by the mestiza (colloquial *tisoy/tisay*) beauty ideal. A few standout non-mestiza actresses occupy a niche as comedians or in typecast roles as maids, villains, or poor women in most cases. The dominance of the mestiza look in Philippine cinema is ironic, as it reflects only a small proportion of the Filipino population, who are mainly brown-skinned in different hues. As the face of multimedia, the mestiza promotes the subtle institutionalization of what I call a "beauty hierarchy" – the more foreign-looking a face is, the greater its commercial value. Filipino cultural historian Doreen Fernandez states: "Contrary to its name, [the mass media] is not usually created by the populous, the people, the majority, the mass, but by 'patrons,' or if you will, 'sponsors,' for the consumption of the masses" (cited in McFerson 2002, 31). Television networks have recently featured white-looking nationals from Korea. How mass media is organized and operated in the Philippines is shaped by certain ideals of beauty that replicate class hierarchies; both in the past and today, "white looks" rule the market. Nationalists may see this trend as the by-product of a colonial mentality – of favouring Western-type looks with light or fair-skinned features as being more marketable for *Pinoy* entertainment (Guerrero 1983; Tolentino 1998). Accordingly, the mestiza look appears consistent with the globalization of the ideal beauty in the mould of Barbie (Grewal and Kaplan 2005; Bosse 2007; Solomon 2010).

Valorization of beauty ideals is reflected in the zealous consumption of skin-whitening products in the Philippines; many of these products are not regulated and potentially cause more harm than good (GMA News 2010). The underlying message of the countless advertisements for these products is: be white and you will succeed. Good-looking women (i.e., those with fair skin or fine facial features) tend to be hired first in many business establishments, a number of which explicitly require a "pleasing personality" in their front-line customer service representatives – "'pleasing personality' means, among other things, youth, good looks and grooming, charm, a gracious manner and a 'well-modulated' voice" (Chant and McIlwaine 1995, 182).

The smallest political units and local organizations have embraced beauty contests and their derivatives with gusto as a time-tested way to capture an audience, and such contests serve multiple agendas in cash-strapped ventures. Schools regularly hold various title competitions based on the highest fund-raiser, who usually has transnational Filipino donors. Crowning of the winner in complete regalia is much anticipated by local participants; an array of singers and dancers and the appearance of a celebrity to crown the winner make up the program. Solicited funds are used to repair buildings, purchase needed equipment and supplies, and accomplish other goals that benefit the wider community. From a feminist perspective, the use of females as a conduit for needed funds is a ground for criticism. The fact that this perspective is not shared by the Filipino women who participate in these contests needs to be understood from the local context. As I see it, this mode of fundraising is a form of negotiation in order to share the resources in the hands of the elites in a community. Female contestants tend to come from upper-middle-class families with established networks to draw in funds for local benefit. This is a practical and effective strategy that serves the interests of the parties involved: the organizers who need money for a good cause, and the elites who need public recognition of their status, including the possibility of gaining popular support in case they run for public office. It appears to be a win/win situation at the cost of giving peculiar titles to women and girls.

National and international broadcast Philippine entertainment crosses two dominant cultural frames in mainstream networks, English and Tagalog. Most television hosts, if not all, effectively use *Taglish* (Tagalog-English) lingo (Rafael 2008), combining both languages to communicate with their audience. By doing so, they bridge a marked class division in Philippine society: Tagalog for the masses and English for the elite. Taglish is a powerful language because it "collapses the hierarchical relationships" of the two colonial languages of Spanish and English as well as the dominant Tagalog as a form of resistance (Ignacio 2003, 167). First-generation immigrant Filipinos from Tagalog regions who live in an English-speaking country like Canada find that the Taglish vernacular of media channels facilitates the transmission of both cultures to their children.

> *Pag nanonood ako sa TFC siyempre naririnig at nakikita ng mga anak ko ang pagka-Pilipino natin. So, natututo din sila.* [Whenever I watch TFC, of course, my children also hear and watch our being Filipino. So, they also learn.]
> – Samantha, a government employee in Regina

Fashion is another aspect of Filipino transnational popular culture. The Philippines is closely linked to various international clothing manufacturers in Hong Kong and China. Filipinos returning to the Philippines find bargains on new outfits in standard petite sizes, and summer clothes purchased in the Philippines can be worn in Canada later in the season. *Balikbayans* arriving with suitcases full of clothes and gifts might leave with empty luggage if not for the fact that Philippine shopping malls are bargain havens. Many *Pinays* in the Prairies claim that new fashion designs come out first in Asia before reaching the stores in Canada.

> *Mura ang bilihin sa atin kung dolyar ang pera mo ... Mga fresh designs na una kong nakita sa SM Megamall kaysa dito sa West Edmonton Mall.* [Cost of goods are cheap in our country if your money is in dollars. I saw fresh designs in SM Megamall before here at West Edmonton Mall.][10]
> – Hosanna, a nurse in Edmonton

Perhaps most patronized by *Pinays* in the Prairies when they return to the Philippines are beauty salon services. The low cost of hairstyling and other services are treats not to be missed.

> *Doon na ako nagpapagupit sa atin. Mura na at maganda pa ang service. Medyo mahal yan sa Canada at hindi ako basta-basta pumupunta sa salon.* [I get my hair cut there in our country. It's cheap and the service is good. It's quite expensive in Canada, and I don't just go to the salon at any time.]
> – Josefina, self-employed in Winnipeg

Female kin provide recommendations on where to get the best-quality service. That the aesthetics industry in the Philippines has thrived despite the global economic recession is due in part to continued tourist arrivals, including *balikbayans* (EnjoyPhilippines 2011).

In simple economics, trade in transnational goods and services occurs during each home visit. *Pinays* as *balikbayans* bring loads of much-desired imported goods as *pasalubong* for families and friends in the Philippines, and help boost the local economy with their spending. Beyond this scale of visible exchange, however, is the apparent perpetuation of a neocolonial mentality in consumption that favours imported goods over locally made products. The appeal of brand labels has contributed to the growth of a counterfeit industry in the Philippines (Chaudhry and Zimmerman 2009, 27). Female *balikbayans* often become walking models of expensive items such as Louis Vuitton (LV) bags, advertising their elite status through the items they take back home. Counterfeit LV bags, copied to perfection, have appeared in the local market at significantly lower prices. Gigantic malls spread across metropolitan cities in the Philippines eye *balikbayans* as customers and OFW families as the new middle class. Goods from the Philippines then become a transnational commodity of use in host societies. However, food products shipped from the Philippines to Canada are subject to much stricter customs enforcement than imported goods arriving at Philippine ports, which suggests that there may be an imbalance in the exchange of commodities between countries (Kuo 1995, 117).

Dual Citizenship and Absentee Voting

Citizenship, according to Marshall (1994, 17), is "a status bestowed on those who are full members of a community," and involves three dimensions of rights: civil, political, and social. He states:

> [The] civil element is composed of the rights necessary for individual freedom – liberty of the person, freedom of speech, thought and faith, and the right to own property and to conclude valid contracts, and the right to justice ... By political element ... [is meant the] right to participate in the exercise of political power ... By social element ... [is meant] the whole range from the right to a modicum of economic welfare and security ... according to the standards prevailing in society. (1994, 9)

Marshall's pioneering liberal conception of modern citizenship is the "cornerstone of the citizenship debate" in the postwar era (Mullard 1999, 14). In the 1980s, citizenship was viewed as an expression of community-introduced communitarianism (Sandel 1982; Walzer 1983), grounded less on formal rights bestowed on citizens and more on their identity and participation – a kind of "cultural democracy" (Delanty 2002, 163) that embeds belonging within a cultural community. The universal conception of citizenship as status and a set of rights led to the equality-difference discussions based on gender, race, and other social markers of identity among historically marginalized groups of people, especially women, since the 1990s (Lister 1997; Voet 1998; Armstrong 2006). Citizenship and the politics of difference remain substantive and poignant matters of debate in public discourses today.

The traditional conception of citizenship was bounded by territory. Rights and obligations accrued in citizenship were premised on one's defined political community. The world has changed dramatically since the 1950s, however, and demographic diversity brought about by immigration now characterizes many countries. One "systematic response to migration" is the granting of dual citizenship (Carter 2001, 110). The number of people with dual or multiple nationalities of belonging has grown rapidly in the last few decades (Bauböck 2006; Faist, Gerdes and Rieple 2007; Sejersen 2008), and about ninety-three countries recognize some form of dual citizenship

(Renshon 2001). In the United States, nineteen of the top twenty source countries of immigrants accept dual citizenship (Spiro 2008). This trend stems from the political integration of multiple nationalities in states, both immigrant-receiving and immigrant-sending countries, in a globalizing world.

Dual citizenship arises in three major ways: (1) gender-neutral citizenship laws allow the transmission of citizenship to children of mixed-nationality relationships from both maternal and paternal filiations; (2) second-generation immigrants acquire their parents' citizenship by *jus soli* (by place of birth) or *jus sanguinis* (by blood); and (3) many immigrants retain their original citizenship of birth on acquisition of new citizenship by naturalization (Brubaker 1992, 144). I opine that dual citizenship is gender-fair, recognizing women's autonomy even after marriage to a non-national, unlike in many countries, where a woman's citizenship follows that of her husband or children's citizenship follows that of their father (Bredbenner 1998; Brysk 2004). Dual citizenship gives women the possibility of choosing citizenship in a country that respects women's rights, especially women coming from repressive or fundamentalist regimes.

Although there is increasing acceptance of nationality as a corpus of human rights in international law (Faist, Gerdes, and Rieple 2007), dual citizenship remains central to the discussion of national identity and allegiance among states (Bauböck, Perchinig, and Sievers 2009). For example, Germany still refuses to grant dual citizenship to non-Germans despite calls to the contrary (Hansen and Weil 2002; Goebel 2010), and multinationalism in Japan is "far from [reaching] acceptance" (Kamiya 2009). The prevailing argument against the granting of dual citizenship concerns the loyalty of those with more than one citizenship; treachery and betrayal are feared as possible outcomes (Brubaker 1992; Schuck 1998b; Faist 2007). Another argument invokes the equality principle, claiming that dual citizens may have more rights than others (Kejžar 2009). Particularly after the 1997 European Convention on Nationality, however, dual nationality is increasingly a reality that needs to be acknowledged by states (Levitt 2003). With more countries easing their citizenship requirements, it appears that "dual citizenship is inevitable" (Hansen and Weil 2002, 9), or at least "frequently necessary," in the face of growing interdependence among nation-states (Harty and Murphy 2005, 89). It is, according to Hammar (1990, 108), a "fair expression" of people's dual or multiple identities.

The formal recognition of Filipinos as transnationals transpired with the granting of dual citizenship under the Citizenship Retention and Reacquisition Act (Republic Act No. 9225) passed by the Philippine Congress in 2003. Its enactment was an acknowledgment of the huge potential for overseas Filipinos to invest in their native country (Rupert and Solomon

2006). Natural-born Filipinos who acquire foreign citizenship do not lose their Philippine citizenship (Lazo 2006). If they have become naturalized citizens of another country and want to become dual citizens, they simply submit an application form and pay the processing fee at Philippine consulates around the world, or to the Bureau of Immigration in the Philippines, and take an oath of allegiance. Filipino dual citizens receive an Identification Certificate from the Bureau of Immigration through the consular office where citizenship was reacquired. Dual citizens have the same rights as other Filipino citizens to own property, enter into business or commerce, practise professionally, vote in the Philippines, and carry a Philippine passport. Property ownership and business ventures are probably the most common reasons for becoming a dual citizen. Filipino dual citizens have been exempt from paying the airport exit fee of 1,200 pesos since April 2009 (Crescini 2009).

The narratives included in this section are snapshots of certain patterns and practices of Filipinos in diaspora. A qualitative study of the numbers of *Pinays* in the Prairies who hold dual citizenship and their reasons for doing so is a topic for future research.

> *Nag-apply ako ng dual citizenship para makabili ng bahay sa amin. At least, hawak ko ang titulo.* [I applied for dual citizenship so that I could buy a house back home. At least, I hold the title.]
> – Dalisay, a retired teacher in Winnipeg

From the 1980s to 1996, the number of Canadians with dual or multiple citizenship grew by 16.6 percent (Bloemraad 2004, 404), but they remain a small portion of the population, about 3 percent (Statistics Canada 1997). In 2006, about 78 percent of Filipinos in Canada were Canadian citizens. Since 1977, they have had the opportunity to gain dual or multiple citizenships under Canada's Citizenship Act.[11] As of August 2008, there were 51,000 Filipinos with dual citizenship, mostly in the United States, Canada, and Australia (*Manila Mail* 2008a). About 30,000 Filipinos regained Philippine citizenship in 2012 alone, with those from Canada comprising the third-largest group, after the United States and the United Kingdom (Diola 2013). The number of Filipinos in the Prairies holding dual citizenship as of 2009 is unknown.

Dual citizenship is consistent with the philosophy of multiculturalism and, unlike in the United States, is "valorized in official government statements" in Canada (Fagan and Munck 2009, 37). However, allegiance to two or more countries is a thorny issue in immigrant political incorporation and integration (Tettey and Puplampu 2005; Bloemraad 2006). Labelle and Salée (2001, 299) note that immigrants are directed "to make Canada their primary, unequivocal site of civic allegiance." While pushing for multiculturalism, the Canadian state "reluctantly continues to allow" diverse citizenships because of ambiguities of adaptation among immigrants (Wong and Satzewich 2006, 12). The issue of dual or multiple citizenship among Canadians, particularly non-white, non-Christian Canadians has become more profound after Muslim extremist attacks in Western countries since 2001 (cf. Stasiulis and Ross 2006). In 2006, the practice of dual citizenship came under government review when, after a costly mass evacuation of fifteen thousand Canadians during the Israeli-Hezbollah conflict, seven thousand of them subsequently returned to Lebanon (CBC News 2006; CTV News 2006).

Filipinos come from a country in Asia with a relatively sparse record of escalated conflict outside its borders. Like the Lebanese, many Filipinos found their way back to their native country when the Philippines recognized dual citizenship in 2003. Dual citizenship makes it possible to have the best of both worlds. I argue that duality of citizenship is hierarchically positioned but flexible based on a person's vested interests at any given time. Filipino-Canadians presumably will not invoke their Philippine citizenship in situations of distress, because of the poor protection it would likely afford compared with their Canadian citizenship. Whether they are in the Philippines or in another country, being a Canadian citizen is perceived as a privileged identity.

Dual citizenship facilitates gender equality and empowerment for Filipino women. While the rights of women are institutionalized in law in both the Philippines and Canada, the practice of gender fairness in many aspects of personal and professional relationships is not the same in both countries. In terms of dissolution of marriages, Canada provides greater security for spouses and children in a well-regulated system. Social rights of citizenship are far better recognized in a developed welfare state than in a developing nation. Although both countries follow the liberal democratic system of rights and governance, there is a gap in terms of practice and the culture within which claims to women's rights can effectively proceed. In short, the "ideal" of gender equality may be written in laws in the Philippines, but the "real" practice is somehow lived in Canada.

> *Of course, gusto ko ang Canadian citizenship. Ang puso ko ay Pinoy pero*
> *mas matimbang ang Canada kung welfare and benefits ang pinag-uusapan.*
> [Of course, I like Canadian citizenship. My heart is Filipino, but Canada
> carries greater weight if we are talking about welfare and benefits.]
> – Norma, a housewife in Saskatoon

An important development for transnational Filipino migrants' grassroots political activism was the institution of absentee voting in February 2003. The Overseas Absentee Voting Act (Republic Act No. 9189) permits qualified

Filipino citizens outside the country to vote in Philippine elections.[12] Absentee voting is supervised by the Commission on Elections (COMELEC) and the Department of Foreign Affairs (DFA). Three modes of overseas absentee voting (OAV) were implemented in the May 2010 elections: personal voting, postal voting, and, in Hong Kong and Singapore, automated voting (Lee-Brago 2010).

Reports from the Overseas Absentee Voting Secretariat show that there were 4,009 registered overseas absentee voters in Canada in 2009 (Inquirer.net 2009). Only 589,830 eligible voters out of 8.1 million OFWs and Filipinos resident in other countries worldwide were registered for the May 2010 national elections (Abano 2010). Of these, only 153,323 actually cast their votes in 2010 (Crisostomo 2011). The number of registered overseas absentee voters in the Prairies is unknown. None of the participants in this study cast an absentee vote during my fieldwork. Despite the low turnout of absentee voting so far, the Overseas Absentee Voting Act provides, according to Maya and Allen (2009, 163), "greater legal protection of the voting rights of overseas citizens than exists in many countries."

The greater significance of overseas absentee voting, however, is the recognition of Filipino migrant or transnational voices in Philippine politics. The Filipino diaspora, or those I call "floating in other borders," have the means to effect change in their native land. Although the tedious process of voter registration remains an obstacle, the issues and concerns of migrant Filipinos are readily publicized in the international media through their allied networks in host societies, bringing pressure to bear on Philippine domestic politics. Female OFWs, with their predominance in gender-segregated occupations, have the tenacity to pursue transnational activism through organizations like the Filipino Domestic Helpers General Union in Hong Kong. Other groups of Filipino women have organized themselves and remain active in promoting women's rights across borders. Examples of these organizations include the Philippine Women Centres in British Columbia and Ontario, PINAY in Quebec, and the Babaylan Philippine Women's Network in Europe. How these transnational groups utilize overseas absentee voting to shape electoral politics is something worth watching.

Pinay Transnational Practices

Overseas Filipino women, like other people in the orbit of globalization and migration, are located in "transnational space" (Hilsdon 2007, 173). Migration because of family, marriage, or work provides the stimulus for engagement in the forms of Filipino transnationalism outlined earlier. However, a close examination of the specific transnational practices undertaken by Filipino women is still lacking in the scholarly literature on migration in Canada. Filipino migrant women's positioning in studies of transnationalism remains focused on their "transnational subaltern" status as "cheap and temporary labor" (Ty 2006, 142) and as the economic underclass of the world. Few have explored their agency, both personal and collective, amid constraining global and national regulatory structures (Barber 2000; Pratt 2004; Swider 2006; Hilsdon 2007). I follow in the women's footsteps to investigate how, living in a transnational world, they find different pathways in negotiating between home country and "other," positioning themselves in a dynamic exchange between sites of new settlement and communities of origin.

The following selection of narratives from *Pinays* in the Prairies presents three types of transnational practices: philanthropy, advocacy, and mission work. Philanthropy loosely refers to voluntary acts of giving financial or material aid to the needy. Advocacy is the act of promoting knowledge on certain issues or defending the rights and welfare of particular groups. Mission work is the act of performing real-time voluntary service in the Philippines, such as medical missions.

Philanthropy

Women have been involved in charitable work since the earliest times (Kroeger and Evans 2002). With women denied full access to education and many professions in many countries even to this day, their role as volunteers was their main public persona aside from that of wife or daughter. Ostrower (1995, 69) notes that philanthropy is a "socially acceptable avenue for the exercise of leadership and public participation" among elite women. Upperclass women used their status and family connections to raise funds for favoured charities (Luddy 1995). Involvement with philanthropic activities continues today and, with the entry of women into the labour market, is no longer the preserve of "rich" women.

Immigrants and migrant women such as *Pinays* have become active in "diaspora philanthropy" or "contributing to countries of origin" (Wason 2004, 308). Millions of people around the world have shown a "natural proclivity to giving back" (Viswanath 2003, xiii) to their homeland (Geithner, Johnson and Chen 2004). Research on Filipino diaspora philanthropy is relatively new in contemporary migration studies, but awareness of this topic is growing (Opiniano 2005; Silva 2006; Amott 2007; Garchitorena 2007), pointing to a strong interest in "converting migration drains to gains" (Asian Development Bank 2006) and underlining the potential of overseas Filipinos in community and national development. The number of Filipinos in the Prairies contributing money to the Philippines through hometown associations and registered charitable organizations is unknown, but I surmise that anyone who is involved in Filipino community associations based on regional origin tends to support these initiatives; the amount collected is usually published, although not the number of people who contributed.

Families and kin networks are often the recipients of financial aid from overseas Filipinos (Johnston, Muñoz, and Alon 2007). This type of personal or private philanthropy to members of the family or clan is not considered in this section. Instead, I highlight the transnational philanthropy of *Pinays* in the Prairies to non-kin groups, communities of origin, and the home country, driven mainly by two motives: (1) alleviation of poverty and (2) response to natural calamities. There is a pressing need for poverty reduction in the Philippines, and transnational Filipinos often work with their hometown or community associations, parishes, and non-governmental organizations to identify recipients of aid.[13] One of the most active programs is Gawad Kalinga (GK), literally, "to give care." GK is a comprehensive poverty reduction program in the Philippines launched by Couples for Christ (CFC) in 2000 and supported by ANCOP (Answering the Cry of the Poor), a worldwide network of charities.[14]

> *In CFC we have ANCOP ... we build houses in the Philippines ... fundraising in Canada in September 2009, the Walk for a Cause in Henderson, Lethbridge ... We have to build twenty GK villages. On our account, we will call it Lethbridge Village. There is now Toronto Village, Calgary Village ... sponsor a child, educate a child under CFC. Para bang [it's like] we pay it back for the good deeds.*
> – Traning, a TFW in Lethbridge

The shelter project is a major component of GK that aims to provide housing to poor Filipinos. So far, about 21,000 homes have been completed in 1,200 GK communities in the Philippines, and GK remains strongly supported by overseas Filipinos. A village is named after its sponsoring group, such as CFC Winnipeg GK Village in Marikina City and the Calgary GK Villages in southern Leyte and Misamis Occidental provinces. Each GK village has about 50 to 100 homes. Other initiatives of the GK program include health care, education, and livelihood (Baggio and Asis 2008). Prominent celebrities and national leaders promote GK and its fundraising activities. In July 2009, former Philippine president Fidel V. Ramos travelled to Calgary to attend a breakfast forum and a GK Gala Night (*Pinoy Times* 2009).

> *In 2006, we built seven houses in Escalante initiated by a youth group in church. People donate money. We support the fundraising and raised $17,000 to build seven houses in Cebu.*
> – Ligaya, a retired factory worker in Winnipeg

> *For Gawad Kalinga we contribute as a group to PCCM [the Philippine Canadian Centre of Manitoba].*
> – Salvacion, a home care worker in Winnipeg

GK has become a catalyst project uniting different Filipino community groups and organizations, both within and beyond the Philippines, who wish to help the poor. The image of 4 million Filipino children growing up in squatter hovels has prompted many to contribute to tangible projects that build houses or provide livelihood opportunities for their parents, giving them the chance to live in "their own homes in beautiful, colorful, thriving communities" (Facun 2009, 129). According to former GK executive director Antonio Meloto, support for the shelter project created a "patriotic philanthropy" demonstrating the "renaissance of love and patriotism of ex-pat Filipinos, expressed in outpourings of care for their underprivileged" country members (Gawad Kalinga n.d.; Lopez 2007). Non-Filipinos have also shown their support for GK program initiatives.

> *CFC has ANCOP and Gawad Kalinga. El Shaddai, members of Filipino Catholic Society, Caring Hands of Jesus where couples coming together for bible study, pray ... own fundraising to help the community.*
> – Marilou, a community worker in Calgary

Couples for Christ, which launched GK, had around 1.4 million members in 2001 (Bouma, Ling, and Pratt 2010, 92) and is characterized by highly gendered practices. There is a strong male leadership tradition for key positions in CFC (Rivera 2008, 101).[15] It follows the patriarchal structure of male headship of the family, which parallels the ideals of Catholic religiosity and structure (ibid., 102). Masculinity is embedded in this ideology and contributes to the perpetuation of gender inequality (Obligacion 1999; Suzuki 2002). According to Abinales and Amoroso (2005, 268), CFC embraces the ideals of "traditional Catholic teachings" and has aligned itself with a "pro-family, nationalist and civic-minded discourse." *Pinays* in the Prairies who are active members of CFC participate with their husbands or with an assigned group such as Singles for Christ. These *Pinays* engage in CFC-inspired philanthropy, not in a female-inspired venture. Migration may offer opportunities for gender equality, but CFC promotes gendered assignments of tasks, including leadership, and the male headship community model.

Besides GK, many *Pinays* in the Prairies are involved with fundraising events in their own parishes. These include support for the education of seminarians and gifts to the poor in the Philippines, especially during Christmas.

> *We invited a missionary priest to celebrate Mass here in Saskatoon so we can help them, the poor in the Philippines. We send four boxes of toys and used clothes. My home is depot of used stuff!*
> – Dahlia, a private employee in Saskatoon

Priest here who is Filipino informed us through church ... As Filipinos, we are represented, speakers – representation for them in fundraising for victims of calamities ... PAS [Philippine Association of Saskatoon] members, kids dance during mosaic, sell spring rolls.
  – Samantha, a government employee in Regina

In areas where Filipino priests hold Masses, the mobilization of support among Filipino parishioners is usually very strong. Women, like Dahlia in Saskatoon, tend to be more involved than men in organizing and information sharing for local fundraising activities (Roces 2003).

Education, child welfare, and livelihood are the most popular projects supported by Filipino women in the Prairies. Social justice issues such as the struggle for equality and empowerment have been significant in women's lives (Jones 1999; Capeheart and Milovanovic 2007). The desire to alleviate the suffering of women, children, and their families is an important motivation for those supporting charitable or development programs in the Philippines. Like the Filipinos in Italy, *Pinays* in the Prairies are "global workers, local philanthropists" (Baggio and Asis 2008).

In FIDWAM [Filipino Domestic Workers Association of Manitoba] we help and support disabled children in Philippines. About four kids already helped in one year ... I contribute towards this.
  – Salvacion, a home care worker in Winnipeg

I was part of the Philippine International Development Council of YMCA and YWCA in Manitoba in the 1990s. I was privileged to go home to Philippines to visit development projects in Cebu – the co-op of women, furniture making, guitar, vegetable gardening, cooking projects, etc. Women are the main participants.
  – Gabriela, a retired government employee in Winnipeg

We did fundraising for victims of Typhoon Thelma. City of Winnipeg gave $60,000 matching donation. We have a fashion show project to help bahay ampunan [adoption house] in the Philippines.
  – Rosie, a sales agent in Winnipeg

Filipino women's philanthropy is also frequently a response to natural disasters in the Philippines. Financial contributions are channelled through their own community organizations as well as Philippine consulates in Canada or the Canadian Red Cross.

About two years ago mayroon [there was] Leyte disaster flash flood ... we raise funds.
  – Siony, a nurse in Calgary

*For typhoon, calamity, we organize and collect money and give to the
Red Cross.*
- Filomena, a government employee in Saskatoon

*With FILCAN [Filipino Canadian Association of Manitoba] we raise funds
for disaster relief in the Philippines.*
- Pilar, a community worker in Winnipeg

Pag may kalamidad [if there is a calamity] *mostly monetary. We send
money for disasters through Philippine associations. We hold dinners ...
disaster relief.*
- Helena, a nurse in Regina

Unlike donations channelled through the Red Cross, direct support to the
Philippines through community organizations usually gains no tax privilege. In 2007, however, the PCCM and the Bicol Association of Manitoba
developed a model of cooperation for their fundraising efforts to assist victims
of Typhoon Reming in the Bicol region. They worked with a Canadian
registered charity, Plan Canada, which accepted the donations and for-
warded them to Plan Philippines; donors were issued tax receipts and were
advised about the flow of funds (*Filipino Journal* 2007).

*Regional groups help their own communities in the Philippines. They are good
to their place ... groups join forces to bring medical supplies to their provinces.
They are never subdivided in practice. We have a GK project to build houses in
my husband's hometown ... We give money to the country for relief, also China
and Italy for earthquake victims.*
- Clemencia, a nurse in Winnipeg

Brinkerhoff (2006, 217) states that "the Filipino diaspora's philanthropic
orientation yields direct assistance to particular regions, hometowns, and
schools, as well as more general service contributions, such as medical missions and teacher training." Philanthropic contributions directed to Philippine hometowns or other causes symbolize continuing transnational ties.
However, these efforts lack consistency among individuals and hometown
associations. Cash is gold among *Pinays* in the Prairies, who remain responsible for the upkeep of the household and other demands to be met on their
own, although they may give a few dollars to charity events or fundraisers
when they can. In his study of Filipino hometown associations in Canada,
Silva (2006) claims that collective remittances are not sent on a regular basis
because of high transaction fees, and organizations have limited capacity to
establish strong ties in the Philippines. Regardless of the sporadic nature of
financial aid provided to others, most *Pinays* in the Prairies and their social

networks do care about development initiatives and relief efforts in the Philippines and show compassion to victims of natural calamities. Like the Filipino community associations in the Prairies, *Pinays* are building the base from which they can embark on wider, more sustained efforts to benefit the poor in the Philippines in the future.

Advocacy

Advocacy work is another transnational practice of activist *Pinays* in the Prairies. Advocacy work challenges existing ideas and beliefs about particular groups and endeavours to effect change through public campaigns or efforts with organizations (Evans 2005). The advocacy work of Filipino women in the Prairies extends across borders. For these women, the political is deeply personal, and they have been connecting with other women in the Philippines to provide guidance on migration to Canada, working for the rights and welfare of OFWs, and responding to international issues affecting women and children.

Improving the status of Philippine-trained nurses in Canada is one example of such advocacy work in the Prairies. Rosal in Winnipeg, through the Philippine Nurses Association of Manitoba, has begun coordinating with nursing schools in the Philippines in order to inform their graduates about their employment prospects on arrival in Canada, and particularly their rights as workers.

> *Philippine Nurses of Manitoba tied up with deans of colleges of nursing in the Philippines ... Spearheaded by UP College of Nursing, one of the goals is to safeguard nursing graduates from being exploited ... they are not a commodity bought from the Philippines! ... Yung action namin* [our action] *will protect the welfare of nurses who are applying here ... bargain with recruiting country for permanent status upon entry. We have ties with Manitoba Labour Relations and Manitoba Multicultural and citizenship community and transmit information to Philippines.*
> – Rosal, a nurse TFW in Winnipeg

Although their transnational advocacy is still in its infancy, Filipino nurses' associations have taken important steps to coordinate with Philippine-based nursing schools as well as with local groups in Canada. Like Rosal, Hosanna in Edmonton has demonstrated personal leadership in this.

> *Filipino nurses from the Philippines are not treated fairly in Canada. Parang iba ang trato sa amin* [it's like they treat us differently] *... We are assessed differently. Gusto nila ang qualities ng mga Filipino nurses* [they like the qualities of Filipino nurses], *but when they arrived here, not treated fairly*

by CARNA [College and Association of Registered Nurses of Alberta] ...
parang Diyos! [like God]
– Hosanna, a nurse in Edmonton

Hosanna expressed frustration about the stiff requirements for professional recognition of foreign-trained nurses in Alberta. She now provides consultation to the health regions in Edmonton that want to directly hire Filipino nurses and liaises with their counterparts in the Philippines. Promoting the rights of TFWs is another aspect of advocacy that spans cross-border relations [Briones 2009]. Knowledge of international conventions protecting workers' rights and of human rights protocols is indispensable. The most significant convention is the International Convention on the Protection of the Rights of All Migrant Workers and Members of Their Families (ICMW),[16] which was adopted by the United Nations in 1990 and came into force in July 2003 (Cholewinski 2005). As of 24 April 2013, there were thirty-five country signatories of the ICMW, mostly sending countries, including the Philippines.[17] However, Canada and other major receiving states have not. The Canadian Council for Refugees (CCR) has called on Canada to ratify the ICMW and undertake the following actions: expand settlement services to TFWs, ensure that TFWs are informed of their rights before coming to Canada and have control over their passports and health cards, and protect the status of TFWs who file complaints against abuses in the workplace (Canadian Council for Refugees 2007). Canada's non-ratification of the ICMW runs counter to its international image as an advocate of human rights.

I advocated for the rights of migrant workers with members of grassroots
women's organizations. Our organization has connections in the Philippines
and knows these challenges.
– Luningning, a community leader in Winnipeg

In Canada, policy of LCP needs improvement. Two years ago BABAE
presented a national women's conference together with live-in caregivers –
a forum theatre. We raise awareness so that audience knows about their
exploitation. We gave a summary recommendation from the conference ...
Why not allow their families?
– Marilou, a community worker in Calgary

The Live-in Caregiver Program (LCP) remains a controversial workers' rights issue in Canada, and progressive organizations and individuals support calls to abolish or reform the program. Filipino women's groups are also caught between these two advocacy lines and at some point take a compromise position. Groups affiliated with Migrante International want to abolish the LCP (Pratt et al. 2010, 82), as does the Philippine Women Centre of British Columbia, which initially held the reformist position but joined in the clamour to abolish the LCP under the banner of the National Alliance of Philippine Women in Canada (NAPWC) (Magkaisa Centre 2010b). On the other hand, some Filipino live-in caregivers in the Prairies tend to accept the reformist agenda because the LCP has provided them with the opportunity to migrate to Canada.

> *Reform lang ngayon. Papaano naman yung ibang Pilipina na gusto din pumunta dito sa Canada?* [Just reform now. How about those other Filipino women who would also like to come to Canada?]
> – Norma, a caregiver in Lethbridge

> *Okay lang naman ang LCP. Ang dapat nilang tutukan ay iyong live-in requirement. Maganda sana kung may option na live-out.* [The LCP is okay. What they need to focus on is the live-in requirement. It would be good if there were a live-out option.]
> – Lara, a caregiver in Lethbridge

As expressed by Lara in Lethbridge, the live-out option would certainly give caregivers more freedom, and they would not be physically accessible to their employers twenty-four hours a day. The "politics of location" (Rich 1986, 210-32) of the current live-in caregivers, graduates of the LCP, and those belonging to moderate and progressive Filipino women's groups diverge in how this immigration program serves their interests, constructs rigid rules to block immediate family unification, and promotes racialized work.

Ethel Tungohan (2010) attended the International Labour Conference held at the United Nations Palais de Nations in Geneva in June 2010 and stated: "I discovered that while the Philippine government was proactive in pushing for stronger labor protections, the Canadian government was reluctant to support provisions that would hold them accountable to the treatment of domestic workers." The LCP has the potential to bring about sustained transnational feminist advocacy among Filipinos, women's groups, and mainstream organizations in Canada. It is working to end the exploitation of live-in caregivers under the LCP and advancing women's rights centres on feminist goals. However, "sisterhood" is far from an effective rallying cry amid the conflicting interests of different groups of women in Canada based on race and class. For example, the Filipino live-in caregivers demanding fair treatment and protection against the Canadian women and their families who make use of their services may not attract empathy from their middle-class employers. The call to abolish the LCP has not received wide support from mainstream women's organizations in Canada.

For now, the most realistic possibility is concerted action by all women's organizations in Canada against the "racist and anti-woman" (National Alliance of Philippine Women in Canada 2009) program of hiring live-in workers. Pratt, in her collaborative work with the Philippine Women Centre of BC and Ugnayan ng Kabataang Pilipino sa Canada (Filipino Canadian Youth Alliance) (2010, 83) notes that "situating an analysis of the LCP within a transnational framework opens a network of sites for action and creates opportunities for building solidarities across national borders."

I still write for a news agency in the Philippines about migrant issues around the globe and not just in Canada.
  – Angela, a hotel worker in Red Deer

I participated in a recent "zero remittance day" for Migrante International as well as a form of protest to the proposed Charter change by the Arroyo regime.
  – Kamuning, a TFW in Edmonton

Transnational advocacy on workers' rights among Filipino women in the Prairies remains individualized and group-specific. Angela in Red Deer writes about the situation of migrant workers for a Philippine newspaper and the Associated Press. Kamuning in Edmonton joined hundreds of OFWs around the world during the annual Zero Remittance Day in October 2009. Damayan Manitoba is allied with Migrante International, whose motto is: "Uphold and advance the rights of overseas Filipinos."[18] OFWs now form a viable sector in Philippine politics (Barber 2010; Nishimori 2010).

Human trafficking facilitated by a global organized network has been linked to the entry of migrant workers in many countries (Aronowitz 2009; Morehouse 2009). It is defined by the United Nations Trafficking Protocol[19] as

the recruitment, transportation, transfer, harboring or receipt of person, by means of the threat or use of force or other forms of coercion, of abduction, of fraud, of deception, of the abuse of power or of a position of vulnerability or of the giving or receiving of payments or benefits to achieve the consent of a person having control over another person, for the purpose of exploitation. (cited in Aronowitz 2009, 1)

The Asia Pacific region, including the Philippines, is considered the most vulnerable region for trafficking of women and children, due to its population size, trends in urbanization, and massive poverty (Cheema, McNally, and Popvski 2011). As of 2007, about 56 percent, or 1.4 million people, of those trafficked for forced labour, including sexual exploitation, came from this region (United Nations Global Initiative to Fight Human Trafficking

[UN.GIFT] n.d.). According to the Department of Foreign Affairs in the Philippines, trafficking syndicates prey on Filipino women and force them into prostitution, drug smuggling, and slave labour (Torres 2010). Most victims of human trafficking are women (about 80 percent) and children (Morehouse 2009, 72). *Pinays* in the Prairies who are strongly opposed to human trafficking have supported various initiatives to eradicate the practice.

> *Yes, transnational project on human trafficking ... we made contacts with Fr. Shay Cullen, an Irish priest from the Missionary Society of St. Columban, on human trafficking and child exploitation.*[20]
> – Marilena, a community worker in Edmonton

Marilena in Edmonton shares her knowledge about human trafficking in the Philippines and around the world by participating in transnational action with other non-profit organizations in Canada and speaking on this topic in various forums. Damayan Manitoba endorsed the Initial Statement of Migrante International to the United Nations Committee on Migrant Workers at the committee's tenth session in Geneva in 2009, which addressed the issue of sex trafficking. The Philippine Women Centre of Manitoba supports the International Purple Rose Campaign against the sex trafficking of Filipino women and children.[21] Filipino women's groups in Canada collaborate with local and international Filipino artists to increase public awareness of sex trafficking, including a gala performance by Alvin Erasga Tolentino in May 2007, the proceeds of which were donated to this campaign (Felipe 2007).

The LCP has also been described as a form of "modern-day slavery" (Pratt 2005, 134) similar to human trafficking. The live-in requirement and the lack of judicial recourse for foreign workers experiencing abuse make the federal migration scheme a kind of formalized human trafficking venture (cf. Langevin and Belleau 2000). Many Filipino live-in caregivers work beyond their contracted hours without additional compensation. While they may have worked willingly as live-in caregivers in the beginning, the working conditions create a power relationship in which the employer can potentially coerce, deceive, or abuse the caregiver. Some Filipino caregivers in the Prairies give moral support to campaigns and sign online petitions launched by Filipino activist groups against the deportation of live-in caregivers who fail to meet the LCP requirements. Although isolated by distance from solidarity actions in metropolitan cities, many of them believe that these activities raise awareness and vigilance regarding the issues affecting TFWs in Canada.

Another important aspect of solidarity among Filipinos in diaspora is their response to crises affecting members of the community, such as the fatal shooting of teenager Jeffrey Reodica by a police officer in 2004 in Toronto (Garcia 2007). Nothing of this magnitude has occurred in the Prairies since my fieldwork in 2009, however, and a more common expression of solidarity there is the provision of financial support to those whose families in Canada or in the Philippines have suffered personal tragedy.

Mission Work

People return home for pleasure or to visit loved ones. But there is an increasingly common homeward journey that involves mission work, a donation of time and skills by immigrant Filipinos who volunteer for service in the Philippines. Although this is generally considered by scholars to be part of diaspora philanthropy, I choose to focus separately on this transnational practice to highlight the direct involvement with the beneficiaries of philanthropic activities such as medical missions.

The Catanduanes International Association, with members from the United States and Canada, conducts medical missions every three years as a way of giving back to the community (Wenning 2006). The University of the Philippines Beta Sigma Fraternity and its Southern California chapter, Canada chapter, and local chapters in the Philippines held a medical and dental mission in 2008 in Sultan Kudarat province in Mindanao. In 2011, a medical mission to the Philippines was organized by the Toronto-based Canadian Aid and Relief Project and was conducted by members of the Filipino-Canadian Medical Association (n.d.; *Philippine Reporter* 2010). A number of Filipino nurses and doctors from the Prairies participated in medical missions in their hometowns and so-called adopted *barangays* in the Philippines (*Filipino Journal* 2008b; McInnis and Holloway 2010).

We attend seminars in the Philippines as part of Volunteers Without Borders. Filipino women went to Philippines, meet sponsored people.
– Lumen, a finance officer in Winnipeg

Yes, we went on a medical mission ... I got to travel but later on I got sick and had surgery [laughs].
– Bella, a retired nurse in Winnipeg

Many types of mission work depend on the professional expertise of Filipino women. Non-medical work is also performed by volunteers. Anyone who is physically able and has time and money to share may participate in medical missions. Spouses and children of doctors or nurses often assist in administrative and distribution tasks. Bella in Winnipeg joined a medical mission as a nurse; she found her experience of serving the poor in the Philippines personally satisfying but physically exhausting. The number of Filipino nurses in the Prairies who have joined medical missions is unknown, but they tend to be older and later in their careers.

A medical mission is neither a one-time activity nor the result of a spur-of-the-moment decision by volunteers. It is a well-coordinated event involving international organizations, professional associations, and local governments in the Philippines. Organizing medical missions has become increasingly problematic amid reports of abduction and deteriorating peace and order in selected areas (ABS-CBN News Global 2010; Balana and Esguerra 2009). Some Filipino nurses participate in smaller-scale hometown medical missions where they find comfort and security among family members and friends. This type of work is usually greatly appreciated and raises the status of the family in the community. Large-scale ventures associated with politicians can be clouded by vested interests, especially if the medical mission is conducted during election time.

Mission work as a transnational practice is a noble exercise for the benefit of millions of poor Filipinos in the countryside. About 36 percent of households in rural Philippines have family members or relatives overseas and receive dollar remittances; the figure for urban areas is 64 percent (Bagasao 2005, 136). Medical missions can be life-changing for poor Filipinos in need of health care. This giving back on the part of immigrant Filipinos continues to be popular across generations.

Another type of mission work in the Philippines (although not one that has been participated in by the participants in this study) involves fact-finding trips by grassroots organizations in Canada for the purpose of investigating extra-judicial killings and violence against civilians (Pratt and Philippines-Canada Task Force on Human Rights 2008). Another type of activity is the participation of some Filipinos in Canada in the electoral campaigns of their relatives in the Philippines.

> *Filipino community is transnational, in transition.*
> – Antonia, a health worker in Edmonton

In sum, philanthropy, advocacy, and mission work engage many women in transnational activities that strongly connect with their Filipino identities. Antonia in Edmonton aptly describes the continuing mobility between homes – the home left behind in the Philippines and the home returned to in Canada – as "transnational [yet] in transition."

Pinays in the Prairies participate in continuing transnational activities that occur at various levels: personal, group, community, hometown, and the state. There are various types of transnational ventures, such as remittances and *balikbayan* boxes, philanthropy, advocacy, and mission work. When migration creates transnational families, alternative forms of mothering and care arise as new information and communication technologies help bridge the physical distance. Philippine television networks with global reach not only connect Filipinos in diaspora to their homeland but are also instrumental in shaping ideals of beauty and normative gender ideologies. Participation of *Pinays* in the Prairies, like that of other Filipinos, is motivated by vested transnationalism, and journeys to the Philippines are made for both personal and collective interests. This is similar to many other pursuits that involve time, money, and personal effort, but vested transnationalism also involves an identification with families and communities in both the Philippines and Canada, and a continuous movement to an imagined "home" and "diasporic location" (Grewal and Kaplan 1994, 16). In each of these spaces, the flow of ideas, sentiments, and goods and services suggests how *Pinays* create or sustain transnational activities.

Conclusion

Migration is a personal journey, a new beginning involving a complex process of finding meanings along the way, especially in societies different from one's own. The feminist dictum that the "personal is political" applies, as the decision to migrate intersects with domestic policies pushing for labour migration, international economic practices searching for cheap labour, and social valuation of people based on gender, race, class, national origin, and immigrant status. Since the second half of the twentieth century, millions of Filipino women have crossed international borders as migrant workers and as immigrants or permanent residents. Using their skills to meet the labour needs of over a hundred countries and territories, they comprise the largest labour diaspora in the world, mostly as caregivers, domestic workers, nannies, nurses, and workers in other feminized occupations. Their work trajectories have shaped the scholarly discourse about them as well as the construction of "Filipino women" in host societies. Recently, new modalities of analysis of Filipino migration have surfaced, offering broader perspectives on the multiple factors of large-scale *Pinay* dispersal and mobility under globalization, its impact on policy and practices, and the intersecting variables in settlement and integration in receiving countries such as Canada.

While I recognize the great personal stress resulting from family separation and the vulnerability to abuse of Filipino women and temporary foreign workers (TFWs), I have embarked in this book on an alternative approach to present a holistic understanding of their migration to Canada, whether as migrant workers or immigrants, with particular emphasis on the Prairie provinces of Alberta, Saskatchewan, and Manitoba. These less popular, non-traditional immigrant destinations that are changing dramatically in different ways counter the scholarly bias of mainstream migration studies focused on the traditional sites of Montreal, Toronto, and Vancouver. The imbalance is no fault of scholars, as metropolitan areas have long captured the imagination of newcomers as providing the best opportunities for work and the presence of established ethnic communities to ease the adaptation process, among other considerations, and the Filipino community in Canada is no exception. The pages of this book, however, offer a wider lens on the settlement experience of Filipino women, both immigrants and TFWs. The Prairie provinces have witnessed a continuous pattern of Filipino migration that has not been fully recognized in Canadian migration discourse. The migrants' experiences of finding and making place, the spatial and scalar dimensions of their experiences as racialized immigrants and outsiders, and the ways in which they practise their understanding of multiculturalism all contribute towards shaping the meanings they find in their diasporic lives. This book highlights the voices of *Pinays* in the Prairies and uses their narratives to understand their negotiation of Filipino or Filipino-Canadian identities in communities they call home. A feminist and culturally sensitive approach informs the presentation of the various aspects of their migration: *Pinay peminism* or *Pinayism*.

Peminism is a new wave of theorizing about Filipino women's lives by mostly Filipino scholars in the United States. Although its conceptualization brings to mind the "imperial trauma" (de Jesus 2005, 6) of Western colonization and the contemporary subject position of the Philippines as a neo-colony of the United States, *peminism* transcends direct postcolonial relations and can be applied to countries with similar white hegemonic discourses, such as Canada. *Pinay peminism* enables Filipino women to claim their own framework for understanding histories of migration, experiences of marginalization, and struggles to belong in constraining social, economic, and political environments in host communities. *Pinayism* draws on the "oppositional politics" (de Jesus 2005, 5) of Filipino women as racialized immigrants in Canada, by challenging the discursive constructs of the "Filipino nanny" and the "victim" phenotype and showing instead women leading productive lives in their communities, as workers, volunteers, and members of Canadian society.

Pinayism also brings to feminist scholarly literature the significance of culture and gender in exploring *Pinay* lives in diaspora, which is quite different from the prevalent white feminist view of culture as anathema to empowerment. This significance is seen in the quotidian lives of *Pinays* in the Prairies. The various chapters in this book have outlined the many ways in which first-generation Filipino women engage with the Canadian public sphere, constrained by exclusionary practices such as discrimination but not so stifled as to limit their abilities to contribute to society as mediated by their own culture. Foremost is the role of shared culture as a means of building social networks and communities where *Pinays* find support in job referrals, housing options, and simply getting together to re-create familiar practices that remind them of home or bind them in transnational ventures. The use of culture as a tool in settlement and integration fosters potential avenues of belonging, such as shared membership in Catholic and other Christian churches in Canada, where the volunteerism of some *Pinays* in the Prairies usually begins. Filipino cultural values as disciplining tools for social inter-actions, participation in the community, and gendered leadership are in-dicative of the intersecting layers of negotiation women have to deal with. Culture is not static and fixed in time, however; *Pinayism* is a lived practice that somehow recognizes a culture-specific consciousness to motivate action in women's personal and public lives. This can take the form of personal politics and grounded volunteerism – for instance, to promote change. Using *Pinayism* as a lens for exploring Filipino women's migration in Canada allows for an in-depth understanding of how racialized (im)migrants make mean-ings of their identities and sense of place. The use of this approach opens up migration discourse to the diversity of non-Western feminism.

Despite the initial angst of employment discrimination due to the non-recognition of their foreign credentials or lack of appropriate Canadian experience, *Pinays* in the Prairies have expressed overall satisfaction with their lives today. Within a constraining social environment, they construct meanings of their identities in the process of settlement and integration based on age, class, regionalism, religion, sexuality, and womanhood. Identities are fluid, culturally constructed, and shaped by particular migra-tion experiences. Although Canadian society considers immigrants as being of low class, *Pinays'* own subject positioning corresponds with the Canadian "middle classness" of having a job, a house, and a car. As women, they iden-tify with the possibility of "making it" for themselves and their families, no matter how difficult a goal that may be. In scholarly literature, the focus tends to be on the challenges and difficulties of initial integration in the labour market and not on the ability of immigrants to potentiate change in other areas. *Pinayism*, therefore, directs us to see how such possibilities are demon-strated in various spheres – personal, group, community, and transnational.

Through the years, *Pinays* in the Prairies have demonstrated a high level of civic consciousness, both within and beyond the Filipino communities. Chapter 5 covered the varied forms of activism, from the personal to the collective, in their lives. I posited the notion of grounded volunteerism stemming from their faith, work, community building, involvement in their children's schools, desire to improve their professions in Canada, social justice, or simply life-changing circumstances. These voluntary civic engage-ments go beyond merely a generous sharing of time and talent because they directly reflect on and impact their lives as immigrants or migrant workers in Canada. The narratives of *Pinay* leaders in Alberta, Saskatchewan, and Manitoba show how racialized immigrant women carve a niche of belonging within their communities and strive to make a difference. Personal politics, motivated by referential experiences both in the Philippines and in Canada, facilitate the volunteerism that fundamentally defines their lives as "activist *Pinays.*" *Pinayism* situates their experiential knowledge as "movers for change" in their own lives and in the communities they now call home. It grounds their personal politics in diaspora, which enables them to become publicly engaged, not in the grand scheme of formal politics (even though involvement in the formal political process has opened up for *Pinays* in Manitoba) but firm in their own beliefs and aspirations to make a difference.

A factor to consider in the process of migration and belonging among Filipino women in the Prairies is the collectivist orientation of Philippine society. The extended kinship system and social network mark out an easier path towards re-creating communities that they are familiar with. The patriarchal value system continues to operate after migration, which even influences the degree to which Filipino women in the Prairies participate in the community. As forms of social control, cultural values provide context-specific ways of exploring women's tendency to engage. Filipino cultural values such as *pakikisama, utang na loob,* and respect for elders contribute to women's participation in community associations. These values comprise an "other-relatedness" that seems to give more consideration to others than to the self. In some ways, they provide a broader schema of the individual in society and facilitate particular social negotiations amid constraints in the women's lives as racialized immigrants in Canada. Smooth interpersonal relations *(pakikisama)* foster positive community relations. Debt of gratitude *(utang na loob)* factors into social reciprocity at all levels, from the individual or family to the group or nation-state. Respect for elders and authority based on hierarchical relationships is still an important cultural value among Filipino women, who are now instrumental in imparting it to their children in Canada. These values may be products of a patriarchal society, but their application fosters community bonds and initiation of activities that help create, in a larger sense, a means for *Pinays* in the Prairies to sustain connection with other Filipinos and Canadians. Although Filipino community associations have historically been led by men, Filipino women are gradually taking charge as leaders, and demonstrating that they are motivated by the noble goal of service and not self-interest. Looking at the interplay of culture and gender roles in Filipino women's migration in the Prairies calls for the use of non-Western perspectives like *Pinayism,* and acknowledgment of the role of culture in Filipino community processes as well as the impact of the values of gender equality in Canada in the lives of racialized women. *Pinayism* integrates Filipino cultural values operating in community participation and emphasizes distinct ways in which hierarchies of power are mitigated.

Migration is a journey that traverses multiple spaces of "home" – the country of origin and the country of residence. In Chapter 6, the concept of vested transnationalism describes the cross-border practices of Filipino men and women in the Prairies that sustain ties to their families and communities in the Philippines, such as regular remittances of cash and shipments of *balikbayan* goods, patronization of global Philippine media and popular culture, and the recognition of dual citizenship and absentee voting. *Pinay* transnational practices involve philanthropy, advocacy, and mission work directed towards recipients in the Philippines – families, hometown communities, and the nation-state. Sharing the material rewards they have gained in Canada is considered a form of giving back, and making a dent in the impoverished lives of those left behind in the Philippines provides the best value to those involved in philanthropy. Mission work, for example, is a way for many to combine a personal visit to family and friends in the Philippines with helping the poor obtain medical care. Transnational advocacy has also been embraced by progressive *Pinays* in the Prairies as a way to improve the rights and welfare of marginalized groups like migrant workers and trafficked women, many of whom are Filipinos. Although Canada's Live-in Caregiver Program has been contested and remains a polarizing issue among different Filipino women's groups that may embrace conflicting agendas, either reform or abolition, it has the potential to lead to alliances among these groups. *Pinayism* recognizes Filipino women's activities, whether local or transnational, towards social justice. It positions the women as active agents in addressing policies and practices that exploit them and others in similar situations.

Exploring the migration, identity, and community of Filipino women in Canada through the voices of *Pinays* in the Prairies enhances our understanding of how representations of their lives are defined by immigration policies and practices, and of how they continue to be subject to varied forms of exploitation and marginalization. Despite their struggles as immigrants or migrant workers, however, they gradually find spaces of inclusion using a complex interplay of identities, culture, and agency to empower themselves and others. *Pinayism* informs us that Filipino women in the Prairies want and will work for change, both in their personal lives and in the communities where they live, although these may be subtle or invisible to others. As *Pinayism* evolves in the scholarly discourse, its ability to contribute to a more nuanced view of Filipino women's migration can only grow.

Notes

Chapter 1: Gender, Migration, and Feminism

1 See Bakan and Stasiulis 1997; Chang 2000; and Lutz 2008.
2 This follows Appadurai's conception (1996, 48) of the "global ethnoscapes" about the non-localized "landscapes of group identity."
3 On domestic workers, see Lan 2000; Brigham 2002; Magat 2003; and Ezquerra 2008. On nurses, see Choy 1998. On sex industry, see Fujieda 2001. On foreign brides, see Crespo 2009.
4 See Beltran and Javate de Dios 1992; Chin 1997; and Ada Cheng 2006.
5 See Pratt 1997, 1999, 2004; Bakan and Stasiulis 1997; McWatt and Neysmith 1998; and Spitzer et al. 2003.
6 See Ball 2004 and Goode 2009.
7 See Piper and Ball 2001; Fuwa and Anderson 2006; and Nuqui 2008.
8 See Cunneen and Stubbs 1997; Woelz-Stirling, Kelaher, and Manderson 1998; Constable 2003; Del Rosario 2005; and Suzuki 2008.
9 See Ramilo and Droescher 1992; Espiritu 1995, 2003; and Posadas 1999.
10 See Anzaldua 1987; Hooks 1989; and Sandoval 2000.
11 The 1987 Constitution recognizes the role of Filipino women in nation building; the Family Code of the Philippines provides for annulment and for legitimacy of children; the Gender and Development Framework of the Philippine Plan for Women, 1989-92, promotes women's welfare; the Philippine Plan for Gender-Responsive Development, 1995-2025, sets goals, policies, and programs related to gender and development; the Barangay-Level Total Development and Protection of Children Act (Republic Act No. 6972) establishes daycare centres in *barangays* (villages); the Rape Victim Assistance and Protection Act of 1998 (Republic Act No. 8505) mandates the establishment of crisis centres; and the Women in Development and National-Building Act (Republic Act No. 7192) provides for, among others, the allocation of resources on gender mainstreaming programs and activites in all government agencies (Pacoy 2013; Tapales n.d., 7-8).
12 "Waray" refers to a group of people living in the provinces of Leyte and Samar in the Visayas; their dialect is also referred to as Waray.

Chapter 2: *Pinay* Migration

1 EDSA is a highway extending about twenty-four kilometres and connecting north and south metropolitan Manila.
2 Enderun, http://www.enderuncolleges.com/.
3 "OFW" is the term used in the Philippines. In Canada, they are known as TFWs (temporary foreign workers).
4 "Irregular residents" refers to Filipinos who are not properly documented, who have no valid residence or work permits, or who have overstayed in a foreign country (CFO 2012).

5 *Japayuki-san* is a term derived from *karayukisan,* a nineteenth-century word for Japanese prostitutes working overseas, especially in China. In the 1980s, the Japanese media used the term to refer to migrant workers. *Japayuki-san* implies work in the sex industry, known as the "water trade" *(mizushobai)* (Lie 1997, 290).
6 The Magna Carta for Migrant Workers and Overseas Filipinos (Republic Act No. 8042) was enacted after the controversial case of Flor Contemplacion, a domestic worker executed in Singapore in 1995 allegedly for double murder. After her execution, President Fidel V. Ramos broke off diplomatic ties and suspended the deployment of Filipinos to Singapore and the Middle East (Martin, Martin, and Weil 2006, 200). Some measures provided by the Magna Carta include legal assistance, deployment, repatriation, and reintegration. However, a number of cases reveal inaction, neglect, and abandonment of many distressed OFWs by the Philippine government (Makilan 2004).
7 Immigration Act, S.C. 1976-77, c. 52; Immigration and Refugee Protection Act, S.C. 2001, c. 27.
8 Statistical data in Canada at this time use "sex" instead of "gender" to refer to males and females. I prefer to use the word "gender" in this book to be consistent with its socially constucted meaning.
9 Provincial Nominee Programs vary from one province to another and are subject to change. The Alberta Immigrant Nominee Program (AINP) offers six streams or categories: skilled worker, international graduate, semi-skilled worker, tradesperson, engineer, and farmer. The Manitoba Provincial Nominee Program (MPNP) has four eligibility areas: TFW, international student graduate, invitation to apply under the Strategic Initiative, and skilled worker with strong family connections in the province. The Saskatchewan Immigrant Nominee Program (SINP) has eight categories: skilled worker, entrepreneur, family referral, farm owner/operator, health professional, hospitality sector pilot project, long-haul truck driver, and student. These categories were in place as of 8 October 2012 (CIC 2012).

Chapter 3: Welcoming Prairies
1 Alberta is the richest province in Canada and the stronghold of the Conservative Party of Canada (Barrie 2006, 50).
2 See http://www.calgarystampede.com.
3 For example, hate crime is a criminal offence specified in the Criminal Code of Canada (Gerstenfeld 2004).
4 Canadian Multiculturalism Act, R.S.C., 1985, c. 24 (4th Supp.).
5 The Multiculturalism Act, S.S. 1997, c. M-23.01.
6 Human Rights, Citizenship and Multiculturalism Act, R.S.A. 2000, c.H-14.
7 The Manitoba Multiculturalism Act, C.C.S.M. 1992, c. M223.
8 Canadian Charter of Rights and Freedoms, Part 1 of the Constitution Act, 1982, being Schedule B to the Canada Act 1982 (U.K.), 1982, c. 11, s. 6.
9 Foreign Credentials Referral Office, http://www.credentials.gc.ca/.

Chapter 4: Making Meanings
1 *Bayanihan* broadly refers to the practice of helping one's neighbour, friend, or community without any expected financial return (David 2011, 131).
2 Quebec took the initiative in recognizing the rights of homosexuals by 1985 (Lahey and Alderson 2004). No other province has followed suit.
3 Under Premier Ralph Klein, the province invoked the notwithstanding clause of the Canadian Charter of Rights and Freedoms "to make sure that same-sex marriages never happen on Alberta soil" (Gudgeon 2003, 190). The Canadian Civil Marriage Act (Bill C-38) recognizing same-sex marriage received royal assent on 20 July 2004 and became law in 2005, and the Alberta government subsequently conceded.
4 Civil Marriage Act, S.C. 2005, c. 33.

Chapter 5: Building Bridges
1 Each *barangay* in the Philippines is mandated to have an SK, whose chairperson automatically sits on the local governing council.

2 Other examples of Filipino community organizations are the Philippine Women Centre of British Columbia, Filipino-Canadian Youth Alliance, Filipino Workers Organization (SIKLAB), British Columbia Committee for Human Rights in the Philippines, Filipino Nurses Support Group in British Columbia, Sinagbayan, and Kabataang Montreal (Magkaisa Centre 2010a).

3 Jomay Amora-Mercado arrived in Edmonton as a temporary foreign worker (TFW) in 2007 and later moved to Winnipeg. She graduated from the University of the Philippines in Baguio City.

4 Tessie Oliva arrived in Canada in 1969. She received her bachelor of science in nursing from the University of Santo Tomas (UST) in the Philippines, and a master of science in administration from Central Michigan University. She is a retired municipal hospital administrator. See also Oliva (n.d.) for her involvement in the Filipino community.

5 In feminist practice, "empowered mothering" refers to "motherhood as a political site wherein mothers can affect social change through the socialization of children and the world through political-social activism" (O'Reilly 2008, 7).

6 Maria Doris Collantes was a retired dean of education in Manila. She received a Certificate of Excellence for outstanding volunteer service as an ESL teacher in 2005 and a Certificate of Recognition – Calgary Learns, Life of Learning Award (LOLA) in 2010.

7 PEAC grants scholarships to teachers and book donations to schools, sends Filipino volunteer teachers to schools, and offers adult literacy services (see also Nethercott, n.d.).

8 Josephine Pallard is a native of Baguio City, Philippines. She arrived in Edmonton in 1967 to pursue studies in education at the University of Alberta and was one of the first Filipinos in the area. She holds a master's degree in education from San Francisco State University and taught at an elementary school for thirty-one years. As a community leader, Josephine received the Governor General's Award in Ottawa in 2005 and was the first winner of the *Western Catholic Reporter*'s Worker in the Vineyard Award in 2007. She received an honorary doctor of laws degree from St. Stephen's College at the University of Alberta, also in 2007 (Gonzalez 2007), and the Citation of Citizenship Award from the federal government and the University of Alberta Alumni Honour Award, both in 2008.

9 Virginia Guiang hails from the province of Nueva Vizcaya, Philippines, and was a trained teacher and librarian. She worked at the acquisitions department of the Elizabeth Dafoe Library at the University of Manitoba and coordinated seven library branches until her retirement in 1999.

10 Perla Javate graduated from the University of the Philippines in 1965 with a degree in social work.

11 PHCM is composed of about thirty-two groups and individuals and coordinates the Philippine Heritage Week (week of 12 June) and other celebrations.

12 She was awarded the Queen Elizabeth II Golden Jubilee Medal in 2002.

13 Gemma Dalayoan obtained two undergraduate degrees, in education and English, in the Philippines, and in Canada earned a bachelor of education and a master of education in English as a second language, both from the University of Manitoba.

14 Estrel Dato obtained her BA with Honours in English Literature and master of arts in English literature from the University of Saskatchewan. She worked for the daily newspaper *Saskatoon StarPhoenix* for twenty-eight years. She served as publication editor of the Filipino newsletter *BALITA*, president of FILCAS for two terms (1998-99 and 2002-3), and cultural director of FILCAS. As president, she made it possible for FILCAS to set up an office in downtown Saskatoon through a steady fundraising drive.

15 In 2007, Folklorico Filipino of Toronto visited Saskatoon and the KFE in turn visited Toronto. Estrel received a grant from the Saskatchewan Arts Board to learn more about Philippine culture by travelling back to that country.

16 Fay Santos-Vargas emigrated from the Philippines in 1980. She obtained a certificate in teaching heritage language from the University of Saskatchewan through a scholarship funded by the Saskatoon Multilingual School. She completed her degree in sociology as a part-time student and has been an employee of the city of Saskatoon since the 1990s.

17 Gemma Dalayoan was a board member of the Manitoba Multicultural Resource Centre at the University of Winnipeg (1988-89); chairperson of the panel of judges for the Mayor's

Volunteer Service Awards (1999); board member of the Assiniboine Credit Union (2001-3); and representative of the Inkster and Seven Oaks area in the Winnipeg Regional Health Authority Advisory Council in 2002. During the 125th anniversary of Confederation in 1992, she received a commemorative medal from Governor General Ramon John Hnatyshyn for her significant contributions to the community.

18 Jean Guiang served as deputy chair of Ethnocultural Community Relations for the United Way for three years. She was a member of the Manitoba Women's Advisory Council for six years, of the federal government's Canadian Race Relations Foundation for two years, and of the City of Winnipeg's Community and Race Relations Committee for four years. She received the Recognition Award for Outstanding Services from the city of Winnipeg in 1990; was the first Filipino recipient of the federal government's Citation of Citizenship Award, in 1991; was named a 1997 YMCA-YWCA Woman of Distinction; and in 2002 received the Queen Elizabeth II Golden Jubilee medal for community volunteerism.

19 Lucenia Ortiz worked as a public health educator in the Philippines after obtaining her bachelor of science degree in hygiene/public health. She received her master's degree in urban and regional planning from the University of the Philippines. She was a recipient of the Doris Badir Graduate Research Fellowship in Human Ecology at the University of Alberta, where she obtained her doctorate in that discipline in 2003. Lucenia has served as board member of the Multicultural Coalition Society for Equity in Health and Well Being since 2008; as a member of the subcommittee on diversity and inclusion in the city of Edmonton since 2007; as a member of the Leadership Council of Vibrant Communities Edmonton (2003-9); and as a board member of Action for Healthy Communities, also in Edmonton (2004-6).

20 Maribel Javier obtained her degree in commerce from Roosevelt College in the Philippines; a master's degree in industrial relations from the University of the Philippines; and, in 2010, a certificate in human resources management from the University of Calgary. She serves as a board member of the Ethno-Cultural Council of Calgary and as volunteer development coordinator for the Centre for Newcomers in Calgary.

21 During the 6 October 2011 Ontario provincial election, Cheryll San Juan and Nerissa Cariño ran as candidates of the Green Party for Etobicoke Centre and of the NDP for Pickering-Scarborough East, respectively (Marquez 2011).

22 Jose Rizal is the national hero of the Philippines, honoured for his role in shaping the revolutionary movement against Spain in the late1800s.

23 Corazon C. Aquino (1986-92) and Gloria Macapagal-Arroyo (2001-10).

24 Linda Cantiveros was a prominent leader of the Filipino community in Winnipeg who died in 2008. She was the editor of the *Filipino Journal* and a founding member of the Manitoba Filipino Business Council. She ran unsuccessfully as the Liberal Party candidate for Point Douglas in the 1995 provincial election (*Filipino Journal* 2007a; CBC News 2008; Gabuna 2008). Ellen Sacoco was one of the founding leaders of the Philippine Circle, the precursor of PAS, together with Dr. Eusebio Koh, Dr. Alex Cunanan, and Dr. Mody Escanlar. She became the first female president of PAS in 1972. Along with Dr. Koh, Ellen founded the Philippine Language School in Regina, and she served as its principal. She led the Filipino community in the Regina Mosaic Festival as dancer, program director, and ambassador for the Philippine Pavilion. Ellen became a board member of the Regina Multicultural Council, treasurer of the Immigrant Women of Saskatchewan, and youth director and public relations officer of the Good Samaritan Parish Council. She taught in the Catholic school system in Saskatchewan until her retirement in 1992 and passed away in 1994 (Koh 1994). Rhoda Abada was co-founder of four Filipino associations and a council in Edmonton; vice-president of the National Council of Canadian Filipino Associations for eight years; and board member of Catholic Social Services. A multi-awarded community leader, she published and edited the *Philippine Canadian Times*. She led the Philippine centennial celebrations in Alberta and the Northwest Territories in the 1990s (Herrera-Maquiling n.d.).

25 The Order of the Knights of Rizal (http://www.knightsofrizal.com/) is an organization of Filipino males honouring the ideals of Dr. Jose Rizal, the Philippine national hero, through programs and activities. It was founded in 1911 in the Philippines.

Chapter 6: Vested Transnationalism

1 The *Balikbayan* Program was instituted by Republic Act No. 6768 in 1989 and amended in 2002. A *balikbayan* enjoys travel tax exemption, visa-free stay for one year for foreign passport holders, and duty-free shopping of up to US$1,500. In 2002, the *kabuhayan* (livelihood) shopping privilege was enacted in Republic Act 9174 (see Arellano Law Foundation, The LAWPHIL Project: Philippine Laws and Jurisprudence Databank, http://www.lawphil. net/), allowing purchase of tax-free livelihood tools to ensure a *balikbayan's* economic self-sufficiency on return to the Philippines. There are five categories of *balikbayan:* (1) a Filipino citizen who has been continuously out of the Philippines for at least one year; (2) an Overseas Filipino Worker (OFW); (3) a former Filipino citizen with a foreign passport; (4) a spouse of and travelling with a former Filipino citizen with a foreign passport; (5) a child of and travelling with a former Filipino citizen with a foreign passport (Templo 2010).

2 About 350-400 million SMS (Short Message Service) text messages are sent daily, an average of twenty text messages per cellphone in 2006 (PhilippineDomain.com n.d.).

3 Ugnayan ng Kabataang Pilipino sa Canada/Filipino-Canadian Youth Alliance (UKPC/FCYA) wrote a play about their experiences of marginalization and social dislocation in Vancouver, including those of Filipino mothers who came as caregivers (Pratt 2003/04).

4 In his view of the social imaginary, Appadurai (2003, 25) presents five separate dimensions of global cultural flows: "Ethnoscapes (people who move between nations, such as tourists, immigrants, exiles, guestworkers, and refugees), technoscapes (technology often linked to multinational corporations), financescapes (global capital, currency markets, stock exchanges), mediascapes (electronic and new media), and ideoscapes (official state ideology and counter-ideologies)."

5 ABS-CBN Global, "Canada: Dealers and Distributors," http://www.abs-cbnglobal.com/Regions/Canada/.

6 Charice Pempengco took third place in the ABS-CBN talent show *Little Big Star* in 2005. When she was fourteen, her renditions of Whitney Houston hit songs were posted on YouTube and she was later offered a recording deal in Sweden. She was invited to appear on prime-time shows in the United States (*The Oprah Winfrey Show* and *The Ellen DeGeneres Show*) and in South Korea. Arnel Pineda is the new lead singer of the American rock band Journey. Lea Salonga is a multi-awarded singer and actress. She was the first Filipino to play the lead role in a musical (*Miss Saigon,* which debuted in London in 1989) and was the singing voices of Princess Jasmine in the Disney animated movie *Aladdin* and *Fa Mulan* (Philippine News Service 2008).

7 Filipino-Norwegian singer Markki (Marcelo Angelo Ledesma) Stroem was a finalist in the first season of *Pilipinas Got Talent* in 2010. Filipino dance groups in the United States performed in *Showtime* with TFC's *One Kapamilya Go* on 12 September 2010, in Santa Clara, California (*Asian Journal* 2010).

8 These include Kirby Ann Basken (Filipino-Norwegian, 2007 Miss Norway Universe), 2006 Mutya ng Pilipinas (Pearl of the Philippines) Asia Pacific; Danielle Castaño (Filipino-American), 2008 Bb. (*Binibining,* or Ms.) Pilipinas World; Marie Ann Bonquin Umali (Filipino-Lebanese), 2009 Bb. Pilipinas World; Melody Gersbach (Filipino-German), 2009 Bb. Pilipinas International; Krista Kleiner (Filipino-American), 2010 Bb. Pilipinas International; and Maria Venus Raj (Filipino-Indian), 2010 Bb. Pilipinas Universe, who subsequently was fourth runner-up in the 2010 Miss Universe pageant in Las Vegas, Nevada.

9 According to the entry form found at http://www.missworldphilippines.com/.

10 West Edmonton Mall is the largest shopping mall in the Americas, with 3.77 million square feet. SM Mall of Asia in Metro Manila has 4.2 million square feet (Touropia 2010).

11 Citizenship Act, R.S.C. 1985, c. C-29.

12 To vote in absentia, a qualified citizen overseas must have filed an approved application for registration in any of the consular offices. A Filipino absentee voter must be included in the certified list from the Commission on Elections and show proof of identity (Lazo 2006).

13 In 2006, over 27.6 million Filipinos were considered poor or unable to provide for the minimum basic needs in health, education, and housing. More than 20 million Filipinos

experience hunger at least once in three months (Pastrana 2009). According to the Human Development Report in 2009, the Philippines ranked 54th out of 135 countries on the Human Poverty Index (United Nations Development Programme 2009).

14 The Canadian organization is ANCOP International (Canada), http://www.ancopcanada. com/.

15 Women occupied leadership roles in key ministries such as Teodora, Tekton Guild, and the CFC Office for Women by 1999, and they were elected to the CFC Board of Elders by 2005 (Rivera 2008).

16 International Convention on the Protection of the Rights of All Migrant Workers and Members of Their Families, New York, 18 December 1990, 2220 U.N.T.S. 3 (entered into force 1 July 2003).

17 See United Nations Treaty Collection, http://treaties.un.org/Pages/ViewDetails.aspx?mtdsg_no=IV-13&chapter=4&lang=en.

18 Migrante International's website is at http://migranteinternational.org.

19 A Protocol to Prevent, Suppress and Punish Trafficking in Persons, Especially Women and Children, supplementing the United Nations Convention against Transnational Organized Crime, New York, 15 November 2000, 2237 U.N.T.S. 319 (entered into force 25 December 2003).

20 Fr. Shay Cullen is an Irish missionary priest in the Philippines who established the PREDA (People's Recovery Empowerment and Development Assistance) Foundation in 1974. He has been nominated three times for the Nobel Peace Prize (PREDA 1997).

21 The International Purple Rose Campaign was launched in the United States in 1999 by GABRIELA Network, a Philippine-US women's solidarity organization (Lindio-McGovern 1997). About 30 percent of Filipino women leaving to work overseas end up in the sex trade: 150,000 Filipino women in *yakuza*-controlled brothels in Japan; 25,000 in brothels, bars, and nightclubs in the United States and in "sex farms" around military bases; and over half a million Filipino women and children in the sex tourism industry in the Philippines (GABRIELA Network USA 2007).

References

Abano, R. 2020. "All about Overseas Absentee Voting." *Philippine Daily Inquirer,* 11 April. http://globalnation.inquirer.net/.

Abinales, P.N. 2000. *Making Mindanao: Cotabato and Davao in the Formation of the Philippine Nation-State.* Quezon City, Philippines: Ateneo de Manila University Press.

Abinales, P.N., and D.J. Amoroso. 2005. *State and Society in the Philippines.* Lanham, MD: Rowman and Littlefield.

ABS-CBN News. 2009. "RP Must Reduce Debt Stock by Half: Teves." 15 May. http://www.abs-cbnnews.com/.

–. 2010. "'Abduction' of Health Workers in Rizal Assailed." 6 February. http://www.abs-cbnnews.com/.

Ackelsberg, M. 2005. "Women's Community Activism and the Rejection of 'Politics': Some Dilemmas of Popular Democratic Movements." In *Women and Citizenship,* edited by M. Friedman, 67-90. New York: Oxford University Press.

Ackerly, B., and J. True. 2010. *Doing Feminist Research in Political and Social Science.* New York: Palgrave Macmillan.

Ada Cheng, S. 2006. *Serving the Household and the Nation: Filipina Domestics and the Politics of Identity in Taiwan.* Lanham, MD: Lexington Books.

Adriano, J.D. 2009. "Remittances Save the Philippines." *Asia Times,* 11 August. http://www.atimes.com/.

Advincula, A.D. 2009. "Profile of the New Filipino Family: House-Husbands Watch the Home Front while Women Fill US Demand for Nurses." *New American Media,* 25 September. AlterNet, http://www.alternet.org/.

Agnew, V., ed. 2009. *Racialized Immigrant Women in Canada: Essays on Health, Violence and Equity.* Toronto: University of Toronto Press.

Aguilar, D. 1998. *Towards a Nationalist Feminism.* Quezon City, Philippines: Giraffe/PALH.

Aguilar, F. Jr., ed. 2002. *Filipinos in Global Migrations: At Home in the World?* Manila: Philippine Migration Research Network and Philippine Social Science Council.

Alama, E.Z. 2009. "The Experience of Sponsored Filipino Seniors in Providing Support to Immigrant Families in Canada: A Grounded Theory Inquiry." PhD diss., University of Calgary.

Alarcon, N., C. Kaplan, and M. Moallem. 1999. "Introduction: Between Woman and Nation." In *Between Woman and Nation: Nationalisms, Transnational Feminisms, and the State,* edited by C. Kaplan, N. Alarcon, and M. Moallem, 1-16. Durham, NC: Duke University Press.

Alberta Community Development. 2002. "Women's Organizations of Alberta," 5th ed. Edmonton: Human Rights and Citizenship Branch. http://www.assembly.ab.ca/lao/library/egovdocs/alcd/2002/135235.pdf.

Alberta Finance. 2007. "2006 Census of Canada: Immigration, Language and Mobility Release." 4 December. http://www.finance.alberta.ca/aboutalberta/census/2006/2007 1210_immigration_language_mobility.pdf.

Alboim, N., R. Finnie, and R. Meng. 2005. "The Discounting of Immigrants' Skills in Canada: Evidence and Policy Recommendations." *IRPP Choices* 11 (2). http://www.irpp.org/.

Alboim, N., and E. McIsaac. 2007. "Making the Connections: Ottawa's Role in Immigrant Employment." *IRPP Choices* 13 (3). http://www.irpp.org/.

Alburo, J. 2005. "Boxed In or Out? Balikbayan Boxes as Metaphors for Filipino American (Dis)Location." *Ethnologies* 27 (2): 137-57.

Alcoff, L.M., and E. Mendieta, eds. 2003. *Identities: Race, Class, Gender, and Nationality.* Oxford: Blackwell.

Alcuitas, T. 2011. "Flexing Our Political Muscle." *Philippine Asian News Today,* 29 September. http://www.philippineasiannewstoday.com/.

Alexander, M.J., and C.T. Mohanty. 2010. "Cartographies of Knowledge and Power: Transnational Feminism as Radical Praxis." In *Critical Transnational Feminist Praxis,* edited by A.L. Swarr and R. Nagar, 23-45. Albany, NY: SUNY Press.

Alibhai-Brown, Y. 2004. "Beyond Multiculturalism." *Canadian Diversity/Diversité Canadienne* 3 (2): 51-54.

Allen, A. 1996. "Foucault on Power: A Theory for Feminists." In *Feminist Interpretations of Michel Foucault,* edited by S.J. Hekman, 265-81. University Park, PA: Pennsylvania State University Press.

The Alliance in Saskatoon. 2003. "Saskatoon Filipino Community Church." http://www.collegeofprayer.ca/.

Almirol, E.B. 1985. *Ethnic Identity and Social Negotiation: A Study of a Filipino Community in California.* New York: AMS Press.

Alston, J.A. 2005. "Climbing Hills and Mountains: Black Female Making It to the Superintendency." In *Sacred Dreams: Women and Superintendency,* edited by C.C. Brunner, 79-90. Albany, NY: SUNY Press.

Alzona, V. 2007. "Bayanihan." *Asia Trend Magazine.* http://www.asiatrendmagazine.com/.

Amott, N. 2007. "Cases for the Philippines in Innovative Philanthropy: An Overview of the Philippines." In *Innovation in Strategic Philanthropy,* edited by H.K. Anheier, A. Simmons, and D. Winder, 61-78. Dordrecht, The Netherlands: Springer.

Andersen, M.L., and H.F. Taylor. 2006. *Sociology: Understanding a Diverse Society,* 4th ed. Belmont, CA: Thomson Wadsworth.

Anderson, B. 1991. *Imagined Communities: Reflections on the Origin and Spread of Nationalism.* London and New York: Verso.

–. 1998. *Spectres of Comparison: Nationalism, Southeast Asia and the World.* London and New York: Verso.

Anderson, C.G., and J.H. Black. 2008. "The Political Integration of Newcomers, Minorities, and the Canadian-Born: Perspectives on Naturalization, Participation, and Representation." In *Immigration and Integration in the Twenty-first Century,* edited by J. Biles, M. Burstein, and J. Frideres, 45-75. Kingston, ON: School of Policy Studies, Queen's University.

Anderson, J. 1999. Filipina Migrants to Japan: Hostesses, House Helpers and Homemakers. *Filipinas* 33: 57-74.

Andres, T.Q.D. 2002. *People Empowerment by Filipino Values.* Manila: Rex Bookstore.

Ang, D. 2005. "The Filipino as Citizen of the World." Speech delivered in Agana, Guam, 14 May. http://www.cfo.gov.ph/.

Ang See, T. 2008. "The State and Public Policies, Civil Society and Identity Formation in Multi-Ethnic Societies: The Case of the Chinese in the Philippines." In *The State, Development and Identity in Multi-Ethnic Societies,* edited by N. Tarling and E.T. Gomez, 154-71. New York: Routledge.

Angeles, L., and S. Sunanta. 2007. "'Exotic Love at your Fingertips': Intermarriage Websites, Gendered Representation, and the Transnational Migration of Filipino and Thai Women." *Kasarinlan: Philippine Journal of Third World Studies* 22 (1): 3-31.

Angeles, L.C. 2003. "Creating Social Spaces for Transnational Feminist Advocacy: The Canadian International Development Agency, The National Commission on the Role of Filipino Women and Philippine Women's NGOs." *Canadian Geographer* 47 (3): 283-302.

Anheier, H.K., E. Hollerweger, C. Badelt, and J. Kendall. 2003. *Work in the Non-Profit Sector: Forms, Patterns and Methodologies.* Geneva: International Labour Organization.

Anthias, F., and G. Lazaridis, eds. 2000. *Gender and Migration in Southern Europe: Women on the Move*. New York: Berg Publishers.

Anti-Slavery International. n.d. "What Is Child Domestic Work?" http://www.antislavery.org/.

Anzaldua, G. 1987. *Borderlands: La Frontera*. San Francisco: Aunt Lute.

Appadurai, A. 1996. *Modernity at Large: Cultural Dimensions of Globalization*. Minneapolis, MN: University of Minnesota Press.

–. 2003. "Disjuncture and Difference in the Global Cultural Economy." In *Theorizing Diaspora*, edited by J.E. Braziel and A. Mannur, 25-48. Oxford: Blackwell.

Aquino, B. 1987. *The Politics of Plunder: The Philippines under Marcos*. Quezon City: University of the Philippines College of Public Administration.

Aranas, M.Q. 1983. *The Dynamics of Filipino Immigrants in Canada*. Edmonton: Coles Printing.

Arat-Koc, S. 1999. "Gender and Race in 'Non-Discriminatory' Immigration Policies in Canada: 1960s to the Present." In *Scratching the Surface: Canadian Anti-Racist Feminist Thought*, edited by E. Dua and A. Robertson, 207-33. Toronto: Women's Press.

Arcenas, M.T. 2006. *Decentralization and Women's Empowerment at the Local Level in the Philippines*. Santo Domingo, Dominican Republic: United Nations International Research and Training Institute for the Advancement of Women (UN-INSTRAW).

Arcibal, C. 2007. "Filipinos 2nd Happiest People in Asia – Study." GMA News Online, 28 November. http://www.gmanews.tv/.

Arcilla, J.S. 1998. *An Introduction to Philippine History*. Loyola Heights, Quezon City: Ateneo Manila University Press.

Arellano-Carandang, M.L., B.A.L. Sison, and C.F.A. Carandang. 2007. *Nawala ang Ilaw ng Tahanan: Case Studies of Families Left Behind by OFW Mothers*. Manila: Anvil Publishing.

Armstrong, C. 2006. *Rethinking Equality: The Challenge of Equal Citizenship*. Manchester and New York: Manchester University Press.

Arnado, J.M. 2008. "Women's Emancipation in the Philippines: A Legacy of Western Feminism?" In *Globalization and Its Counter-Forces in Southeast Asia*, edited by T. Chong, 296-312. Singapore: Institute of Southeast Asian Studies.

Arnett, J.J., ed. 2007. *International Encyclopedia of Adolescence*. New York: Routledge.

–. 2009. *Adolescence and Emerging Adulthood: A Cultural Approach*, 4th ed. Englewood Cliffs, NJ: Prentice Hall.

Aronowitz, A.A. 2009. *Human Trafficking, Human Misery: The Global Trade in Human Beings*. Westport, CT: Praeger.

Arya, S., and A. Roy, eds. 2006. *Poverty, Gender, and Migration*. New Delhi: Sage.

ASEAN Affairs. 2009. "Philippine Economy to Grow 3.7% in 2009." 14 February. http://www.aseanaffairs.com/.

Åseskog, B. 2008. "The National Commission on the Role of Filipino Women, the Women's Movement and Gender Mainstreaming in the Philippines." In *Mainstreaming Gender, Democratising the State: Institutional Mechanisms for the Advancement of Women*, edited by S. Rai, 131-45. Manchester: Manchester University Press.

Asian Development Bank (ADB). 2006. *Converting Migration Drains to Gains: Harnessing the Resources of Overseas Professionals*. Manila: Asian Development Bank.

–. 2011. "Asian Development Bank and Philippines: Fact Sheet." http://www.adb.org/Documents/Fact_Sheets/PHI.pdf.

Asian Journal. 2010. "Calendar of Events: TFC's One Kapamilya Go sa California's Great America." 29 August. http://www.asianjournal.com/.

Asian Legal Resource Centre. 2009. "Philippines: Violations of Rights under Failing Land Reforms." 27 February. http://www.alrc.net/.

Asian Pacific Post. 2009. "Filipinos Are No. 1!" 8 January. http://www.asianpacificpost.com/.

Asian Political News. 2004. "Tougher Japan Visa Rules for Entertainers Worry Filipinos." BNet Breaking News, 24 November. Highbeam Business, http://business.highbeam.com/.

AsiaOne News. 2010. "Overseas Filipinos Send More Money Home Despite Crisis." 15 February. http://www.asiaone.com/.

Asis, M.B., S. Huang, and B.S.A Yeoh. 2004. "When the Light of the Home Is Abroad: Unskilled Female Migration and the Filipino Family." *Singapore Journal of Tropical Geography* 25 (2): 198-215.

Asis, M.M.B. 2006. "The Philippines' Culture of Migration." Migration Information Source Country Profile. http://www.migrationinformation.org/.

Austria, J. 2008. "Multicultural Education from the Private Sphere: Growing Up Filipino-Canadian in a Third-Tier City School." MA thesis, Ryerson University. http://digital commons.ryerson.ca/diss.s/79.

Bach, J., and M.S. Solomon. 2008. "Labors of Globalization: Emergent State Responses." *New Global Studies* 2 (2), DOI: 10.2202/1940-0004.1025.

Bacungan, F., and R. Ofreneo. 2002. "The Development of Labour Law and Labour Market Policy in the Philippines." In *Law and Labour Market Regulation in East Asia*, edited by S. Cooney, T. Lindsey, R. Mitchell, and Y. Zhu, 91-121. London and New York: Routledge.

Bagasao, I.F. 2005. "Migration and Development: The Philippine Experience." In *Remittances: Development Impact and Future Prospects*, ed. S.M. Maimbo and D. Ratha, 133-42. Washington, DC: World Bank.

Baggio, F., and M.M.B. Asis. 2008. "Global Workers, Local Philanthropists in Italy and the Tug of Home." In *Global Migration and Development*, edited by T. van Naerssen, E. Spaan, and E.B. Zoomers, 130-49. New York and London: Routledge.

Bakan, A., and D. Stasiulis, eds. 1997. *Not One of the Family: Foreign Domestic Workers in Canada*. Toronto: University of Toronto Press.

Balakrishnan, Z.T.R., R. Ravanera, and T. Abada. 2005. "Spatial Residential Patterns and Socio-Economic Integration of Filipinos in Canada." *Canadian Ethnic Studies* 37 (2): 67-76.

Balana, C., and C.V. Esguerra. 2009. "Palace Orders Probe into FilAm's Abduction." *Philippine Daily Inquirer*, 1 July. http://globalnation.inquirer.net/.

Baldwin, A., L. Cameron, and A. Kobayashi, eds. 2011. *Rethinking the Great White North: Race, Nature and the Historical Geographies of Whiteness*. Vancouver: UBC Press.

Bales, K. 1999. *Disposable People: New Slavery in the Global Economy*. Los Angeles: University of California Press.

Balisacan, A.M., and E.M. Pernia. 2002. "Probing beneath Cross-National Averages: Poverty, Inequality, and Growth in the Philippines." ERD Working Paper Series No. 7. Manila: Economics and Research Department, Asian Development Bank.

Balita. 2008. "Pasko '08 Mini Newsletter." December.

–. 2009. "Pride in Being Filipino – What Does It Mean?" 1 April. http://www.balita.ca/.

Ball, R. 2004. "Divergent Development, Racialized Rights: Globalized Labour Markets and the Trade of Nurses: The Case of the Philippines." *Women's Studies International Forum* 27 (2): 119-33.

Ballescas, M. R. P. 1992. *Filipino Entertainers in Japan: An Introduction*. Quezon City: Foundation for Nationalist Studies.

Bangko Sentral ng Pilipinas. n.d. "Overseas Filipinos' Cash Remittances by Country, by Source." http://www.bsp.gov.ph/.

Bankoff, G., and K. Weekley. 2002. *Post-Colonial National Identity in the Philippines: Celebrating the Centennial of Independence*. Aldershot, UK: Ashgate.

Bannerji, H. 2000a. "The Paradox of Diversity: The Construction of a Multicultural Canada and 'Women of Color.'" *Women's Studies International Forum* 23 (5): 537-60.

–. 2000b. *The Dark Side of the Nation: Essays on Multiculturalism, Nationalism and Gender*. Toronto: Canadian Scholars' Press.

Barber, P.G. 1997. "Transnationalism and the Politics of 'Home' for Philippine Domestic Workers." *Anthropologica* 39 (1/2): 39-52.

–. 2000. "Agency in Philippine Women's Labour Migration and Provisional Diaspora." *Women's Studies International Forum* 23 (4): 399-411.

–. 2006. "Locating Gendered Subjects in Vocabularies of Citizenship." In *Women, Migration and Citizenship: Making Local, National and Transnational Connections*, edited by E. Tastsoglou and A. Dobrowolsky, 61-83. Aldershot, UK: Ashgate.

–. 2008. "The Ideal Immigrant? Gendered Class-Subjects in Philippine-Canadian Migration." *Third World Quarterly* 29 (7): 1265-85.

–. 2010. "Cell Phones, Politics, and the Philippine Labor Diaspora." In *Class, Contention, and a World in Motion*, edited by W. Lem and P.G. Barber, 138-62. New York: Berghahn Books.

Barrie, D. 2006. *The Other Alberta: Decoding a Political Enigma*. Regina: Canadian Plains Research Center, University of Regina.

Barry, B. 2001. *Culture and Equality: An Egalitarian Critique of Multiculturalism*. Cambridge, MA: Harvard University Press.

Basch, L., N. Glick Schiller, and C. Szanton Blanc. 1994. *Nations Unbound: Transnational Projects, Postcolonial Predicaments, and Deterritorialized Nation-States*. London: Routledge.

Bauböck, R., ed. 2006. *Migration and Citizenship: Legal Status, Rights and Political Participation*. Amsterdam: Amsterdam University Press.

Bauböck, R., B. Perchinig, and W. Sievers, eds. 2009. *Citizenship Policies in New Europe: Expanded and Updated Edition*. Amsterdam: Amsterdam University Press.

Bauder, H. 2006. *Labor Movement: How Migration Regulates Labor Markets*. New York: Oxford University Press.

Bauer, E., and P. Thompson. 2004. "'She's Always the Person with a Very Global Vision': The Gender Dynamics of Migration, Narrative Interpretation and the Case of Jamaican Transnational Families." *Gender and History* 16 (20): 334-75.

Bautista, C. 2001. "Composition and Origins of the Philippine Middle Classes." In *Exploration of the Middle Classes in Southeast Asia*, edited by H.M. Hsiao, 91-149. Taipei: Program for Southeast Asian Area Studies, Academia Sinica.

Bautista, V. 2002. *The Filipino Americans (1763-present): Their History, Culture, and Traditions*, 2nd ed. Naperville, IL: Bookhaus.

Beckett, H. 2001. *Manitoba*. Calgary: Weigl Educational Publishers.

Behnia, B. 2009. "Immigrant Volunteers: Their Characteristics, Contributions, and Experience." *INSCAN: International Settlement Canada* 23 (1): 1, 3-4.

Bélanger, A., and È. Caron Malenfant. 2005. *Population Projections of Visible Minority Groups, Canada, Provinces and Regions, 2001 to 2017*. Ottawa: Statistics Canada.

Bello, W., H. Docena, M. de Guzman, and M. Malig. 2005. *The Anti-Development State: The Political Economy of Permanent Crisis in the Philippines*. New York: Zed Books.

Beltran, R., and A. Javate de Dios, eds. 1992. *Filipino Overseas Contract Workers: At What Cost?* Manila: Goodwill Trading Bookstore.

Bernstein, R. 2009. *The East, the West, and Sex: A History of Erotic Encounters*. New York: Alfred A. Knopf.

Berry, J.W., J.S. Phinney, D.L. Sam, and P. Vedder. 2006. *Immigrant Youth in Cultural Transition: Acculturation, Identity, and Adaptation across National Contexts*. Mahwah, NJ: Lawrence Erlbaum Associates.

Bessell, S. 2009. "Children's Participation in Decision-Making in the Philippines: Understanding the Attitudes of Policy-Makers and Service Providers." *Childhood* 16 (3): 299-316.

Bhavnani, K., and A. Phoenix, eds. 1994. *Shifting Identities Shifting Racism: A Feminism and Psychology Reader*. London: Thousand Oaks; New Delhi: Sage.

Biery, R.E. 1990. *Understanding Homosexuality: The Pride and the Prejudice*. Austin, TX: Edward-William Publishing.

Billig, M.S. 2003. *Barons, Brokers, and Buyers: The Institutions and Cultures of Philippine Sugar*. Honolulu: University of Hawai'i Press.

Bilodeau, A., and M. Kanji. 2010. "The New Immigrant Voter, 1965-2004: The Emergence of a New Liberal Partisan?" In *Voting Behaviour in Canada*, edited by C.D. Anderson and L.B. Stephenson, 65-85. Vancouver: UBC Press.

Bissoondath, N. 1994. *Selling Illusions: The Cult of Multiculturalism in Canada*. London: Penguin.

Blackmore, J. 2002. "Educational Leadership: A Feminist Critique and Reconstruction." In *Critical Perspectives on Educational Leadership*, edited by J. Smyth, 93-130. London and New York: Routledge.

Bloemraad, I. 2004. "Who Claims Dual Citizenship? The Limits of Postnationalism, the Possibilities of Transnationalism, and the Persistence of Traditional Citizenship." *International Migration Review* 38 (2): 389-426.

–. 2006. *Becoming a Citizen: Incorporating Immigrants and Refugees in the United States and Canada*. Berkeley: University of California Press.

Böhlmark, A. 2009. "Integration of Childhood Immigrants in the Short and Long Run – Swedish Evidence." *International Migration Review* 43 (2): 387-409.

Bojar, K. 1998. Volunteerism in Women's Lives: A Lens for Exploring Conflicts in Contemporary Feminist Thought, Historical Importance and Socio-Economic Value of Women's Contributions as Volunteers." In *Women's Studies in Transition: The Pursuit of Interdisciplinarity*, edited by K. Conway-Turner, S. Cherrin, J. Schiffman, and K.D. Turkel, 36-56. Cranbury, NJ: Associated University Press.

Bonifacio, G. 2003. "Filipino Women and Their Citizenship in Australia: In Search of Political Space." PhD diss., University of Wollongong, Australia.

–. 2005. "Filipino Women in Australia: Practising Citizenship at Work." *Asian and Pacific Migration Journal* 14 (3): 293-326.

–. 2008. "I Care for You, Who Cares for Me? Transitional Services of Filipino Live-in Caregivers in Canada." *Asian Women: Gender Issues in International Migration* 24 (1): 25-50.

–. 2009. "Migration and Maternalism: (Re)Configuring Ruddick's Maternal Thinking." In *Maternal Thinking: Philosophy, Politics, Practice*, edited by A. O'Reilly, 160-72. Toronto: Demeter Press.

–, ed. 2012. *Feminism and Migration: Cross-Cultural Engagements*. Dordrecht, The Netherlands: Springer.

Bonifacio, G., and V. Angeles. 2010a. "Building Communities through Faith: Filipino Catholics in Philadelphia and Alberta." In *Gender, Religion and Migration: Pathways of Integration*, edited by G.T. Bonifacio and V. Angeles, 257-73. Lanham, MD: Lexington Books.

–, eds. 2010b. *Gender, Religion and Migration: Pathways of Integration*. Lanham, MD: Lexington Books.

Bonus, R. 2000. *Locating Filipino Americans: Ethnicity and the Cultural Politics of Space*. Philadelphia: Temple University Press.

Borras, S.M. Jr. 2005. "The Philippine Land Reform in Comparative Perspective: Some Conceptual and Methodological Implications." *Journal of Agrarian Change* 6 (1): 69-101.

Bosse, C.L. 2007. *Becoming and Consumption: The Contemporary Spanish Novel*. Lanham, MD: Lexington Books.

Bottomley, G. 2010. *From Another Place: Migration and the Politics of Culture*. Cambridge: Cambridge University Press.

Bouma, G.D., R. Ling, and D. Pratt. 2010. *Religious Diversity in Southeast Asia and the Pacific: National Case Studies*. New York: Springer.

Bourdieu, P. 1991. *Language and Symbolic Power*, translated by G. Raymond and M. Adamson. Cambridge, MA: Harvard University Press.

Bower, S.S. 2011. *Wet Prairies: People, Land and Water in Agricultural Manitoba*. Vancouver: UBC Press.

Boyd, M., and J. Yiu. 2009. "Immigrant Women and Earnings Inequality in Canada." In *Racialized Migrant Women in Canada: Essays in Health, Violence, and Equity*, 208-31.Toronto: University of Toronto Press.

Boyle, P., and K. Halfacree. 1999. "Introduction: Gender and Migration in Developed Countries." In *Migration and Gender in the Developed World*, 1-29. London and New York: Routledge.

Bozett, F.W., ed. 1989. *Homosexuality and the Family*. Binghamton, NY: Haworth Press.

Brah, A., and A. Phoenix. 2004. "Ain't I a Woman? Revisiting Intersectionality." *Journal of International Women's Studies* 5 (3): 75-86.

Bramadat, P. 2009. "Socio-Economic Conditions – Manitoba and Saskatchewan." *Canadian Journal for Social Research* 2 (1): 229-36.

Brandl, B., C.B. Dyer, C.J. Heisler, J.M. Otto, L.A. Stiegel, and R.W. Thomas, eds. 2007. *Elder Abuse Detection and Intervention: A Collaborative Approach*. New York: Springer.

Bredbenner, C.L. 1998. *A Nationality of Her Own: Women, Marriage, and the Law of Citizenship*. Berkeley: University of California Press.

Bretell, C. 2000. "Theorizing Migration in Anthropology: The Social Construction of Networks, Identities, Communities and Globalscapes." In *Migration Theory: Talking across Disciplines*, edited by C. Bretell and J.F. Hollifield, 97-136. New York and London: Routledge.

Brigham, S.M. 2002. "Women Migrant Workers in the Global Economy: The Role of Critical Feminist Pedagogy for Filipino Domestic Workers." PhD diss., University of Alberta.

Brinkerhoff, J.M. 2006. "Diaspora Mobilization Factors and Policy Options." In *Converting Migration Drains to Gains: Harnessing the Resources of Overseas Professionals*, 127-48. Manila: Asian Development Bank.

Briones, L. 2009. "Reconsidering the Migration-Development Link: Capability and Livelihood in Filipina Experiences of Domestic Work in Paris." *Population, Space and Place* 15 (2): 133-45.

Brooks, A. 2007. "Feminist Standpoint Epistemology: Building Knowledge and Empowerment through Women's Lived Experience." In *Feminist Research Practice: A Primer*, edited by S.N. Hesse-Biber and P.L. Leavy, 53-82. London: Sage.

Brooks, A., and S.N. Hesse-Biber. 2007. "An Invitation to Feminist Research." In *Feminist Research Practice: A Primer*, edited by S.N. Hesse-Biber and P.L. Leavy, 1-24. London: Sage.

Brotz, H. 1980. "Multiculturalism in Canada: A Muddle." *Canadian Public Policy* 6 (1): 41-46.

Broussine, M. 2009. "Public Leadership." In *Public Management and Governance*, 2nd ed., edited by T. Bovaird and E. Löffler, 261-78. New York: Routledge.

Brozowski, K., and D.R. Hall. 2004. "Growing Old in a Risk Society: Elder Abuse in Canada." *Journal of Elder Abuse and Neglect* 16 (3): 65-81.

Brubaker, R. 1992. *Citizenship and Nationhood in France and Germany*. Cambridge, MA: Harvard University Press.

Brunero, S., J. Smith, and E. Bates. 2008. "Expectations and Experiences of Recently Recruited Overseas Qualified Nurses in Australia." *Advances in Contemporary Transcultural Nursing* 28 (1-2): 101-10.

Brush, B., and J. Sochalski. 2007. "International Nurse Migration: Lessons from the Philippines." *Policy, Politics, and Nursing Practice* 8 (1): 37-46.

Bryceson, D., and U. Vuorela. 2002. "Transnational Families in the Twenty-First Century." In *The Transnational Family: New European Frontiers and Global Networks*, edited by D. Bryceson and U. Vuorela, 3-29. Oxford: Berg.

Brysk, A. 2004. "Children across Borders: Patrimony, Property, or Persons." In *People Out of Place: Globalization, Human Rights, and the Citizenship Gap*, edited by A. Brysk and G. Shafir, 153-76. New York and London: Routledge.

Buchan, J. 2006. "Filipino Nurses in the UK: A Case Study in Active International Recruitment." *Harvard Health Policy Review* 7 (1): 113-20.

Bueker, C.S. 2006. *From Immigrant to Naturalized Citizen: Political Incorporation in the United States*. New York: LFB Scholarly Publishing.

Buell, E.C., E. Luluquisen, L. Galedo, E.H. Luis, and Filipino American National Historical Society East Bay Chapter. 2008. *Filipinos in the East Bay*. San Francisco: Arcadia Publishing.

Bumsted, J.M. 2003. *Canada's Diverse Peoples: A Reference Sourcebook*. Santa Barbara, CA: ABC-CLIO.

Bureau of East Asian and Pacific Affairs. 2009. "US Relations with the Philippines." US Department of State, http://www.state.gov/.

Burgess, R., and V. Haksar. 2005. *Migration and Foreign Remittances in the Philippines*. Washington, DC: International Monetary Fund.

Burgoon, J.K., and A.E. Bacue. 2008. "Nonverbal Communication Skills." In *Handbook of Communication and Interaction Skills*, edited by J.O. Greene and B.R. Burleson, 179-220. Mahwah, NJ: Lawrence Erlbaum Associates.

Bustos, A.S., N.I. Malolos, E.E. Ramirez, E.C. Ramos, and M.A. Bustos-Orosa. 1999. *Introduction to Psychology*, 3rd ed. Quezon City: Katha Publishing.

Cahill, D. 1990. *Intermarriages in International Contexts: A Study of Filipina Women Married to Australian, Japanese and Swiss Men*. Quezon City: Scalabrini Migration Center.

Campbell, C.D. 2000. "Social Structure, Space, and Sentiment: Searching for Common Ground in Sociological Conceptions of Community." In *Community Structure and Dynamics at the Dawn of the New Millennium*, edited by D.A. Chekki, 21-58. Stamford, CT: JAI Press.

Canadian Council for Refugees. 2007. "Protecting the Rights of Migrant Workers in Canada." http://www.ccrweb.ca/.

Cannell, F. 1999. *Power and Intimacy in the Christian Philippines*. Cambridge: Cambridge University Press.

Cantú, L. Jr. 2009. *The Sexuality of Migration: Border Crossings and Mexican Immigrant Men*. New York: New York University Press.

Capeheart, L., and D. Milovanovic. 2007. *Social Justice: Theories, Issues and Movements*. Piscataway, NJ: Rutgers University Press.

Capili, R.A. 2010. "The Dual Citizenship Law (I)," *Sun Star*, 16 February. http://www.sunstar.com.ph/.

Caplan, P., ed. 1987. *The Cultural Construction of Sexuality*. New York: Routledge.

Carter, A. 2001. *The Political Theory of Global Citizenship*. London and New York: Routledge.

Cashmore, E. 1996. *Dictionary of Race and Ethnic Relations*, 4th ed. New York: Routledge.

Castles, S., and M.J. Miller. 1998. *The Age of Migration: International Population Movements in the Modern World*. Basingstoke, UK: Macmillan.

Castro, J.R., F.R. Dado, and C.I. Tubesa. 2006. "When Dad Becomes Mom: Communication of Househusbands with Breadwinner Wives." *Far Eastern University Communication Journal* 2: 1-11.

Catalyst. 2012. "Quick Take: Visible Minorities." 28 June. http://www.catalyst.org/knowledge/visible-minorities.

Catholic Institute for International Relations. 1987. *The Labour Trade: Filipino Migrant Workers around the World*. London: Catholic Institute for International Relations.

Catholic News Agency. 2008. "Filipino Priest's Healing Ministry under Observation after Two Die." 27 January. http://www.catholicnewsagency.com/.

CBC News. 2006. "Ottawa Reviewing Rules of Dual Citizenship: Solberg." 7 November. http://www.cbc.ca/.

–. 2008. "Cancer Claims Winnipeg Philippine Leader." 5 March. http://www.cbc.ca/.

–. 2009a. "48 Arrested at Police-Brutality Protest in Montreal." 15 March. http://www.cbc.ca/.

–. 2009b. "Same-Sex Marriage Disparaged in Alberta Benefits Booklet, Man Says." 20 April. http://www.cbc.ca/.

CBS News. 2010. "Miss Philippines Venus Raj Stumbled on Question." 24 August. http://www.cbsnews.com/.

Center for Migrant Advocacy and Friedrich Ebert Stiftung (FES). 2009. The Philippines: A Global Model on Labor Migration? 2nd ed. June. www.qdocuments.com/The-Global-Context-and-Migration-DOC.html (accessed July 29, 2011).

Center for People Empowerment in Governance (CenPEG). 2008. "Labor Migration in the Philippines: A Dangerous Doctrine." *Pinoy Press*, http://www.pinoypress.net/.

Chagnon, N.A. 2000. "Yanomamö: The Last Days of Eden." In *Moral Disagreements: Classic and Contemporary Readings*, edited by C.W. Gowans, 91-101. London: Routledge.

Chang, G. 2000. *Disposable Domestics: Immigrant Women Workers in the Global Economy*. Cambridge, MA: South End Press.

Chang, K.A., and J. Groves. 1997. "'Saints and Prostitutes:' Sexual Discourse in the Filipina Domestic Worker Community in Hong Kong." Working Papers in the Social Sciences, No. 20. Hong Kong: Division of Social Science, Hong Kong University of Science and Technology.

Chang, K.A., and L.H.M. Ling. 2000. "Globalization and Its Intimate Other: Filipina Domestic Workers in Hong Kong." In *Gender and Global Restructuring: Sightings, Sites and Resistances*, edited by M.H. Marchand and A.S. Runyan, 27-43. New York: Routledge.

Chant, S. 1997. "Gender and Tourism Employment in Mexico and the Philippines." In *Gender, Work and Tourism*, edited by M.T. Sinclair, 120-79. London: Routledge.

Chant, S., and C. McIlwaine. 1995. *Women of a Lesser Cost: Female Labor, Foreign Exchange and Philippine Development*. East Haven, CT: Pluto Press.

Chappell, N.L., L. McDonald, and M. Stones. 2008. *Aging in Contemporary Canada*, 2nd ed. Toronto: Pearson Education Canada.

Chaudhry, P., and A.S. Zimmerman. 2009. *The Economics of Counterfeit Trade: Governments, Consumers, Pirates and Intellectual Property Rights*. Heidelberg, Germany: Springer.

Cheema, G.S., C.A. McNally, and V. Popvski, eds. 2011. *Cross-Border Governance in Asia: Regional Issues and Mechanisms*. Tokyo: United Nations University Press.

Chell, V. 2000. "Female Migrants in Italy: Coping in a Country of New Migration." In *Gender and Migration in Southern Europe: Women on the Move*, edited by F. Anthias and G. Lazaridis, 103-24. New York: Berg.

Chelladurai, P. 2006. *Human Resource Management in Sport and Recreation*. Champaign, IL: Human Kinetics.

Chen, A.B. 1998. *From Sundown to Snowbelt: Filipinos in Canada*. Calgary: Canadian Ethnic Studies Association, University of Calgary.

–. 1999. "Filipinos." In *Encyclopedia of Canada's Peoples*, edited by P.R. Magocsi, 501-13. Toronto: University of Toronto Press.

Cheng, S.A. 2006. *Serving the Household and the Nation: Filipina Domestics and the Politics of Identity in Taiwan*. Lanham, MD: Lexington Books.

Chiang, L.N. 2008. "'Astronaut Families:' Transnational Lives of Middle-Class Taiwanese Married Women in Canada." *Social and Cultural Geography* 9 (5): 505-18.

Chin, C.B.N. 1997. "Walls of Silence and Late Twentieth Century Representation of the Foreign Female Domestic Worker: The Case of Filipina and Indonesian Female Servants in Malaysia." *International Migration Review* 31: 353-85.

Chin, J.L., B. Lott, J.K. Rice, and J. Sanchez-Hucles, eds. 2007. *Women and Leadership: Transforming Visions and Diverse Voices*. Malden, MA: Blackwell.

Chisanga, B. 2003. "Community Participation and the Status of Women in Developing Countries: The Case of Community Service Provision in Zambia." *Journal of Social Work Research and Evaluation* 4 (1): 83-94.

Chiswick, B.R., and P.W. Miller. 2010. "An Explanation for the Lower Payoff to Schooling for Immigrants in the Canadian Labour Market." In *Canadian Immigration: Economic Evidence for a Dynamic Policy Environment*, edited by T. McDonald, E. Ruddick, A. Sweetman, and C. Worswick, 41-75. Montreal and Kingston: McGill-Queen's University Press.

Cholewinski, R. 2005. "Protecting Migrant Workers in a Globalized World." Migration Information Source, http://www.migrationinformation.org/.

Choy, C.C. 1998. "The Export of Womanpower: A Transitional History of Filipino Nurse Migration to the United States." PhD diss., University of California at Los Angeles.

–. 2003a. *Empire of Care: Nursing and Migration in Filipino American History*. Durham, NC: Duke University Press.

–. 2003b. "Relocating Struggle: Filipino Nurses Organize in the United States." In *Asian/Pacific Islander American Women: A Historical Anthology*, edited by S. Hune and G.M. Nomura, 335-49. New York and London: New York University Press.

Chui, T., K. Tran, and H. Maheux. 2008. *Canada's Ethnocultural Mosaic, 2006 Census*. Ottawa: Statistics Canada.

CIC News. 2008. "Canada – The Most Welcoming Country in the World." December. http://www.cicnews.com/.

Citizenship and Immigration Canada (CIC). 2005. "Immigration statistics = Statistique de l'immigration (PDF)," 1966-1996. Library and Archives Canada Electronic Collection, http://epe.lac-bac.gc.ca/.

–. 2009. "Facts and Figures 2009 – Immigration Overview: Permanent and Temporary Residents." http://www.cic.gc.ca/.

–. 2011a. *Canada Facts and Figures. Immigration Overview: Permanent and Temporary Residents 2010*. Ottawa: Research and Evaluation Branch, Citizenship and Immigration Canada.

–. 2011b. "Facts and Figures 2011 – Immigration Overview: Permanent and Temporary Residents." http://www.cic.gc.ca/.

–. 2012. "Provincial Nominees." http://www.cic.gc.ca/.

City of Winnipeg. 2006. "Census Data – City of Winnipeg." http://winnipeg.ca/Census/2006/City%20of%20Winnipeg/City%20of%20Winnipeg/City%20of%20Winnipeg.pdf.

Clarke, G., and M. Sison. 2005. "Voices from the Top of the Pile: Elite Perceptions of Poverty and the Poor in the Philippines." In *Elite Perceptions of Poverty and Inequality,* edited by E.P. Reis and M. Moore, 57-90. New York and London: Zed Books.

Claussen, H.L. 2001. *Unconventional Sisterhood: Feminist Catholic Nuns in the Philippines.* Ann Arbor: University of Michigan Press.

Clément, D. 2008. *Canada's Rights Revolution: Social Movements and Social Change, 1937-82.* Vancouver: UBC Press.

Clymer, K.J. 1976. "Humanitarian Imperialism: David Prescott Barrows and the White Man's Burden in the Philippines." *Pacific Historical Review* 45 (4): 495-517.

Code, L. 1991. *What Can She Know? Feminist Theory and the Construction of Knowledge.* Ithaca, NY: Cornell University Press.

Cohen, T. 2008. "Middle Class Stagnant, Rich and Poor Increasing Numbers." CBC News, 1 May. http://www.cbc.ca/.

Coleman, M. 2003. "Gender and Orthodoxies of Leadership." *School Leadership and Management* 23 (3): 325-39.

Comerford, M. 2005a. "Why Nurses Leave the Philippines." *Daily Herald* (Arlington Heights, IL), 18 April. http://www.questia.com/.

–. 2005b. "'It Breaks Your Heart': The Poorest of the Philippines' Poor Live among Mountains of Garbage." *Daily Herald* (Arlington Heights, IL), 17 April. http://www.questia.com/.

Commission on Filipinos Overseas (CFO). 2011. "Number of Registered Filipino Emigrants by Sex: 1981-2010." http://www.cfo.gov.ph/images/stories/pdf/by_sex.pdf.

–. 2012. "Stock Estimate of Overseas Filipinos as of December 2010." http://www.cfo.gov.ph/pdf/statistics/Stock%202010.pdf.

–. 2013a. "Statistical Profile of Registered Filipino Emigrants." http://www.cfo.gov.ph/.

–. 2013b. "Highlights of the 2011 Stock Estimate of Filipinos Overseas." http://www.cfo.gov.ph/.

Committee on the Rights of the Child (CRC). 2009. "Committee on Rights of Child Examines Report of the Philippines." ReliefWeb, http://www.reliefweb.int/.

Conklin Frederking, L. 2007. *Economic and Political Integration in Immigrant Neighborhoods: Trajectories of Virtuous and Vicious Cycles.* Cranbury, NJ: Rosemont Publishing and Printing.

Connolly, W.E. 2002. *Identity/Difference: Democratic Negotiations of Political Paradox,* expanded ed. Minneapolis: University of Minnesota Press.

Constable, N. 1997. *Maid to Order in Hong Kong: Stories of Filipina Workers.* Ithaca, NY: Cornell University Press.

–. 1998. "At Home but Not at Home: Filipina Narratives of Ambivalent Returns." *Cultural Anthropology* 14 (2): 203-28.

–. 2000. "Dolls, T-Birds, and Ideal Workers: The Negotiation of Filipino Identity in Hong Kong." In *Home and Hegemony: Domestic Service and identity Politics in South and Southeast Asia,* edited by K.M. Adams and S. Dickey, 221-48. Ann Arbor: University of Michigan Press.

–. 2003. *Romance on a Global Stage: Pen Pals, Virtual Ethnography, and "Mail-Order" Marriages.* Berkeley and Los Angeles: University of California Press.

–. 2006. "Brides, Maids, and Prostitutes: Reflections on the Study of 'Trafficked' Women." *PORTAL: Journal of Multidisciplinary International Studies* 3 (2): 1-25.

Constantino, R. 1982. *The Miseducation of the Filipino.* Quezon City, Philippines: Foundation for Nationalist Studies.

Cooke, T.J. 2003. "Family Migration and the Relative Earnings of Husbands and Wives." *Annals of the Association of American Geographers* 93 (2): 338-49.

Coronel, S.S. 1998. *Pork and Other Perks: Corruption and Governance in the Philippines.* Pasig, Metro Manila: Philippine Center for Investigative Journalism, Evelio B. Javier Foundation, and the Institute for Popular Democracy.

Cowan, T.L. 2008. "Genealogies of Sex and Landscape in Poetry by Robert Kroetsch and Shane Rhodes." In *The Body and the Book: Writings on Poetry and Sexuality,* edited by G. Byron and A.J. Sneddon, 113-34. Amsterdam and New York: Rodopi.

Crescini, D. 2009. "Filipino Foreign Passport Holders Exempt from Manila Airport Exit Fees." *Philippine Tribune,* 16 October. http://www.philippinesentinel.org/.

Crespo, M.J.C. 2009. "Online Marriage and 'Buhay Ko' (My Life): Views from Filipino Prospective Brides, Wives, and their US/British/Australian Husbands." PhD diss., University of New Mexico.

Crisostomo, S. 2011. "Comelec Eyes 1 Million Absentee Voters for 2013 Elections." *Philippine Star*, 3 November. http://www.philstar.com/.

Crocker, R. 2010. "Program Aims to Curb Elder Abuse in Asian Community." *Winnipeg Free Press*, 25 March. http://www.winnipegfreepress.com/.

Cruz, J. 1994. "Filipino-American Community Organizations in Washington, 1900s-1930s." In *Peoples of Color in the American West*, edited by S. Chan, D.H. Daniels, M. Garcia, and T. Wilson, 235-45. Lexington, MA: Heath.

CTV Montreal. 2010. "Filipino-Canadian Student Wins Human Rights Case." 23 April. http://montreal.ctv.ca/.

CTV News. 2004. "Manitoba Gay Marriage Rules Violate Rights: MP." 11 November. http://www.ctv.ca/.

–. 2006. "Canadian Evacuation from Lebanon Cost $85 M: CTV." 20 September. http://www.ctv.ca/.

Cunneen, C., and J. Stubbs. 1997. *Gender, Race and International Relations: Violence against Filipino Women in Australia*. Sydney: Institute of Criminology.

Curry-Stevens, A. 2008. "Building the Case for the Study of the Middle Class: Shifting Our Gaze from Margins to Centre." *International Journal of Social Welfare* 17 (4): 379-89.

Cushner, N. 1971. *Spain in the Philippines: From Conquest to Revolution*. Quezon City: Institute of Philippine Culture, Ateneo de Manila University.

D'Appollonia, A.C., and S. Reich. 2008. *Immigration, Integration and Security: America and Europe in Comparative Perspective*. Pittsburgh, PA: University of Pittsburgh Press.

Dalayoan, G., L. Enverga-Magsino, and L. Bailon. 2008. *The First Filipino Immigrants in Manitoba (1959-1975)*. Winnipeg: Manitoba Filipino Writers Guild.

Dancel, F. 2005. "*Utang na Loob* [Debt of Gratitude]: A Philosophical Analysis." In *Filipino Cultural Traits: Claro R. Ceniza Lectures*, edited by R.M. Gripaldo, 109-28. Washington, DC: Council for Research in Values and Philosophy.

Darden, J.T. 2009. "Filipinos in Canada and the United States – Comparison of Socio-economic Equality." Paper presented at the Canadian Studies Center, Michigan State University, 14 April. http://canadianstudies.isp.msu.edu/docs/filipinos%20in%20 canada%20and%20the%20United%20States%20(4-28-09).pdf.

Dato, E.A. 2004. "FILCAS: Celebrating 31 Years of Volunteerism." In *Celebrating 31 Years: Fiesta Filipiniana Araw ng Kalayaan Memorabilia*, 13-14. Saskatoon: FILCAS.

David, E.J.R. 2011. *Filipino-/American Postcolonial Psychology: Oppression, Colonial Mentality, and Decolonization*. Bloomington, IN: AuthorHouse.

Davis, K. 2006. "Feminist Politics of Location." In *Handbook of Gender and Women's Studies*, edited by K. Davis, M. Evans, and J. Lorber, 476-80. London: Sage.

–. 2008. "Intersectionality as Buzzword: A Sociology of Science Perspective on What Makes a Feminist Theory Successful." *Feminist Theory* 9 (1): 67-85.

De Castro, L.D. 2000. "*Kagandahang Loob*: A Filipino Concept of Feminine Bioethics." In *Globalizing Feminist Bioethics: Crosscultural Perspectives*, edited by R. Tong with G. Anderson and A.F. Santos, 51-61. Boulder, CO: Westview Press.

De Castro, R.C. 2007. "The 1997 Asian Financial Crisis and the Revival of Populism/ Neo-Populism in 21st Century Philippine Politics." *Asian Survey* 47 (6): 930-51.

de Jesus, M., ed. 2005. *Pinay Power: Theorizing the Filipina/American Experience*. New York and London: Routledge.

De la Cruz, J. 2009. "Filipino Nurses in Canada Vulnerable to Exploitation, Misleading and Abusive Policies." *Bulatlat*, 1 November. http://www.bulatlat.com/.

De la Torre, V.R. 2002. *Cultural Icons of the Philippines*. Makati, Philippines: Tower Book House.

De Lauretis, T. 1987. *Technologies of Gender: Essays on Theory, Film, and Fiction*. Bloomington, IN: Indiana University Press.

Del Rio-Laquian, E., and A. Laquian. 2008. *Seeking a Better Life Abroad: A Study of Filipinos in Canada, 1957-2007*. Manila: Anvil.

Del Rosario, T.C. 2005. "Bridal Diaspora: Migration and Marriage among Filipino Women." *Indian Journal of Gender Studies* 12 (2-3): 253-73.

DeLamater, J., and J.S. Hyde. 2004. "Conceptual and Theoretical Issues in Studying Sexuality in Close Relationships." In *Handbook of Sexuality in Close Relationships*, edited by J.H. Harvey, A. Wenzel, and S. Sprecher, 7-30. Hillsdale, NJ: Lawrence Erlbaum Associates.

Delanty, G. 2002. "Communitarianism and Citizenship." In *Handbook of Citizenship Studies*, edited by E.F. Isin and B.S. Turner, 159-74. London: Sage.

Delos Reyes, E. 2010. "A Concert in Review ... One Kapamilya Go! Canada 2010." *Pinoy Times*, 21 June. http://pinoytimes.ca/.

Department of Labor and Employment, Republic of the Philippines. 2011. "Summary of Current Regional Daily Minimum Wage Rates, Non-Agriculture, Agriculture as of July 2011." National Wages and Productivity Commission. http://www.nwpc.dole.gov.ph/.

DeSantis, L. 1998. "Reproductive Health." In *Handbook of Immigrant Health*, edited by S. Loue, 449-76. New York: Plenum Press.

Dewey, J. 1938. *Experience and Education.* New York: Collier Books.

Dewing, M. 2009. "Canadian Multiculturalism." Parliament of Canada, Parliamentary Information and Research Service. http://www.parl.gc.ca/Content/LOP/ResearchPublications/prb0920-e.pdf.

Dhruvarajan, V., and J. Vickers. 2002. *Gender, Race, and Nation: A Global Perspective.* Toronto: University of Toronto Press.

Dib, K., I. Donaldson, and B. Turcotte. 2008. "Integration and Identity in Canada: The Importance of Multicultural Common Spaces." *Canadian Ethnic Studies* 40 (1): 161-87.

Dickerson, M.O., T. Flanagan, and B. O'Neill. 2010. *An Introduction to Government and Politics: A Conceptual Approach,* 8th ed. Toronto: Nelson Education.

Dictaan-Bang-oa, E. 2004. "The Question of Peace in Mindanao, Southern Philippines." In *Beyond the Silencing of the Guns*, edited by C.K. Roy, V. Tauli-Corpuz, and A. Romero-Medina, 153-83. Baguio City, Philippines: Tebtebba Foundation, Indigenous Peoples International Center for Policy Research and Education.

Digal, S. 2009. "Philippines: Over 6 Million Young People Drop Out of School." AsiaNews. it, 5 November. http://www.asianews.it/.

Dill, B.T. 1987. "The Dialectics of Black Womanhood." In *Feminism and Methodology*, edited by S. Harding, 97-108. Bloomington: Indiana University Press.

Diola, C. 2013. "30,000 ex-Filipinos Regained Citizenship in 2012." *Philippine Star,* 3 January. http://www.philstar.com/.

Dion, K.L. 2001. "Immigrants' Perceptions of Housing Discrimination in Toronto: The Housing New Canadians Project." *Journal of Social Issues* 57 (3): 523-39.

DiPalma, C., and K. Ferguson. 2006. "Clearing Ground and Making Connections: Modernism, Postmodernism, Feminism." In *Handbook of Gender and Women's Studies*, edited by K. Davis, M. Evans, and J. Lorber, 127-45. London: Sage.

Dobrowolsky, A. 2008. "Interrogating 'Invisibilization' and 'Instrumentalization': Women and the Current Citizenship Trends in Canada." *Citizenship Studies* 12 (5): 465-79.

Docot, M.L.B. 2009. "On Identity and Development: Filipino Women Entertainers in Transition in Japan." In *Development in Asia: Interdisciplinary, Post-neoliberal, and Transnational Perspectives*, edited by D.M. Nault, 107-34. Boca Raton, FL: Brown Walker Press.

Dolan, R.E., ed. 1991. *Philippines: A Country Study.* Washington, DC: Government Printing Office for the Library of Congress. http://countrystudies.us/philippines/.

Domingo, E.V. 2008. "Pinoy Graduates: Whither Thou Goeth?" National Statistical Co-ordination Board, http://www.nscb.gov.ph/.

Donato, K., G. Gabaccia, J. Holdaway, M. Manalansan IV, and P. Pessar. 2006. "A Glass Half Full? Gender in Migration Studies." *International Migration Review* 40 (1): 3-26.

Dreby, J. 2009. "Gender and Transnational Gossip." *Qualitative Sociology* 32 (1): 33-52.

Driedger, L., and S.S. Halli. 2000. "The Race Challenge." In *Race and Racism: Canada's Challenge,* edited by L. Driedger and S.S. Halli, 1-18. Montreal and Kingston: McGill-Queen's University Press.

Duerst-Lahti, G., and R.M. Kelly, eds. 1995. *Gender Power, Leadership, and Governance.* Ann Arbor: University of Michigan Press.

Ebaugh, H.R.F., and J.S. Chafetz. 2000. *Religion and the New Immigrants: Continuities and Adaptations in Immigrant Congregations.* Walnut Creek, CA: AltaMira Press.

Eckstein, S. 2001. "Community as Gift-Giving: Collectivistic Roots of Volunteerism." *American Sociological Review* 66 (6): 829-51.

Eclarin Azada, J.M. 2006. "Asian and Pacific American Catholic Women." In *Encyclopedia of Women and Religion in North America,* vol. 1, edited by R.S. Keller and R.R. Ruether, 178-86. Bloomington: Indiana University Press.

Economic Times. 2010. "Canada to Open Office in India for Degree Recognition." 19 February. Toronto Region Immigrant Employment Council, http://triec.ca/.

Eder, J. 2006. "Gender Relations and Household Economic Planning in the Rural Philippines." *Journal of Southeast Asian Studies* 37: 397-413.

Edgar, B., J. Doherty, and H. Meert. 2007. *Immigration and Homelessness in Europe.* Bristol, UK: Policy Press.

Edgerton, R.K. 1984. "The Society and Its Environment." In *Philippines: A Country Study,* edited by F.M. Bunge, 57-110. Washington, DC: Department of the Army.

Edmonton Journal. 2008. "Alberta Has Come a Long Way on Same-Sex Marriage." 8 November. http://www.canada.com/edmontonjournal/.

Edwards, L., and M. Roces, eds. 2004. *Women's Suffrage in Asia: Gender, Nationalism and Democracy.* New York: RoutledgeCurzon.

Ehrenreich, B., and A.R. Hochschild, eds. 2002. *Global Woman: Nannies, Maids and Sex Workers in the New Economy.* New York: Henry Holt.

Ellerman, D. 2005. "Labour Migration: A Development Path or a Low-Level Trap?" *Development in Practice* 15 (5): 617-30.

England, K. 2003. "Towards a Feminist Political Geography?" *Political Geography* 22: 611-16.

England, K., and B. Stiell. 1997. "'They Think You're Stupid as Your English Is': Constructing Foreign Domestic Workers in Toronto." *Environment and Planning A* 29: 195-215.

EnjoyPhilippines. 2011. "Beauty and Healthcare Industry in the Philippines Thrives." http://www.enjoyphilippines.com/.

Enloe, C. 1990. *Bananas, Beaches and Bases: Making Feminist Sense of International Politics.* Berkeley and Los Angeles: University of California Press.

Ennaji, M., and F. Sadiqi. 2008. *Migration and Gender in Morocco: The Impact of Migration on the Women Left Behind.* Trenton, NJ: Red Sea Press.

Enriquez, C. 2009. *Filipinos Are Rich.* Maitland, FL: Xulon Press.

Enriquez, V.G. 1992. *From Colonial to Liberation Psychology: The Philippine Experience.* Quezon City: University of the Philippines Press.

–. 1993. "Developing a Filipino Psychology." In *Indigenuous Psychologies: Research and Experience in Cultural Context,* edited by U. Kim and J.W. Berry, 152-69. London: Sage.

Erlinghagen, M., and K. Hank. 2006. "The Participation of Older Europeans in Volunteer Work." *Ageing and Society* 26 (4): 567-84.

Escobar, A. 2001. "Culture Sits in Places: Reflections on Globalism and Subaltern Strategies of Localization." *Political Geography* 20: 139-74.

Escobar, P. 2004. "Poverty, Corruption: The Ties that Bind." *Asia Times Online,* 5 October. http://www.atimes.com/.

Esguerra, M.P.G. 2011. "Filipino Immigrants." In *Multicultural America: An Encyclopedia of the Newest Americans,* edited by R.H. Bayor, 701-52. Santa Barbara, CA: ABC-CLIO.

Esman, M.J. 1990. "Language Policy and Political Community in Southeast Asia." In *Language Policy and Political Development,* edited by B. Weinstein, 185-201. Norwood, NJ: Ablex Publishing.

Espinosa, H. 2010. "Fil-Ams Angry Over Undelivered Balkibayan Boxes." ABS-CBN News, 9 July. http://www.abs-cbnnews.com/.

Espiritu, Y.L. 1995. *Filipino American Lives.* Philadelphia: Temple University Press.

–. 1997. *Asian American Women and Men: Labor, Laws and Love.* London: Sage.

–. 2003a. *Home Bound: Filipino American Lives across Cultures, Communities, and Countries.* Berkeley and Los Angeles: University of California Press.

–. 2003b. "'We Don't Sleep around Like White Girls Do': Family, Culture, and Gender in Filipino American Lives." In *Gender and US Immigration: Contemporary Trends,* edited by P. Hondagneu-Sotelo, 263-86. Berkeley and Los Angeles: University of California Press.

–. 2005. "Colonial Oppression, Labour Importation and Group Formation: Filipinos in the United States." In *A Companion to Asian American Studies,* edited by K.A. Ono, 332-49. Malden, MA: Blackwell.

Esplanada, J.E. 2009. "Male Teachers an Endangered Species?" *Philippine Daily Inquirer,* 23 November. http://newsinfo.inquirer.net/.

Esses, V.M., L.K. Hamilton, C. Bennett-AbuAyyash, and M. Burstein. 2010. "Characteristics of a Welcoming Community." Report prepared for the Integration Branch, Citizenship and Immigration Canada. http://www.welcomebc.ca/local/wbc/docs/characteristics_welcoming_community.pdf.

Essess, V.M., and R.C. Gardner. 1996. "Multiculturalism in Canada: Context and Current Status." *Canadian Journal of Behavioural Science* 28 (3): 145-52.

Esteves, E. 2002. "The New Wageless Worker: Volunteering and Market-Guided Health Care Reform." In *Is Anyone Listening? Women, Work and Society,* edited by M. Jacobs, 227-50. Toronto: Women's Press.

Estimo, R.C. Jr. 2007. "Philippine Envoy Expresses Concern over Failed OFW Marriages." *Arab News,* 16 November. http://archive.arabnews.com/.

Evans, K. 2005. "A Guide to Feminist Advocacy." *Gender and Development* 13 (3): 10-20.

Eviota, E.V. 1992. *The Political Economy of Gender: Women and the Sexual Division of Labor in the Philippines.* London: Zed Books.

–, ed. 1994. *Sex and Gender in Philippine Society: A Discussion of Issues on the Relations between Women and Men.* Manila: National Commission on the Role of Filipino Women.

Ezquerra, S. 2008. "The Regulation of the South-North Transfer of Reproductive Labor: Filipino Women in Spain and the United States." PhD diss., University of Oregon.

Facun, A.O. 2009. *Yes! The Secrets Work: Discover Your Unlimited Potential and Purpose in Life.* Garden City, NY: Morgan James Publishing.

Fagan, G.H., and R. Munck. 2009. *Globalization and Security: Social and Cultural Aspects.* Santa Barbara, CA: Greenwood Publishing Group.

Faist, T., ed. 2007. *Dual Citizenship in Europe: From Nationhood to Social Integration.* Aldershot, UK: Ashgate.

Faist, T., J. Gerdes, and B. Rieple. 2007. "Dual Citizenship as a Path-Dependent Process." In *Rethinking Migration: New Theoretical and Empirical Perspectives,* edited by A. Portes and J. DeWind, 90-121. New York: Berghahn Books.

Fanon, F. [1952] 2008. *Black Skin, White Masks,* translated by Richard Philcox. New York: Grove Press.

Farrales, L.L., and G. Chapman. 1999. "Filipino Women Living in Canada: Constructing Meanings of Body, Food and Health." *Health Care for Women International* 20 (2): 179-94.

Farrell, A. 1999. "Fairytales and Feminism: Volunteering in the Gender Team." In *Gender Works: Oxfam Experience in Policy and Practice,* edited by F. Porter, I. Smyth, and C. Sweetman, 196-202. Oxford: Oxfam.

Faulks, K. 2003. "Defining Politics." In *Politics,* edited by K. Faulks, K.M. Phillips, and A. Thomson, 3-59. Edinburgh: Edinburgh University Press.

Fay, T.J. 2005. "From the Tropics to the Freezer: Filipino Catholics Acclimatize to Canada, 1972-2002." *Historical Studies* 71: 29-59.

Fee, M.H. [1910] 2009. *A Woman's Impressions of the Philippines.* Charleston, SC: BiblioLife.

Feliciano, M.S. 1996. "The Filipina: A Historical Legal Perspective." In *Women's Role in Philippine History: Selected Essays,* edited by P.D. Tapales, 22-51. Quezon City: University of the Philippines Press.

Felipe, A. 2007. "Request for Art: Stop the Sex Trafficking of Filipino Women (Canada). *Sariling Atin* B&W (SAB&W)/Discuss. Flickr.com, http://www.flickr.com/.

Fernandez, E.S. 2006. "The Quest for Power: The Military in Philippine Politics, 1965-2002." *Asia Pacific: Perspectives* 6 (1): 38-47.

FILCAS. 2004. Memorabilia. Saskatoon: FILCAS.

Filipino Journal. 2007. "PCCM – Bicol Assn. Pilot Project on Fundraising for Philippine Disaster Victims ... A Model of Cooperation." 18 May-6 June. http://www.filipinojournal.com/.

–. 2007a. "Brief Statement from the PCCM President Linda Natividad Cantiveros." 5-20 November. http://www.Filipinojournal.com/.

–. 2008a. "'Dr. Jose Rizal Way' Keeps Filipino Pride of Country Alive." 20 June-5 July. http://www.filipinojournal.com/.

–. 2008b. "Myrna Evaristo and Dance for Life Group Raises $4,000." 5-20 December. http://www.filipinojournal.com/.

–. 2009a. "FIDWAM Celebrates 18 Years of Advocacy, Caring and Community Volunteerism." 5-20 June. http://filipinojournal.com/.

–. 2009b. "A Group of Filipino Leaders Form the Manitoba Council of Filipino Associations." 5-20 February. http://filipinojournal.com/.

Filipino-Canadian Medical Association (FCMA). n.d. "President's Message." http://www.fcma.ca/.

Fine, M. 2007. "Women, Collaboration, and Social Change: An Ethics-Based Model of Leadership." In *Women and Leadership: Transforming Visions and Diverse Voices,* edited by J.L. Chin, B. Lott, J.K. Rice, and J. Sanchez-Hucles, 177-91. Oxford: Blackwell.

–. 2009. "Women Leaders' Discursive Constructions of Leadership." *Women's Studies in Communication* 32 (2): 180-202.

Fischer, F. 2003. *Reframing Public Policy: Discursive Politics and Deliberative Practices.* New York: Oxford University Press.

Fleras, J. 1997. "Reclaiming Our Historic Rights: Gays and Lesbians in the Philippines." In *We Are Everywhere: A Historical Sourcebook in Gay and Lesbian Politics,* edited by M. Blasius and S. Phelan, 823-33. New York: Routledge.

Flores-Oebanda, M.C., R.R. Pacis, and V.P. Montano. 2003. *The Kasambahay, Child Domestic Work in the Philippines: A Living Experience.* Manila: Visayan Forum Foundation and the International Labour Organization.

Foster, L. 2008. "Foreign Credentials in Canada's Multicultural Society." In *Daily Struggles: The Deepening Racialization and Feminization of Poverty in Canada,* edited by M.A. Wallis and S. Kwok, 129-42. Toronto: Canadian Scholars' Press.

Francisco, J.S. 2000. "Women, Trade Liberalization and Food Security." *Development* 43 (2): 88-90.

–. 2007. "Gender Inequality, Poverty and Human Development in South East Asia." *Development* 50 (2): 103-14.

Fraser, N. 1995. "Politics, Culture, and the Public Sphere: Toward a Postmodern Conception?" In *Social Postmodernism,* edited by L. Nicholson and S. Seidman, 287-312. Cambridge: Cambridge University Press.

–. 2003. "Social Justice in the Age of Identity Politics: Redistribution, Recognition, and Participation." In *Redistribution or Recognition? A Political-Philosophical Exchange,* edited by N. Fraser and A. Honneth, 7-109. New York: Verso.

Fraser, N., and A. Honneth. 2003. "Introduction: Redistribution or Recognition?" In *Redistribution or Recognition? A Political-Philosophical Exchange,* edited by N. Fraser and A. Honneth, 1-6. New York: Verso.

Freedman, J., ed. 2003. *Gender and Insecurity: Migrant Women in Europe.* Aldershot, UK: Ashgate.

Freire, P. 2007. *Education for Critical Consciousness.* London and New York: Continuum.

Fresnoza-Flot, A. 2009. "Migration Status and Transnational Mothering: The Case of Filipino Migrants in France." *Global Networks* 9 (2): 252-70.

Frideres, J. 2008. "Creating an Inclusive Society: Promoting Social Integration in Canada." In *Immigration and Integration in the Twenty-First Century,* edited by J. Biles, M. Burstein, and J. Frideres, 77-101. Kingston, ON: School of Policy Studies, Queen's University.

Fryling, T., R. Summers, and A. Hoffman. 2006. "Elder Abuse: Definition and Scope of the Problem." In *Elder Abuse: A Public Health Perspective*, edited by R.W. Summers and A.M. Hoffman, 5-18. Washington, DC: American Public Health Association.

Fuchs, S. 2001. *Against Essentialism: A Theory of Society and Culture*. Cambridge, MA: Harvard University Press.

Fujieda, E. 2001. "Filipino Women's Migration to Japan's Sex Industry: A Case of Transnational Gender Subjection." PhD diss., University of Illinois at Urbana-Champaign.

Fujimoto, N. 2006. "Trafficking in Persons and the Filipino Entertainers in Japan." *Focus Asia Pacific News* 43 (March). HURIGHTS Osaka, http://www.hurights.or.jp/.

Fuwa, N., and J.N. Anderson. 2006. "Filipina Encounters with Japan: Beyond the Stereotype from a Pangasinan Barangay." *Philippine Studies* 54 (1): 111-41.

Gabbacia, D.R. and V.I. Ruiz. 2006. "Migrations and Destinations: Reflections on the Histories of US Immigrant Women." *Journal of American Ethnic History* 26 (1): 3-19.

GABRIELA Network USA. 2007. "The Purple Rose Campaign." http://www.gabnet.org/.

Gabuna, B. 2008. "Linda: A Gentle Spirit." *Filipino Journal*, 5-20 June. http://www.filipinojournal.com/.

Galicano-Adanza, E., R.N. Padua, J.G. Pulumbarit Jr., and V.S. Pinili. 1991. *Integrated Mathematics: Textbook for Third Year High School*. Manila: Rex Bookstore.

Gamolo, N. 1985. "Maria Wants a Barbie Doll, a Blonde Seatmate and Alien Citizenship." *Sunday Malaya*, 26 May, 8.

Garcea, J. 2008. "Postulations on the Fragmentary Effects of Multiculturalism in Canada." *Canadian Ethnic Studies* 40(1): 141-59.

Garcea, J., A. Kirova, and L. Wong. 2009. "Introduction: Multiculturalism Discourses in Canada." *Canadian Ethnic Studies* 40 (1): 1-10.

Garchitorena, V. P. 2007. "Diaspora Philanthropy: The Philippine Experience." http://www.tpi.org/downloads/pdfs/Philippines_Diaspora_Philanthropy_Final.pdf.

Garcia, M.A. 2007. *The Road to Empowerment in Toronto's Filipino Community: Moving from Crisis to Community Capacity-Building*. CERIS Working Paper No. 54. Toronto: Joint Centre of Excellence for Research on Immigration and Settlement – Toronto. http://www.ceris.metropolis.net/wp-content/uploads/pdf/research_publication/working_papers/wp54.pdf.

Gardner, C.B. 2009. "Gender Discrimination in Employment." In *Encyclopedia of Gender and Society*, vol. 1, edited by J. O'Brien, 350. Thousand Oaks, CA: Sage.

Garzon, E.D. 1999. "An Ethnography of Technology Transfer in the Philippines: A Case Study of the Agricultural Sector." In *Civic Discourse: Intercultural, International and Global Media*, edited by M.H. Prosser and K.S. Sitaram, 323-48. Stamford, CT: Ablex Publishing.

Gawad Kalinga. n.d. "Patriotic Philanthropy." http://jonathan.rickard.nz.googlepages.com/PatrioticPhilanthropyinGawadKalinga.pdf.

Geithner, P.F., P.D. Johnson, and L.C. Chen, eds. 2004. *Diaspora Philanthropy and Equitable Development in China and India*. Cambridge, MA: Global Equity Initiative, Asian Center, Harvard University Press.

Gelb, J., and M. L. Palley. 2009. *Women and Politics around the World: A Comparative History and Survey*, vol. 1. Santa Barbara, CA: ABC-CLIO.

George, U. 2010. "Canada: Immigration to Canada." In *Immigration Worldwide: Policies, Practices and Trends*, edited by U.A. Segal, D. Elliott, and N.S. Mayadas, 95-111. New York: Oxford University Press.

Gerstenfeld, P.B. 2004. *Hate Crimes: Causes, Controls, and Controversies*. Thousand Oaks, CA: Sage.

Gidengil, E., and D. Stolle. 2009. "The Role of Social Networks in Immigrant Women's Political Incorporation." *International Migration Review* 43 (4): 727-63.

Gilligan, C. 2000. "Selection from *In a Different Voice*." In *Ethical Theory: A Concise Anthology*, edited by H. Geirsson and M.R. Holmgren, 273-84. Peterborough, ON: Broadview Press.

Gilmore, J. 2008. *The Canadian Immigrant Labour Market in 2006: Analysis by Region or Country of Birth*. Ottawa: Statistics Canada.

Gingrich, F.C. 2002. "Pastoral Counseling in the Philippines." In *International Perspectives on Pastoral Counseling*, edited by J.R. Farris, 5-56. Binghamton, NY: Haworth Press.

GMA News. 2008. "'Zero Remittance Day' to Cost Govt Millions – Group." GMA News Online, 21 October. http://www.gmanews.tv/.

–. 2010. "Group: Banned Skin Whitening Products Still Sold in Baclaran." GMA News Online, 11 September. http://www.gmanews.tv/.

Goebel, N. 2010. "German NGOs Urge Government to Allow Full Dual Citizenship." Deutsche Welle, 23 August. http://www.dw.de/.

Goldin, L.R. 1999. *Identities on the Move: Transnational Processes in North America and the Caribbean Basin.* Boulder, CO: University of Colorado Press.

Goode, A.S. 2009. "Global Economic Changes and the Commodification of Human Capital: Implications of Filipino Nurse Migration." *East Asia* 26 (2): 113-31.

Gonzales, J.L. III. 1998. *Philippine Labour Migration: Critical Dimensions of Public Policy.* Singapore: Institute of Southeast Asian Studies.

Gonzales, M.A. 1998. *Filipino Migrant Women in the Netherlands.* Quezon City: Giraffe Books.

Gonzalez, A. 1992. "Higher Education, Brain Drain and Overseas Employment in the Philippines: Towards a Differentiated Set of Solutions." *Higher Education* 23 (1): 21-31.

Gonzalez, G.G., R.A. Fernandez, V. Price, D. Smith, and L. Trinh Võ. 2004. *Labor versus Empire: Race, Gender, and Migration.* New York: Routledge.

Gonzalez, J.J. III. 2009. *Filipino American Faith in Action: Immigration, Religion and Civic Engagement.* New York and London: New York University Press.

Gonzalez, R. 2006. "Gary Lee Dreamt about Being a Priest." *Western Catholic Reporter,* 10 April. http://wcr.ab.ca/.

–. 2007. "Pallard's Passion Is to Do Small Things for Newcomers." *Western Catholic Reporter,* 24 December, 1.

Gordon, M.M. 1964. *Assimilation in American Life: The Role of Race, Religion, and National Origins.* New York: Oxford University Press.

Gorospe, V.R. 1994. "Understanding the Filipino Value System." In *Values in Philippine Culture and Education,* edited by M.B. Dy, 66-70. Washington, DC: Council for Research in Values and Philosophy.

Gorospe-Jamon, G., and M.G.P. Mirandilla. 2007. "Religion and Politics." In *Whither the Philippines in the 21st Century,* edited by R. Severino and L.C. Salazar, 100-26. Singapore: Institute of Southeast Asian Studies.

Government of Alberta. 2011. *Alberta Immigration Progress Report 2011.* http://eae.alberta.ca/documents/WIA/WIA-IM-immigration-progess-report.pdf.

Government of Canada. 2005. *Canada's Action Plan against Racism: A Canada for All.* Gatineau, QC: Department of Canadian Heritage.

Greve, A., and J.W. Salaff. 2005. "Social Network Approach to Understand the Ethnic Economy: A Theoretical Discourse." *GeoJournal* 64 (1): 7-16.

Grewal, I., and C. Kaplan. 1994. "Introduction: Transnational Feminist Practices and Questions of Postmodernity." In *Scattered Hegemonies: Postmodernity and Transnational Feminist Practices,* edited by I. Grewal and C. Kaplan, 1-33. Minneapolis: University of Minnesota Press.

–, ed. 2005. *An Introduction to Women's Studies: Gender in a Transnational World,* 2nd ed. Columbus, OH: McGraw-Hill.

Gripaldo, R.M. 2005. "Cultural Traditions, the Person, and Contemporary Change: The Filipino Experience." In *Cultural Traditions and Contemporary Challenges in Southeast Asia: Hindu and Buddhist,* edited by W. Sriwarakuel, M.B. Dy, J. Haryatmoko, N. Trong Chuan, and C. Yiheang, 283-311. Washington, DC: Council for Research in Values and Philosophy.

Gross, A. 1999. "Human Resources in the Philippines." Pacific Bridge Recruiting, http://www.pacificbridge.com/.

Guarnizo, L. 1997. "The Emergence of a Transnational Social Transformation and the Mirage of Return among Dominican Transmigrants." *Identities* 4: 281-322.

Gudgeon, C. 2003. *The Naked Truth: The Untold Story of Sex in Canada.* Vancouver: Greystone Books.

Guerrero, R.M. 1983. *Readings in Philippine Cinema.* Manila: Experimental Cinema of the Philippines.

Gunn, G.C. 2003. *First Globalization: The Eurasian Exchange, 1500 to 1800.* Lanham, MD: Rowman and Littlefield.

Haan, M. 2007. "The Homeownership Hierarchies of Canada and the United States: The Housing Patterns of White and Non-White Immigrants of the Past Thirty Years." *International Migration Review* 41 (2): 433-65.

–. 2010. "Assimilation or Stratification? The Sources of Early Differentiation of Immigrant Ethno-Racial Groups in the Canadian Housing Market." In *Canadian Immigration: Economic Evidence for a Dynamic Policy Environment,* edited by T. McDonald, E. Ruddick, A. Sweetman, and C. Worswick, 235-55. Montreal and Kingston: McGill-Queen's University Press.

Haddow, R., and T. Klassen. 2006. *Partisanship, Globalization, and Canadian Labour Market Policy.* Toronto: University of Toronto Press.

Hall, M.A. 2003. "Girls and Women Sport in Canada: From Playground to Podium." In *Sport and Women: Social Issues in International Perspective,* edited by I. Hartmann-Tews and G. Pfister, 161-78. London: Routledge.

Hammar, T. 1990. *Democracy and the Nation State: Aliens, Denizens and Citizens in a World of International Migration.* Aldershot, UK: Avebury.

Haney López, I.F. 2006. *White by Law: The Legal Construction of Race.* New York and London: New York University Press.

Hansen, R., and P. Weil. 2002. "Dual Citizenship in a Changed World: Immigration, Gender and Social Rights." In *Dual Nationality, Social Rights and Federal Citizenship in the US and Europe: The Reinvention of Citizenship,* edited by R. Hansen and P. Weill, 1-18. New York: Berghahn Books.

Haraway, D. 2004. "Situated Knowledges: The Science Question in Feminism and the Privilege of Partial Perspective." In *The Feminist Standpoint Theory Reader: Intellectual and Political Controversies,* edited by Sandra Harding, 81-101. New York and London: Routledge.

Harding, S.G. 1987. *Feminism and Methodology: Social Science Issues.* Bloomington: Indiana University Press and Open University Press.

–, ed. 2004. *The Feminist Standpoint Theory Reader: Intellectual and Political Controversies.* New York and London: Routledge.

Harris, P.R., R.T. Moran, and S.V. Moran. 2004. *Managing Cultural Differences: Global Leadership Strategies for the Twenty-First Century,* 6th ed. Oxford: Butterworth-Heinemann.

Harrison, W.C. 2006. "The Shadow and the Substance: The Sex/Gender Debate." In *Handbook of Gender and Women's Studies,* edited by K. Davis, M. Evans, and J. Lorber, 35-52. London: Sage.

Harty, S., and M. Murphy. 2005. *In Defence of Multinational Citizenship.* Vancouver: UBC Press.

Hawkes, R. 2012. "Filipino TV Channel GMA Launches in UAE." *RAPIDTVNews,* 15 February. http://www.rapidtvnews.com/.

Hawkesworth, M.E. 2006. *Globalization and Feminist Activism.* Lanham, MD: Rowman and Littlefield.

Hawthorne, L. 2008. "The Impact of Economic Selection Policy on Labour Market Outcomes for Degree-Qualified Migrants in Canada and Australia." *IRPP Choices* 14 (5). http://www.irpp.org/choices/archive/vol14no5.pdf.

Heald, S. 2008. "Embracing Marginality: Place-Making vs Development in Gardenton, Manitoba." *Development in Practice* 18 (1): 17-29.

Health Alliance for Democracy. 2006. "Export of Filipino Nurses: From Brain Drain to National Hemorrhage to NLE Leakage." SlideShare, http://www.slideshare.net/.

Hedman, E.E. 2006. *In the Name of Civil Society: From Free Election Movements to People Power in the Philippines.* Honolulu: University of Hawai'i Press.

Hedman, E.E., and J.T. Sidel. 2000. *Philippine Politics and Society in the Twentieth Century: Colonial Legacies, Post-Colonial Trajectories.* London: Routledge.

Helgesen, S. 1995. *Female Advantage: Women's Ways of Leadership.* New York: Doubleday.

Henderson, K.A. 1984. "Women as Volunteers." *The Humanist* 44 (4): 26-27, 36.

Henderson, N. 2005. *Rediscovering the Prairies: Journeys by Dog, Horse and Canoe.* Surrey, BC: TouchWood Editions.

Herrera-Maquiling, H. n.d. "Abada to Lead the Centennial Celebrations in Alberta and Northern Territories." *Philippine Canadian Times.* http://philcan.tripod.com/mainn.htm.

Hesse-Biber, S.N. 2007. "The Practice of Feminist In-Depth Interviewing." In *Feminist Research Practice: A Primer*, edited by S.N. Hesse-Biber and P.L. Leavy, 111-48. Thousand Oaks, CA: Sage.

Hesse-Biber, S.N., P. Leavy, and M. Yaiser. 2004. "Feminist Approaches to Research as a *Process:* Reconceptualizing Epistemology, Methodology, and Method." In *Feminist Perspectives on Social Research*, edited by S.N. Hesse-Biber and M. Yaiser, 3-26. New York and Oxford: Oxford University Press.

Hewitt, R. 2005. *White Backlash and the Politics of Multiculturalism*. Cambridge: Cambridge University Press.

Hicap, J.M. 2009. "Koreans Flock to the Philippines to Learn English." *Korea Times*, 13 September. http://www.koreatimes.co.kr/.

Hiebert, D. 2009. "Newcomers in the Canadian Housing Market: A Longitudinal Study, 2001-2005." *Canadian Geographer* 53 (3): 268-87.

Hier, S.P., and B. Singh Bolaria, eds. 2007. *Race and Racism in 21st Century Canada: Continuity, Complexity and Change*. Toronto: UTP Higher Education.

Higham, N. 2007. "Skilled Workers Desert Philippines." BBC News, 7 January. http://news.bbc.co.uk/.

Highmore, B. 2011. *Ordinary Lives: Studies in the Everyday*. New York: Routledge.

Hilhorst, D. 1997. "Discourse Formation in Social Movements: Issues of Collective Action." In *Images and Realities of Rural Life: Wagenigen Perspectives on Rural Transformations*, edited by H. de Haan and N. Long, 121-52. Assen, The Netherlands: Van Gorcum.

Hill, S.D. 2002. "The Unspeakability of Racism: Mapping Law's Complicity in Manitoba's Racialized Spaces." In *Race, Space, and the Law: Unmapping a White Settler Society*, edited by S. Razack, 157-84. Toronto: Between the Lines.

Hill, T.L. 2002. *Canadian Politics, Riding by Riding*. Minneapolis, MN: Prospect Park Press.

Hillier, J., and E. Rooksby, eds. 2005. *Habitus: A Sense of Place*. Aldershot, UK: Ashgate.

Hilsdon, A. 1995. *Madonnas and Martyrs: Militarism and Violence in the Philippines*. Quezon City: Ateneo de Manila University Press.

–. 2007. "Transnationalism and Agency in East Malaysia: Filipina Migrants in the Nightlife Industries." *Australian Journal of Anthropology* 18 (2): 172-93.

Hodder, R. 2009. "Political Interference in the Philippine Civil Service." *Environment and Planning C: Government and Policy* 27 (5): 766-82.

Holroyd, E.A. 2007. "Chinese Women and Cancer as Contagious: Screening Implications." In *New Research on Cervical Cancer*, edited by G.Z. Rolland, 189-216. New York: Nova Science Publishers.

Hom, S. 2008. "Housekeepers and Nannies in the Homework Economy: On the Morality and Politics of Paid Housework." In *Global Feminist Ethics*, edited by R. Whisnant and P. DesAutels, 23-42. Lanham, MD: Rowman and Littlefield.

Hondagneu-Sotelo, P. 2001. *Domestica: Immigrant Women Cleaning and Caring in the Shadows of Affluence*. Berkeley: University of California Press.

Hondagneu-Sotelo, P., and E. Avila. 1997. "'I'm Here but There': The Meanings of Trans-national Motherhood." *Gender and Society* 11 (5): 548-71.

Hondagneu-Sotelo, P., and C. Cranford. 1999. "Gender and Migration." In *Handbook of the Sociology of Gender*, edited by J.S. Chafetz, 105-26. New York: Plenum.

Hooghe, M., and D. Stolle. 2005. "Youth Organisations within Political Parties: Political Recruitment and the Transformation of Party Systems." In *Revisiting Youth Political Participation*, edited by J. Forbig, 43-52. Strasbourg: Council of Europe.

Hooks, B. 1989. *Talking Back: Thinking Feminist, Thinking Black*. Cambridge, MA: South End Press.

Howard Ecklund, E., and J. Z. Park. 2007. "Religious Diversity and Community Volunteerism among Asian Americans." *Journal for the Scientific Study of Religion* 46 (2): 233-44.

Huang, F. 1997. *Asian and Hispanic Immigrant Women in the Workforce: Implications of the United States Immigration Policies since 1965*. New York: Routledge.

Huang, S., and B. Yeoh. 2008. "Heterosexualities and the Global(ising) City in Asia." *Asian Studies Review* 32 (1): 1-6.

Huffington, C. 2004. "What Women Leaders Can Tell Us." In *Working Below the Surface: The Emotional Life of Contemporary Organizations,* edited by C. Huffington, D. Armstrong, W. Halton, L. Hoyle, and J. Pooley, 49-66. London: H. Karnac (Books).

Hulchanski, J.D. 2004. "A Tale of Two Canadas: Homeowners Getting Richer, Renters Getting Poorer." In *Finding a Room: Policy Options for a Canadian Rental Strategy,* edited by J.D. Hulchanski and M. Shapcott, 81-88. Toronto: CUCS Press.

Hum, D., and W. Simpson. 2004. "Economic Integration of Immigrants to Canada: A Short Survey." *Canadian Journal of Urban Research* 13 (1): 46-61.

Human Resources and Skills Development Canada (HRSDC). 2012. "Archived – A Profile of Filipinos in Canada." http://www.hrsdc.gc.ca/.

Human Trafficking Project. 2008. "Filipina Domestic Workers Losing Out to Indonesians in HK Job Market." 15 February. http://traffickingproject.blogspot.com/.

Hunt, C.L., and R.W. Coller. 1957. "Intermarriage and Cultural Change: A Study of Philippine-American Marriages." *Social Forces* 35 (3): 223-30.

Huo, F. 2004. "Recent Immigration and the Formation of Visible Minority Neighbourhoods in Canada's Large Cities." Business and Labour Market Analysis Division, Analytical Studies Branch Research Paper No. 221, Statistics Canada. http://www.statcan.gc.ca/pub/11f0019m/11f0019m2004221-eng.pdf.

Hutchcroft, P.D. 2008. "The Arroyo Imbroglio in the Philippines." *Journal of Democracy* 19 (1): 141-55.

Iacovetta, F. 1995. "Remaking Their Lives: Women, Immigrants, Survivors, and Refugees." In *A Diversity of Women: Ontario, 1945-1980,* edited by J. Parr, 135-67. Toronto: University of Toronto Press.

ICON Group International. 2008. *ABS: Webster's Quotations, Facts and Phrases.* San Diego, CA: ICON Group International.

Ignacio, E.N. 2003. "Laughter in the Rain: Jokes as Membership and Resistance." In *Asian American.Net: Ethnicity, Nationalism and Cyberspace,* edited by R.C. Lee and S.C. Wong, 158-76. New York and London: Routledge.

–. 2005. *Building Diaspora: Filipino Community Formation on the Internet.* Piscataway, NJ: Rutgers University Press.

Ileto, R.C. 1998. *Filipinos and Their Revolution: Event, Discourse, and Historiography.* Quezon City: Ateneo de Manila University Press.

Informetrica Limited. 2001. *Canada's Recent Immigrants: A Comparative Portrait Based on the 1996 Census.* Ottawa: Citizenship and Immigration Canada.

Ingraham, C. 2006. "Thinking Straight, Acting Bent." In *Handbook of Gender and Women's Studies,* edited by K. Davis, M. Evans, and J. Lorber, 307-21. London: Sage.

Inquirer.net. 2009. "Overseas Filipino Voters Exceed 100,000 Mark." 18 June. http://newsinfo.inquirer.net/.

Institute of Philippine Culture. 2005. *The Vote of the Poor: Modernity and Traditions in People's Views of Leadership and Elections.* Quezon City: Ateneo de Manila University Press.

International Bank for Reconstruction and Development (IBRD) and World Bank (WB). 2006. *Global Economic Prospects 2006: Economic Implications of Remittances and Migration.* Washington, DC: IBRD/WB.

International Organization for Migration (IOM). 2006. *World Migration 2005: Costs and Benefits of International Migration.* New Delhi: Academic Foundation.

Irving, K. 2000. *Immigrant Mothers: Narratives of Race and Maternity, 1890-1925.* Champaign: University of Illinois Press.

Israel-Sobritchea, C.I. 1990. "The Ideology of Female Domesticity: Its Impact on the Status of Filipino Women." *Review of Women's Studies* 1 (1): 26-41.

–. 1996. "American Colonial Education and Its Impact on the Status of Filipino Women." In *Women's Role in Philippine History: Selected Essays,* edited by P.D. Tapales, 79-108. Quezon City: University Center for Women's Studies, University of the Philippines Press.

Itzigsohn, J., and S. Giorguli-Saucedo. 2005. "Incorporation, Transnationalism, and Gender: Immigrant Incorporation and Transnational Participation and Gendered Processes." *International Migration Review* 39 (4): 895-920.

Iwanaga, K. 2008. *Women's Political Participation and Representation in Asia: Obstacles and Challenges*. Copenhagen: NIAS-Nordic Institute of Asian Studies.

Jackson, M. 2005. "The Limits of Connectivity: Technology and 21st-Century Life." In *From Work-Family Balance to Work-Family Interaction: Changing the Metaphor*, edited by D.F. Halpern and S.E. Murphy, 135-50. Mahwah, NJ: Lawrence Erlbaum Associates.

Jackson, S. 2004. *Differently Academic? Developing Lifelong Learning for Women in Higher Education*. Dordrecht, The Netherlands: Kluwer Academic Publishers.

Jaggar, A. 2007. *Just Methods: An Interdisciplinary Feminist Reader*. Boulder, CO: Paradigm Publishers.

Jain, H.C. 2008. "The Recruitment and Selection of Visible Minorities in Canadian Police Organizations, 1985-1987." *Canadian Public Administration* 31 (4): 463-82.

James, E. 1991. "Private Higher Education: The Philippines as a Prototype." *Higher Education* 21 (2): 189-206.

James, S.B. 2007. *Filipino Labour Migration to Nigeria: A Study in Labour and Bilateral Relations*. Ibadan, Nigeria: Loud Books.

Janoff, D. 2005. *Pink Blood: Homophobic Violence in Canada*. Toronto: University of Toronto Press.

Jasinska-Lahti, I., and K. Liebkind. 2000. "Predictors of the Actual Degree of Acculturation of Russian-Speaking Immigrant Adolescents in Finland." *International Journal of Intercultural Relations* 24 (4): 503-18.

Jenkins, R. 1992. *Pierre Bourdieu*. Rev. ed. London: Routledge.

Johansson, T. 2007. *The Transformation of Sexuality: Gender and Identity in Contemporary Youth Culture*. Aldershot, UK: Ashgate.

Johnston, J.P., J. Mark Muñoz, and I. Alon. 2007. "Filipino Ethnic Entrepreneurship: An Integrated Review and Proposition." *International Entrepreneurship Management Journal* 3: 69-85.

Jones, N. 1999. "Culture and Reproductive Health: Challenges for Feminist Philanthropy." In *Embodying Bioethics: Recent Feminist Debates*, edited by A. Donchin and L.M. Purdy, 223-38. Lanham, MD: Rowman and Littlefield.

Kalbach, M.A. and W.E. Kalbach. 2000. *Perspectives on Ethnicity in Canada: A Reader*. Toronto: Harcourt Canada.

Kamboureli, S. 2009. *Scandalous Bodies: Diasporic Literature in English Canada*. Waterloo, ON: Wilfrid Laurier University Press.

Kamiya, S. 2009. "The Many Faces of Citizenship: Multinationalism Remains Far from Acceptance in Japan." *Japan Times*, 4 January. http://info.japantimes.co.jp/.

Kang, D.C. 2002. *Crony Capitalism: Corruption and Development in South Korea and the Philippines*. Cambridge: Cambridge University Press.

Karan, P.P. 2005. *Japan in the 21st Century: Environment, Economy, and Society*. Lexington, KY: University Press of Kentucky.

Karnow, S. 1989. *In Our Image: America's Empire in the Philippines*. New York: Random House.

Kawahara, D.M. 2007. "'Making a Difference': Asian American Women Leaders." *Women and Therapy* 30 (3/4): 17-33.

Kejžar, B. 2009. "Dual Citizenship as an Element of the Integration Process in Receiving States: The Case of Slovenia." In *Illiberal States: Immigration, Citizenship and Integration in the EU*, edited by E. Guild, K. Groenendijk, and S. Carrera, 131-48. Surrey, UK: Ashgate.

Kelaher, M., G. Williams, and L. Manderson. 2001. "The Effect of Partner's Ethnicity on the Health of Filipinas in Australia." *International Journal of Intercultural Relations* 25 (5): 531-43.

Kelley, N., and M. Trebilcock. 2010. *The Making of the Mosaic: A History of Canadian Immigration Policy*, 2nd ed. Toronto: University of Toronto Press.

Kelly, P., M. Astorga-Garcia, E.F. Esguerra, and the Community Alliance for Social Justice. 2009. "Explaining the Deprofessionalized Filipino: Why Filipino Immigrants Get Low-Paying Jobs in Toronto." CERIS Working Paper No. 75. Toronto: CERIS – The Ontario Metropolis Centre.

Kelly, P., S. Park, C. de Leon, and J. Priest. 2011. "Profile of Live-in Caregiver Immigrants to Canada, 1993-2009." TIEDI Analytical Report 18. Toronto Immigrant Employment Data Initiative, http://www.yorku.ca/tiedi/doc/AnalyticalReport18.pdf.

Kelly, P.F. 2006. "Filipinos in Canada: Economic Dimensions of Immigration and Settlement." CERIS Working Paper No. 48 (revised). Joint Centre of Excellence for Research on Immigration and Settlement – Toronto, http://www.ceris.metropolis.net/wp-content/uploads/pdf/research_publication/working_papers/wp48.pdf.

–. 2007a. "Transnationalism and Political Participation among Filipinos in Canada." In *Organizing the Transnational: Labour, Politics, and Social Change*, edited by L. Goldring and S. Krishnamurti, 215-31. Vancouver: UBC Press.

–. 2007b. "Filipino Migration, Transnationalism and Class Identity." Working Paper Series No. 90. Asia Research Institute, National University of Singapore. http://www.ari.nus.edu.sg/docs/wps/wps07_090.pdf.

–. 2010. "Filipino Migration and the Spatialities of Labour Market Subordination." In *Handbook of Employment and Society: Working Space*, edited by S. McGrath-Champ, A. Herod, and A. Rainnie, 159-76. Northampton, MA: Edward Elgar Publishing.

Kelly, P.F., and T. Lusis. 2006. "Migration and the Transnational Habitus: Evidence from Canada and the Philippines." *Environment and Planning A* 38 (5): 831-47.

Kelsky, K. 2001. *Women on the Verge: Japanese Women, Western Dreams*. Durham, NC: Duke University Press.

Kerkvliet, B.J. 1995. "Toward a More Comprehensive Analysis of Philippine Politics: Beyond the Patron-Client, Factional Framework." *Journal of Southeast Asian Studies* 26 (2): 401-19.

Kessler, S. 1998. *Lessons from the Intersexed*. New Brunswick, NJ: Rutgers University Press.

Kessler, S., and W. McKenna. 1978. *Gender: An Ethnomethodological Approach*. Chicago: University of Chicago Press.

Kheiriddin, T., and A. Daifallah. 2005. *Rescuing Canada's Right: Blueprint for a Conservative Revolution*. Mississauga, ON: John Wiley and Sons Canada.

Kilgour, D. 2009. "Canada and 'Diasporas' – The Case of Filipinos." http://www.david-kilgour.com/.

Kim, Y. 1997. "'Asian-Style Democracy': A Critique from East Asia." *Asian Survey* 37 (12): 1119-34.

Kimura, M. 2003. "The Emergence of the Middle Classes and Political Change in the Philippines." *Developing Economies* 41 (2): 264-84.

King, V.T. 2008. *The Sociology of Southeast Asia: Transformations in a Developing Region*. Copenhagen: NIAS Press.

Klaszus, J. 2008. "Tory Candidate Links Immigrants with Crime, Expresses Regret." *Fast Forward Weekly*, 25 September. http://www.ffwdweekly.com/.

Knight, J. 2004. "Quality Assurance and Recognition of Qualifications in Post-Secondary Education in Canada." In *Quality and Recognition in Higher Education: The Cross-Border Challenge*, 43-53. Paris: Centre for Educational Research and Innovation, Organisation for Economic Co-operation and Development.

Knörr, J., and B. Meier, eds. 2000. *Women and Migration: Anthropological Perspectives*. New York: Campus Verlag and St. Martin's Press.

Ko, V. 2012. "What Is Driving the Philippines' Surprisingly Strong Growth?" CNN, 12 July. http://www.cnn.com/.

Koenig, H.G., D.M. Lawson, and M. McConnell. 2004. *Faith in the Future: Healthcare, Aging and the Role of Religion*. West Conshohocken, PA: Templeton Foundation Press.

Kofman, E. 2004. "Gendered Global Migrations." *International Feminist Journal of Politics* 6 (4): 643-65.

Koh, E. 1994. "For Ellen. Eulogy." *Filipino Journal*, 8-21 October.

Korinek, V.J. 2010. "A Queer Eye View of the Prairies: Reorienting Western Canadian Histories." In *The West and Beyond: New Perspectives on an Imagined Region*, edited by A. Finkel, S. Carter, and P. Fortna, 278-96. Athabasca, AB: Athabasca University Press.

Kosnick, K. 2011. "Sexuality and Migration Studies: The Invisible, the Oxymoronic and Heteronormative Othering." In *Framing Intersectionality: Debates on a Multi-Faceted Concept in Gender Studies,* edited by H. Lutz, M.T. Herrera Vivar, and L. Supik, 121-36. Surrey, UK: Ashgate.

Kreuzer, P. 2005. *Political Clans and Violence in the Southern Philippines.* PRIF Report No. 71. Frankfurt: Peace Research Institute Frankfurt.

Kriaski, C. 2009. "CCIS (Calgary Catholic Immigration Society) Together with Centre for Newcomers." *Pinoy Times,* 13 September. http://pinoytimes.ca/.

Krinks, P. 2002. *The Economy of the Philippines: Elites, Inequalities and Economic Restructuring.* New York: Routledge.

Kroeger, C.C., and M.J. Evans, eds. 2002. *The IVP Women's Bible Commentary.* Downers Grove, IL: Intervarsity Press.

Kunz, R. 2011. "The 'Making Women Productive' Strategy: Uncovering Gendered Sightings, Sites, and Resistances to Global Restructuring in Rural Mexico." In *Gender and Global Restructuring: Sightings, Sites, and Resistances,* 2nd ed., edited by M.M. Marchand, 163-82. New York: Routledge.

Kuo, C. 1995. *Global Competitiveness and Industrial Growth in Taiwan and the Philippines.* Pittsburgh, PA: University of Pittsburgh Press.

Kwok, A. 2008. "Low Education Budget Blamed for High Drop-out Rate." Inquirer.net, 15 July. http://newsinfo.inquirer.net/.

Kwok, S., and D.M. Tam. 2008. "Deliquency of Asian Youth in Canada." In *Daily Struggles: The Deepening Racialization and Feminization of Poverty in Canada,* edited by M.A. Wallis and S. Kwok, 197-208. Toronto: Canadian Scholars' Press.

Kymlicka W. 1998. *Finding Our Way: Rethinking Ethnocultural Relations in Canada.* Don Mills, ON: Oxford University Press.

–. 2007a. *Multicultural Odysseys: Navigating the New International Politics of Diversity.* New York: Oxford University Press.

–. 2007b. "Ethnocultural Diversity in a Liberal State: Making Sense of the Canadian Model(s)." In *Belonging? Diversity, Recognition and Shared Citizenship in Canada,* edited by K. Banting, T.J. Courchene, and F. Leslie Seidle, 39-86. Montreal: Institute for Research on Public Policy.

–. 2009. "The Current State of Multiculturalism in Canada." *Canadian Journal for Social Research* 2 (1): 15-34.

Kyungwon Hong, G. 2006. *The Ruptures of American Capital: Women of Color, Feminism and the Culture of Immigrant Labor.* Minneapolis: University of Minnesota Press.

Labelle, M., and D. Salée. 2001. "Immigrant and Minority Representations of Citizenship in Quebec." In *Citizenship Today: Global Perspectives and Practices,* edited by T.A. Aleinikoff and D. Klusmeyer, 278-315. Washington, DC: Brookings Institution Press.

Lacquian, E.R. 2011. "Filipinos." *The Canadian Encyclopedia,* http://www.thecanadian encyclopedia.com/.

Lahey, K.A. and K. Alderson. 2004. *Same-Sex Marriage: The Personal and the Political.* Toronto: Insomniac Press.

Lan, P. 2000. "Global Divisions, Local Identities: Filipina Migrant Domestic Workers and Taiwanese Employers." PhD diss., Northwestern University.

–. 2003. "Maid or Madam? Filipina Migrant Workers and the Continuity of Domestic Labor." *Gender and Society* 17 (2): 187-208.

Langevin, L., and M. Belleau. 2000. *Trafficking in Women in Canada: A Critical Analysis of the Legal Framework Governing Immigrant Live-in Caregivers and Mail-Order Brides.* Ottawa: Status of Women Canada.

Lanzona, V.A. 2009. *Amazons of the Huk Rebellion: Gender, Sex, and Revolution in the Philippines.* Madison: University of Wisconsin Press.

Larsen, J., and J. Urry. 2008. "Networking in Mobile Societies." In *Mobility and Place: Enacting Northern European Peripheries,* edited by J.O. Bærenholdt and B. Granås, 89-102. Aldershot, UK: Ashgate.

Lassiter, S.M. 1998. *Cultures of Color in America: A Guide to Family, Religion and Health.* Westport, CT: Greenwood Press.

Lau, Y. 2007. "Change, Community, and Politics: Shifting Agendas among Chicago's Filipino Americans." Paper presented at the American Sociological Association 102nd annual meeting, 11 August, New York.

Lauby, J., and O. Stark. 1988. "Individual Migration as a Family Strategy: Young Women in the Philippines." *Population Studies* 42 (3): 473-86.

Laurent, E. 2005. "Sexuality and Human Rights: An Asian Perspective." *Journal of Homosexuality* 48 (3-4): 163-225.

Lawsin, E.P. 1998. "Empowering the Bayanihan Spirit: Teaching Filipina/o American Studies." In *Teaching Asian America: Diversity and the Problems of Community*, edited by L.R. Hirabayashi, 187-98. Lanham, MD: Rowman and Littlefield.

Lawson, A., R. Francis, P. Russell, and J. Veitch. 2008. "Equality and Access to Human Rights for People with Both Learning Disability and Mental Illness Needs." *Advances in Mental Health and Learning Disabilities* 2 (2): 3-8.

Lazaridis, G. 2000. "Filipino and Albanian Women Migrant Workers in Greece: Multiple Layers of Oppression." In *Gender and Migration in Southern Europe: Women on the Move*, edited by F. Anthias and G. Lazaridis, 49-79. New York: Berg Publishers.

Lazo, R. 2006. *Philippine Governance and the 1987 Constitution*. Manila: Rex Bookstore.

Lee, D.R. 1998. "Mail Fantasy: Global Sexual Exploitation in the Mail-Order Bride Industry and Proposed Legal Solutions." *Asian Law Journal* 5 (1): 139-79.

Lee, K. 2008. "Immigrant Women Workers in the Immigrant Settlement Sector." In *Daily Struggles: The Deepening Racialization and Feminization of Poverty in Canada*, edited by M.A. Wallis and S. Kwok, 103-12. Toronto: Canadian Scholars' Press.

Lee, M. 2006. "Filipino Village in South Korea." *Community, Work and Family* 9 (4): 429-40.

Lee Guy, M. 2005. "Moralities in Conflict: Ambiguities of Identity and Social Control for Filipina Domestic Helpers in Malaysia." In *Contesting Moralities: Science, Identity, Conflict*, edited by N. Redclift, 135-52. London: UCL Press.

Lee-Brago, P. 2010. "Overseas Absentee Voting Starts Today." *Philippine Star*, 10 April. http://www.philstar.com/.

LeGates, M. 2001. *In Their Time: A History of Feminism in Western Society*. New York and London: Routledge.

Leoncini, D.L.P. 2005. "A Conceptual Analysis of *Pakikisama* (Getting Along Well with People)." In *Filipino Cultural Traits: Claro R. Ceniza Lectures*, edited by R.M. Gripaldo, 157-84. Washington, DC: Council for Research in Values and Philosophy.

Levitt, P. 2001. *The Transnational Villagers*. Berkeley: University of California Press.

–. 2003. "Transnational Villagers." In *Race and Ethnicity: Comparative and Theoretical Perspectives*, edited by J. Stone and R. Dennis, 260-73. Oxford: Blackwell.

Li, P. 2008. "The Market Value and Social Value of Race." In *Daily Struggles: The Deepening Racialization and Feminization of Poverty in Canada*, edited by M.A. Wallis and S. Kwok, 21-33. Toronto: Canadian Scholars' Press.

Lie, J. 1997. "The 'Problem' of Foreign Workers in Contemporary Japan." In *The Other Japan: Conflict, Compromise, and Resistance*, edited by J. Moore, 288-300. Armonk, NY: M.E. Sharpe.

Lim, F.C., and B. Makani-Lim. 2006. "Intercultural Communications in the Asian Operations Setting." In *Negotiating Globalization in Asia*, edited by Ateneo Center for Asian Studies, 105-44. Quezon City: Ateneo de Manila University Press.

Lim, T., and D. Pangan-Specht. 2010. *Images of America: Filipinos in the Willamette Valley*, with the Filipino American National Historical Society Oregon Chapter. Charleston, SC: Arcadia Publishing.

Lindio-McGovern, L. 1997. *Filipino Peasant Women: Exploitation and Resistance*. Philadelphia: University of Pennsylvania Press.

–. 2003. "Labor Export in the Context of Globalization: The Experience of Filipino Domestic Workers in Rome." *International Sociology* 18 (3): 513-34.

Lindsay, C. 2007. *The Filipino Community in Canada, 2001*. Ottawa: Statistics Canada.

Lipszyc, C. 2004. "The Feminization of Migration: Dreams and Realities of Migrant Women in Four Latin American Countries." Diputació Barcelona, http://www.diba.es/urbal12/PDFS/CeciliaLipszyc_en.pdf.

Lister, R. 1997. *Citizenship: Feminist Perspectives*. London: Macmillan.

Little, A. 2002. *The Politics of Community: Theory and Practice*. Edinburgh: Edinburgh University Press.

Llorito, D. 2007. "The Vanishing Middle Class." Philippines without Borders, 29 October. http://davidllorito.blogspot.com/.

Loewen, R., and G. Friesen. 2009. *Immigrants in the Prairies: Ethnic Diversity in Twentieth-Century Canada.* Toronto: University of Toronto Press.

Long Marler, P. 2008. "Religious Change in the West: Watch the Women." In *Women and Religion in the West: Challenging Secularization,* edited by K. Aune, S. Sharma, and G. Vincett, 23-56. Hampshire, UK: Ashgate.

Lopez, A. 2007. "Being Pinoy Is Fashionable Once Again." *Philippine Daily Inquirer,* 1 July. http://newsinfo.inquirer.net/.

Lopez, M. 2009. "Nursing Graduates in Contact Center Jobs: Philippines and India." Articlesbase, 5 May. http://www.articlesbase.com/.

Lopez, M.L. 2006. *A Handbook of Philippine Folklore.* Quezon City: University of the Philippines Press.

Lott, J.T. 2006. *Common Destiny: Filipino American Generations.* Lanham, MD: Rowman and Littlefield.

Lovell, T. 2004. "Bourdieu, Class and Gender: 'The Return of the Living Dead?'" In *Feminism after Bourdieu,* edited by L. Adkins and B. Skeggs, 37-56. Oxford: Blackwell.

Luddy, M. 1995. *Women and Philanthropy in Nineteenth-Century Ireland.* Cambridge: Cambridge University Press.

Lund, D. 2006. "Social Justice Activism in the Heartland of Hate: Countering Extremism in Alberta." *Alberta Journal of Educational Research* 52 (2): 181-94.

Lusis, T. n.d. "Filipino Immigrants in Canada: A Literature Review and Directions for Further Research on Second-Tier Cities and Rural Areas." Department of Geography, University of Guelph, http://www.geography.ryerson.ca/hbauder/Immigrant%20Labour/filipino Settlement.pdf.

Lutz, H. 1997. "The Limits of European-ness: Immigrant Women in Fortress Europe." *Feminist Review* 57(Autumn): 93-111.

–, ed. 2008. *Migration and Domestic Work: A European Perspective on a Global Theme.* Aldershot, UK: Ashgate.

Lynch, F. 1973. "Social Acceptance Reconsidered." In *Four Readings on Philippine Values,* edited by F. Lynch and A. de Guzman II, 1-68. Quezon City: Ateneo de Manila University Press.

Lyon, D. 2000. "Introduction." In *Rethinking Church, State, and Modernity: Canada between Europe and America,* edited by D. Lyon and M. Van Die, 3-19. Toronto: University of Toronto Press.

Maas, M. 2008. "Door-to-Door Cargo Agents: Cultivating and Expanding Filipino Transnational Space." In *Tales of Development: People, Power and Space,* edited by P. Hebinck, S. Slootweg, and L. Smith, 135-48. Assen, The Netherlands: Royal Van Gorum B.V.

Mackey, E. 2002. *The House of Difference: Cultural Politics and National Identity in Canada.* Toronto: University of Toronto Press.

Mackie, V. 1998. "Japayuki Cinderella Girl: Containing the Immigrant Other." *Japanese Studies* 18 (1): 45-63.

Macklin, A. 2009. "Particularized Citizenship: Encultured Women and the Public Sphere." In *Migrations and Mobilities: Citizenship, Borders and Gender,* edited by S. Benhabib and J. Resnik, 276-303. New York: New York University Press.

Madibbo, A.I. 2006. *Minority within a Minority: Black Francophone Migrants and Their Dynamics of Power and Resistance.* New York: Routledge.

Magalit Rodriguez, R. 2008. "The Labor Brokerage State and the Globalization of Filipina Care Workers." *Signs: Journal of Women in Culture and Society* 33 (4): 794-800.

–. 2010. *Migrant for Export: How the Philippine State Brokers to the World.* Minneapolis: University of Minnesota Press.

Magat, M.C. 2003. "Transnational Lives, Cosmopolitan Women: Filipina Domestic Workers and Expressive Culture in Rome, Italy." PhD diss., University of Pennsylvania.

Magkaisa Centre. 2010a. "Creating and Nurturing a New Path for the Progressive Filipino-Canadian Community." http://www.magkaisacentre.org/wp-content/uploads/2011/08/CPFC-Declaration.pdf.

–. 2010b. "Towards Genuine Women's Equality, Development and Liberation." http://www.magkaisacentre.org/.

Mahalingam, R., S. Balan, and J. Haritatos. 2008. "Engendering Immigrant Psychology: An Intersectionality Perspective." *Sex Roles* 59 (5-6): 326-36.

Mahalingam, R., S. Balan, and K. Molina. 2009. "Transnational Intersectionality: A Critical Framework for Theorizing Motherhood." In *Handbook of Feminist Family Studies*, edited by S. Lloyd, A. Few, and K.R. Allen, 69-82. Thousand Oaks, CA: Sage.

Mahalingam, R., and J. Leu. 2005. "Culture, Essentialism, Immigration and Representations of Gender." *Theory and Psychology* 15 (6): 839-60.

Mahler, S.J., and P.R. Pessar. 2001. "Gendered Geographies of Power: Analyzing Gender across Transnational Spaces." *Identities: Global Studies in Culture and Power* 7: 441-59.

–. 2006. "Gender Matters: Ethnographers Bring Gender from the Periphery toward the Core of Migration Studies." *International Migration Review* 40 (1): 27-63.

Mahlum, E. 2009. "Squatter's Demolition Delayed." *Manila Bulletin*, 14 August. http://www.mb.com.ph/.

Mahr, K. 2008. "The Motherless Generation." *Time*, 13 November, 42-44.

Mai, N., and R. King. 2009. "Love, Sexuality and Migration: Mapping the Issue(s)." *Mobilities* 4 (3): 298-307.

Makilan, A. 2004. "2003: A Tough Year for OFWs and Their Families." *Bulatlat*, 4-10 January. http://bulatlat.com/.

Makosky, D. 2010. "Philippines Supreme Court Certifies Gay Rights Party for Election." JURIST Paper Chase Newsburst, 8 April. http://jurist.org/paperchase/.

Man, G. 2004. "Gender, Work and Migration: Deskilling Chinese Immigrant Women in Canada." *Women's Studies International Forum* 27 (2): 135-48.

Manalansan, M.F. IV. 2003. *Global Divas: Filipino Gay Men in the Diaspora*. Durham, NC: Duke University Press.

–. 2006. "Queer Intersections: Sexuality and Gender in Migration Studies." *International Migration Review* 40 (1): 224-49.

Mananzan, M.J., ed. 1987a. *Essays on Women*. Manila: Institute of Women's Studies, St. Scholastica's College.

–. 1987b. "The Filipino Woman: Before and after the Spanish Conquest of the Philippines." In *Essays on Women*, edited by M.J. Mananzan, 6-35. Manila: Institute of Women's Studies, St. Scholastica's College.

–. 1997. *The Woman Question in the Philippines*. Manila: Institute of Women's Studies, St. Scholastica's College.

Mangahas, F.B., and J. Llaguno, eds. 2006. *Centennial Crossings: Readings on Babaylan Feminism in the Philippines*. Manila: C and E Publishing.

Manila Mail. 2008a. "51,000 Acquire Dual Citizenship." 29 August. http://www.manilamaildc.net/.

–. 2008b. "TNT's Drop Due to Economic Crisis." 20 October. http://www.manilamaildc.net/.

–. 2009. "RP Needs 175 Years before It Becomes 1st World." 27 May. http://www.manilamaildc.net/.

Maningas, C. 2004. "Is FILCAS Relevant?" *Celebrating 31 Years: Fiesta Filipiniana Araw ng Kalayaan Memorabilia*, 11. Saskatoon: FILCAS.

Maniquet, S. 2011. "Marriage Commissioners Can't Refuse Same-Sex Ceremonies: Sask. Court." *National Post*, 10 January. http://life.nationalpost.com/.

Manlove, R.F. 2004. "A Taxonomy of Esteem Values in the Philippines." In *Narrative Themes in Comparative Context*, vol. 2, edited by G.A. De Vos and E.S. De Vos, 399-436. Lanham, MD: Rowman and Littlefield.

Mannarini, T., and A. Fedi. 2009. "Multiple Senses of Community: The Experience and Meaning of Community." *Journal of Community Psychology* 37 (2): 211-27.

Marchand, M. 2003. "Challenging Globalisation: Feminism and Resistance." *Review of International Studies* 29 (3): 145-60.

Marger, M.N. 2006. *Race and Ethnic Relations: American and Global Perspectives*, 7th ed. Belmont, CA: Thompson Higher Education.

Margold, J.A. 2004. "Filipina Depictions of Migrant Life for Their Kin at Home." In *Coming Home? Refugees, Migrants, and Those Who Stayed Behind*, edited by L.D. Long and E. Oxfeld, 49-64. Philadelphia: University of Pennsylvania Press.

Marquez, C.R.C. 2005. "Medical Schools Rake in Profits – but Health System Is in Crisis." *Bulatlat*, 23-29 January. http://www.bulatlat.com/.

Marquez, R.M. 2011. "Two Filipino Mothers in Oct. 6 Ontario Election." *Digital Journal*, 27 September. http://digitaljournal.com/.

Marshall, T.H. 1994. "Citizenship and Social Class." In *Citizenship*, vol. 2, edited by B. Turner and P. Hamilton, 5-44. London and New York: Routledge.

Martin, P.L., S.F. Martin, and P. Weil. 2006. *Managing Migration: The Promise of Cooperation.* Lanham, MD: Lexington Books.

Masaaki, S. 2008. "At the Core of Filipina-Japanese Intercultural Marriages: Family, Gender, Love and Cross-Cultural Understanding." In *The Past, Love, Money, and Much More: Philippines-Japan since the Second World War*, edited by L.N. Yu-Jose, 111-37. Quezon City, Philippines: Ateneo de Manila University.

Massey, D.B. 1994. *Space, Place and Gender.* Minneapolis: University of Minnesota Press.

Masson, D. 2010. "Transnationalizing Feminist and Women's Movements: Toward a Scalar Approach." In *Solidarities beyond Borders: Transnationalizing Women's Movements*, edited by P. Dufour, D. Masson, and D. Caouette, 35-55. Vancouver: UBC Press.

Maya, M., and B. Allen. 2009. "Voter Registration." In *International Election Principles: Democracy and the Rule of Law*, edited by J.H. Young, 135-64. Chicago: ABA Publishing.

McClelland, S. 2009. "Nanny's Other Family: Canada's Live-in Caregiver Immigration Program May Not be Good for the Kids." *The Walrus*, September. http://www.susan mcclelland.com/.

McCourt, T. 2008. "National Public Radio." In *Battleground: The Media*, vol. 1, edited by R. Andersen and J. Gray, 277-83. Westport, CT: Greenwood Press.

McCoy, A.W., ed. 2009. *An Anarchy of Families: State and Family in the Philippines.* Madison: University of Wisconsin Press.

McCracken, J. 2001. *Taste and the Household: The Domestic Aesthetic and Moral Reasoning.* Albany, NY: SUNY Press.

McDonald, T., and C. Worswick. 2010. "Visible Minority Status, Immigrant Status, Gender, and Earnings in Canada: A Cohort Analysis." In *Canadian Immigration: Economic Evidence for a Dynamic Policy Environment*, edited by T. McDonald, E. Ruddick, A. Sweetman, and C. Worswick, 111-45. Montreal and Kingston: McGill-Queen's University Press.

McFerson, H.M. 2002. "Filipino Identity and Self-Image in Historical Perspective." In *Mixed Blessing: The Impact of the American Colonial Experience on Politics and Society in the Philippines*, edited by H.M. McFerson, 13-42. Westport, CT: Greenwood Press.

McGhee, D. 2008. *The End of Multiculturalism? Terrorism, Integration and Human Rights.* Maidenhead, UK: Open University Press.

McGowan, M.G. 2008. "Roman Catholics (Anglophone and Allophone)." In *Christianity and Ethnicity in Canada*, edited by P. Bramadat and D. Seljak, 49-100. Toronto: University of Toronto Press.

McInnis and Holloway (Funeral Homes). 2010. "Quitzon – Erlinda (Linda) Gilo." http://www.mhfh.com/.

McIntyre, S. 2009. "Under the Radar: The Sexual Exploitation of Young Men – Western Canadian Edition." http://www.hindsightgroup.com/Resources/Documents/UnderThe Radar%20Low%20Res.pdf.

McKay, D. 2003. "Filipinas in Canada – De-skilling as a Push Toward Marriage." In *Wife or Worker? Asian Women and Migration*, edited by N. Piper and M. Roces, 23-52. Lanham, MD: Rowman and Littlefield.

–. 2004. "Everyday Places – Philippine Place-Making and the Translocal Quotidian." Paper presented at the "Everyday Transformations: The 21st Century Quotidian" Cultural Studies

Association of Australia annual conference, Murdoch University. http://wwwmcc.murdoch. edu.au/cfel/docs/McKay_FV.pdf.

McMullin, J. 2010. *Understanding Social Inequality: Intersections of Class, Age, Gender, Ethnicity, and Race in Canada*, 2nd ed. New York: Oxford University Press.

McNeill, D. 2005. "Japan's Laborious Dilemma." *Yale Global Online*, 13 January. http://yaleglobal.yale.edu/.

McWatt, S., and S. Neysmith. 1998. "Enter the Filipina Nanny: An Examination of Canada's Live-in Caregiver Policy." In *Women's Caring: Feminist Perspectives on Social Welfare*, 2nd ed., edited by C. Baines, P. Evans, and S. Neysmith, 218-32. Toronto: Oxford University Press.

Medalla, F. 2007. "Economic Integration in East Asia: A Philippine Perspective." In *East Asian Visions: Perspectives on Economic Development*, edited by I. Gill, Y. Huang, and H. Kharas, 203-30. Washington and Singapore: International Bank for Reconstruction and Development/World Bank and Institute of Policy Studies.

Medeiros, E.S., K. Crane, E. Heginbotham, N.D. Levin, J.F. Lowell, A. Rabasa, and S. Seong. 2008. *Pacific Currents: The Responses of US Allies and Security Partners in East Asia to China's Rise*. Santa Monica, CA: Rand Corporation.

Medina, B.T.G. 2005. *The Filipino Family: A Text with Selected Readings*. Quezon City: University of the Philippines Press.

Meinardus, R. 2003. "The Crisis of Public Education in the Philippines." Friedrich Naumann Foundation for Liberty, Philippine Office. http://www.fnf.org.ph/.

Mellner, C., G. Krantz, and U. Lundberg. 2006. "Symptom Reporting and Self-Rated Health among Women in Mid-life: The Role of Work Characteristics and Family Responsibilities." *International Journal of Behavioral Medicine* 13 (1): 1-7.

Mellyn, K. 2003. *Worker Remittances as a Development Tool: Opportunity for the Philippines*. Manila: Asian Development Bank.

Mendez, P., D. Hiebert, and E. Wyly. 2006. "Landing at Home: Insights on Immigration and Metropolitan Housing Markets from the Longitudinal Survey of Immigrants to Canada." *Canadian Journal of Urban Research* 15 (2): 82-104.

Mendoza, S.L.L. 2002. *Between the Homeland and the Diaspora: The Politics of Theorizing Filipino and Filipino American Identities*. New York and London: Routledge.

Meng, X., and D. Meurs. 2009. "Intermarriage, Language, and Economic Assimilation Process: A Case Study of France." *International Journal of Manpower* 30 (1/2): 127-47.

Mercene, F.L. 2007. *Manila Men in the New World: Filipino Migration to Mexico and the Americas*. Quezon City: University of the Philippines Press.

Messias, D.K.H. 2011. "The Health and Well-Being of Immigrant Women in Urban Areas." In *Women's Health and the World's Cities*, edited by A. Ibrahim Meleis, E.L. Birch, and S.M. Wachter, 144-67. Philadelphia: University of Pennsylvania Press.

Messias, D.K.H., M.K. DeJong, and K. McLoughlin. 2005. "Expanding the Concept of Women's Work: Volunteer Work in the Context of Poverty." *Journal of Poverty* 9 (3): 25-47.

Migrant Rights. 2009. "Interview with Helen O'Reilly: Blogging about Migration and Domestic Helpers." http://www.migrant-rights.org/.

Milan, L. 2009. "A Disastrous Oversupply of Unemployable Graduates." *Planet Philippines*, 19 June. http://planetphilippines.com/.

Mitchell, B.A. 2009. *Family Matters: An Introduction to Family Sociology in Canada*. Toronto: Canadian Scholars' Press.

Mohanty, C.T. 1988. "Under Western Eyes." *Feminist Review* 30: 238-51.

–. 2003. *Feminism without Borders: Decolonizing Theory, Practicing Solidarity*. Durham, NC: Duke University Press.

Morehouse, C. 2009. *Combating Human Trafficking: Policy Gaps and Hidden Political Agendas in the USA and Germany*. Wiesbaden, Germany: VS Verlag.

Moreno, A.F. 2006. *Church, State, and Civil Society in Postauthoritarian Philippines: Narratives of Engaged Citizenship*. Quezon City: Ateneo de Manila University Press.

Morokvasic, M. 1984. "Birds of Passage Are Also Women." *International Migration Review* 18 (4): 886-907.

Mulder, M., and B. Korenic. 2005. *Portraits of Immigrants and Ethnic Minorities in Canada: Regional Comparisons*. Edmonton: Prairie Centre of Excellence for Research on Immigration and Integration.

Mullard, M. 1999. "Discourses on Citizenship: The Challenge to Contemporary Citizenship." In *Citizenship and Welfare State Reform in Europe*, edited by J. Bussemaker, 13-28. London and New York: Routledge.

Musick, M.A., and J. Wilson. 2008. *Volunteers: A Social Profile*. Bloomington: Indiana University Press.

Mwale, S. 2008. "What Contributions Have Biological Approaches Made to Our Understanding of Gender and Sexuality?" *Journal of Social and Psychological Sciences* 1 (2): 88-97.

Nadal, K.L. 2009. *Filipino American Psychology: A Handbook of Theory, Research and Clinical Practice*. Bloomington, IN: Author House.

Nagar, R. 2002. "Footloose Researchers, Travelling Theories, and the Politics of Transnational Feminist Praxis." *Gender, Place and Culture* 92 (2): 179-86.

Nam, H.J. 2006. *Mission Strategies of Korean Presbyterian Missionaries in Central and Southern Philippines: In Light of Paul's Mission Strategies*. Norwalk, CA: Hermit Kingdom Press.

Nanda, S. 2000. *Gender Diversity: Crosscultural Variations*. Long Grove, IL: Waveland Press.

Naples, N. 2003. *Feminism and Method: Ethnography, Discourse Analysis and Activist Research*. New York and London: Routledge.

Narayan, U. 1998. "Essence of Culture and Sense of History: A Feminist Critique of Cultural Essentialism." *Hypatia* 13 (2): 86-106.

–. 2004. "The Project of Feminist Epistemology: Perspectives from a Nonwestern Feminist." In *The Feminist Standpoint Theory Reader*, edited by S. Harding, 213-24. New York and London: Routledge.

National Alliance of Philippine Women in Canada. 2009. "Scrap Canada's Live-in Caregiver Program: End Violence Against Filipino Women!" Statement, 20 May. TMLDaily Internet Edition, 14 July 14. http://cpcml.ca/.

National Statistics Office (NSO). 2002. "Philippines: Population Expected to Reach 100 Million Filipinos in 14 Years." Press release, 16 October. http://www.census.gov.ph/.

–. 2005. "2002 Scenario of the Agriculture Sector in the Philippines." http://www.census.gov.ph/.

–. 2006. "Table D. Basic Literacy Rate of Population 10 Years Old and Over, by Sex, Age Group and Region, Philippines, 2003." http://www.census.gov.ph/.

–. 2008. "Official Population Count Reveals ..." Press release, 16 April. http://www.census.gov.ph/.

–. 2009a. "Overseas Filipino Women." http://www.census.gov.ph/.

–. 2009b. "2008 Survey on Overseas Filipinos." http://www.census.gov.ph/.

–. 2009c. "Unemployment Rate Posted at 7.6 Percent in July 2009 Results from the July 2009 Labor force Survey (LFS)." http://www.census.gov.ph/.

–. 2011. "2010 Annual Labor and Employment Status." Press release, 8 February. http://www.census.gov.ph/.

–. 2012. "Employment Situation in January 2011." http://www.census.gov.ph/.

–. 2013. "National Quickstat – March 2013." http://www.census.gov.ph/.

National Statistics Office – Gender and Development Committee. 2009a. "Gender Fact Sheet: Unemployed Women." March, No. 09-05. http://www.census.gov.ph/.

–. 2009b. "Gender Fact Sheet: Underemployed Women." March, No. 09-06. http://www.census.gov.ph/.

Neher, C.D. 1994. "Asian Style Democracy." *Asian Survey* 34 (11): 949-61.

Nethercott, P. n.d. "St. Patrick's School Filipino Language and Culture Club." Calgary: Pilipino Educators Advocated Council.

Ng, R. 1981. "Constituting Ethnic Phenomenon: An Account from the Perspective of Immigrant Women." *Canadian Ethnic Studies* 13 (1): 97-108.

–. 1988. *The Politics of Community Service: Immigrant Women, Class and the State.* Toronto: Garamond Press.

–. 1990. "Immigrant Women: The Construction of a Labour Market Category." *Canadian Journal of Women and the Law* 4 (1): 96-112.

–. 1991. "Finding Our Voices: Reflections on Immigrant Women's Organizing." In *Women and Social Change: Feminist Activism in Canada,* edited by J. Wine and J. Ristock, 184-97. Toronto: James Lorimer.

Nie, J. 2007. "The Specious Idea of an Asian Bioethics: Beyond Dichotomizing East and West." In *Principles of Health Care Ethics,* edited by R.E. Ashcroft, A. Dawson, H. Draper, and J. McMillan, 143-50. West Sussex, UK: John Wiley and Sons.

Nishimori, M.A.N. 2010. "Will OFWs Finally Win Party-List Seats This Year?" ABS-CBN News, 5 April. http://www.abs-cbnnews.com/.

Nolais, J. 2011. "Mom Takes Action on Homophobia." *Metro Calgary,* 23 August. http://www.metronews.ca/calgary/.

Northouse, P.G. 2010. *Leadership Theory and Practice,* 5th ed. Thousand Oaks, CA: Sage.

Nuqui, C.G. 2008. "International Migration, Citizenship, Identities and Cultures: Japanese-Filipino Children (JFC) in the Philippines." *Gender, Technology, and Development* 12 (3): 483-507.

O'Boyle, L.G., and R.G. Alejandro. 1988. *Philippine Hospitality: A Gracious Tradition of the East.* New York: Acacia Corporation.

O'Connor, K., ed. 2010. *Gender and Women's Leadership: A Reference Handbook.* London: Sage.

O'Donnell, L., and A. Stueve. 1985. "Community Demands and Supports for Childrearing Related Volunteer Work." *Sociological Focus* 18 (2): 127-42.

O'Neill, B. 2005. "Canadian Women's Religious Volunteerism: Compassion, Connections, and Comparisons." In *Gender and Social Capital,* edited by B. O'Neill and E. Gidengil, 185-211. New York and London: Routledge.

O'Reilly, A. 2008. "Introduction." In *Feminist Mothering,* edited by A. O'Reilly, 1-24. Albany, NY: SUNY Press.

Obligacion, F.R. 1999. "Cognitive Consequences of Faith in God among Filipino Women." In *Research in the Social Scientific Study of Religion,* edited by J.M. Greer and D.O. Moberg, 117-36. Stamford, CT: JAI Press.

Oishi, N. 2005. *Women in Motion: Globalization, State Policies, and Labour Migration.* Stanford, CA: Stanford University Press.

Okamoto, D., and K. Ebert. 2010. "Beyond the Ballot: Imagined Collective Action in Gateways and New Destinations in the United States." *Social Problems* 57 (4): 529-58.

Okamura, J.Y. 1998. *Imagining the Filipino Diaspora: Transnational Relations, Identities and Communities.* New York: Garland Publishing.

Okin, S.M. 1999. "Is Multiculturalism Bad for Women?" In *Is Multiculturalism Bad for Women?* edited by J. Cohen, M. Howard, and M.C. Nussbaum, 9-24. Princeton, NJ: Princeton University Press.

Olea, R.V. 2008. "Undocumented Workers Most Vulnerable among Migrants." GMA News Online, 6 November. http://www.gmanews.tv/.

Olin Wright, E. 2005. "Introduction." In *Approaches to Class Analysis,* edited by E. Olin Wright, 1-3. Cambridge: Cambridge University Press.

Oliva, T.P. n.d. Council of Edmonton Filipino Associations (CEFA), What Is It For Me or the Filipino community? http://www.geocities.com/filcefa/aboutcefa.html?200917 (accessed March 3, 2009).

Ong, A. 2004. "Cultural Citizenship as Subject-Making: Immigrants Negotiate Racial and Cultural Boundaries in the United States." In *Life in America: Identity and Everyday Experience,* edited by L.D. Baker, 156-78. Malden, MA: Blackwell.

Ongsotto, R.R., and R.R. Ongsotto. 2002. *Philippine History I Module-Based Learning.* Manila: Rex Bookstore.

Opiniano, J.M. 2004a. *Our Future beside the Exodus: Migration and Development Issues in the Philippines.* Manila: Friedrich Ebert Stiftung.

–. 2004b. *Within Reach: Philippine Nonprofit Organization's Approaches in Tapping Overseas Filipinos for Philanthropy.* Quezon City: Institute on Church and Social Issues.

–. 2005. "Filipinos Doing Diaspora Philanthropy: The Development Potential of Transnational Migration." *Asia Pacific Migration Journal* 14 (1-2): 225-41.

–. 2010. "OFW Families Spending Less on Food, More on Health – ADB Study." Philippines Today, 23 March. http://www.philippinestoday.net/.

Ordinario, C.U. 2009. "Human-Development Gaps Still Haunt RP." *Business Mirror*, 5 October. United Nations Development Programme, Philippines, http://www.undp.org.ph/.

Ore, T.E. 2008. *The Social Construction of Difference and Inequality: Race, Class, Gender and Sexuality.* New York: McGraw-Hill.

Organisation for Economic Co-operation and Development (OECD). 1998. *Immigrants, Integration and Cities: Exploring the Links.* Paris: OECD.

–. 2006. *From Immigration to Integration: Local Solutions to a Global Challenge.* Paris: OECD.

Osnes, B. 2008. "Performing Mother Activism." In *The Maternal Is Political,* edited by S.M. Strong, 280-84. Berkeley, CA: Seal Press.

Ostrower, F. 1995. *Why the Wealthy Give: The Culture of Elite Philanthropy.* Princeton, NJ: Princeton University Press.

Owusu, T.Y. 1999. "Residential Patterns and Housing Choices of Ghanaian Immigrants in Toronto, Canada." *Housing Studies* 14 (1): 77-97.

Pablo, C. 2008. "Vancouver Filipino Women Are Finding a Voice." Straight.com, 12 June. http://www.straight.com/.

Pacoy, E.P. 2013. "Reducing Gender Gaps through Gender-Responsive Budgeting in Davao City, Philippines." In *Millennium Development Goals and Community Initiatives in the Asia Pacific,* edited by A. Singh, E.T. Gonzalez, and S.B. Thomson, 97-106. New Delhi: Springer.

Padilla, Malu D. 2007. "Women Changing Our Lives, Making HERstory: Migration Experiences of Babaylan Philippine Women's Network in Europe." In *In De Olde Worlde: Views of Filipino Migrants in Europe,* edited by F.M. Hoegsholm, 83-109. Manila: Philippine Migration Research Network and Social Science Council.

Pagaduan, M.C. 2006. "Leaving Home: Filipino Women Surviving Migration." In *Poverty, Gender and Migration,* edited by S. Arya and A. Roy, 72-86. New Delhi: Sage.

Pagliaro, J., and J. Mahoney. 2010. "Funding Cuts Threaten Immigrant Agencies." *Globe and Mail,* 23 December. http://www.theglobeandmail.com/.

Palatino, M. 2009. "The Tragedy of Philippine Education: Privilege Speech of Kabataan Party List Representative Mong Palatino at the Batasang Pambansa, on May 18, 2009." Advocacy for Philippine Arts and Culture, http://asiancenter.multiply.com/.

Panopio, I.S., and R.S. Rolda. 2007. *Society and Culture: Introduction to Sociology and Anthropology.* Rev. ed. Quezon City: Katha Publishing.

Paragas, F. 2006. "Eccentric Networks: Patterns of Interpersonal Communication, Organizational Participation, and Mass Media Use among Overseas Filipino Workers." PhD diss., College of Communication, Ohio University.

Park, H. 2006. "Scoping the Issues of Elder Abuse among Asian Migrants." In *Prevention, Protection and Promotion: Proceedings of the Second International Asian Health and Wellbeing Conference,* edited by S. Tse, M.E. Hoque, K. Rasanathan, M. Chatterji, R. Wee, S. Garg, and Y. Ratnasabapathy, 50-56. Auckland, New Zealand: University of Auckland.

Parker, P.S. 2005. *Race, Gender, and Leadership: Re-envisioning Organizational Leadership from the Perspectives of African American Women Executives.* Mahwah, NJ: Lawrence Erlbaum Associates.

Parr, J. 1995. *A Diversity of Women: Ontario, 1945-1980.* Toronto: University of Toronto Press.

Parreñas, R.S. 2000. "Migrant Filipina Domestic Workers and the International Division of Reproductive Labor." *Gender and Society* 14 (4): 560-80.

–. 2001a. *Servants of Globalization: Women, Migration, and Domestic Work.* Stanford, CA: Stanford University Press.

–. 2001b. "Mothering from a Distance: Emotions, Gender and Intergenerational Relations in Filipino Transnational Families." *Feminist Studies* 27 (2): 361-90.

–. 2005a. *Children of Global Migration: Transnational Families and Gendered Woes.* Stanford, CA: Stanford University Press.

–. 2005b. "Long Distance Intimacy: Class, Gender and Intergenerational Relations between Mothers and Children in Filipino Transnational Families." *Global Networks* 5 (4): 317-36.

–. 2006. "Migrant Filipina Domestic Workers and the International Division of Reproductive Labor." In *Global Dimensions of Gender and Carework*, edited by M.K. Zimmerman, J.S. Litt, and C.E. Bose, 48-64. Stanford, CA: Stanford University Press.

–. 2008a. *The Force of Domesticity: Filipina Migrants and Globalization.* New York and London: New York University Press.

–. 2008b. "Breaking the Code: Women, Labor Migration, and the 1987 Family Code of the Republic of the Philippines." In *Gender and Globalization in Asia and the Pacific: Method, Practice, Theory,* edited by K.E. Ferguson and M. Mironesco, 176-94. Honolulu: University of Hawai'i Press.

Pastrana, D. 2009. "Rising Unemployment and Poverty in the Philippines." World Socialist Web Site, 6 April. http://www.wsws.org/.

Patterson, J. 2006. "Top 10 Reasons for Dating a Filipina Girl." SearchWarp.com, 2 July. http://searchwarp.com/.

Pauleen, D., ed. 2007. *Cross-Cultural Perspectives on Knowledge Management.* Westport, CT: Greenwood Publishing.

Pe-Pua, R., and P. Perfecto-Ramos. 2012. "Philippines." In *The Oxford Handbook of the History of Psychology: Global Perspectives,* edited by D.B. Baker, 395-411. New York: Oxford University Press.

Pedraza, S. 1991. "Women and Migration: The Social Consequences of Gender." *Annual Review of Sociology* 17: 303-25.

Pegiña, J.P. 2009. *The Portrait of the 21st Century Filipina.* Cavite, Philippines: Kamalayan Publishing.

Pendakur, R. 2000. *Immigrants and the Labour Force: Policy, Regulation, and Impact.* Montreal and Kingston: McGill-Queen's University Press.

Penner, L.A. 2000. "Promoting Prosocial Actions: The Importance of Culture and Values." *Journal of Social Philosophy* 31 (4): 477-87.

Perez, E. 1999. *The Decolonial Imaginary: Writing Chicana into History.* Bloomington and Indianapolis: Indiana University Press.

Pessar, P.R. 1999. "The Role of Gender, Households, and Social Networks in the Migration Process: A Review and Appraisal." In *The Handbook of International Migration: The American Experience,* edited by C. Hirschman, P. Kasinitz, and J. DeWind, 53-70. New York: Russell Sage Foundation.

Pessar, P.R., and S.J. Mahler. 2003. "Transnational Migration: Bringing Gender in." *International Migration Review* 37 (3): 812-46.

Peterson, V.S. 2010. "International/Global Political Economy." In *Gender Matters in Global Politics: A Feminist Introduction to International Relations,* edited by L.J. Shepherd, 204-17. New York: Routledge.

Philippine Asian News Today. 2008. "Hiring Filipino Nurses Pays Off for Saskatchewan." 27 November.

Philippine Commission on Women. 2012. "Statistics on Filipino Women and Men's Overseas Employment." 2 October. http://pcw.gov.ph/.

Philippine Heritage Council of Manitoba (PHCM). 2009. "Celebrating 50 Years with the Filipino Canadian Community in Winnipeg." Souvenir program.

Philippine News Service. 2008. "Filipino Singers Breaking into International Stardom." *Philippines Today,* 19 January. http://www.philippinestoday.net/.

Philippine Overseas Employment Administration (POEA). 2007. "GB Resolutions/Memorandum Circulars on HSWs." http://www.poea.gov.ph/.

–. 2008. "OFW Statistics." http://www.poea.gov.ph/.

–. 2009. "OFW Deployment per Skill and Country – New Hires for the Year 2009." http://www.poea.gov.ph/.

–. 2010. "Overseas Employment Statistics 2010." http://www.poea.gov.ph/stats/2010_Stats.pdf.

Philippine Reporter. 2010. "CARP Raises Funds for RP Poor." 31 March. http://www.philippinereporter.com/.

Philippine Women Centre of BC. 2009. "Filipino Live-in Caregivers Share Stories and Struggles of Family Separation under the LCP during the Holiday Season." 24 December. *Northern Philippine Times,* http://www.northphiltimes.com/.

PhilippineDomain.com. n.d. "Facts about the Philippines." http://www.philippinedomain.com/.

Phoenix, A., and P. Pattynama. 2006. "Editorial: Intersectionality." *European Journal of Women's Studies* 13 (3): 187-92.

Pietrobruno, S. 2006. *Salsa and Its Transnational Moves.* Lanham, MD: Lexington Books.

Pilcher, J., and I. Whelehan. 2004. *50 Key Concepts in Gender Studies.* London: Sage.

Pinoy Overseas. 2008. "Overseas Filipino Worldwide." http://www.pinoyoverseas.net/.

Pinoy Times. 2009. "GK/ANCOP Brings FVR to Calgary." 17 August. http://pinoytimes.ca/.

Piper, N., ed. 2008. *New Perspectives on Gender and Migration: Livelihood, Rights and Entitlements.* New York and London: Routledge.

Piper, N., and R. Ball. 2001. "Globalisation of Asian Migrant Labour: The Philippine-Japan Connection." *Journal of Contemporary Asia* 31 (4): 533-54.

Piper, N., and M. Roces, eds. 2003. *Wife or Worker? Asian Women and Migration.* Lanham, MD: Rowman and Littlefield.

Pojmann, W. 2006. *Immigrant Women and Feminism in Italy.* Hampshire, UK: Ashgate.

Poole, R. 2003. "National Identity and Citizenship." In *Identities: Race, Class, Gender, and Nationality,* edited by L.M. Alcoff and E. Mendieta, 271-80. Oxford: Blackwell.

Population Reference Bureau. 2007. *2007 World Population Data Sheet.* Washington, DC: Population Reference Bureau.

Portes, A., and J. DeWind, eds. 2007. *Rethinking Migration: New Theoretical and Empirical Perspectives.* New York: Berghahn Books.

Portes, A., L.E. Guarnizo, and P. Landolt. 1999. "The Study of Transnationalism: Pitfalls and Promise of an Emergent Research Field." *Ethnic and Racial Studies* 22 (2): 217-37.

Posadas, B.M. 1999. *The Filipino Americans.* Westport, CT: Greenwood Publishing.

Posadas, B.M., and R.L. Guyotte. 2008. "Filipino Families in the Land of Lincoln: Immigrant Incorporation in Springfield, Illinois, since 1965." In *From Arrival to Incorporation: Migrant to the US in a Global Era,* edited by E.R. Barkan, H. Diner, and A.M. Kraut, 143-62. New York and London: New York University Press.

Pratt, G. 1997. "Stereotypes and Ambivalence: The Construction of Domestic Workers in Vancouver, British Columbia." *Gender, Place and Culture: A Journal of Feminist Geography* 4 (2): 159-78.

–. 1999. "From Registered Nurse to Registered Nanny: Discursive Geographies of Filipina Domestic Workers in Vancouver, BC." *Economic Geography* 75 (3): 215-36.

–. 2003/2004. "Between Homes: Displacement and Belonging for Second-Generation Filipino-Canadian Youths." *BC Studies: The British Columbian Quarterly* 140 (Winter): 41-68.

–. 2004. *Working Feminism.* Philadelphia: Temple University Press.

–. 2005. "From Migrant to Immigrant: Domestic Workers Settle in Vancouver, Canada." In *A Companion to Feminist Geography,* edited by L. Nelson and J. Seager, 123-37. Malden, MA: Blackwell.

Pratt, G., Philippine Women Centre, and Ugnayan Kabataan Pilipino sa Canada/The Filipino-Canadian Youth Alliance. 2010. "Seeing beyond the State: Toward Transnational Feminist Organizing." In *Critical Transnational Feminist Praxis,* edited by A. Lock Swarr and R. Nagar, 65-86. Albany, NY: SUNY Press.

Pratt, G., and Philippines-Canada Task Force on Human Rights. 2008. "International Accompaniment and Witnessing State Violence in the Philippines." *Antipode: A Radical Journal of Geography* 40 (5): 751-79.

Pratt, G., and B. Yeoh. 2003. "Transnational (Counter) Topographies." *Gender, Place and Culture* 10 (2): 159-66.

PREDA. 1997. "Profile: Father Shay Cullen." http://www.preda.org/.

Putzel, J. 1992. *A Captive Land: The Politics of Agrarian Reform in the Philippines.* London: Catholic Institute for International Relations; New York: Monthly Review Press; Quezon City, Philippines: Ateneo de Manila University Press.

Quezada-Reyes, Z. 2003. "An Agenda for Gender-Fair Education." *Human Rights Education in Asia* 3: 89-94.

Quilop, R.J.G. 2006. "Nation-State Formation in the Philippines." In *Philippine Politics and Governance: An Introduction,* edited by N.M. Morada and T.S. Encarnacion Tadem, 1-12. Quezon City: Department of Political Science, University of the Philippines.

Quimpo, N.G. 2008. *Contested Democracy and the Left in the Philippines after Marcos.* New Haven, CT: Yale University, Council on Southeast Asian Studies.

Rafael, V.L. 2008. "Taglish, or the Phantom Power of the Lingua Franca." In *Philippine English: Linguistic and Literary Perspectives,* edited by M.L.S. Bautista and K. Bolton, 101-28. Aberdeen, Hong Kong: Hong Kong University Press.

Ralston, M., and E. Keeble. 2009. *Reluctant Bedfellows: Feminism, Activism and Prostitution in the Philippines.* Sterling, VA: Kumarian Press.

Ramilo, C., and R. Droescher. 1992. *Filipino Women: Challenges and Responses.* New South Wales: Ethnic Affairs Commission.

Ravenstein, E.G. 1885. "The Laws of Migration." *Journal of the Royal Statistical Society* 48: 167-235.

Rebullida, M.L.G. 2006. "Religion, Church, and Politics in the Philippines." In *Philippine Politics and Governance: An Introduction,* edited by N.M. Morada and T.S. Encarnacion Tadem, 63-85. Quezon City: Department of Political Science, University of the Philippines.

Reilly, K., S. Kaufman, and A. Bodino, eds. 2003. *Racism: A Global Reader.* Armonk, NY: M.E. Sharpe.

Reinharz, S. 1992. *Feminist Methods in Social Research.* New York: Oxford University Press.

Reitz, J.G. 2001. "Immigrant Skill Utilization in the Canadian Labour Market: Implications of Human Capital Research." *Journal of International Migration and Integration* 2 (3): 347-78.

–. 2004. "Canada: Immigration and Nation-Building in the Transition to a Knowledge Economy." In *Controlling Immigration: A Global Perspective,* 2nd ed., edited by W.A. Cornelius, T. Tsuda, P.L. Martin, and J.F. Hollified, 97-133. Stanford, CA: Stanford University Press.

–. 2009. "Assessing Multiculturalism as a Behavioural Theory." In *Multiculturalism and Social Cohesion: Potentials and Challenges of Diversity,* edited by J.G. Reitz, R. Breton, K.K. Dion, and K.L. Dion, 1-48. New York: Springer.

Remo, A.R., and C. Avendaño. 2008. "Land Conversion Moratorium Eyed." *Philippine Daily Inquirer,* 29 March. http://newsinfo.inquirer.net/.

Remo, M. 2010. "NSCB: Poverty Rate Was Stagnant in 2009." *Philippine Daily Inquirer,* 28 May. http://newsinfo.inquirer.net/.

–. 2012. "OFW Remittances Grew by 7.2% to $20.1-B in 2011 – BSP." *Philippine Daily Inquirer,* 15 February. http://business.inquirer.net/.

Remollino, A.M. 2009. "Another Shameful Arroyo Legacy: Highest Dropout Rates in Years." *Bulatlat,* 6 June. http://www.bulatlat.com/.

Renshon, S.A. 2001. *Dual Citizenship and American National Identity.* Washington, DC: Center for Immigration Studies.

Ribas-Mateos, N. 2008. *Gender, Remittances and Development: The Case of Filipino Migration to Italy.* Santo Domingo, Dominican Republic: United Nations International Research and Training Institute for the Advancement of Women (INSTRAW).

Rich, A. 1986. *Blood, Bread, and Poetry: Selected Prose, 1979-1985.* New York: W.W. Norton.

Riedinger, J.M. 1995. *Agrarian Reform in the Philippines: Democratic Transitions and Redistributive Justice.* Stanford, CA: Stanford University Press.

Rivera, R.E.N. 2008. "The Couples for Christ: Suborganizational Framing and Sociopolitical Mobilization in the Catholic Charismatic Renewal." PhD diss., University of Notre Dame.

Rivera, T.C. 1994. *Landlords and Capitalists: Class, Family, and State in Philippine Manufacturing.* Quezon City: University of the Philippines and Center for Integrative and Development Studies.

–. 2000. "Middle Class Politics: The Philippine Experience." *Journal of Social Science* 45: 1-22.

Roberts, J.A., D. Boyington, and S.S. Kazarian. 2008. *Diversity and First Nations Issues in Canada.* Toronto: Emond Montgomery.

Robinson, A.M. 2007. *Multiculturalism and the Foundations of Meaningful Life.* Vancouver: UBC Press.

Robles, D.G. 2001. *America the Great: Footprints on the Sands of Time.* Victoria, BC: Trafford Publishing.

Rocamora, J. 2007. "From Regime Crisis to System Change." In *Whither the Philippines in the 21st Century?* edited by R. Severino and L.C. Salazar, 18-42. Singapore: Institute of Southeast Asian Studies.

Roces, M. 1998. *Women, Power, and Kinship Politics: Female Power in Post-War Philippines.* Westport, CT: Praeger.

–. 2000. "Negotiating Modernities: Filipino Women 1970-2000." In *Women in Asia: Tradition, Modernity and Globalisation,* edited by L. Edwards and M. Roces, 112-38. Ann Arbor: University of Michigan Press.

–. 2003. "Sisterhood Is Local: Filipino Women in Mount Isa." In *Wife or Worker? Asian Women and Migration,* edited by N. Piper and M. Roces, 73-100. Lanham, MD: Rowman and Littlefield.

–. 2005. "The Militant Nun as Political Activist and Feminist in Martial Law Philippines." In *Women, Activism and Social Change,* edited by M. Mikula, 136-56. London and New York: Routledge.

–. 2010. "Rethinking 'the Filipino Woman': A Century of Women's Activism in the Philippines, 1905-2006." In *Women's Movements in Asia: Feminisms and Transnational Activism,* edited by M. Roces and L. Edwards, 34-52. New York: Routledge.

–. 2012. *Women's Movements and the Filipina.* Honolulu: University of Hawai'i Press.

Rodis, R. 2009. "Divorce, Philippines-Style." Inquirer Global Nation, 12 June. http://globalnation.inquirer.net/.

Rodriguez, L. 1990. "Patriarchy and Women's Subordination in the Philippines." *Review of Women's Studies* 1 (1): 15-25.

Rodriguez, R. 2008. "Domestic Debates: Constructions of Gendered Migration from the Philippines." *S&F Online* 6 (3).

Roffey, B. 1999. "Filipina Managers and Entrepreneurs: What Leadership Models Apply?" *Asian Studies Review* 23 (3): 375-405.

Roncesvalles, C.I., and B.S. Sto. Domingo. 2012. "Filipino Workers Surpass Indonesians." *Hong Kong News,* 12 October. http://hongkongnews.com.hk/.

Rothausen, T.J., J.A. Gonzalez, and A.E.C. Griffin. 2009. "Are All Parts There Everywhere? Fact Job Satisfaction in the United States and the Philippines." *Asia Pacific Journal of Management* 26 (4): 681-700.

Rothenberg, P.S. 2007. *Race, Class, and Gender in the United States,* 7th ed. New York: Worth Publishers.

Rotolo, T., and J. Wilson. 2007. "Sex Segregation in Volunteer Work." *Sociological Quarterly* 48 (3): 559-85.

Rousseau, C., G. Hassan, T. Measham, N. Moreau, M. Lashley, T. Castro, C. Blake, and G. McKenzie. 2009. "From the Family Universe to the Outside World: Family Relations, School Attitude, and Perception of Racism in Caribbean and Filipino Adolescents." *Health and Place* 15 (3): 751-60.

Roy, P. 2001. "At Home in the World? The Gendered Cartographies of Globality." *Feminist Studies* 27 (3): 709-31.

Royeca, J.E. 2010. "Crab Mentality is Universal." *Philippine Studies,* 19 January, http://emanila.com/philippines/.

Rubrico, J.G.U. 1998. "The Metamorphosis of Filipino as National Language." Center for Southeast Asian Studies, Northern Illinois University, http://www.seasite.niu.edu/Tagalog/.

Ruddick, S. 2007. "Maternal Thinking." In *Maternal Theory: Essential Readings,* edited by A. O'Reilly, 96-113. Toronto: Demeter Press.

Rupert, M., and M.S. Solomon. 2006. *Globalization and International Political Economy: The Politics of Alternative Futures.* Lanham, MD: Rowman and Littlefield.

Saeed, A. 2010. "Reflections on the Establishment of Shari'a Courts in Australia." In *Shari'a in the West,* edited by R. Ahdar and N. Aroney, 223-38. New York: Oxford University Press.

Salamanca, B.S. 1968. *The Filipino Reaction to American Rule, 1901-1913*. Hamden, CT: Shoe String Press.

Salcedo, L., A.R. Peralta, A.A. Ronquillo, and S.C. Espiritu. 1999. *Social Issues*. Quezon City, Philippines: Katha Publishing.

Salcedo, M. 2007. "HRM Gets a Global Retouch." Inquirer.net, 10 June. http://www.inquirer.net/.

Salih, R. 2001. "Moroccan Migrant Women: Transnationalism, Nation-States and Gender." *Journal of Ethnic and Migration Studies* 27(4): 655-71.

Salmer, J., and C. de Leon. 2003. "Culture and Management in the Philippines." In *Culture and Management in Asia*, edited by M. Warner, 152-70. London: RoutledgeCurzon.

San Juan, E. Jr. 2006. "Globalization and the Emergent Filipino Diaspora." Philippines Matrix Project, http://philcsc.wordpress.com/.

Sandel, M. 1982. *Liberalism and the Limits of Justice*. New York: Cambridge University Press.

Sandoval, C. 2000. *Methodology of the Oppressed*. Minneapolis: University of Minnesota Press.

Sanford, N. 2006. *Self and Society: Social Change and Development*. New Brunswick, NJ: Transaction Publishers.

Santiago, L.Q. 1995. "Rebirthing Babaye: The Women's Movement in the Philippines." In *The Challenge of Local Feminisms*, edited by A. Basu, 110-28. Boulder, CO: Westview Press.

–. 1996. "Roots of Feminist Thought in the Philippines." *Review of Women's Studies* 5 (2): 159-72.

Saptari, R. 2008. "Studying Asian Domestic Labour within Global Processes: Comparisons and Connections." In *Global Labour History: A State of the Art*, edited by J. Lucassen, 479-512. Berne: Peter Lang.

Sassen, S. 2004. "Countergeographies of Globalization: Feminization of Survival." In *Feminist Post-Development Thought: Rethinking Modernity, Post-Colonialism and Representation*, edited by K. Saunders, 89-104. London and New York: Zed Books.

Satz, D. 2010. *Why Some Things Should Not Be for Sale: The Moral Limits of Markets*. New York: Oxford University Press.

Schaefer, R.T. 2008. *Encyclopedia of Race, Ethnicity, and Society*, vol. 3. Thousand Oaks, CA: Sage.

Schenk, C. n.d. "Bishops' Conference Discusses Priest Shortage." Future Church, http://www.futurechurch.org/.

Schein, L. 2008. "Text and Transnational Subjectification: Media's Challenge to Anthropology." In *Ethnographica Moralia: Experiments in Interpretive Anthropology*, edited by N. Panourgia and G.E. Marcus, 188-212. Bronx, NY: Fordham University Press.

Schuck, P.H. 1998a. "Plural Citizenships." In *Immigration and Citizenship in the 21st Century*, edited by N.M. J. Pickus, 149-92. Lanham, MD: Rowman and Littlefield.

–. 1998b. *Citizens, Strangers, and In-Betweens: Essays on Immigration and Citizenship*. Boulder, CO: Westview Press.

Seekins, D.M. 1983. "Historical Setting." In *Philippines: A Country Study*, 3rd ed., edited by F.M. Bunge, 1-56. Washington, DC: US Department of the Army.

Sefa Dei, G.J. 2008. "The Social Construction of a 'Drop Out': Dispelling the Myth." In *Daily Struggles: The Deepening Racialization and Feminization of Poverty in Canada*, edited by M.A. Wallis and S. Kwok, 263-73. Toronto: Canadian Scholars' Press.

Seidman, S. 2009. *The Social Construction of Sexuality*, 2nd rev. ed. New York: W.W. Norton.

Sejersen, T.B. 2008. "'I Vow to Thee My Countries' – the Expansion of Dual Citizenship in the 21st Century." *International Migration Review* 42 (3): 523-49.

Sellek, Y. 2001. *Migrant Labour in Japan*. New York: Palgrave Macmillan.

Selmer, J., and C. de Leon. 2003. "Culture and Management in the Philippines." In *Culture and Management in Asia*, edited by M. Warner, 152-70. London and New York: RoutledgeCurzon.

Señeres, R.V. 2010. "The Price of Working Abroad: Abandoned Wives, Orphaned Children." Inquirer Global Nation, 7 February. http://globalnation.inquirer.net/.

Seniors Council. n.d. "Filipino Community." http://www.seniorscouncil.net/uploads/files/Issues/Mobilizing_Action_Report/FILIPINO%20COMMUNITY.pdf.

Shaafsma, J., and A. Sweetman. 2001. "Immigrant Earnings: Age at Immigration Matters." *Canadian Journal of Economics* 34 (4): 1066-99.

Shachar, A. 2009. "What We Owe Women: The View from Multicultural Feminism." In *Toward a Humanist Justice: The Political Philosophy of Susan Moller Okin,* edited by D. Satz and R. Reich, 143-65. New York: Oxford University Press.

Shapiro, E.R. 2005. "Because Words Are Not Enough: Latina Re-visionings of Transnational Collaborations Using Health Promotion for Gender Justice and Social Change." *NWSA Journal* 17 (1): 141-72.

Sharma, N. 2005. *Home Economics: Nationalism and the Making of "Migrant Workers" in Canada.* Toronto: University of Toronto Press.

Shaver Hughes, S., and B. Hughes. 2001. "Women in Ancient Civilizations." In *Agricultural and Pastoral Societies in Ancient and Classical History,* edited by M. Adas, 116-50. Philadelphia: Temple University Press.

Shelton, B.A. 1999. "Gender and Unpaid Work." In *Handbook of the Sociology of Gender,* edited by J.S. Chafetz, 375-90. New York: Kluwer Academic/Plenum Publishers.

Shields, S.A. 2008. "Gender: An Intersectionality Perspective." *Sex Roles* 59: 301-11.

Sidel, J.T. 1998. "The Underside of Progress: Land, Labor and Violence in Two Philippine Growth Zones, 1985-1995." *Bulletin of Concerned Scholars* 30 (1): 3-12.

Silva, J. 2006. "Engaging Diaspora Communities in Development: An Investigation of Filipino Hometown Associations in Canada." Master of Public Policy thesis, Simon Fraser University.

Silvera, M. 1996. "Man Royals and Sodomites: Some Thoughts on the Invisibility of Afro-Caribbean Lesbians." In *Lesbian Subjects: A Feminist Studies Reader,* edited by M. Vicinus, 167-77. Bloomington: Indiana University Press.

Silvey, R. 2004. "Power, Difference and Mobility: Feminist Advances in Migration Studies." *Progress in Human Geography* 28 (4): 490-506.

Simoes, M.B. 2006. "Latina Immigrant Women in the Washington, DC Metropolitan Area: Transnationalism and Identity." *Journal of Latino/Latin American Studies* 2 (2): 79-95.

Simms, M. 1989. "Democracy, Freedom and the Women's Movement in the Philippines." In *Politics of the Future,* edited by C. Jennett and R. Stewart, 340-54. Melbourne: Macmillan Company of Australia.

Singh Roy, A. 2006. "Philippines Is 'SMS Capital of the World.'" *Business Daily,* 6 October. Hindu Business Line, http://www.thehindubusinessline.com/.

Skinner, L., K. Steel, D. Fisher, and L. Zahnd. 1995. "The Changing World of Volunteer Management: A Practical Guide to Cultural Diversity in Volunteer Management." Calgary: Calgary ADVR (Association of Directors of Volunteer Resources). http://wayback.archive-it.org/2217/20101208173443/http://www.abheritage.ca/volunteer/issues/articles/Changing_World_Volunteer_Management.pdf.

Smith, B. 2007. *The Psychology of Sex and Gender.* Boston: Pearson.

Smith, B., S. Shue, J.L. Vest, and J. Villareal. 1999. *Philanthropy in Communities of Color.* Bloomington: Indiana University Press.

Smith, M., ed. 2008. *Political Institutions and Lesbians and Gay Rights in the United States and Canada.* New York: Routledge.

Sobhan, S. 1994. "National Identity, Fundamentalism and the Women's Movement in Bangladesh." In *Gender and National Identity: Women and Politics in Muslim Societies,* edited by V.M. Moghadam, 63-80. London: Zed Books

Solomon, M.R. 2010. *Consumer Behavior: Buying, Having, and Being,* 9th ed. Englewood Cliffs, NJ: Prentice Hall.

Somodio, J. 2008. "Pinoy Priest to OFWs in Australia: Be Faithful to Your Spouses." ABS-CBN News, 8 September. http://www.abs-cbnnews.com/.

Song, M. 2006. "Gender in a Global World." In *Handbook of Gender and Women's Studies,* edited by K. Davis, M. Evans, and J. Lorber, 185-95. London: Sage.

Sook Kim, H. 2007. "The Politics of Border Crossings: Black, Postcolonial, and Transnational Perspectives." In *Handbook of Feminist Research: Theory and Praxis,* edited by S.N. Hesse-Biber, 107-22.California: Sage.

Spiro, P.J. 2008. *Beyond Citizenship: American Identity after Globalization.* New York: Oxford University Press.

Spitzberg, B.H. 2003. "Methods of Interpersonal Skill Assessment." In *Handbook of Communication and Social Interaction Skills,* edited by J.O. Greene and B.R. Burleson, 93-134. Mahwah, NJ: Lawrence Erlbaum Associates.

Spitzer, D., A. Neufeld, M. Harrison, and K. Hughes. 2003. "Caregiving in Transnational Context: My Wings Have Been Cut; Where Can I Fly?" *Gender and Society* 17 (2): 267-86.

Spivak, G. 1989. "The Political Economy of Women as Seen by a Literary Critic." In *Coming to Terms: Feminism, Theory, Politics,* edited by E. Weed, 218-29. New York: Routledge.

Sprenger, G. 2004. "Encompassment and Its Discontents: The Rmeet and the Lowland Lao." In *Grammars of Identity/Alterity: A Structural Approach,* edited by G. Baumann and A. Gingrich, 173-91. New York: Berghahn Books.

Staeheli, L.A., E. Kofman, and L.J. Peake, ed. 2004. *Mapping Women, Making Politics: Feminist Perspectives on Political Geography.* New York: Routledge.

Stanley, L., ed. 1990. *Feminist Praxis: Research, Theory and Epistemology in Feminist Sociology.* London: Routledge.

Stanley, L., and S. Wise. 1983. *Breaking out: Feminist Consciousness and Feminist Research.* London: Routledge and Kegan Paul.

Star Phoenix. 2008a. "Sask. Recruiters Lure 297 Filipino Nurses." 12 March. http://www.canada.com/.

–. 2008b. "Sask. Attractive to Filipino Nurses." 17 March. http://www.canada.com/.

Stasiulis, D.K. 1999. "Relational Positionalities of Nationalisms, Racisms, and Feminisms." In *Between Woman and Nation: Nationalisms, Transnational Feminisms, and the State,* edited by C. Kaplan, N. Alarcón, and M. Moallem, 182-218. Durham, NC: Duke University Press.

Stasiulis, D.K., and A.B. Bakan. 2005. *Negotiating Citizenship: Migrant Women in Canada and the Global System.* Toronto: University of Toronto Press.

Stasiulis, D., and D. Ross. 2006. "Security, Flexible Sovereignty, and the Perils of Multiple Citizenship." *Citizenship Studies* 10 (3): 329-48.

Statistics Canada. 1997. "1996 Census: Immigration and Citizenship." *The Daily,* 4 November. http://www.statcan.gc.ca/dai-quo/index-eng.htm.

–. 2005. *Longitudinal Survey of Immigrants to Canada: A Portrait of Early Settlement Experiences.* Ottawa: Statistics Canada.

–. 2006. *Census of Population.* Statistics Canada Catalogue No. 97-564-XCB2006007. http://www40.statcan.gc.ca.

–. 2007. "Study: Rising Education of Women and the Gender Earnings Gap, 1981-2001." *The Daily,* 12 June. http://www.statcan.gc.ca/dai-quo/index-eng.htm.

–. 2008. "Study: The 2006 Canadian Immigrant Labour Market: Analysis by Region or Country of Birth." *The Daily,* 13 February. http://www.statcan.gc.ca/dai-quo/index-eng.htm.

–. 2009. "Mobility 5: Mobility Status – Place of Residence 5 Years Ago." http://www12.statcan.gc.ca/.

–. 2012. "Population Clock." http://www.statcan.gc.ca/.

Stein, J.G., D.R. Cameron, J. Ibbitson, W. Kymlicka, J. Meisel, H. Siddiqui, and M. Valpy. 2007. *Uneasy Partners: Multiculturalism and Rights in Canada.* Waterloo, ON: Wilfrid Laurier University Press.

Stevens, G. 1999. "Age at Immigration and Second Language Proficiency among Foreign-Born Adults." *Language in Society* 28: 555-78.

Straits Times. 2009. "Philippine Foreign Debt Down." 31 March. http://www.straitstimes.com/.

Stratton, J. 2005. "Lost in Music: Popular Music, Multiculturalism and Australian Film." In *Reel Tracks: Australian Feature Film Music and Cultural Identities,* edited by R. Coyle, 74-94. Eastleigh, UK: John Libbey Publishing.

Stretton, H. 2005. *Australia Fair.* Sydney: UNSW Press.

Stuckart, D.W., and J. Glanz. 2010. *Revisiting Dewey: Best Practices for Educating the Whole Child Today.* Lanham, MD: Rowman and Littlefield Education.

Suárez-Orozco, C., and D. Baolian Qin. 2006. "Gendered Perspectives in Psychology: Immigrant Origin Youth." *International Migration Review* 40 (1): 165-98.

Sun Star. 2008. "Nursing Schools Warned to Implement New Curriculum." 27 June.

Suter, K. 2007. "The Philippines: What Went Wrong with One Asian Economy." *Contemporary Review* 289 (1684): 53-59.

Suzuki, N. 2002. "Gendered Surveillance and Sexual Violence in Filipina Pre-migration Experiences to Japan." In *Gender Politics in the Asia-Pacific Region*, edited by B.S.A. Yeoh, P. Teo, and S. Huang, 99-119. London and New York: Routledge.

–. 2008. "Between Two Shores: Transnational Projects and Filipina Wives in/from Japan." In *Transcultural Japan: At the Borderlands of Race, Gender, and Identity*, edited by D.B. Willis and S. Murphy-Shigematsu, 65-85. New York: Routledge.

Swartz, D. 1997. *Culture and Power: The Sociology of Pierre Bourdieu.* Chicago: University of Chicago Press.

Sweetman, C., ed. 1998. *Gender and Migration.* Oxford: Oxfam.

Swider, S. 2006. "Working Women of the World Unite? Labor Organizing and Transnational Gender Solidarity among Domestic Workers in Hong Kong." In *Global Feminism: Transnational Women's Activism, Organizing and Human Rights*, edited by M.M. Ferree and A.M. Tripp, 110-40. New York: New York University Press.

Sworden, P.J. 2006. *An Introduction to Canadian Law*, 2nd ed. Toronto: Emond Montgomery.

Sy, A. 2009. "Reasons that Make a Filipino Maid Agency the Best Source for Housemaids." Website Profit/Make Money from Internet, 15 October. PopularArticles.com, http://www.populararticles.com/.

Taborda, J. 2013. "Philippine Unemployment Rate Up to 7.1% in January." *Trading Economics*, http://www.tradingeconomics.com/.

Tadiar, N.X.M. 2004. *Fantasy-Production: Sexual Economies and Other Philippine Consequences for the New World Order.* Aberdeen, Hong Kong: Hong Kong University Press.

Tan, K.J., and R. Concha. 2009. "Palace: Repatriation of 121 OFWs from Jeddah Hastened by Arroyo Visit." GMA News Online, 24 September. http://www.gmanews.tv/.

Tan, M.L. 2001. "Survival through Pluralism: Emerging Gay Communities in the Philippines." In *Gay and Lesbian Asia: Culture, Identity and Community*, edited by G. Sullivan and P.A. Jackson, 117-42. Binghamton, NY: Harrington Park Press.

Tapales, P.D. 1992a. "Filipino Women in Politics and Public Affairs: Activism in the Patriarchal System." In *Filipino Women and Public Policy*, edited by P.D. Tapales, 13-19. Manila: Kalikasan Press.

–. 1992b. "Women's Political Participation in the Philippines: The Cultural Dimension." In *Filipino Women and Public Policy*, edited by P.D. Tapales, 109-15. Manila: Kalikasan Press.

–. 2005. "Women in Contemporary Philippine Politics." Lecture delivered at the University of California at Los Angeles Center for Southeast Asian Studies Colloquium Series, 11 October. University of California eScholarship, http://escholarship.org/.

–. n.d. "Gender Policies and Responses towards Greater Women's Empowerment in the Philippines." United Nations Public Administration Network, http://unpan1.un.org/intradoc/groups/public/documents/eropa/unpan014236.pdf.

Tardiff-Williams, C.Y., and L. Fisher. 2009. "Clarifying the Link between Acculturation Experiences and Parent-Child Relationships among Families in Cultural Transition: The Promise of Contemporary Critiques of Acculturation Psychology." *International Journal of Intercultural Relations* 33 (2): 150-61.

Tastsoglou, E. 2006. "Gender, Migration and Citizenship: Immigrant Women and the Politics of Belonging in the Canadian Maritimes." In *Women, Migration and Citizenship: Making Local, National and Transnational Connections*, edited by E. Tastsoglou and A. Dobrowolsky, 201-30. Hampshire, UK: Ashgate.

Tastsoglou, E., and P.S. Jaya. 2011. *Immigrant Women in Atlantic Canada: Challenges, Negotiations, Reconstructions.* Toronto: Canadian Scholars' Press.

Tastsoglou, E., and B. Miedema. 2003. "Immigrant Women and Community Development in the Canadian Maritimes: Outsiders Within?" *Canadian Journal of Sociology* 28 (2): 203-34.

Tekin, B.C. 2010. *Representations and Othering in Discourse: The Construction of Turkey in the EU Context.* Amsterdam: John Benjamins Publishing.

Templo, M. 2010. "Duty-Free Shopping in the Philippines for Balikbayans." ABS-CBN News, 21 April. http://www.abs-cbnnews.com/.

Terrazas, A. 2008. "Filipino Immigrants in the United States." Migration Information Source, http://www.migrationinformation.org/usfocus/display.cfm?id=694 (accessed August 13, 2010).

Tettey, W., and K.P. Puplampu, eds. 2005. *The African Diaspora in Canada: Negotiating Identities and Belonging.* Calgary: University of Calgary Press.

Thapan, M., ed. 2005. *Transnational Migration and the Politics of Identity.* New Delhi: Sage.

Thobani, S. 2003. "War and Politics of Truth-Making in Canada." *International Journal of Qualitative Studies in Education* 16 (3): 399-414.

–. 2007. *Exalted Subjects: Studies in the Making of Race and Nation in Canada.* Toronto: University of Toronto Press.

Thomas, R.K. 2003. *Society and Health: Sociology for Health Professionals.* New York: Kluwer Academic/Plenum Publishers.

Thompson, E. 2008. "Immigration Policies Boosting Number of Degree Holders in Canada: Study." *Victoria Times-Colonist,* 26 May. http://www.canada.com/victoriatimescolonist/.

Thompson, R.M. 2003. *Filipino Taglish and Taglish.* Amsterdam: John Benjamins Publishing.

Tilly, C., and C. Tilly. 1994. "Capitalist Work and Labor Markets." In *Handbook of Economic Sociology,* edited by N. Smelser and R. Swedberg, 283-313. Princeton, NJ: Princeton University Press.

Tintiangco-Cubales, A.G. 2005. "Pinayism." In *Pinay Power: Theorizing the Filipina/American Experience,* edited by M. de Jesus, 137-48. New York and London: Routledge.

Tolentino, C.P. 2004. "Filipino Children and Families." In *Culturally Competent Practice with Immigrant and Refugee Children and Families,* edited by R. Fong, 60-80. New York and London: Guilford Press.

Tolentino, R.B. 1998. "Nations, Nationalisms, and *Los Ultimos de Filipinas:* An Imperialist Desire for Colonialist Nostalgia." *Kasarinlan: Philippine Journal of Third World Studies* 14 (2): 107-26.

Torres, E. 2010. "Trafficking Syndicates Prey on Filipino Women." ABS-CBN News, 22 July. http://www.abs-cbnnews.com/.

Torres, T. 2011. "World Bank: Philippines 4th Biggest Remittance Recipient in 2010." ABS-CBN News, 7 March. http://www.abs-cbnnews.com/.

Tosone, C. 2009. "Sotto Voce: Internalized Misogyny and the Politics of Gender in Corporate America." *Psychoanalytic Social Work* 16 (1): 1-11.

Touropia. 2010. "10 Largest Malls in the World." http://www.touropia.com/.

Trager, L. 1984. "Family Strategies and the Migration of Women: Migrants to Dagupan City, Philippines." *International Migration Review* 18 (4): 1264-77.

TransWorldNews. 2009. "Nursing Salaries in Saudi Arabia Are on Rise." 12 March. http://www.transworldnews.com.

Tropman, J.E. 2002. *The Catholic Ethic and the Spirit of Community.* Washington, DC: George Washington University Press.

Tucker, S.C., ed. 2009. *The Encyclopedia of the Spanish-American and Philippine-American Wars.* Santa Barbara, CA: ABC-CLIO.

Tullao, T.S., and J.P.R. Rivera. 2008. "The Impact of Temporary Labor Migration on the Demand for Education: Implications on the Human Resource Development in the Philippines." UNESCO, http://portal.unesco.org/education/es/files/58051/12246685645Tullao_and_Rivera.pdf/Tullao%2Band%2BRivera.pdf.

Tung, C. 2003. "Caring across Borders: Motherhood, Marriage, and Filipina Domestic Workers in California." In *Asian/Pacific Islander American Women: A Historical Anthology,* edited by S. Hune and G.M. Nomura, 301-18. New York and London: New York University Press.

Tungohan, E. 2010. "Canada Reluctant to Promote Domestic Workers' Rights." *Philippine Reporter,* 2 July. http://www.philippinereporter.com/.

Ty, E. 2006. "Abjection, Masculinity, and Violence in Brian Roley's *American Son* and Han Ong's *Fixer Class.*" In *Transnational Asian American Literature: Sites and Transits,* edited by

S. Lim, J.B. Gamber, S.H. Sohn, and G. Valentino, 142-58. Philadelphia: Temple University Press.

Tyner, J.A. 2000. "Global Cities and Circuits of Global Labour: The Case of Manila, Philippines." *Professional Geographer* 52 (1): 61-74.

–. 2004. *Made in the Philippines: Gendered Discourses and the Making of Migrants*. London and New York: RoutledgeCurzon.

–. 2007. "Filipinos: The Invisible Ethnic Community." In *Contemporary Ethnic Geographies in America*, edited by I.M. Miyares and C.A. Airriess, 251-70. Lanham, MD: Rowman and Littlefield.

Ubac, M.L. 2009. "Senator Escudero Says High Dropout Rates in Schools Alarming." *Philippine Daily Inquirer*, 3 July. http://newsinfo.inquirer.net/.

United Nations Children's Fund (UNICEF). 2003. "At a Glance: Philippines Statistics." http://www.unicef.org/infobycountry/.

–. 2011. *The State of the World's Children 2011. Adolescence: An Age of Opportunity*. New York: UNICEF.

United Nations Development Programme (UNDP). 2005. *Taking Action: Achieving Gender Equality and Empowering Women*. London: Earthscan.

United Nations Global Initiative to Fight Human Trafficking (UN.GIFT). n.d. "Human Trafficking: The Facts." United Nations Global Compact, http://www.unglobalcompact. org/docs/issues_doc/labour/Forced_labour/HUMAN_TRAFFICKING_-_THE_FACTS_-_final. pdf.

Uy, V. 2007. "Incest on the Rise with Feminization of Overseas Labor." Inquirer Global Nation, 9 March. http://globalnation.inquirer.net/.

Vachon, M., and W. Toews. 2008. "A Geography of the Filipino Migration to Winnipeg." *Canadian Journal of Urban Research* 17 (1): 107-29.

Valiani, S. 2009. "The Shift in Canadian Immigration Policy and Unheeded Lessons of the Live-in Caregiver Program." http://www.ccsl.carleton.ca/~dana/TempPermLCPFINAL.pdf.

Vasquez, D.C. 2007. "Amazing Beauties. The Amazing Ladyboys of the Philippines." Life Funtastique! http://jaynir.wordpress.com/.

Veneracion-Rallonza, L. 2008. "Women and the Democracy Project: A Feminist Take on Women's Political Participation in the Philippines." In *Women's Political Participation and Representation in Asia: Obstacles and Challenges*, edited by K. Iwanaga, 210-52. Copenhagen: Nordic Institute of Asian Studies

Verba, S., K.L. Schlozman, and H.E. Brady. 2002. *Voice and Equality: Civic Voluntarism in American Politics*. Cambridge, MA: Harvard University Press.

Vergara, B.M. Jr. 2009. *Pinoy Capital: The Filipino Nation in Daly City*. Philadelphia: Temple University Press.

Verma, R.B.P., and K.B. Chan. 2000. "Economic Adaptation of Asian Immigrants." In *Race and Racism: Canada's Challenge*, edited by L. Driedger and S.S. Halli, 116-33. Montreal and Kingston: McGill-Queen's University Press.

Vertovec, S. 2009. *Transnationalism*. London and New York: Routledge.

Vertovec, S., and S. Wessendorf, eds. 2010. *The Multiculturalism Backlash: European Discourses, Policies and Practices*. New York: Routledge.

Vickers, A. 2005. *A History of Modern Indonesia*. Cambridge: Cambridge University Press.

Villadiego, R. 2002. "'Return to RP!': Envoy Urges Undocumented Filipinos to Go Back to R.P. to Avoid Detention and Deportation." *Filipino Express*, 29 December.

Villareal, C.D., L.R.R. Tope., and P.M.B. Jurilla, eds. 2002. *Ruptures and Departures: Language and Culture in Southeast Asia*. Papers presented at the Second International Conference on Southeast Asia, University of the Philippines, Quezon City, 19-21 January, 2000. Quezon City: Department of English and Comparative Literature, University of the Philippines.

Villegas, B. 1986. "The Economic Crisis." In *Crisis in the Philippines: The Marcos Era and Beyond*, edited by J. Bresnan, 145-75. Princeton, NJ: Princeton University Press.

Villegas, C.M. 2010. "Revolution 'from the Middle': Historical Events, Narrative, and the Making of the Middle Class in the Contemporary Developing World." In *Political Power and Social Theory*, vol. 21, edited by J. Go, 299-312. Bingley, UK: Emerald Group Publishing.

Virola, R.A. 2007. "Antipoverty? How about Pro-Middle Class?" Statistically Speaking, National Statistical Coordination Board, http://www.nscb.gov.ph/.

Visayan Daily Star. 2010. "TFC Expands Canada Coverage." 29 April. http://www.visayandailystar.com/.

Vissandjée, B., A. Apale, and S. Wieringa. 2009. "Exploring Social Capital among Women in the Context of Migration: Engendering the Public Policy Debate." In *Racialized Migrant Women in Canada: Essays on Health, Violence, and Equity,* edited by V. Agnew, 187-203. Toronto: University of Toronto Press.

Viswanath, P. 2003. *Diaspora Indians – on the Philanthropy Fast-Track.* Mumbai: Centre for Advancement of Philanthropy.

Voet, R. 1998. *Feminism and Citizenship.* London: Sage.

Voicu, M., and B. Voicu. 2003. "Volunteering in Romania: A Rara Avis." In *The Values of Volunteering: Cross-Cultural Perspectives,* edited by P. Dekker and L. Halman, 143-59. New York: Kluwer Academic/Plenum Publishers.

Volpp, L. 2001. "Feminism versus Multiculturalism." *Columbia Law Review* 101 (5): 1181-1218.

Von Meien, J. 2006. *The Multiculturalism vs. Integration Debate in Great Britain.* Norderstedt, Germany: GRIN Verlag.

Wajcman, J. 2000. "It's Hard to Be Soft: Is Management Style Gendered?" In *Work and Society: A Reader,* edited by K. Grint, 254-76. Cambridge: Polity Press.

Walker, B., ed. 2008. *The History of Immigration and Racism in Canada: Essential Readings.* Toronto: Canadian Scholars' Press.

Walsh, K., H. Shen, and K. Willis. 2008. "Heterosexuality and Migration in Asia." *Gender, Place and Culture* 15 (6): 575-79.

Warburton, J., and D. McLaughlin. 2006. "Doing It from Your Heart: The Role of Older Women as Informal Volunteers." *Journal of Women and Aging* 18 (2): 55-72.

Wason, S.D. 2004. *Webster's New World Grant Writing Handbook.* Hoboken, NJ: Wiley.

Waterman, S. 2001. "Forever Immigrants: Cultural Politics and the Israeli Cultural Canon." In *The Territorial Factor: Political Geography in a Globalizing World,* edited by G. Dijkink and H. Knippenberg, 377-98. Amsterdam: Amsterdam University Press.

Waters, J.L. 2002. "Flexible Families? 'Astronaut' Households and the Experiences of Lone Mothers in Vancouver, British Columbia." *Social and Cultural Geography* 3 (2): 117-34.

Weininger, E.B. 2005. "Foundations of Pierre Bourdieu's Class Analysis." In *Approaches to Class Analysis,* edited by E.O. Wright, 82-118. Cambridge: Cambridge University Press.

Wekerle, G.R. 1997. "The Shift to the Market: Gender and Housing Disadvantage." In *Women and the Canadian Welfare State: Challenges and Changes,* edited by P.M. Evans and G.R. Wekerle, 170-96. Toronto: University of Toronto Press.

Wesley, J.J. 2011. *Code Politics: Campaigns and Cultures on the Canadian Prairies.* Vancouver: UBC Press.

Wesley, J.J., and L. Summerlee. 2011. "Voter Turnout in Manitoba: An Ecological Analysis." Paper presented at the annual meeting of the Canadian Political Science Association, 16 May. http://www.cpsa-acsp.ca/papers-2011/Wesley-Summerlee.pdf.

Walzer, M. 1983. *Spheres of Justice: A Defense of Pluralism and Equality.* New York: Basic Books.

Weegender. 2009. "Get to Know the Filipina Lesbian: Tomboy and Other Names We Go By." *Weegender: LGBTQ Travel and Lifestyle Magazine,* 1 November. http://weegender.com/.

Weiss, P.A. 1998. *Conversations with Feminism: Political Theory and Practice.* Lanham, MD: Rowman and Littlefield.

Wenning, E. 2006. "Catanduanes International Association Gears Up for Its 7th Medical Missions." *Insider Reports,* 20 May. http://www.insiderreports.com/.

Werbner, P. 2003. "The Politics of Multiculturalism in the New Europe." In *Whither Multiculturalism? A Politics of Dissensus,* edited by B. Saunders and D. Haljan, 47-58. Leuven, Belgium: Leuven University Press.

Whelehan, I. 1995. *Modern Feminist Thought: From the Second Wave to "Post-Feminism."* Edinburgh: Edinburgh University Press.

White, C., and T. Walker. 2008. *Tooning In: Essays on Popular Culture and Education.* Lanham, MD: Rowman and Littlefield.

White, P. 1995. "Geography, Literature and Migration." In *Writing across Worlds: Literature and Migration,* edited by R. King, J. Connell, and P. White, 1-19. New York: Routledge.

Wilding, R. 2006. "Virtual Intimacies? Families Communicating across Transnational Contexts." *Global Networks* 6 (2): 125-42.

Wilson, J., and M. Musick. 1997. "Who Cares? Toward an Integrated Theory of Volunteer Work." *American Sociological Review* 62 (5): 694-713.

–. 2003. "Doing Well by Doing Good: Volunteering and Occupational Achievement among American Women." *Sociological Quarterly* 44 (3): 433-50.

Wilson, K. 2011. "Boom in Remittances Has Hidden Cost Back in the Philippines." *The National* (Abu Dhabi), 25 January. http://www.thenational.ae/.

Winzeler, R. 1996. "Sexual Status in Southeast Asia: Comparative Perspectives on Women, Agriculture and Political Organization." In *Women of Southeast Asia,* edited by P. van Esterik, 139-69. DeKalb, IL: Center for Southeast Asian Studies, Northern Illinois University.

Wise, A., and S. Velayutham, eds. 2009. *Everyday Multiculturalism.* Basingstoke, UK: Palgrave Macmillan.

Wiseman, N. 2007. *In Search a Canadian Political Culture.* Vancouver: UBC Press.

Woelz-Stirling, N., M. Kelaher, and L. Manderson. 1998. "Power and the Politics of Abuse: Rethinking Violence in Filipina-Australian Marriages." *Health Care for Women International* 19 (4): 289-301.

Wolf, D.L. 2002. "Family Secrets: Transnational Struggles among Children of Filipino Immigrants." In *Filipinos in Global Migrations: At Home in the World?* edited by F.V. Aguilar, 347-49. Quezon City, Philippines: Philippine Migration Research Network.

Wolff, L. 1992. *Little Brown Brother: How the United States Purchased and Pacified the Philippines.* New York: Oxford University Press.

Wong, L., and V. Satzewich. 2006. "Introduction: The Meaning and Significance of Transnationalism." In *Transnational Identities and Practices in Canada,* edited by L. Wong and V. Satzewich, 1-15. Vancouver: UBC Press.

Woods, D.L. 2006. *The Philippines: A Global Studies Handbook.* Santa Barbara, CA: ABC-CLIO.

Woodward, K. 2004. "Introduction." In *Questioning Identity: Gender, Class, Ethnicity,* 2nd ed., edited by K. Woodward, 1-4. London: Open University Press.

World Bank. 2011. "Philippines: Robust Growth, Stubborn Poverty." *Philippine Quarterly Update,* January. Pasig City, Philippines: World Bank.

–. 2012. "Philippines." http://data.worldbank.org/.

Wurfel, D. 1988. *Filipino Politics: Development and Decay.* Ithaca, NY: Cornell University Press.

Wuthnow, R. 2009. *Boundless Faith: The Global Outreach of American Churches.* Berkeley and Los Angeles: University of California Press.

Wymer, W.W. Jr., and D.R. Self. 1999. "Major Research Studies: An Annotated Bibliography of Marketing to Volunteers." In *Volunteerism Marketing: New Vistas for Nonprofit and Public Sector Management,* edited by D.R. Self and W.W. Wymer Jr., 106-64. Binghamton, NY: Haworth Press.

Xue, L. 2010. "A Comprehensive Look at the Employment Experience of Recent Immigrants during Their First Four Years in Canada." In *Canadian Immigration: Economic Evidence for a Dynamic Policy Environment,* edited by T. McDonald, E. Ruddick, A. Sweetman, and C. Worswick, 11-40. Montreal and Kingston: McGill-Queen's University Press.

Yamanaka, K. 2005. "Changing Family Structures of Nepalese Transmigrants in Japan: Split-Households and Dual Wage Earners." *Global Networks* 5 (4): 337-58.

Yang, D. 2008. "Can Enforcement Backfire? Crime and Displacement in the Context of Customs Reform in the Philippines." *Review of Economics and Statistics* 90 (1): 1-14.

Yengoyan, A.A., and P.Q. Makil, eds. 2004. *Philippine Society and the Individual: Selected Essays of Frank Lynch.* Quezon City: Institute of Philippine Culture, Ateneo de Manila University.

Yinger, N.V. 2007. "The Feminization of Migration: Limits of the Data." Population Reference Bureau, February. http://www.prb.org/.

Yijälä, A., and A. Jasinskaja-Lahti. 2009. "Pre-Migration Acculturation Attitudes among Potential Ethnic Migrants from Russia to Finland." *International Journal of Intercultural Relations* (in press).

Yorgason, E.R. 2003. *Transformation of the Mormon Culture Region.* Chicago: University of Illinois Press.

Young, M.A. 2005. *Negotiating the Good life: Aristotle and Civil Society.* Surrey, UK: Ashgate.

Yuval-Davis, N. 1997. *Gender and Nation.* London: Sage.

Zaman, H. 2006. *Breaking the Iron Wall: Decommodification and Immigrant Women's Labor in Canada.* Lanham, MD: Lexington Books.

Zenkoku Ippan Tokyo General Union. 2011. "Number of Local Entertainers in Japan Down." 15 February. http://tokyogeneralunion.org/.

Zheng, T., ed. 2010. *Sex Trafficking, Human Rights and Social Justice.* New York: Routledge.

Zialcita, F. 2000. "Self-Expression and Mutual Sympathy in Farming Villages." In *Old Ties and New Solidarities: Studies on Philippine Communities,* edited by C.J.-H. Macdonald and G.M. Pesigan, 177-91. Quezon City, Philippines: Ateneo de Manila University Press.

Zlotnik, H. 2003. "The Global Dimensions of Female Migration." Migration Information Source, http://www.migrationinformation.org/.

Zontini, E. 2010. *Transnational Families, Migration and Gender: Moroccan and Filipino Women in Bologna and Barcelona.* New York: Berghahn Books.

Index

Printed and bound in Canada by Friesens
Set in Stone by Artegraphica Design Co. Ltd.
Copy editor: Frank Chow
Proofreader: Shirarose Wilensky
Cartographer: Eric Leinberger